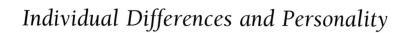

Individual Differences and Personality

Individual Differences and Personality

Michael C. Ashton

PROFESSOR
DEPARTMENT OF PSYCHOLOGY
BROCK UNIVERSITY
ST. CATHARINES, ONTARIO
CANADA

ELSEVIER

AMSTERDAM • BOSTON • HEIDELBERG
LONDON • NEW YORK • OXFORD • PARIS
SAN DIEGO • SAN FRANCISCO • SINGAPORE
SYDNEY • TOKYO
Academic Press is an imprint of Elsevier

Elsevier Academic Press

30 Corporate Drive, Suite 400, Burlington, MA 01803, USA
525 B Street, Suite 1900, San Diego, California 92101-4495, USA
84 Theobald's Road, London WC1X 8RR, UK

This book is printed on acid-free paper. ∞

Library of Congress Cataloging-in-Publication Data
APPLICATION SUBMITTED

British Library Cataloguing in Publication Data
A catalogue record for this book is available from the British Library

ISBN: 978-0-12-374129-5

For all information on all Elsevier Academic Press publications visit our Web site at www.books.elsevier.com
Printed in

09   10   9   8   7   6   5   4   3

Table of Contents

Acknowledgments   *xv*
Preface   *xvii*

Introduction

The Study of Personality   xix
The Universal, the Unique, and the In-Between   xx
Idiographic versus Nomothetic Approaches   xxi
Outline of This Book   xxiii

Chapter 1:   Basic Concepts in Psychological Measurement

Some Simple Statistical Ideas   2
  Levels of Measurement   2
  Standard Scores   3
  BOX 1-1: The Normal Distribution   4
  Correlation Coefficients   5
  BOX 1-2: Calculating the Correlation Coefficient   8
Assessing Quality of Measurement: Reliability and Validity   9
  Reliability   9
    Internal-Consistency Reliability   10
    BOX 1-3: Calculating Internal-Consistency Reliability   13
    Interrater (Interobserver) Reliability   14
    Test–Retest Reliability   15
  Validity   16
    Content Validity   16
    Criterion Validity: Convergent and Discriminant   18
    Construct Validity   19
Methods of Measurement: Self- and Observer Reports, Direct Observations,
  Biodata   20
  Self-Reports   20

Observer Reports   21
Direct Observations   22
Biodata (Life-Outcome Data)   23
Comparing the Methods of Measurement   23
Summary and Conclusions   24

Chapter 2:   Personality Traits and the Inventories That Measure Them

The Idea of a Personality Trait   27
Differences among Individuals   28
In a Typical Tendency to Behave, Think, or Feel   28
In Some Conceptually Related Ways   28
Across a Variety of Relevant Situations   29
Over Some Fairly Long Period of Time   29
Personality Traits and Other Psychological Characteristics   29
Do Personality Traits Exist?   30
Research Studies Testing the Existence of Traits   30
The Importance of Aggregation: Some Familiar Examples   32
BOX 2-1: Variance Due to Situations, Persons, and Person-by-Situation Interactions   33
Measuring Traits by Self- or Observer Report: Structured Personality Inventories   34
Strategies of Personality Inventory Construction   36
The Empirical Strategy   36
The Factor-Analytic Strategy   39
The Rational Strategy   39
Comparisons of the Three Strategies   41
BOX 2-2: Some Widely Used Personality Inventories   41
Self- and Observer Reports on Personality Inventory Scales   45
Agreement between Self- and Observer Reports   45
Why Do Self- and Observer Reports Tend to Agree?   46
The Validity of Self- and Observer Reports in Predicting Behavior   48
BOX 2-3: Projective Tests   49
Summary and Conclusions   51

Chapter 3:   Personality Structure: Classifying Traits

Which Traits to Measure? Completeness without Redundancy   53
A Gentle Introduction to Factor Analysis   54
Factor Analysis of Personality Traits: How to Find a Representative Set of Traits?   59
The Idea of the Lexical Approach   60
The Early Use of the Lexical Approach   61
Lexical Studies in the English Language: The Big Five Personality Factors   62

The Big Five   62
Personality Inventories and the Five-Factor Model   64
Lexical Studies in Many Languages: The HEXACO Personality
  Factors   66
Different Languages, Same Six Factors   66
BOX 3-1: Many Traits Are Blends of Two or More Factors   70
The HEXACO Model of Personality Structure   70
What It All Means: A Few Dimensions, but Many Personalities   72
Summary and Conclusions   73
BOX 3-2: Broad Factors versus Narrow Traits   74

Chapter 4: *Developmental Change and Stability of Personality*

Defining Change and Stability   77
Developmental Changes in Mean Levels of Personality Traits   79
Longitudinal Research Studies   79
Patterns of Life Span Change: Increasing Maturity?   80
Stability of Traits across the Years (and the Life Span)   82
Stability across a Period of Several Years during Adulthood   82
Stability across Longer Periods of Time during Adulthood   83
Stability during Adolescence and Young Adulthood   84
Personality in Childhood and Infancy: Measurement and Structure   86
Personality Structure during Childhood   86
Developmental Change in Personality Traits during Childhood   88
Stability of Traits during Childhood   89
BOX 4-1: The Development of Self-Esteem across the Life Span   89
Summary and Conclusions   90

Chapter 5: *Biological Bases of Personality*

Early Ideas: The Four "Humors" and Personality   93
BOX 5-1: Physique and Personality   95
Neurotransmitters   96
Cloninger's Theory   97
  Dopamine and Novelty Seeking   97
  Serotonin and Harm Avoidance   98
  Norepinephrine and Reward Dependence   98
  Empirical Tests of Cloninger's Theory   99
Brain Structures   99
Gray's Theory   99
  The Behavioral Activation System   100
  The Behavioral Inhibition System   100
  The Fight-or-Flight System   100
Eysenck's Theory   101
  Extraversion   101

Neuroticism   102
Psychoticism   102
Comparing Gray's and Eysenck's Dimensions   102
Empirical Evidence and the Theories of Gray and Eysenck   103
Zuckerman's Model   105
BOX 5-2: Some Biological Bases for Conscientiousness?   106
Hormones   106
Testosterone   107
Cortisol   108
Oxytocin   109
BOX 5-3: Is Personality Related to Blood Type, Handwriting Style, or Astrological Sign?   110
Summary and Conclusions   111

Chapter 6:   *Genetic and Environmental Influences on Personality*

The Question: Nature versus Nurture   114
Examining the Similarity of Relatives   114
Separating Heredity and Environment   116
Examining the Similarity of Identical Twins Raised Apart   116
Examining the Similarity of Other Relatives Raised Apart   116
Additive and Nonadditive Heritability   117
Comparing the Similarity of Different Kinds of Relatives   119
Examining the Similarity of Adoptive Relatives: Common and Unique Environment   120
The Answers   121
Similarities between Relatives   121
Strong Genetic Influences (Both Additive and Nonadditive), with Weak Common Environment Influence   122
Assumptions Underlying Heritability Studies in General   124
Are Relatives' Personalities Really Measured Independently?   124
Is There Really No Assortative Mating for Personality?   127
Assumptions Underlying Twin-Based Heritability Studies in Particular   128
Are Twins' Early Environments Really Separate?   128
Are Twins' Adoptive Households Really Very Different?   129
Are Identical Twins Really Treated Differently by Others?   131
Effects of the Unique Environment on Personality? Parental Treatment, Peer Groups, and Birth Order   132
Parental Treatment and Peer Groups   132
Birth Order   133
BOX 6-1: Identifying Specific Genes That Influence Personality: Molecular Genetic Studies   134
Summary and Conclusions   134
Appendix: Difficulties in Separating the Effects of Heredity and Environment   135

Genotype–Environment Interactions   135

Genotype–Environment Correlations: Passive, Reactive,
and Active   137

Chapter 7:   The Evolutionary Function of Personality

The Idea of Evolution by Natural Selection   142

Why Are We Not All the Same? Fluctuating Optimum and
Frequency-Dependence   144

Several Reasons Why Variation Does Not Go Away   144

Fluctuating Optimum: Ideal Levels of a Characteristic Vary across Places
and Times   145

Frequency Dependence: The Advantages of Doing What Others Are Not
Doing   146

The Operation of the Fluctuating Optimum and Frequency Dependence:
Genetic and Developmental Routes   147

Adaptive Trade-offs between High and Low Levels of the HEXACO Personality
Factors   148

Honesty–Humility   148

Agreeableness   149

Emotionality   149

Summary for Honesty–Humility, Agreeableness, and Emotionality:
Altruism versus Aggression   150

BOX 7-1: Sex Differences in Personality Traits: The Emotionality
Factor   151

Extraversion   151

Conscientiousness   151

Openness to Experience   152

Summary for Extraversion, Conscientiousness, and Openness to Experience:
Engagement in Areas of Endeavor   152

BOX 7-2: Adaptive Trade-offs from the Perspective of the Big Five
Personality Dimensions   153

The Operation of the Fluctuating Optimum and Frequency Dependence:
Some Examples   153

Honesty–Humility and Agreeableness   153

Emotionality   156

Extraversion   157

Conscientiousness   158

Openness to Experience   158

Summary and Conclusions   160

BOX 7-3: Cross-Generational and Cross-National Differences in Mean
Levels of Personality Traits   160

BOX 7-4: How "Old" Are Personality Characteristics? Evidence from
Studies of Animal Personality   161

Chapter 8:   *Personality Disorders*

The Idea of a Personality Disorder   163
The DSM-IV Personality Disorders   165
   Schizoid   165
   Schizotypal   165
   Paranoid   166
   Antisocial   166
   Borderline   166
   Histrionic   167
   Narcissistic   167
   Avoidant   167
   Dependent   167
   Obsessive-Compulsive   168
Classifying the DSM-IV Personality Disorders: Clusters A, B,
   and C   168
Disorders Considered for Inclusion in DSM-IV but Rejected   169
   Depressive   169
   Passive-Aggressive (Negativistic)   170
   Self-Defeating   170
   Sadistic   170
Other Personality-Related Disorders Not Included as DSM-IV Personality
   Disorders   171
   Attention-Deficit/Hyperactivity Disorder   171
   Separation Anxiety Disorder   172
   Oppositional Defiant Disorder   172
   Specific Phobias   173
   Summary   174
Problems with the Concept of Personality Disorders   174
Alternative Systems for Personality Disorder Diagnosis   176
Origins of Personality Disorders: Development, Biological Bases,
   Heredity and Environment, and Evolutionary Function   178
Summary and Conclusions   179

Chapter 9:   *Personality and Life Outcomes*

Does Personality Predict Features of One's Life Story?   181
Relationships and Marriage   182
   Are Spouses Similar in Personality?   182
   Marital Satisfaction   183
   Attachment Styles   185
   Parenting Styles   186
Peer Relationships: Friendships and Status   186
Health-Related Outcomes   187
   Substance Use   188

Longevity 189
Heart Disease (and "Type A" Personality) 192
Academic Performance 193
Job Performance 194
How to Assess Job Performance? 195
The Role of Conscientiousness 195
Specific Traits: The Case of Proactivity 196
Integrity Tests 197
The Problem of Faking 198
BOX 9-1: Personality and Occupational Choice 199
Law-Abidingness versus Criminality 200
The Role of Self-Control 200
Primary and Secondary Psychopathy 201
BOX 9-2: Self-Esteem, Narcissism, and Aggression 203
Life Satisfaction 203
BOX 9-3: Job Satisfaction 205
Summary and Conclusions 205

Chapter 10: *Mental Ability*

The Domain of Mental Ability 210
The Structure of Mental Ability: One Dimension or Many? 211
Spearman and the g *Factor* 214
Thurstone and Group Factors 217
g *Plus Group Factors* 218
Developmental Change and Stability in Mental Abilities 220
Developmental Changes in Mean Levels of Mental Ability 220
Stability of Mental Ability across the Life Span 221
Biological Bases of Mental Ability 222
Brain Size 222
Nerve Conduction Velocity 223
Reaction Time 224
Inspection Time 226
Brain Waves: Averaged Evoked Potentials 227
Brain Glucose Metabolism 228
Genetic and Environmental Influences on Mental Ability 228
Genetic Influences 228
Womb Environment Influences 230
Other Environmental Influences: Nutrition 231
**BOX 10-1: Chorion Type as an Example of Womb Environment Influences
on Mental Ability** 232
Evolutionary Function of Mental Ability 234
Mental Ability and Life Outcomes 237
Academic Achievement and Performance 237
Job Performance, Occupational Status, and Income 240

Longevity and Health   242
Law-Abidingness versus Criminality   243
Marriage: Assortative Mating   245
Not All *g*-Loaded Tasks Are the Same   245
Novel versus Familiar Tasks: Fluid and Crystallized Intelligence   246
Generational Changes in Mental Abilities: The Flynn Effect   246
Reasoning with Numbers and Shapes versus Understanding Verbal Concepts:
    Different Relations with Personality   248
Alternative Ideas about Mental Abilities   249
Gardner's "Theory of Multiple Intelligences"   249
Sternberg's "Triarchic Theory of Intelligence"   251
Emotional Intelligence   253
Summary and Conclusions   255

Chapter 11:   Religion and Politics

Religion   260
Is Religiosity a Personality Characteristic?   260
BOX 11-1: Cross-Generational and Cross-National Differences in
    Religiosity   261
Religiosity and the Major Dimensions of Personality   261
Developmental Change and Stability in Religiosity   264
Religiosity and Paranormal Beliefs   265
Religiosity and Life Outcomes   266
Politics   267
Right-Wing Authoritarianism   267
Social Dominance Orientation   269
Relations between Right-Wing Authoritarianism and Social Dominance
    Orientation   270
BOX 11-2: Right-Wing Authoritarianism and Social Dominance
    within Minority Groups   271
Two Dimensions of Political Attitudes   272
Political Attitudes and the Major Dimensions of Personality   273
Political Attitudes, Social Values, and Religion   274
Developmental Change and Stability in Political Attitudes   276
Origins of Religious Beliefs and Political Attitudes: Biological Bases, Genetic and
    Environmental Influences, and Evolutionary Function   278
Biological Bases   278
Genetic and Environmental Influences   278
Evolutionary Function   281
Summary and Conclusions   281

Chapter 12:   Sexuality

Major Dimensions of Sexuality   285
Sexuality and Personality   287

Sexual Arousal and Personality   287
Sexual Commitment and Personality   288
Sexual Orientation and Personality   289
BOX 12-1: Cross-Generational and Cross-National Differences in Sexuality   292
Origins of Variation in Sexuality: Genetic and Environmental Influences, Biological Bases, and Evolution   292
BOX 12-2: Religiosity and Sexuality   293
Sexual Commitment (or Restricted versus Unrestricted Sociosexuality)   294
Genetic and Environmental Influences   294
Biological Bases   294
Evolutionary Function   295
Sexual Orientation   297
Genetic and Environmental Influences and Biological Bases   297
Difficulties in Estimating the Heritability of Sexual Orientation   297
Causes of Sexual Orientation? "Exotic Becomes Erotic"   298
Causes of Sexual Orientation? Number of Older Brothers   299
Evolutionary Function   301
BOX 12-3: The Evolution of Sex Differences in Vocational Interests?   302
Sexual Arousal   302
Genetic and Environmental Influences   302
Biological Bases   303
Evolutionary Function   303
Summary and Conclusions   304

Conclusion

What We Have Learned So Far   305
What We Have Yet to Learn   309
Final Remarks   311

References   *313*
Index   *331*

Acknowledgments

Writing a textbook is a big job, and I want to thank many people for the help of various kinds that they have given me.

I would like to thank several people at Elsevier/Academic Press. My publisher, Nikki Levy, received my textbook proposal with enthusiasm and gave much help and advice throughout the publication process. My developmental editor, Barbara Makinster, and my production managers, Christie Jozwiak and Julie Ochs, were highly efficient and very patient in their work of converting the original manuscript into a textbook.

I should also thank several individuals who were generous in allowing me to include their test items or not-yet-published data in this book. Ted Jackson of Sigma Assessment Systems kindly permitted me to reproduce example items from the Nonverbal Personality Questionnaire and the Multidimensional Aptitude Battery. Lew Goldberg shared the data from his Eugene-Springfield Community Sample. David Schmitt provided further analyses of his data on personality and sexuality. Erik Noftle and Richard Robins shared their current work on personality and academic aptitude.

I would also like to thank my colleagues in the Department of Psychology at Brock University for their support. I especially appreciate the helpful advice of John Mitterer, Stan Sadava, and Sid Segalowitz concerning the textbook publishing process. My graduate students, Beth Visser and Julie Pozzebon, also deserve my thanks for their patience throughout the writing of this book. I also thank Linda Pidduck for her help in preparing figures.

This textbook reflects my thinking about personality psychology, which has been influenced by the teachers who supervised me during my years as a student. I thank Jerry Hogan, the late Doug Jackson, and Sam Paunonen for sharing their learning with me.

There are also a few friends and colleagues whose encouragement was of great help in motivating me to undertake and persist with this project. I thank Reinout de Vries, Paul Tremblay, and Gordon Hodson for their support and also for their advice on several aspects of the book.

A special thanks goes to my friend and colleague Kibeom Lee. His detailed comments on a previous full draft were invaluable, as was his advice on the organization and content of the book more generally. I thank Kibeom for his intellectual input, but also for his very helpful moral support throughout the writing of this book.

Most of all, I would like to thank my parents for the enormous encouragement that they have always given, and for the special interest that they took in this latest project of mine. I also give a special thanks to my sister and brother-in-law, whose three "projects" have helped me to keep mine in perspective. This book is dedicated to John, Michael, and Caroline.

Preface

The central aim of personality psychology is to understand differences between people. With this in mind, my purpose in writing this textbook was to describe the main questions about the nature of personality variation, and to explain the answers that have been learned so far.

The organization of this textbook largely follows from this aim, and differs from that of most other textbooks in this discipline. In the past, most authors structured their textbooks around the theorists who had written about personality psychology, with each chapter being devoted to the work of a different theorist. More recently, some authors have organized their textbooks in terms of several distinct "domains" or "approaches" within the discipline of personality psychology. The structure of this textbook is closer to the latter than to the former, in the sense of being organized around issues rather than around theorists. But the present textbook emphasizes the unity of the discipline, by treating the diverse areas of research in personality psychology as efforts to answer a series of related questions about the same basic phenomenon—human personality variation.

This book begins with some basic orientation to the discipline, by explaining the *nomothetic approach* to personality and by introducing the basic principles of personality *measurement*. The idea of a *personality trait* is then described, along with the evidence for the existence (and the measurability) of those traits. At this point, the stage is set for an examination of the big questions of personality psychology.

The first issue to be examined is that of *personality structure*—of finding the basic dimensions that summarize personality traits. The next topic is that of the *development* of personality, in terms of stability and change in personality trait levels across the life span. Then follows an examination of the *origins* of personality variation, in the sense of its proximal biological *causes* (i.e., in brain structures and substances) and its more distal *sources* (i.e., in genes and environmental features). This leads to the question of the *function* of personality variation throughout human *evolution*, and of the *consequences* of personality variation in modern society, with attention to *personality disorders* and also to diverse *"life outcomes"*—involving relationships, work, health, and so on—that are influenced by personality.

All of those chapters deal with personality variation as defined in a somewhat narrow sense, and thereby leave aside some important areas of psychological variation, including *mental abilities* as well as *religious beliefs and political attitudes* in addition to various aspects of *sexuality*. These individual differences are often omitted altogether from personality textbooks, but I have included them here in recognition of their importance to personality in a broader sense of the term. Each of the remaining chapters of the textbook examines a different one of these domains, discussing its relations with the major personality dimensions and also addressing the same questions as those considered for personality traits throughout the earlier chapters of the book. Finally, a concluding chapter summarizes and integrates the previous sections of the book, drawing attention to the major findings of personality research as well as the important questions that remain to be answered.

A few brief notes to the instructor: It is strongly recommended that the Introduction be assigned as required reading. The chapter on genetic and environmental influences contains an appendix about genotype–environment interactions and genotype–environment correlations, two rather advanced topics that may be considered optional. The chapter on mental abilities is about twice as long as the others, and might therefore be assigned to students over a longer period of time. Finally, the chapter on personality disorders is to some extent a departure from the framework of addressing questions about the nature of personality variation, and is included chiefly for its practical and clinical relevance; the decision to assign this chapter will thus depend on the aims of the course.

Introduction

The Study of Personality   xix
The Universal, the Unique, and the
   In-Between   xx

Idiographic versus Nomothetic
   Approaches   xxi
Outline of This Book   xxiii

The Study of Personality

Welcome to the fascinating world of personality psychology!

One of the most intriguing aspects of life is the variety that we notice in the people around us. People differ, of course, in their outward physical characteristics. But the variety among human beings is not just "skin deep": People also differ in their typical ways of behaving, thinking, and feeling. And it is these differences in psychological characteristics—these differences in *personality*—that seem so important to us for defining who a person is. All around the world, people notice the personalities of the people around them, and all around the world, people find it useful to describe each other's personalities: Is this person outgoing or shy? Sensitive or tough? Creative or conventional? Quick-tempered or patient? Sincere or deceitful? Disorganized or self-disciplined?

You have probably observed these differences in personality all throughout your life. Even when you were a young child playing in the playground, you probably realized very early that the other kids had very different styles of playing: Some shared their toys more than others did, some would "tattle-tale" more than others would, some liked to compete more than others did, and so on. (You probably also realized that the adults who supervised that playground were not all the same either: Some punished more severely than others did, some watched the playground more closely than others did, and so on.) And ever since that time, you have no doubt noticed the different personalities of the people around you—relatives, friends, classmates, co-workers, or anyone else you have encountered.

But have you ever *wondered* about personality? Have you ever been struck by the sheer variety of people's personalities—by the many ways that one person can be similar to and different from another person? Have you ever speculated about *why* people have such varied personalities—about what causes the differences between one person and the next? Have you ever wondered whether personality really matters in life—whether someone's personality will influence their relationships, their career, their health? If so, then you have come to the right place: These are exactly the kinds of questions that we will try to answer in this book.

Of course, these questions are not new: People have speculated and debated about them for centuries. More than 2000 years ago, the ancient Greeks were fascinated by the variety of personalities that people exhibit. One philosopher, Theophrastus, even wrote a book describing the many characteristics he observed in others. Greek doctors, such as Hippocrates and Galen, wrote that different bodily fluids were responsible for the major personality characteristics. But the first attempts to examine personality in a systematic, scientific way were not undertaken until much more recently: There were some promising beginnings in the late nineteenth century, then some scattered progress leading up to the late twentieth century, and then an explosion of discoveries that continues into the twenty-first century. And this is what makes the field of personality research so exciting: It examines fundamental, age-old questions about the human condition—questions whose answers are only now finally being revealed.

The Universal, the Unique, and the In-Between

Before going any further, we should examine what kinds of questions this book will consider, and what kinds of questions it will not. A good way to summarize this is to consider three categories of topics that psychologists can study in regard to human behavior.

At one extreme, some psychologists study the *universal* aspects of human nature—the ways in which everyone tends to be similar in their behavior. That is, some researchers investigate the circumstances in which people in general are likely to behave in a certain way. For example, one could try to find the conditions that cause all (or almost all) people to show a particular reaction, such as conforming to group norms, retaliating against an attacker, feeling closely attached to one's parents, helping a person in distress, rebelling against authority, changing opinions on a topic, boasting about achievements, feeling sexually attracted to someone, and so on.

At the other extreme, some psychologists examine the *unique* combinations of very specific features that make a given person different from everyone else. That is, some researchers investigate the ways in which each person behaves differently when confronted with various situations or circumstances. For example, perhaps one of your friends can relax and reduce stress by listening to music not by exercising, whereas the opposite may be true for another of your friends. Perhaps the first friend is irritated by criticisms of his or her physical appearance but not of the quality of his or her work, whereas the opposite may be true for the second friend. And perhaps the first friend would be tempted to eat too much chocolate but not too much pizza, whereas the opposite may be true for the second friend.

In between these two extremes, some psychologists explore the ways in which any given person can be similar to some people yet different from other people. That is, some researchers investigate the important characteristics (or traits) along which people vary, with the aim of measuring those characteristics, and of learning about their causes and their consequences. For example, how can we measure (and thus compare) different people's overall levels of honesty or of creativity? What are the reasons why people differ from one another in their usual levels of fearfulness or of impulsiveness? What are the consequences—for relationships or for work or for health—of differences among people in their typical levels of cheerfulness or of stubbornness?

The focus of this book will be on this third, intermediate category of topics. The first category—that of the universal features of human nature—is studied in great detail by researchers in many areas of psychology, particularly social psychology. The topics of that category are obviously very interesting, and they are certainly relevant to an understanding of personality. But because those topics have been so thoroughly investigated by researchers in other areas of psychology, we will not consider them here.

The second category—that of the unique aspects of each individual—is examined in a subjective way by many insightful observers of the human condition, including novelists, playwrights, poets, philosophers, biographers, and historians. In addition, the topics of that category are also studied in a more systematic way by some personality psychologists. However, many personality psychologists believe that we can learn much more about personality by studying the third category of topics. To understand the reason for this opinion, consider two different ways in which we could approach the study of personality: The *idiographic* approach and the *nomothetic* approach (e.g., Allport, 1937).

Idiographic versus Nomothetic Approaches

As noted before, one way of studying personality is to examine individual persons in detail, with the aim of identifying the unique features of each individual's personality. You have already encountered this approach used many times, whenever you have read or watched a biography or a "case study" of a person's life.

Let us consider an example of how this approach might work. Suppose that we wanted to write a detailed description of the personality of our classmate, Alice. To do so, we would study Alice's personality in depth. For example, we might conduct interviews with her, with her family members, and with her friends, and we might observe her behavior directly, across many situations and over a long period of time. (We will assume that Alice would agree to some invasions of her privacy.)

After all of this careful investigation, we might conclude that the most striking features of Alice's personality are her fear of the disapproval of others and her strong sense of responsibility in her dealings with others. So, when writing our biography of Alice, we would draw attention to these aspects of her personality, and we would illustrate them with various episodes from her life. But in writing this biography, we might also want to try to *explain* why these are the outstanding features of her personality. In looking for clues, we might notice that Alice's parents had a very strict style of raising their children, and expressed strong disapproval whenever Alice behaved "badly" as a child. From these observations, we might decide that it was Alice's strict upbringing that caused her fear of disapproval of others, and that this fear of disapproval in turn caused her to be a very responsible person. It might be difficult to prove this conclusively, but we could certainly make a persuasive argument to support this explanation of how these prominent aspects of Alice's personality had developed.

This strategy of studying the many unique details of an individual's personality is called the idiographic approach, and it has some obvious strengths. By its very nature, it can give us some interesting insights into the really distinctive features of an individual's personality, and it can even give us some fascinating clues as to the origins of those features. These strengths might help to explain why most of us find the biographies of famous people and the stories of fictional characters to be so captivating.

On the other hand, the idiographic approach also has some weaknesses. One obvious shortcoming is inefficiency: It would simply be too expensive and too time-consuming to study a large number of people in so much detail, and as a result our knowledge of personality would be based on a very small number of cases. This inefficiency is also seen in the relatively small segment of "personality" that really stands out in any one person. Remember that Alice did not strike us as being, say, especially ambitious, or especially artistic. So, if we had been hoping to learn more about those particular aspects of personality, we would need to keep looking for other individuals to study.

But perhaps an even more serious shortcoming of the idiographic approach is that it does not easily allow us to figure out any *general laws* about personality. Recall that when we studied Alice, we decided that her very responsible and dependable nature was caused by her need for approval of others, which was in turn the result of the strict upbringing given to her by her parents. But, do we really know for sure that people who are very responsible also tend to be very fearful of the disapproval of others? And do we really know that people whose upbringing was strict also tend to be responsible, or to be afraid of disapproval? Perhaps if we looked at a large number of people, we would find that, on average, responsible people are no more afraid of others' disapproval than irresponsible people are. And maybe we would find that people raised by strict parents are no more fearful of disapproval than are people raised by very permissive parents. So, although the idiographic approach can give us some interesting ideas about personality, it does not allow us to test whether or not those ideas are actually correct.

Because of these drawbacks associated with the idiographic approach, most personality researchers now prefer the other strategy, which is called the nomothetic approach. In the nomothetic approach, the researcher studies certain features of the personalities of many different people, and then compares those people in an effort to figure out some general rules about personality. The nomothetic approach usually involves measuring some interesting variables in a large group of people, and then finding out how those variables are related. For example, our study of Alice might suggest to us that traits such as responsibility and fear of disapproval might be worth measuring in a large sample of people, to find out whether or not those traits usually go together. Using the nomothetic approach, we could also study the hypothesized causes of one's personality, such as parental child-rearing style or the levels of a certain hormone or neurotransmitter chemical; likewise, we could also study the hypothesized consequences of one's personality, such as job performance, marital satisfaction, or criminal record.

The great strength of the nomothetic approach is that it *does* allow us to find general laws of personality. Because the aim of any scientific research is to discover the laws that govern nature, the nomothetic approach is clearly the best choice for researchers who wish to understand the laws of personality. For example, we can use the nomothetic approach to find out whether two personality characteristics are related to each other, or to find out whether some presumed "causes" or "consequences" of a personality characteristic are really related to that trait. By using the nomothetic approach, we can gradually learn more and more about the personality characteristics that differentiate people, and about the origins and the effects of those personality differences. But in addition, the nomothetic strategy can also teach us a great deal about the personalities of individual persons. For example, if we can assess an individual's personality in terms of several important characteristics, then the overall pattern produced by this combination of variables is likely to be very informative, and to give a description that is virtually unique.

Thus, it is for these reasons that we will study personality using the nomothetic approach, rather than using the idiographic approach. By focusing on the ways in which people differ from (and are similar to) each other, we can learn some general laws about personality. Moreover, we can also learn a great deal about any individual person, perhaps more than we could learn by trying to study individuals one at a time.

Of course, all of this is not to say that idiographic approaches are not valuable, or that a study of the unique features of an individual is uninteresting. On the contrary, a creative personality scientist will probably derive some of his or her original insights from making observations made in daily life, from reading great works of fiction, or from studying the biographies of famous persons.

Outline of This Book

Now that we have established the general approach that we will adopt in our study of personality, let us have a brief overview of the major questions to be addressed in this book.

First, we will start with some basic concepts in psychological measurement, and with some basic issues about the existence of personality: How do we know that personality traits really exist? How can we measure those characteristics? What are the main traits that make up our personalities?

Then we will look at the nature of personality: How does personality change throughout the life span? In what ways do the workings of our brains and bodies influence our personalities? Is personality shaped more by genes or by environments? How did personality evolve in our early ancestors?

Next we will consider the practical importance of personality: Are there "disorders" of personality? What is the role of personality in aspects of life such as relationships, work, health, the law, and satisfaction with life?

Finally, we will look at personality in relation to some other important psychological characteristics—characteristics that we will also examine in their own right. How does personality relate to mental abilities? To religious beliefs and political attitudes? To sexuality?

Personality psychology is surely one of the most exciting fields of knowledge—get ready to enjoy studying it for the first time!

Chapter 1

Basic Concepts in Psychological Measurement

Some Simple Statistical Ideas   2
  Levels of Measurement   2
  Standard Scores   3
  Correlation Coefficients   5
**Assessing Quality of Measurement:
  Reliability and Validity   9**
  Reliability   9
  Validity   16

**Methods of Measurement: Self- and
  Observer Reports, Direct
  Observations, Biodata   20**
  Self-Reports   20
  Observer Reports   21
  Direct Observations   22
  Biodata (Life Outcome Data)   23
  Comparing the Methods of
    Measurement   23
Summary and Conclusions   24

Before we can really begin to understand personality, we need to figure out how to measure it. And before we can measure personality, it would be useful to have some common terms for describing our measurements.

In this chapter, we will introduce some basic concepts that allow us to describe psychological measurements. By using these concepts, we will have some quick and simple ways of understanding the results of personality research. For example, if a researcher reports that women have a higher level than do men of some personality characteristic, you would probably want to know *how much* higher. Or, if a researcher reports that a given personality characteristic is related to enjoyment of a particular kind of music, you would probably want to know *how much* they are related.

Also in this chapter, we will consider the basic ways of evaluating whether or not our measurements are accurate. Whenever we try to measure a psychological characteristic, we need to make sure (a) that we really have measured some meaningful characteristic, and (b) that this characteristic really is the same one that we are trying to measure. Measuring psychological characteristics accurately can be tricky, so it is important to have some ways of expressing *how well* we have measured those characteristics.

And finally, we will also explore in this chapter some of the methods that psychologists use when measuring personality and related characteristics. As you will see later in this chapter, there exists a variety of methods, each of which has its advantages and disadvantages.

Some Simple Statistical Ideas

Levels of Measurement

One difficulty in psychological measurement, as opposed to measurement in other areas of science, is that there is usually not a meaningful "zero" level of a psychological trait. When physicists describe a variable such as distance, it is easy to imagine what zero distance is. But when psychologists describe a characteristic such as intelligence or rebelliousness or irritability, it is difficult to imagine what a zero level would be. Even if someone has a score of zero on an intelligence test, it does not seem meaningful to say that the person has zero intelligence—presumably, he or she would get a score higher than zero if the test were easier. Because there is no clear zero point, we cannot really say that one person is "three times" more rebellious or "50%" less irritable than another, in the way that a physicist might say that one object has twice as much mass as another. That is, in psychology we are usually not able to describe *ratios* between people's levels of a variable or a person's *absolute amount* of a variable.

But the lack of a true zero level of psychological characteristics does not mean that we cannot measure those characteristics. In fact, there are several different ways by which we could compare people's levels of any given trait. One of these is simply to rank people: For example, we could measure people's levels of ambition, and then record their positions relative to each other, such as 1st, 2nd, 3rd, . . . , 654th, ... This is a sensible approach, but it has some shortcomings. One difficulty is that the *differences* between the ranks are not always meaningful. For example, the person with the highest level of a trait in a given sample might be just slightly higher than the person with the 2nd highest level, but the person who is 2nd highest might be far, far ahead of the person in 3rd. This fact means that ranks are less than ideal for calculating statistics based on our measurements. For example, when we want to compute the average level of a trait, our computation is much more meaningful if the differences (or "intervals") between the numbers always mean the same thing. So, the numbers provided by ranks are not as useful as we might like them to be.

In measuring people's characteristics, therefore, psychologists would like to obtain scores that have meaningful *differences* between them (even though the *ratios* need not be meaningful). For example, if we are trying to measure the trait of "assertiveness," we would like to be confident that a score of 60 really does mean a level of the trait that is halfway between the levels indicated by a 50 and a 70. Note that assertiveness is not really being measured in any particular "units," and that it does not matter if the average score is 60, or 360, or −60, or whatever. The important thing, for the purpose of making meaningful comparisons among people and of being able to calculate statistics, is simply that equal differences, or intervals, between scores represent roughly equal differences in the level of the trait. For example, when psychologists measure intelligence using an "IQ" test, they would hope that the difference between an IQ of 110 and an IQ of 120 really does have the same meaning as the difference between an IQ of 130 and an IQ of 140. (Note again, by the way, that an IQ of 0 does not indicate zero intelligence; note also that the average IQ level has been set arbitrarily at 100, even though any other value could have been chosen as the average instead.)

How do psychologists know if their measurements meet the requirement of having meaningful differences? The methods for testing this are beyond the scope of this textbook, but we can say here that most well-designed psychological measurements are close enough to this ideal to be useful for statistical analysis.

Standard Scores

It was mentioned before that psychological characteristics are not measured in any particular "units," and that it does not matter how high or low the "scores" on a characteristic tend to be, as long as the differences between scores are meaningful. But differences in the numbers used for measuring variables might cause difficulties when we want to compare someone's scores across two or more traits. For example, suppose that Bob has an IQ of 90 (where the average person's IQ is 100) and that Bob also has a score of 60 on a "sociability" scale (which, let us say, has an average score of 50). At first glance, it seems that Bob's IQ score (90) is higher than his sociability score (60), but in fact Bob is below the average on IQ and above the average on sociability. Therefore, we need some way to relate scores on one scale to scores on another scale, so that we can compare levels of one characteristic with levels of another, or to compare scores on the *same* characteristic as measured by different scales.

Psychologists are able to make meaningful comparisons across different kinds of measurement scales by converting scores into *standard scores*. The first step in calculating a standard score is to take an individual's score on a given scale, and then subtract the mean score (i.e., the average score) for the persons who have been measured. This difference between the individual's score and the mean score tells us whether the person is above the average (if the difference is positive) or below the average (if the difference is negative).

But this is not the only step. If we merely subtract the mean score from the individual's score, we still might not have a meaningful idea of *how far* above or below the average that person is. This is because different scales of measurement differ in terms of how "spread out" people's scores are. For example, on a typical IQ test, about two-thirds of people are within 15 points of the average (i.e., between 85 and 115), and about 95% of people are within 30 points of the average (i.e., between 70 and 130). So, a person who has an IQ of 110 is above average, but not by an especially large distance. But imagine that we have another IQ test, on which people's scores are much more tightly bunched (say, two-thirds of people between 95 and 105, and 95% of people between 90 and 110). On this scale, an IQ of 110 would be very high. So, we need some way to compare scales that have different amounts of *variability* in people's scores, as well as different average scores.

In order to do this, psychologists use a second step, after having first subtracted the average score on a scale from the individual's score on that scale. They then divide this difference by the standard deviation, a number that indicates how much variability there

BOX 1-1
The Normal Distribution

The examples in the text are based on what is called a *normal distribution* of scores; when drawn as a graph, this produces the well-known bell-shaped curve (see Figure 1-1). For many physical and psychological characteristics, the distribution of scores is roughly normal: Most people have scores close to the average value, with relatively few people being far above or far below that average. Notice that a person whose score is equal to the mean will have a score that is higher than that of 50% of people. If a person's score is one standard deviation above the mean, then his or her score is higher than that of about 84% of people; if it is two standard deviations above, then it is higher than that of about 98% of people. Conversely, a score that is one standard deviation below the mean is higher than that of about 16% of people, and a score that is two standard deviations below is higher than that of about 2% of people.

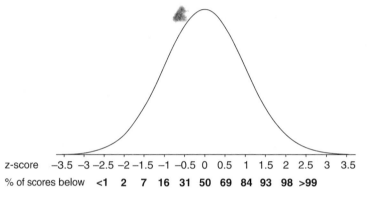

z-score	−3.5	−3	−2.5	−2	−1.5	−1	−0.5	0	0.5	1	1.5	2	2.5	3	3.5
% of scores below		<1	2	7	16	31	50	69	84	93	98	>99			

FIGURE 1-1.   The normal distribution of scores.

is among people on a variable.[1] For many psychological characteristics, about two-thirds of people are within one standard deviation above or below the mean, and about 95% of people are within two standard deviations above or below the mean. (For example, in the situation mentioned before for the typical IQ test, the standard deviation is 15.)

---

[1] The standard deviation is calculated by, first, finding the difference between each person's score and the average score across all persons, then squaring each of these values, then adding up all of the squared values, then dividing this sum by the number of people who were measured, and then finding the square root of this result. Suppose that there are N individuals, and each of the individuals, i, has a score of X_i on variable X, with a mean score of μ for those individuals. The formula for the standard deviation, σ, will then be as follows:

$$\sigma = \sqrt{\left[\frac{\sum_{i=1\,to\,N} (X_i - \mu)^2}{N} \right]}$$

If we do not take the square root, then we have the *square* of the standard deviation of scores, which is called the *variance* of scores, σ^2.

The result of the preceding two steps—finding the difference between the individual's score and the average score, and then dividing this difference by the variability (standard deviation) of the scores—is to give a universal or standard way of expressing people's scores on a given characteristic, regardless of the original distribution of scores on that characteristic. These scores, known as standard scores, have two special properties: First, the average score on a standard-score scale is exactly zero, and second, the standard deviation of a standard-score scale is exactly one. So, after we have calculated standard scores for our variables, we can meaningfully compare a person's scores across different variables. This applies not only to different scales measuring the same variable (e.g., two different IQ test scales), but also to scales measuring different variables (e.g., an IQ test scale and a sociability scale, or an "orderliness" scale and an "originality" scale).[2]

Correlation Coefficients

When we have measured people on two variables, and when we have calculated standard scores of those persons on the variables, we can then easily figure out the extent to which the two variables "go together," or correlate, with each other. Psychologists are frequently interested in the extent to which people who have a high level of a given personality trait are also likely to have a high level of some other variable. For example, to what extent do people with higher levels of hostility also have higher levels of anxiety? To what extent is a high level of hostility associated with a strict, authoritarian upbringing? To what extent is a high level of hostility associated with heart disease? In each of these cases, we need to calculate the *correlation* between the pair of variables in question.

The correlation coefficient, known by the symbol r, can have values ranging anywhere from a maximum of +1 to a minimum of −1. A correlation of +1 means that the two variables go together perfectly; for example, if height and intelligence had a correlation of +1, then a person's height and intelligence would correspond perfectly: A person who was 2 standard deviations above the mean for height would have to be 2 standard deviations above the mean for intelligence, whereas a person who was half a standard deviation below the mean for height would have to be half a standard deviation below the mean for intelligence, and so on.

A correlation of −1 also means that the two variables go together perfectly, but that they go together *in the opposite direction*. So, if height and intelligence had a correlation of −1, then a person's height and intelligence would correspond in a perfectly *opposite* way: A person who was 2 standard deviations above the mean for height would have to

---

[2] Sometimes, standard scores are converted from their basic form, in which the mean is zero and the standard deviation is one, into some other form. As mentioned above, IQ scores are nowadays calculated as standard scores, but with the mean set to 100 and the standard deviation set to 15. Many other tests use a form of standard scores called T-scores, whereby the mean is set to 50 and the standard deviation to 10. Scores on the well-known SAT or GRE tests, which are used in admissions to higher education in the United States, were originally standard scores for which the mean was set to 500 and the standard deviation to 100.

be 2 standard deviations *below* the mean for intelligence, whereas a person who was half a standard deviation below the mean for height would have to be half a standard deviation *above* the mean for intelligence, and so on.

To summarize, a correlation of +1 means a perfect relation in the positive direction: the higher the level of one variable, the higher the level of the other. Conversely, a correlation of −1 means a perfect relation in the negative direction: the higher the level of one variable, the lower the level of the other. By now, you may have guessed that when two variables are completely unrelated to each other, the value of the correlation between them is exactly 0. So, suppose now that height and intelligence are completely uncorrelated—that is, that they correlate 0 with each other. Then, if a person is 2 standard deviations above the mean in height, we have no idea what that person's level of intelligence would be. It could be 3 standard deviations above the mean, or 1 standard deviation below the mean, or anywhere at all. If height and intelligence correlate 0, then knowing the person's height gives us no clue at all about that person's intelligence, and vice versa.

When psychologists investigate the correlations between variables, they rarely find values of exactly +1, or −1, or even 0. Instead, they usually get values that are in between, such as +.34, −.65, +.27, or −.08. Generally, psychologists consider correlations that are fairly close to zero—say, between +.20 and −.20—to be weak or small. Correlations that are somewhat larger—say, between +.20 and +.50, or between −.20 and −.50—are considered to be moderate in size. Correlations that are more extreme—say, above +.50, or below −.50—are considered to be strong or large. But this classification does not really give a very clear idea or "feel" of what a correlation of a given size actually tells us. To appreciate the meaning of a correlation of a given size, we can consider the *binomial effect size display* (Rosenthal & Rubin, 1982).

The binomial effect size display (BESD) is a table that helps to give us an intuitive understanding of the meaning of a correlation of a given size. The BESD table (see Table 1-1) contains two rows and two columns. One row represents the set of people who have a "high" or above-average level of one variable (variable A), and the other row represents the set of people who have a "low" or below-average level of that variable. Similarly, one column represents the set of people who have a "high" or above-average level of a second variable (variable B), and the other column represents the set of people who have a "low" or below-average level of that second variable. The four cells of this table represent the set of people who have each of the four possible combinations of levels of the two variables: high and high; high and low; low and high; low and low. For the sake of simplicity, let us assume that 200 people have been measured on these two variables, so that we will have 100 "low" and "100" high people for each variable.

Now, suppose that we have two variables that are perfectly correlated with each other in the positive direction; that is, the correlation between the variables is 1.00. If this is the case, then everyone who has a high level of variable A must have a high level of variable B, and everyone who has a low level of variable A must have a low level of variable B. Notice, then, that in the BESD table representing this case, we have 100 people in the top right cell, 100 people in the bottom left cell, 0 people in the top left cell, and 0 people in

TABLE 1-1
Examples of Binomial Effect Size Display

$r = 1.00 = (100 - 0) / 100$		Variable B	
		Low	High
Variable A	High	0	100
	Low	100	0
$r = .20 = (60 - 40) / 100$		Variable B	
		Low	High
Variable A	High	40	60
	Low	60	40
$r = -.40 = (30 - 70) / 100$		Variable B	
		Low	High
Variable A	High	70	30
	Low	30	70
$r = .60 = (80 - 20) / 100$		Variable B	
		Low	High
Variable A	High	20	80
	Low	80	20
$r = -.80 = (10 - 90) / 100$		Variable B	
		Low	High
Variable A	High	90	10
	Low	10	90
$r = .00 = (50 - 50) / 100$		Variable B	
		Low	High
Variable A	High	50	50
	Low	50	50

The panels illustrate the meaning of correlations of various sizes by showing the proportions of individuals having high or low levels of one variable who have high or low levels of the other variable.

the bottom right cell. In fact, if we take the number of people in the top right, and subtract the number of people in either the bottom right or the top left, we get $100 - 0 = 100$. This difference, 100, represents the correlation between the two variables (1.00) multiplied by 100. In fact, we can calculate the correlation between any two variables in this way; all we need to do is to subtract the value in the top left or bottom right quadrant from the value in the top right or bottom left quadrant.

Let us consider some other examples (see Table 1-1). Suppose that there are 100 people who are above the median on one variable, and that of these people there are 60 who are above the median on the other and 40 who are below, then the correlation is $60 - 40 = 20$, or .20. If instead only 30 of those 100 people had been above the median on the second variable, and 70 below, then the correlation would be $30 - 70 = -.40$.

It is also possible to use a given correlation value to estimate what proportion of the people who are above the median on one variable will be above (or below) the median on the other. We can do this simply by taking the proportion that corresponds to a zero correlation (i.e., 50%), and then adding and subtracting half of the value of the correlation coefficient. So, if the correlation is .60, then we can estimate that $50 + (60/2) = 50 + 30 = 80\%$ of the people who are above the median on one variable will be above the median on the other, whereas $50 - (60/2) = 50 - 30 = 20\%$ of the people who are above the median on one variable will be below the median on the other.

Similarly, if the correlation is $-.80$, then we can estimate that $50 + (-80/2) = 50 - 40 = 10\%$ of the people who are above the median on one variable will be above the median on the other, whereas $50 - (-80/2) = 50 + 40 = 90\%$ of the people who are above the median on one variable will be below the median on the other. Or, to take an easy example, if the correlation is zero, then we can estimate that $50 + (0/2) = 50 + 0 = 50\%$ of the people who are above the median on one variable will be above the median on the other, whereas $50 - (0/2) = 50 - 0 = 50\%$ of the people who are above the median on one variable will be below the median on the other.

Thus, the usefulness of the BESD is that it gives you a quick and easy way of imagining roughly what a correlation coefficient of a given size actually means, in terms of the extent to which two variables go together. When you hear that there exists a correlation of a given size between two variables, you can use the BESD to visualize how strong that correlation actually is.

BOX 1-2
Calculating the Correlation Coefficient

The BESD is a very useful way to let us imagine what a correlation of a given size actually means. But the BESD was developed for situations in which there really are only two levels of each variable (i.e., "high" and "low"), with people being equally divided between those levels. For most psychological characteristics, however, there are usually not just two levels of "high" and "low"; instead, there are many different levels that a person might have. (The same is true of physical characteristics: A person's height is not simply "tall" or "short"; instead, it can be expressed in terms of centimeters or inches.) When we have variables that have many different levels, as opposed to just two levels, then the results from the BESD for a given correlation coefficient will not be perfectly accurate; that is, they will not exactly match the numbers of persons who are above and below the median on each variable. Nevertheless, the results from the BESD are generally very close to the true values, which means that the BESD still gives a handy guide for interpreting the meaning of a given correlation coefficient.

When researchers actually calculate the correlation coefficient, they use a method that does allow for many different levels of each variable. This method takes into account *how* high or *how* low is an individual's level of a variable, instead of simply relying on whether the individual is above or below the median. The formula for calculating the correlation, r, between two variables, x and y, is as follows when Zx_i and Zy_i are standard scores on those variables for each of N individuals, i:

$$r_{xy} = \frac{\sum_{i=1\,to\,N} Zx_i Zy_i}{N}$$

The idea is that for each of the N individuals we have measured, we find the product of his or her standard scores on the two variables. Then we add together the products obtained from each individual, and we divide this total by N, the number of individuals we have measured. Notice that, if most people tend to have positive z-scores on both variables or negative z-scores on both variables—rather than a positive z-score on one variable and a negative z-score on the other—then the products will be positive, and their sum will be a positive number, thereby producing a positive correlation. If instead many people have a positive z-score on one variable and a negative z-score on the other, then the products will be negative, and their sum will be a negative number, thereby producing a negative correlation.

Note that the correlation coefficient is sometimes used to express how much two groups differ on a variable, even if the groups are not really "above-average" or "below-average" in any sense. For example, we could calculate the correlation between adults' sex (man or woman) and their height. If we found that 70% of men (but only 30% of women) were above the average height for adults, then this would suggest a correlation of about .40 between sex and height (or a −.40 correlation, depending on which sex we arbitrarily treat as "high" in the BESD). However, there is another way to express the relation between people's sex and people's height.

Differences between two groups (such as men and women) on variables such as height, weight, or psychological characteristics can be expressed in terms of standard deviation units. For example, if the standard deviation of adults' height is 10 centimeters (4 inches), and if the average man is 10 centimeters taller than the average woman, then we can say that the difference in height between men and women equals 1 standard deviation unit. Similarly, we could use standard deviation units to express the difference between men and women in any other variable that we can measure.

This method of expressing the differences between groups is still related to the correlation coefficient, however. Consider the following examples: If the difference between two groups is 0.5 standard deviation units, then the correlation is about .20 (giving a 60/40 ratio in the BESD; see Table 1-1). If the group difference is 1.0 standard deviation units, the correlation is about .40 (a 70/30 ratio in the BESD). If the group difference is 1.5 standard deviation units, the correlation is about .60 (an 80/20 ratio in the BESD). These conversions allow a ready grasp of what a group difference of a given size actually means.

Assessing Quality of Measurement: Reliability and Validity

The preceding sections have described some of the basic statistical concepts that are used by psychologists who measure people's levels of various characteristics. But now we need to consider the question of how to assess the *quality* of those measurements: When we try to measure a characteristic in a sample of people, how do we know whether or not we have been successful? In other words, how can we know *how accurately* we have measured that characteristic? There are several aspects of measurement quality to be considered, but these are generally classified into two broad properties known as reliability and validity.

Reliability

The *reliability* of a measurement is the extent to which it agrees with other measurements of the same variable. When there is good agreement between measurements, this tells us that they are assessing some real characteristic, rather than just being meaningless random numbers. It is important to evaluate the reliability of our measurements, because whenever we try to measure a variable, there is likely to be some random error in those measurements.

There are several different ways in which reliability can be assessed, depending on the kind of random error that we consider. For example, there is error in the sense that the various questions on a test are not perfectly accurate in measuring the intended characteristic.

There is also error in the sense that different observers of individuals' levels of a characteristic are not able to assess the characteristic perfectly. And there is also error in the sense that measurements of a given characteristic on any one occasion do not perfectly reflect an individual's actual level of that characteristic. Let us consider the different aspects of reliability, which deal with these different kinds of error in measurement.

Internal-Consistency Reliability

When evaluating the quality of a psychological measurement, we need to consider the error that results from differences among the "items" or parts of the measurement, such as the various questions on a test or a scale. Whenever we try to measure a characteristic, we use a limited number of possible questions or statements, which we call "items." These items are combined to produce an overall score for the test or scale. (You are already familiar with this idea: For example, your instructor combines your scores on the different parts of an examination to get your overall score; similarly, a golfer adds up his or her scores for each of the 18 holes to get his or her overall score for the round of golf.)

But the problem is that any particular item is not a pure measure of the characteristic that we are trying to assess. Instead, each item will assess that characteristic only partially, and will also assess some other variable that is specific to that item. To the extent that an item measures some specific variable of its own, rather than the characteristic that we are trying to assess, we say that the item has "error" variance. If a test or scale overall has a large proportion of error variance, then it cannot be measuring any single, common characteristic very reliably.

To understand this idea more clearly, consider the following example. Suppose that we want to measure the extent to which people have a "sweet tooth"—that is, a preference for various sweet-tasting foods and beverages—and that we plan to measure this variable by asking people how much they like various kinds of sweet foods. So, suppose we ask people to rate, on a scale of 0 to 10, how much they like (a) maple ice cream, (b) blueberry pie, and (c) ginger ale. We then add up each individual's response on the three items in order to find their overall level of "sweet toothedness."

Now, you might already have realized that this three-item test would not be an ideal measure of how much of a "sweet tooth" a person has. Let us examine what these questions measure. First, all three items probably are related to the overall tendency to enjoy sweet foods, at least to some small extent. That is, people who really do have a sweet tooth will probably like each of these foods, on average, somewhat more than the people who do not have a sweet tooth will like these foods. But how much do these items really measure a person's level of sweet toothedness? It seems likely that each question would probably measure, in large part, the enjoyment of the *specific* flavor or type of food or beverage, rather than enjoyment of sweet things in general. The first item probably measures liking of maple flavor and of ice cream, in addition to liking of sweet foods. Similarly, the second item probably measures liking of blueberry flavor and of pie crusts, in addition to liking of sweet foods. Finally, the third item probably measures liking of ginger flavor and of carbonated drinks, in addition to liking of sweet foods.

How can we tell *how much* these items are measuring the liking of sweet foods in general, as opposed to measuring the liking of the specific flavors and types of foods described in each item? The way to determine this is to find the correlations among people's liking of the three foods, which will tell us the extent to which persons who especially like any one of these foods will also tend to like any of the others. To the extent that the three items measure something in common—which would very likely be sweet toothedness—these correlations should be rather high. To the extent that the three items each measure something unique, these correlations should be very small, that is, only slightly above zero. Now, I have not actually measured these variables, but my prediction is that the correlations among them would be pretty small: A person who especially likes any one of these three foods would only be slightly more likely than the average person to like any of the other two foods. In other words, I expect that people's liking of these three foods depends more on their liking of the specific flavors and types of food involved than on the overall tendency to enjoy sweet foods in general.

But even if people's liking of each specific type of food depends only slightly on their sweet toothedness, we might still get a fairly good measure of that characteristic, when we find an average score for each person across all three questions. This is a crucial point: By averaging out the three responses, we get an overall score that tends to represent the common element of the three items, more than it represents the specific elements of the items. That is, when we find a person's responses to the three questions, what we begin to see is his or her level of whatever characteristic that the three questions have in common—in this case, sweet toothedness. The average score will still also tell us about the unique aspect of each question—in this case, preference for the specific flavors and types of food described—but these unique elements have a weaker influence than they did for each question individually. Think of it this way: If two people differ greatly in their *overall* liking of maple ice cream, blueberry pie, and ginger ale, the main reason is probably the difference between those two people in their liking of sweet foods generally.

Now, remember that the idea of assessing the reliability of a measurement is that we want to know the extent to which the scores measure a common characteristic, as opposed to "error" variance, which includes whatever characteristics influence responses to the individual items. The reliability of a score that is found by averaging responses to several items (where the items have similar standard deviations) basically depends on two things: the number of items, and the correlations among the items. If you think about this for a moment, you will understand why these things matter.

First, if we are averaging out people's responses to items that have something in common, that common element will become stronger and stronger when we add more and more items. In the example considered here, a person's average liking of maple ice cream, blueberry pie, and ginger ale probably does indicate his or her sweet toothedness, but his or her liking for each of those three specific flavors and food types is also important. However, if we average out across a larger number of items—say, by also including items about liking of chocolate-chip cookies, apple fritters, and caramel pudding, in addition to the original three foods—then the common element of sweet toothedness becomes even stronger, and the unique elements of liking each individual food (there are now six of them instead of just three) become relatively weaker. So, by averaging out across a larger number of items, we get a more reliable overall score—in other words, we get a better measurement of whatever characteristic the items are measuring in common.

Second, if we are averaging out people's responses to items that have something in common, that common element will be stronger to the extent that the items are correlated with each other, because those correlations tell us how much each individual item is measuring the common characteristic. If the items are very weakly correlated with each other, then they do not do a very good job of measuring that common characteristic. In the sweet-toothedness example, considering the original three foods—maple ice cream, blueberry pie, and ginger ale—the average correlation among them might be, say, .30. But if we had taken three other foods that were less sugary, and hence less likely to be preferred simply on the basis of one's sweet toothedness, then these correlations would have been weaker. For example, if we had chosen three moderately sweet foods, such as orange juice, corn (maize) bread, and arrowroot cookies, then probably we would have found weaker correlations among them, because liking of each of these foods would depend less on sweet toothedness, and more on enjoyment of the specific aspects of each food, such as orange, corn, and arrowroot flavors. So, by averaging an individual's responses to these three items, we would only get a fairly weak indication of his or her sweet toothedness, at least in relation to average responses for the original three items. On the other hand, if we had taken three very sugary foods—let us say, white sugar, brown sugar, and icing sugar—then we would have found very strong correlations among them, because these foods are very similar in taste. So, by averaging an individual's responses to these three items, we would get a very strong indication of a characteristic that would probably represent his or her sweet toothedness. (Even if people do not like plain sugar as much as they like sugary foods, the differences among people in their liking of different kinds of sugar might still be a good indication of people's relative levels of sweet toothedness.)

To maximize reliability—in other words, to obtain a very strong measure of the common characteristic measured by the items of your scale—it is better to have both a large number of items and a high level of correlations among the items. But to some extent, a large number of items can compensate for low correlations among items, and high correlations among items can compensate for a small number of items.

Table 1-2 shows the level of reliability that results when tests have different numbers of items, and different average correlations among the items. Notice that the reliability values are all between zero and one. This index of reliability has a special property, in that

TABLE 1-2

Internal-Consistency Reliability of a Measurement, as a Function of the Number of Items (k) and the Mean Correlation among Items (r)

Mean correlation among items (r)	Number of items (k)				
	2	5	10	20	50
.05	.10	.21	.34	.51	.72
.10	.18	.36	.53	.69	.85
.20	.33	.56	.71	.83	.93
.50	.67	.83	.91	.95	.98

BOX 1-3
Calculating Internal-Consistency Reliability

There are various formulas for estimating the internal-consistency reliability of a test by using the number of items and the average correlation among the items. The following is one of the simpler formulas, known as the *Spearman–Brown formula*; it is less precise than some of the others, but it is good enough for our purposes. In this formula, r_{xx} is internal-consistency reliability, k is the number of items, and $\bar{r}$ is the average correlation among the items.

$$r_{xx} = \frac{k\bar{r}}{1+(k-1)\,\bar{r}}$$

A somewhat more complicated formula for calculating internal-consistency reliability is called *Cronbach's alpha*, or *coefficient alpha*. Unlike the Spearman–Brown formula, the formula for Cronbach's alpha (α) takes into account the differences in correlations among items, and the differences in the items' standard deviations. Because the alpha formula is somewhat more accurate, it is the method of calculating reliability that is most widely used. In case you are curious, the formula is as follows, where α is internal-consistency reliability, where k is the number of items in the test, where σ_i^2 is the variance of each item i, and where σ_x^2 is the variance of the entire test:

$$\alpha = \frac{k}{k-1}\left[1 - \frac{\sum_{i=1\,\text{to}\,k} \sigma_i^2}{\sigma_x^2}\right]$$

A simpler method of calculating internal-consistency reliability is simply to split the items of a test into two halves, and to calculate each individual's score on each half of the test, so that one can then find the correlation between the two halves. In this *split-half* method of calculating the reliability of a test, the Spearman–Brown formula is than applied to this correlation, using 2 as the value of k. This method is easy to use, but it is less accurate than are the previous methods, in which scores on each item are considered separately.

An even simpler method of calculating internal-consistency reliability is to take two different but comparable versions of a test—that is, two "parallel forms" of a test—and to calculate the correlation between them. The idea of this *parallel forms* method is that the reliability of a test is given by the correlation of the whole test with another test that is meant to measure the same characteristic, but using a different set of items. This is a useful method, but it can only be applied in the somewhat unusual case when one actually has two parallel forms of a test.

it represents the proportion of variance in the measurement that is due to the common element. Conversely, if we subtract the reliability value from one, then we obtain the proportion of variance in the measurement that is due to "error," or to the unique aspects of the various items individually. To the extent that the reliability value is high, it tells us that our scale does measure a common characteristic, not just a collection of unrelated characteristics.

The kind of reliability described above is called *internal-consistency reliability*, because it depends in part on the extent to which the items in a test are correlated with each other, or "internally consistent." As noted before, internal-consistency reliability represents the proportion of variance in a test that is due to the variance that is common to the various items of the test. This is the kind of reliability that is most commonly reported in research on personality characteristics and related individual differences.

Interrater (Interobserver) Reliability

Another kind of reliability is analogous to internal-consistency reliability, but instead of being based on the items of a test, it is based on the observers or raters of a characteristic. To understand this other kind of reliability, known as *interrater reliability* (or as *interobserver reliability*), let us consider the sweet-toothedness example again. But this time, let us suppose that we measure sweet toothedness in a very different way.

Imagine that we obtain ratings of each individual's sweet toothedness, on a scale from 0 to 10, from three people who know the individual fairly well—for example, a summer job co-worker, a sports teammate, and a college classmate. Now, for any given individual, each of these three raters is likely to have at least some idea of how much of a sweet tooth the individual has, because each rater is likely to have observed the individual's eating habits on some at least some occasions. But the ratings are likely to be somewhat inaccurate, because each of these persons is unlikely to have observed the individual's eating habits thoroughly enough, across a wide enough variety of situations, to know exactly how much the person likes sweet foods overall. So, we would expect the three ratings of sweet toothedness to be somewhat correlated with each other, because the three raters presumably have some vague knowledge of the individual's level of sweet toothedness. But the correlations would not be extremely high, because there is some error: That is, each rater is to some extent guessing, based on a limited amount of information. By averaging the three ratings, we should obtain a more reliable overall rating of the individual's sweet toothedness, because the common element of the three ratings—presumably, the individual's true level of sweet toothedness—would become fairly strong. In contrast, the specific, "error" aspects of each rating—that is, each rater's own subjective sense of the individual's sweet toothedness—would become relatively weak.

Notice that, similar to the situation when we calculate internal-consistency reliability, we will have higher reliability if we have more raters. (In the case of interrater reliability, these raters take the place of the items that are used in computing internal-consistency reliability.) If we added three more people who are acquainted with the individual, and based our estimates of reliability on the average response from all six, then the common element of true sweet toothedness would be even more strongly represented.

Also, and again similar to the situation when we calculate of internal-consistency reliability, we will have higher reliability if our raters' ratings are more highly correlated with each other. (This is similar to the situation in which items are highly correlated with each other when computing internal-consistency reliability.) So, if we had selected three people who knew the individual very well—say, his or her sister, mother, and daughter—then the correlations among the three raters' ratings would be very high, because each rater would have observed the individual's eating preferences across the full range of sweet foods. But if we had selected three people who had barely interacted with the individual at all, and had only a very limited basis for estimating his or her sweet toothedness, then each of them would largely be guessing, and the correlations among the three ratings would be weak, giving a low level of reliability.

Thus, whenever we obtain some ratings of individuals' levels of characteristic as made by different observers, we can calculate the interrater (or interobserver) reliability of those ratings. This interobserver reliability represents the proportion of variance in the overall ratings that is common to the different observers' ratings; the remaining proportion of variance is the error that is specific to each of the different observers.[3]

Test–Retest Reliability

Another kind of error in our measurements is due to random fluctuations across short periods of time. If we measure some characteristic of people at a given time, and then we measure that same characteristic again a few days or weeks later, we will probably find that people's scores, relative to each other, will not be exactly the same: Some people will have standard scores a bit higher, and some will have standard scores a bit lower, than they were when the variable was measured the first time.

The fluctuations in people's scores on psychological characteristics across short periods of time are usually not very large, but psychologists like to have some indication of the extent to which those scores fluctuate—that is, of the extent to which there is error across occasions of measurement. To obtain this information, psychologists measure the characteristic in the same group of individuals on two different occasions, usually separated by a few days or a few weeks. The correlation between the two measurements is called the *test–retest reliability* of the measurements. If individuals' relative levels of the characteristic tend to be consistent across different occasions of measurement, then the correlation will be high; this indicates that there is little error due to the occasion of measurement, and that there is a high level of test–retest reliability.

Note that when evaluating test–retest reliability, the measurements are taken at relatively short time intervals. If, instead, these time intervals were much longer, then changes in individuals' relative scores might not be due to random fluctuations. Instead, the shifting positions of individuals might be due to real differences among them in their long-term development of the characteristic. As an example, consider the trait of height in children. If we measured children's heights on one occasion, and then measured the same children's heights again a few weeks later, then the correlation between the two sets of measurements would tell us about the test–retest reliability of our measurement. However, if the time interval separating the measurements were much longer, say several years, then the correlation between the two measurements would not necessarily tell us about the reliability of our measurement. Instead, it would probably tell us more about the long-term stability of the characteristic of height. That is, a low correlation would tell us that different children were growing at different rates during the years between the two measurements, which would cause changes in the children's standard scores for height. (In Chapter 4, we will discuss the extent to which personality characteristics are stable across long periods of time.)

As noted before, most measurements of psychological characteristics tend to show relatively little fluctuation across short periods of time, so test–retest reliability tends to be quite high. However, test–retest reliability can be low under some circumstances. For

---

[3] The calculation of interrater reliability, and the interpretation of the resulting values, is the same as in the case of internal-consistency reliability, except that we have raters instead of items. For example, in the Spearman–Brown formula described before, k now represents the number of raters, and $\bar{r}$ represents the average correlation among the raters.

example, suppose that we are interested in measuring an individual's level of some emotion, such as anxiety, anger, fatigue, joy, sadness, or sentimentality. If the items used to measure these variables are phrased in such a way as to ask about the individual's current, temporary state, then there might be quite low correlations between scores obtained one week apart (or one day apart, or even one hour apart). These low correlations would reflect the tendency for most people's moods to fluctuate at least somewhat over short periods of time. So, if we were interested in measuring an individual's typical level of these emotions, we would need to make sure that the items ask how much the individual *generally* experiences these emotions, over the long run. In this way, test–retest reliability will likely be high, because an individual's perceptions of his or her *typical* level of the emotions will not be influenced so much by his or her temporary mood.

Validity

The *validity* of a measurement is the extent to which it assesses variation in the *same* characteristic that it is supposed to assess. Notice that this definition is different from, and more restrictive than, the definition of reliability. When we evaluate reliability, we are concerned only with the extent to which our measurements represent *some* meaningful characteristic, whatever that might be, rather than error. By contrast, when we evaluate validity, we are concerned with precisely *which* characteristic is being assessed.

You might wonder why we consider reliability at all, given that validity would seem to be more important. But there are two reasons for considering reliability. First, by knowing the reliability of a scale, we get an idea of the maximum possible validity of a scale: If a scale has poor reliability—that is, if it is not measuring any characteristic at all—then we know that it cannot have a very high level of validity—that is, it cannot be measuring the characteristic we had in mind. This is important to know, because we might sometimes realize that a scale having moderate validity could potentially have much higher validity, if its reliability could be improved (e.g., by adding more items or by slightly modifying the items already included). This contrasts with the situation in which a scale with high reliability has low validity, in which case we know that the scale is measuring something, but something different from what we had in mind. In the latter case, we need to make some major changes to the scale, by using items that are quite different; it will not help just to supplement or modify the items already included.

There are different ways of evaluating the validity of a measurement of a characteristic. One way involves examining the *content* of the scale, and another involves examining the relations of scores on the scale with other variables (which are called *criterion* variables). Let us consider these aspects of validity.

Content Validity

An important aspect of the validity of a measurement is the extent to which its components—for example, the items or questions of a scale or test—are relevant to the characteristic that is supposed to be measured. For a measurement to have *content validity*, it should assess *all* of the features of the intended characteristic, and it should *not* assess the features of other, irrelevant characteristics.

Consider the example of the sweet-toothedness scale that was described in our discussion of reliability. Suppose that we constructed a sweet-toothedness scale containing 10 items, each of which assessed the individual's liking for a different type of sweet food or beverage. We would hope that these items would describe a wide variety of different flavors and kinds of sweet food, so that the scale would assess sweet toothedness in general, rather than just liking for one or two kinds of sweet foods. For example, if all of the sweet-tooth items described fruit-flavored foods, then the content validity of our sweet-toothedness scale would be rather weak, because the scale probably measures liking of fruit just as much as it measures liking of sweet foods. In a less extreme case, even if a wide variety of sweet foods were included, but if some kinds seemed to be much more heavily represented than others, then the content validity would also be limited. (This might happen, for example, if we had several items about chocolate-flavored foods, but only one item about any kind of fruit-flavored foods.) In addition, we would hope that none of the sweet-toothedness items described foods that were not sweet at all (e.g., chips, nachos); if these irrelevant kinds of foods were included, then the content validity of the scale would also be poor.

In thinking about these examples, it might seem to you that achieving good content validity is fairly easy, and that simple common sense can prevent us from constructing a scale that has poor content validity. But sometimes there are some subtle and difficult issues involved in making sure that content validity is strong. One difficulty is that it can often be tricky to decide exactly what kinds of content ought to be included, and what ought not to be included, in our definition of a characteristic. This might not be much of a problem for the trait of sweet toothedness, but for other traits, it often is a challenge. For example, suppose that we wanted to measure the trait of athletic ability. (This is not a psychological characteristic, but it is a good example anyhow.) We would probably decide that our athletic ability test should assess individuals' speed, power, agility, balance, and coordination. But what about cardiovascular endurance? Strength? Flexibility? Should these characteristics be viewed as aspects of athletic ability? Or do they represent something different? If they are aspects of athletic ability, then we would only achieve content validity by including them; but if they are not, then we would only achieve content validity by excluding them. Sometimes it is difficult to decide exactly which content should be considered as part of the characteristic to be measured, and which content should be considered as something separate.

Difficulties with content validity can sometimes arise when we try to achieve a high level of internal-consistency reliability. Recall from the earlier section about reliability that the items of a scale should be substantially correlated with each other, so that the scale will have a high level of internal-consistency reliability. But it is possible to go too far in selecting items that show high correlations with each other, because we could end up with a set of very similar items that would only represent a small part of the range of content that our characteristic is supposed to include. To return to our example of sweet toothedness, we might achieve very high internal-consistency reliability by including only a few items, all of which assess the liking of a particular kind of sweet food—perhaps sugar itself. But if we did this, we would then have sacrificed the content validity of our scale, because our items would no longer assess the liking of the full range of sweet foods. So, even though it is important to achieve high internal-consistency reliability, we should be just as careful to make sure that we also maintain the content validity of our scale.

In my own work, I have occasionally had to find a compromise between internal-consistency reliability and content validity. When my colleague and I were developing a scale to measure "aesthetic appreciation" (i.e., appreciation of beauty in art and nature), we noticed that the best items, from the point of view of internal-consistency reliability, were those related to the visual arts, such as painting and sculpture. But we did not want our scale to reflect only the appreciation of visual art, so we included only a few of the visual art items, and instead added some other items assessing appreciation of other art forms, such as music and poetry, and also of various natural wonders. In this way, we were able to have an aesthetic appreciation scale that had good internal-consistency reliability but also had good content validity.

Criterion Validity: Convergent and Discriminant

Another aspect of the validity of a measurement of a characteristic involves the correlations between that measurement and some other, outside variables. This is known as *criterion validity*, because the outside variables are called criteria (the word "criteria" is plural for "criterion"). The idea of criterion validity is that, if our scale is really measuring the characteristic that it is intended to measure, then it should correlate in certain specified ways with criterion variables. The sizes of these correlations should correspond closely to the degree of similarity between the characteristic to be measured by our scale and the characteristic measured by the criterion variables.

One aspect of criterion validity is called *convergent validity*. When we test the convergent validity of a scale, we investigate how strongly it correlates with criterion variables that measure characteristics similar (or *opposite*) to the one that our scale is intended to measure. If there is a criterion variable that is known to measure something very similar to what our scale is supposed to measure, then we would expect our scale to show strong positive correlations with that variable. If so, then this would support the convergent validity of our scale. But if we failed to find such a result, then this would be evidence against the convergent validity of our scale; it would suggest that perhaps our scale was not measuring the characteristic that we had intended it to measure. Similarly, if there is a criterion variable that is known to measure something rather *opposite* to what our scale is supposed to measure, then we would expect our scale to show strong negative correlations with that variable. If so, then this would support the convergent validity of our scale. But again, if we failed to find such a result, then this would again be evidence against the convergent validity of our scale; it would suggest that perhaps our scale was not measuring the characteristic that we had intended it to measure. So, keep in mind that convergent validity involves the correlations of our scale with criterion variables measuring related characteristics: This includes strong negative correlations with opposite variables, as well as strong positive correlations with similar variables.

The other aspect of criterion validity is called *discriminant validity*. When we test for the discriminant validity of a scale, we investigate how strongly it correlates with criterion variables that measure characteristics *unrelated* to the one that our scale is intended to measure. If there is a criterion variable that is known to measure something neither similar nor opposite to what our scale is supposed to measure, then we would expect our scale to show weak correlations with that variable; in other words, the observed correlation, whether positive or negative, would be quite close to zero. If so, then this would support the discriminant validity of our scale. But if we instead found a strong correlation (either positive or negative), then this would be evidence against the discriminant validity of our scale; it would suggest that perhaps our scale was measuring some characteristic other than the one that we had intended it to measure.

Let us think about how we might evaluate the convergent validity—both convergent and discriminant—of our sweet-toothedness scale. If our sweet-toothedness scale really measured sweet toothedness, we would expect good convergent validity, as observed in strong correlations with other indicators of having a sweet tooth. For example, sweet-toothedness scores should correlate positively with how much sugar the person consumes (from all food sources) in each week. Similarly, sweet-toothedness scores should correlate negatively with observations of how frequently the person declines to eat dessert. In addition, sweet-toothedness scores should correlate positively with relatives' or friends' ratings of the person's sweet toothedness. Of course, it is unlikely that any of these correlations would be extremely high, because variables other than sweet toothedness would also influence these criterion variables. For example, people who have a very sweet tooth but who are on a low-carbohydrate diet would probably not consume much sugar, and probably would often decline dessert. But in general, we would expect people who have a very sweet tooth to eat more sweet foods than do people who have a less sweet tooth.

With regard to discriminant validity, we would expect our sweet-toothedness scale to correlate weakly with several variables. If our sweet-toothedness scale really did measure sweet toothedness, then we would expect it to correlate weakly (i.e., to show only a *small* positive or a *small* negative correlation) with the consumption of nonsweet foods. For example, we would expect a near-zero correlation with the amount of meat consumed in a week, or with the amount of vegetables consumed in a week. Similarly, we would also expect the scale to correlate weakly with relatives' or friends' ratings of the person's liking of these various nonsweet foods.

Construct Validity

Sometimes researchers describe a kind of validity called *construct validity*. The word construct is used to indicate that the property being measured is something that is imagined or "constructed," and is not something that is concrete or tangible. So, sweet toothedness is a construct, as are other variables such as intelligence or sociability or impulsivity. (In the same way, many variables assessed in the physical sciences—such as temperature, mass, and length—are also constructs.) Thus, when we say that a measurement has construct validity, we are saying that the evidence indicates that this measurement really does assess the same construct that we are trying to assess.

As described in the preceding way, "construct validity" essentially just means the same thing as "validity," which includes the two aspects described before: Content validity and criterion validity (where criterion validity itself consists of both convergent and discriminant validity). But if construct validity is simply the same thing as validity, then you might wonder why we would even consider it as an aspect that is separate from content validity or criterion validity. For the purpose of this book, we will not: Instead, we will treat "construct validity" as being identical to "validity."

But still, why is construct validity sometimes considered as a separate, third aspect of validity? The reason is that some researchers prefer to define criterion validity somewhat more narrowly than we have defined it here. Specifically, they use the term criterion validity only when referring to the relations between the measurement and some criterion variable that is of *practical* usefulness (e.g., job performance, health outcomes). Those researchers instead use the term construct validity when referring to the relations between the measurement of some criterion variable that is of *theoretical* interest (e.g., other measurements of the same or different traits). Thus, according to this alternative view, much evidence of convergent or of discriminant validity would be considered as part of construct validity, rather than as part of criterion validity.

Methods of Measurement: Self- and Observer Reports, Direct Observations, Biodata

In the previous sections we considered the mathematical meaning of psychological measurements, but here we will discuss *how* psychological measurements are actually made. When we want to know about someone's personality—his or her patterns of behavior, thought, and emotion—we have several strategies for making our measurements.

Self-Reports

One simple approach is simply to ask the person a series of questions about his or her actions, thoughts, and feelings in various situations. An important feature of this approach is that the observations are "standard" or "objective," in the sense (a) that every person is asked the same set of questions, and also (b) that there is a fixed set of response alternatives for every question (e.g., yes/no, or a number from 1 to 7). In this way, we can make meaningful comparisons of the responses that different persons provide. If we ask a series of questions that involve related behaviors (e.g., talking on the phone, visiting friends, inviting guests, attending parties), then we can make some inference about the person's level of some underlying characteristic (e.g., sociability).

This method is known as *self-report*, and it is the most widely used method of measuring personality. Perhaps the main reason for the popularity of self-report is the belief that it usually allows a fairly accurate and efficient measurement, and at a rather low cost. The accuracy of self-report depends on a couple of important assumptions: First, that people generally know their behaviors, thoughts, and feelings fairly well, and second, that people are willing (at least under some circumstances) to report those behaviors, thoughts, and feelings. Of course, these assumptions are probably not entirely true: Most people are unlikely to be able to report all aspects of their personality with near-perfect accuracy, and some people may be quite poor at judging their own personality. Moreover, at least some people are likely to distort their responses intentionally, to a greater or lesser extent, in order to present a good impression (or even, in some cases, to present a bad impression).

As described before, the self-report method of assessing personality involves asking an individual about his or her behaviors, thoughts, and feelings, and then inferring that individual's personality on the basis of the responses. But sometimes, the self-reports can simply involve an overall rating of the individual's level of a personality trait. For example, an individual might be asked to rate his or her own level of impulsivity, perhaps a number from 0 to 10. These self-ratings might have an advantage relative to self-reports, insofar as the rating is a more direct indication of the trait. To the extent that people agree about what is actually meant by a given trait name, this method could be quite accurate. But on the other hand, people might differ in their understandings of which behaviors, thoughts, and feelings would indicate an individual's level of a given trait. (For example, one person might interpret impulsivity as a kind of spontaneous fun-loving tendency, whereas another person might interpret impulsivity as an inability to control one's urges.) To the extent that these understandings may differ, the accuracy of self-ratings would be limited, relative to self-reports of the kind described before. For many purposes, however, the distinction between "reports" and "ratings" is not so clear; many personality questionnaires, for example, contain a mixture of items that represent reports of behaviors, thoughts, and feelings, and items that represent direct ratings of traits.

Observer Reports

Another method of assessing an individual's personality is analogous to self-report, but instead of asking the individual about his or her own behaviors, thoughts, and feelings, it involves asking someone else for that information. Ideally, this other person should be someone who knows the individual fairly well, for example, a spouse, a close relative, or a close friend, but for some purposes and some traits a co-worker or classmate might be a suitable rater. Compared with self-report, this *observer report* method (also called *other report* or *peer report*) has the advantage that an individual's personality might in some cases be judged more objectively by someone who actually *observes* that individual from the outside. But then again, the people who know an individual very well might be just as strongly inclined to present a good impression for that individual as the individual he or she would be—for example, your parents might overestimate your level of desirable traits, and underestimate your level of undesirable ones. Also, it is likely that even the other people who know the individual very well still do not know that person quite as well as the individual himself or herself does; there are some aspects of his or her thoughts and feelings, and even behaviors, that others might never really observe. This is particularly true when the other people are only acquainted with the individual in a limited range of contexts, such as in the workplace or at school. (Note that, just as we distinguished between self-reports and self-ratings in the previous section, we can also distinguish between observer reports and observer ratings in the same way.)

Direct Observations

Another method of measuring personality, quite different from self- and observer reports or ratings, is to observe a person's behavior directly. If the behaviors that indicate a given personality trait are known to the observer, then it is possible to measure that trait by observing the frequency or intensity with which the individual performs those behaviors. These observations might be made by watching the individual in his or her own natural habitat. For example, I could try to assess your level of a trait such as sociability by actually watching how frequently you talk on the phone, visit friends, invite guests, and attend parties. Alternatively, the individual could be observed in an artificial setting: For example, I could try to assess your sociability level by observing your behavior in a social situation created in my laboratory, in which you would have the opportunity to interact and converse (or to *avoid* interacting and conversing) with other research participants or with my research assistants. By observing various features of your behavior, such as how much talking you did, how many questions you asked, how many people you spoke with, and how closely you stood to the other people, I might be able to estimate your level of sociability.

The method of direct observation has sometimes been used in personnel selection. One example of this occurred in the United States during World War II, when the Office of Strategic Services (OSS)—the former name of today's Central Intelligence Agency (CIA)—used direct observations to assess personality when selecting secret agents for overseas assignments. In one of the OSS selection tests, the (male) applicant was observed in a role-playing scenario. In this scenario, he was told to imagine that he had just been caught looking through secret documents at a government building, and that he was not authorized to do so. The applicant was then given 10 minutes to come up with a detailed explanation that would justify what he had been caught doing and would preserve his "cover" as an agent. Subsequently, the applicant was interrogated by several officers who would try to confuse and intimidate him, to catch him in contradictions, to make him feel stressed, and to trick him into breaking his cover. The OSS officials who made this selection test observed the extent to which the applicant could maintain his composure and poise during the interrogation, and how well he was able to maintain a plausible cover story. Some applicants did these things well; others plainly did not. (In a few cases, the OSS officials were impressed by some applicants who had fooled the interrogators by pretending to break down emotionally, giving a fake but irrelevant "confession" that actually maintained their cover.)

As you might have noticed, the method of direct observation is potentially very informative, but it has the disadvantage that it requires a lot of time and effort to use, and is therefore very expensive. To observe an individual's behavior, either in natural or artificial settings, can be a very large undertaking, particularly if one hopes to measure many different individuals, or to measure many different traits. Moreover, when observing in natural settings, it might be necessary to observe over a long period of time in order to get a really accurate idea of the individual's typical behavior, and hence his or her level of a personality trait. And, when observing in artificial settings, it might be necessary to observe over a variety of artificial situations, again in order to ensure that one can assess the individual's typical behavior related to a given trait. These considerations make direct observation very difficult to use on a large scale. However, an important advantage is the fact that one really is observing behavior directly. This gives the observer some confidence that he or she really is assessing personality, as long as the behaviors really are valid indicators of the characteristic that he or she wants to measure.[4]

Biodata (Life Outcome Data)

Yet another method for assessing personality is to obtain "biodata"—that is, to obtain some records of the person's life which seem likely to be relevant to an individual's personality. For example, I might use your phone bill as an indication of your sociability, your grade point average (GPA) as an indication of your industriousness, or your speeding tickets as an indication of your recklessness. These records have the advantage that they often represent important outcomes in a person's life, and that they are objective indicators of behavior rather than merely reports. But on the other hand, it is not always clear that a particular piece of information about an individual's life is really an accurate indication of his or her level of the personality trait that we hope to assess. Instead, a particular outcome might be influenced by other traits, or by a variety of circumstances that are unrelated to one's personality. For example, a sociable person whose friends live nearby (or whose money is limited) might have a low phone bill; an industrious person who has no interest or aptitude for schoolwork might have a low GPA; and a reckless person who has no car might have few speeding tickets. Nevertheless, it seems likely that many kinds of life outcome data will give at least some information about an individual's personality.

Comparing the Methods of Measurement

How do we know that any of the previous methods actually provide valid indicators of individuals' levels of various personality traits? The main source of evidence on this question has been the convergent validity correlations among measures of the same or similar traits, as assessed by different methods or by different versions of the same method. As we will discuss in more detail in Chapter 2, there are generally rather strong correlations between self-report and observer report measurements of personality characteristics, and strong correlations also between observer report measurements of personality characteristics as provided by different observers. In addition, self-report and observer report measurements generally show good convergent validity with regard to direct observations of

---

[4] In some sense, certain kinds of tests of ability or achievement can also be considered as examples of direct observations within artificial settings. For example, consider tests of mental abilities: Here, the individual being measured is placed into an artificial setting (specifically, the situation of taking the test) and his or her behavior is observed simply by recording his or her answers to the test questions. In other words, the researcher is able to measure the individual's level of ability by directly observing that individual's performance on the test. Notice that this is quite different from the self-report or observer report methods, which in this case would involve *asking* about the individual's level of ability.

behavior and with regard to biodata; we will discuss these latter results in more depth in Chapter 9.

Some researchers have criticized the heavy reliance on personality reports (especially self-reports) by other researchers. However, it is easy to see why self- and observer reports are so widely used: They provide extremely quick, cheap, and efficient methods of measuring a wide array of traits, with generally good levels of reliability and validity. Although some researchers view direct observation as the ideal method—as a kind of "gold standard" for personality measurement—it is likely that self- and observer reports will provide better measures of personality overall. This is because of the extreme difficulty of obtaining enough observations of individuals, across a wide enough variety of situations, and involving a wide enough variety of different behaviors, for each of the traits that researchers would like to measure.

Summary and Conclusions

In this chapter, we have introduced some basic statistical concepts, some ways of assessing the quality of measurement, and some methods for measuring psychological characteristics. Here we will briefly summarize these points.

First, most psychological measurements are reported using numbers that show which people have higher or lower levels of a characteristic, and also show how large the difference is between any two people. However, those numbers do not show an absolute "zero" level of a characteristic, nor do they allow us to talk about ratios between people's levels—for example, it would not make sense to say that one person is twice as organized as another. Also, measurements of psychological characteristics are generally reported in terms of standard scores, where the mean level is given as zero (or some other round number) and the standard deviation is one (or some other round number). In addition, the relations between psychological characteristics are reported in terms of correlation coefficients, whose possible values range from -1 (perfect negative relation) through 0 (no relation) to $+1$ (perfect positive relation). By knowing the correlation coefficient, we gain a clear idea of the extent to which people with relatively high levels of one characteristic are likely to have high levels of another characteristic.

Next, let us review the concepts that are used in evaluating the quality of psychological measurements. The reliability of a measurement is the extent to which it really does measure some meaningful characteristic. Reliability can be evaluated by examining different parts of a measurement to see how much people's scores on those parts are correlated. In a similar way, reliability can be evaluated by comparing different observers who make ratings of individuals on a characteristic, to see how much the observers' ratings are correlated. Another way of evaluating reliability is to determine whether people's scores are stable across time, by finding out how much people's scores on different occasions are correlated. The validity of a measurement is the extent to which it really does measure the intended characteristic. Validity can be evaluated by examining the extent to which the content of the measurement (e.g., items on a personality inventory scale) corresponds to the concept of the characteristic that is supposed to be measured. Another way of evaluating validity is to find out the extent to which scores on this measurement are (a) strongly correlated with other variables that are known to be good indicators of the same characteristic, and (b) weakly correlated with other variables that are known to be unrelated to this characteristic.

Finally, we considered some of the basic methods used in evaluating personality. Self-report methods ask the individual to describe his or her own behaviors, thoughts, and feelings, and from this the researcher can figure out the individual's levels of various characteristics. Observer report methods ask some other person to describe the behaviors, thoughts, and feelings of the person to be measured. (Sometimes, the person who provides personality descriptions is asked to make self- or observer *ratings*, whereby he or she makes a direct estimate of the level of a given characteristic, rather than a report of some behavior that is relevant to the characteristic.) With direct observation methods, the researcher watches and records the behavior of the person whose personality is to be assessed, and infers that person's level of a characteristic from his or her behaviors. (Direct observations can be made both in "natural" settings—such as the person's home or workplace, or in "artificial" situations, such as the psychologist's laboratory.) Biodata (or life outcome data) methods involve the use of records about various aspects of a person's life to make inferences about his or her personality characteristics. Each of the preceding methods has its advantages and disadvantages, but self- and observer report methods are used most frequently because of their great efficiency in providing accurate measurements.

Chapter 2

Personality Traits and the Inventories That Measure Them

The Idea of a Personality Trait   27

Differences among Individuals   28

In a Typical Tendency to Behave, Think, or Feel   28

In Some Conceptually Related Ways   28

Across a Variety of Relevant Situations   29

Over Some Fairly Long Period of Time   29

Personality Traits and Other Psychological Characteristics   29

Do Personality Traits Exist?   30

Research Studies Testing the Existence of Traits   30

The Importance of Aggregation: Some Familiar Examples   32

Measuring Traits by Self- or Observer Report: Structured Personality Inventories   34

Strategies of Personality Inventory Construction   36

The Empirical Strategy   36

The Factor-Analytic Strategy   39

The Rational Strategy   39

Comparisons of the Three Strategies   41

Self- and Observer Reports on Personality Inventory Scales   45

Agreement between Self- and Observer Reports   45

Why Do Self- and Observer Reports Tend to Agree?   46

The Validity of Self- and Observer Reports in Predicting Behavior   48

Summary and Conclusions   51

The Idea of a Personality Trait

In the previous chapter, we used terms such as "personality trait" or "personality characteristic" simply in the way that you would use those terms in everyday conversation. This familiar meaning is pretty close to what psychologists have in mind when they discuss personality traits, but it would be useful to have at least a rough definition. Briefly, a personality trait refers to *differences among individuals in a typical tendency to behave, think, or feel in some conceptually related ways, across a variety of relevant situations and across some fairly long period of time*. But this definition has several parts, some of which could be stated more precisely. Let us discuss this definition a bit further.

Differences among Individuals

First, the idea of "differences among individuals" is important, because the description of an individual's personality is meaningful only to the extent that it gives us, directly or indirectly, a comparison with others. For example, if we are told that Bob tends to show signs of fatigue after concentrating intensely for a long time, this does not really tell us very much, because the same is true of everyone. What is more informative is to know the degree to which Bob shows fatigue after having concentrated for a long time, relative to that shown by other people. This would give us some indication of how "fatigable" Bob is.

In a Typical Tendency to Behave, Think, or Feel

Next, "in a tendency to behave, think, or feel" refers to a *likelihood* of showing some behaviors or of having some thoughts or feelings. When we say that a person has a high (or low) level of a trait, we do not suggest that a person always (or never) exhibits certain behaviors, thoughts, of feelings; instead, we suggest that they have a relatively strong (or weak) inclination or predisposition to exhibit those behaviors, thoughts, or feelings. For example, when we say that Bob is very optimistic, we do not mean that he is always optimistic about everything; instead, we just mean that he is frequently optimistic or is optimistic about many things. Note also that "a tendency to behave, think, or feel" includes not only the external or behavioral aspects of a trait, as shown by the person's actions or words, but also the internal aspects, as shown by the person's ideas and emotions. Some traits might be expressed in all of these ways; for example, the trait of optimism might be shown by what a person does (e.g., taking on difficult challenges) and what a person says (e.g., telling others that things will turn out well), but also what a person thinks (e.g., estimating the likelihood of success to be high) and what a person feels (e.g., experiencing excitement rather than anxiety when confronted by difficulties).

In Some Conceptually Related Ways

In the next phrase, "in some conceptually related ways," the idea is that a trait is expressed by various behaviors, thoughts, and feelings that appear to have some common psychological cause. Sometimes, those expressions of the trait might share some obvious similarities to each other: For example, a person with a high level of the trait of "thrill seeking" might enjoy activities such as skydiving, bungee jumping, motorcycle racing, and jet-skiing. But sometimes, a trait can be expressed in ways that superficially appear to be quite different: For example, consider behaviors such as wearing fancy clothes, complimenting others loudly, stating extreme opinions, performing magic tricks, or giving large tips at a restaurant. These behaviors all look rather different from each other, but they might all reflect the same underlying trait of "showing off." (Related to this point, note that a given behavior might be related to two or more different traits: For example, some people who give large tips at a restaurant may be show-offs, but others may be very generous people, and still others may be careless with money.)

Across a Variety of Relevant Situations

The phrase "across a variety of relevant situations" is important, because a personality trait is not simply a habit that is confined to one specific situation; instead, it is shown across a variety of settings in which people differ in the ways that the trait is expressed. Suppose that we describe Bob as inquisitive: We mean that he is curious across a wide range of situations in which a person might feel this curiosity. But if Bob reads books *only* about mathematics, or asks questions *only* about sports, or watches documentaries *only* about gardening, then we probably would not describe him as inquisitive.

Over Some Fairly Long Period of Time

Finally, the phrase "over some fairly long period of time" means that there is some pattern that can be observed over the long run, rather than simply on a temporary basis. For example, a person who is generally very cheerful might be quite subdued for a few weeks after a very depressing event, such as the loss of a loved one. But this would not necessarily mean that the person's level of the *trait* of cheerfulness had actually changed; instead, it would probably mean that this temporary condition was interfering with the normal expression of that trait. The idea of a trait is that there is some reasonably stable, long-lasting tendency to show the relevant pattern of behaviors. It is difficult to specify exactly what a "fairly long period of time" should be, but it can probably be considered as a period of at least a few years. Note, though, that the idea of a trait does not require that the person show the same tendency across the entire life span: Instead, it is possible that even the rather stable, long-run tendencies of an individual might change considerably during the course of a lifetime. For example, we could at least imagine that a person might have a stable tendency to be lazy throughout his or her adolescence, but then a stable tendency to be hardworking throughout his or her early adulthood, and then a stable tendency to be "in between" these levels during middle age. During each of these three stages, it would have been meaningful to describe this individual in terms of the personality trait of being lazy versus hardworking, even though her level of that trait did change across this long period. The question of whether personality traits tend to be stable across the life span is an interesting one, and in Chapter 4 we will look at the results of studies that have compared people's personalities across very long periods of time.

Personality Traits and Other Psychological Characteristics

Using the preceding definition of a personality trait, we can also consider the issue of which kinds of individual differences should be considered as personality traits, and which kinds should be considered separately from personality traits, as distinct categories of psychological characteristics. For the purpose of this textbook, we will treat several important individual differences as belonging to categories different from the category of personality traits. For example, mental abilities—such as verbal or mathematical skills—differ from personality traits by representing one's maximum level of performance in some tasks, rather than one's typical way or style of behaving, thinking, or feeling. As another example, beliefs and attitudes differ from personality traits by being focused on some particular "object"—such as a specific set of religious or political issues—rather than standing alone as a general style of behaving, thinking, or feeling. A similar point can also be made about individual differences in sexuality. This is not to say that these "other" kinds of individual differences—mental abilities, beliefs and attitudes, and sexuality—are not important parts of one's personality; on the contrary, we will consider these individual differences in some depth in later chapters of this textbook. However, we will examine those individual differences as characteristics that are somewhat different in nature from the more general personality traits that will be the focus of the next few chapters of this book.

In those following chapters, we will explore several interesting questions about personality traits: How are those traits related to each other? What are the causes of individual differences in personality traits? What are the "real-world" consequences of those differences? But first, we need to discuss another issue—one that occupied much of the attention of personality psychologists between the late 1960s and the early 1980s. This issue involves a fundamental question: Do personality traits really exist?

Do Personality Traits Exist?

By the 1960s, psychologists were conducting many research studies aimed at understanding and measuring a variety of personality traits. But some psychologists—most notably, a researcher named Walter Mischel—argued that the results of those studies indicated that personality traits were of limited value for predicting behavior (e.g., Mischel, 1968). One important reason why some researchers reached this conclusion was that, in several studies, results showed that behaviors supposedly related to the same underlying trait were weakly correlated across situations.[1] Mischel and others argued that these results contradicted the idea that personality traits would be useful for predicting or explaining people's behaviors.

Research Studies Testing the Existence of Traits

Let us consider an example of the findings that led some psychologists to doubt the value of personality traits. An early research study by Hartshorne and May (1928) examined

---

[1] Notice that the issue here is about behavior in *different situations*, and not just about behavior in the same situation on different occasions. Even though any given person may vary from one occasion to the next in his or her response to the same situation, his or her typical response to the same situation becomes clear over the long run (see discussion by Fleeson, 2004). Mischel and others understood this, and their concern was instead about behavior in different situations.

the behaviors of 11,000 elementary- and high school students, who were observed in a variety of situations in which individual differences in traits of "moral character" would emerge. For example, Hartshorne and May watched to see whether each child would perform various behaviors related to altruism (e.g., voting to spend class money on a charity rather than on oneself, donating to charity various items from a pencil-case given to the child), self-control (e.g., resisting temptation to eat candy, persisting in a puzzle-solving task), and honesty (e.g., not stealing coins from a puzzle-box, not cheating in various contests). The children were observed several times in each situation, so that for each child, a reliable score could be calculated to indicate his or her tendencies to be altruistic, self-controlled, or honest. (The researchers designed each situation so that the observations would be subtle, to prevent the children from realizing that their moral character was being assessed.) What Hartshorne and May found was that the correlations between altruistic behaviors in any two situations were rather weak, generally not much above .20. That is, there was only a weak tendency for the children who were highly altruistic in one situation (compared with their peers) to be highly altruistic in another situation. Instead, many children who were relatively altruistic in one situation were not particularly altruistic in another. Similar results were obtained for self-controlled behaviors and for honest behaviors.

On the basis of this and similar findings, Mischel (1968) and others concluded that personality traits were much less important than had previously been thought. Instead, those researchers argued, individual differences in a given kind of behavior depend overwhelmingly on the specific situation involved. But soon after Mischel's points were published, other psychologists disputed his conclusions. Although the facts cited by Mischel were true, other researchers disagreed with the interpretation of what those facts meant. The chief problem, they suggested, was that Mischel had failed to notice the cross-situational consistency that can be shown when observations of behavior are *aggregated*, or averaged, across many situations. For example, even though altruistic behavior (or self-controlled behavior, or honest behavior, etc.) may depend heavily on the situation involved, it is still possible that individuals will differ consistently from each other when we consider their *overall* level of altruism (or self-control, or honesty), as based on their average behavior across many situations.

To illustrate this point, Epstein (1979) and Rushton, Brainerd, and Pressley (1983) calculated each child's *average* level of altruism within each of two sets of *several* situations, and then found the correlation between the scores on the two sets. They found that the children's overall scores for altruism on one set correlated about .50 or .60 with their overall scores for altruism on the other set. This is obviously a much higher value than the .20 correlation observed for any two *single* situations; it suggests that if a person is above average in altruism as averaged across one set of several situations, then there is a 75 or 80% chance that the same person will be above average in altruism as averaged across another set of several situations.

The meaning of the aggregated results is that, even though an individual's level of altruism (or self-control, or honesty) in one kind of situation is not a particularly accurate indicator of his or her level of altruism (or self-control, or honesty) in another kind of situation, people still differ consistently in their overall level as observed across many situations. The important point is that, even though behavior in any one situation does depend a great deal on the nature of that specific situation, we can still see the importance of traits when we consider people's overall patterns of behavior, as shown by their typical tendencies, averaged across many situations. (For example, a child who is usually honest but who is worried about failing a course in school might be tempted to cheat on a test; or, a child who is usually dishonest but doesn't much like sweet foods might not feel much urge to steal a particular kind of candy. But when we consider the "big picture" of how honestly those children usually behave, we could see the consistent differences between the two of them.) The effect of aggregating is important, because even though we may have a difficult time in predicting people's behavior in any one specific situation, we can still be rather successful in predicting people's overall patterns of behavior, which is usually our primary aim.

In addition to citing the results of previous research, such as the Hartshorne and May study, Mischel also conducted some investigations of his own to address the question of whether or not personality traits existed. Mischel and Peake (1982) made detailed observations of the behaviors of a sample of college students, with attention to behaviors that might be considered as indicators of a trait of conscientiousness. Mischel and Peake observed each student on repeated occasions to measure many conscientiousness-related variables, such as class attendance, appointment attendance, assignment neatness, class-note neatness, desk neatness, bed neatness, assignment punctuality, class reading punctuality, lecture punctuality, class reading completion, note thoroughness, and others. What Mischel and Peake found was that each of these indicators of conscientiousness tended to be only weakly correlated with the others, with an average correlation of only .13. They interpreted this finding as evidence that there was no important trait of conscientiousness, but that instead a student's "conscientiousness" depended very strongly on the situation.

Other researchers reached different conclusions, however. Jackson and Paunonen (1985) showed, using the data from the Mischel and Peake study, that the trait of conscientiousness emerges more clearly when one aggregates across the various behaviors assessed by Mischel and Peake. For example, if the 19 variables are randomly divided into two roughly equal sets, the correlations between overall conscientiousness levels on the two sets would typically be in the .50s. This again shows that, even though situations have an important influence on behavior, we can still see the very strong influence of traits when we consider people's typical behavior, as averaged across many different situations.

The Importance of Aggregation: Some Familiar Examples

One way to appreciate the importance of aggregation, or averaging, in understanding the existence of traits is to think about some examples from everyday life. For example, consider "academic performance," which in some ways resembles a trait, even though it is not exactly a personality trait. You would probably agree that there is some cross-situational consistency in academic performance, in the sense that some students tend to obtain higher grades than others, across a variety of courses. And yet, the relative standings of students in any given course will depend in part on the specific features of that course, such as the subject matter, the instructor, and the methods used in evaluating student performance. As a result, correlations between grades obtained in any two different courses may be rather low. For example, there might be only a weak or modest tendency for higher grades in geography to be associated with higher grades in math, or for higher grades in biology to be associated with higher grades in French. But, if we consider each student's *average* grades across two sets of several courses each, we should see that there are quite strong correlations between the two sets. That is, students who have higher *average* grades in one set of courses will very likely have higher average grades in the other set of courses. In other words, even though the situation is important, there are still some very consistent differences between individuals when we take an average of their behavior across many situations.

As one final example, consider also "athletic ability," which of course is mainly a physical trait rather than a psychological one. Again, you would probably agree that there is some cross-situational consistency to athletic ability, as some people tend to be more athletic than other people are, across a variety of sports. But nevertheless, the relative abilities of people in a given sport will depend a lot on the specific demands of that sport: The amount of specific experience or practice in that sport, the ideal body size and shape, the role of speed versus endurance, and so on. Consequently, correlations between ability levels in any two sports might be weak or modest: The best soccer players might be only slightly better than average at tennis, or the best golf players might be only slightly better than average at basketball. Nevertheless, if we look at people's overall athletic ability more broadly, by averaging out each person's level of ability across several quite different sports, we would find that *average* athletic ability level in one set of several diverse sports would correlate highly with *average* athletic ability level in another set of several diverse sports. In other words, we would be able to identify some people as being consistently better all-around athletes.

The main messages of this section should be clear. First, differences among people in their tendencies to behave in ways related to a given trait will depend a great deal on the situation. As a result, we cannot guess very accurately how individuals will behave in one situation just by knowing how they behave in another situation. However, if we know how individuals typically behave across several situations, then we can guess very accurately how they typically behave across several other situations. In other words, even though the situation is important, we can still see very consistent differences among people when we consider their overall behavior as observed across many different situations: Traits clearly do exist.

BOX 2-1
Variance Due to Situations, Persons, and Person-by-Situation Interactions

One way to understand the question of whether or not traits exist is to think of it in terms of "analysis of variance," the statistical technique that you have likely learned about in your statistics class. As an example, suppose that we observe each of many people as they experience various situations that might cause them to feel and express some anger toward another person. In doing so, we are likely to find that the level of anger is not the same for every person in every situation; that is, there will be some variance in angry behavior. Some of this variance is likely due to the situation alone, because different situations can provoke more or less anger: For example, pretty much everyone will feel more anger in response to being intentionally insulted than in response to being accidentally (and gently) bumped

(continues)

into. The idea that some variance is due to situations is considered obvious by all personality psychologists, regardless of whether or not they believe that personality traits are important. In fact, they tend to ignore this source of variance as a rather uninteresting one, focusing instead on the other two possible sources of variance.

Another potential source of variance involves the interaction between persons and situations. To see this, let us continue with our example of anger-related behaviors. Some people tend to become angry when a driver "cuts them off" in traffic but not when a retail salesperson is very slow, whereas other people show the opposite tendencies. As was the case for variance due to situations, all personality psychologists agree that person-by-situation interactions can be important. (When we say that specific situations have an important influence on behavior, we are referring not only to the effects of situations alone, but also to person-by-situation interactions.)

But personality psychologists have disagreed about the question of whether or not the person-by-situation interactions can account for pretty much all of the variance that is not already accounted for by situations alone. Researchers who consider personality traits to be unimportant believe that person-by-situation interactions can account for nearly all of that variance. In contrast, researchers who consider personality traits to be important believe that there is a considerable amount of variance that is attributable to another source, namely, that of *persons* alone.

Consider our example of anger-related behaviors. Some researchers believe that, when we take an average across various situations of each person's amount of anger-related behavior, we will find that some people have been much more angry than others overall. In other words, researchers who believe that there is a trait of anger would expect to find that some people tend to get angry much more easily than others do. In contrast, researchers who do not believe that there is a trait of anger would expect to find very little difference among people in the overall tendency to become angry. Thus, the debate about the existence of personality traits is a debate about the question of whether or not there is any considerable amount of variance in behavior due to persons.

Measuring Traits by Self- or Observer Report: Structured Personality Inventories

Self- and observer reports are the methods most frequently used by psychologists to assess personality. Given this wide use, it is worth considering how psychologists construct the questionnaires that are used for obtaining self- and observer reports of personality. These questionnaires are generally known as "structured personality inventories." They are structured in the sense that the individuals being measured are given a predetermined set of options for responding to the "items" (i.e., the statements or questions) that make up the test: For example, they might answer questions on a yes/no basis, or they might indicate level of agreement with statements using a 1 to 5 scale, and so on. (In contrast, an inventory would be *unstructured* if it allowed individuals to respond freely rather than requiring them to choose one of several specified options. Later in this chapter, we will consider some methods of personality assessment that are unstructured in nature.)

Most personality inventories assess several different personality traits. Each trait is assessed by its own "scale," which contains several different "items."[2] An individual's responses to the items of a given scale are averaged out (or added up) to produce an overall score, which can then be compared to the scores of other individuals on that scale. The reason why each trait is measured by a scale containing several different items is that this allows for good reliability and good content validity. When a scale has several related items, the scores on that scale will largely represent whatever is common to those items; if the items really do assess the trait that is supposed to be measured, then this common element will correspond to that trait. Also, a scale containing several items can assess the various features of the trait, because each item can capture a different aspect of the trait. Consider as an example a scale that measures the trait of intellectual curiosity: Such a scale might contain items describing interests in history, in geography, in literature, in the arts, in life sciences, and in physical sciences. This scale would probably show good reliability, because the average response to these items would likely be a good indicator of the element that is common to those items (presumably, intellectual curiosity). This scale would also have good content validity, because the items describe a wide array of interests, all of which are intellectual interests.

Most scales contain some items for which responses indicating greater agreement will contribute to higher scores on the trait. For example, a sociability scale might contain items about greatly enjoying parties or about frequently going out with friends, and individuals who agree with those statements will tend to get high scores on that sociability scale. But one interesting feature of personality inventory scales is that many of the scales contain some items that suggest the *opposite* of the trait in question. That is, most scales also contain some items for which responses indicating greater *disagreement* will contribute to higher scores on a trait. To use the example of the sociability scale again, such a scale might contain some items about preferring to be alone or about rarely engaging in small talk, and individuals who *disagree* with those statements will tend to get high scores on the sociability scale. Such items are generally known as "negatively keyed" or "reverse-coded" items, among other names.[3]

---

[2] Note that the word "scale" is used in different ways. Scale sometimes refers to a group of several items that are averaged out or added up to give an overall score for a given trait. However, scale sometimes refers to the set of options that an individual can use in responding to a given item; for example, an item might have a *response scale* with options ranging from 1 (very inaccurate) to 5 (very accurate).

[3] Doing the math of reverse-coded items is very easy. Suppose that we have a trait scale from an inventory whose items use a 1-to-5 response scale. For regular items, an individual's responses can simply be averaged (or added). For reverse-coded items, an individual's responses must first be "reversed," so that a 1 is converted to a 5, a 2 to a 4, a 3 to a 3, a 4 to a 2, and a 5 to a 1. After the reversal of these negatively keyed items, scores on all items can then be averaged (or added) to give the overall scale score.

Why do psychologists bother to include reverse-coded items in their scales? The main reason is that there are differences among individuals in their general tendency to agree with statements (or to say "yes" or "true" to questions), independently of the content of those statements (or questions). For example, when individuals respond to the items of a personality inventory, there will frequently be some items for which they are not absolutely sure of their precise responses. When faced with such items, some people usually tend to respond in the direction of greater agreement; other people, however, usually tend to respond in the direction of greater disagreement. As a result, some people will tend to have substantially higher scores than other people when we average responses across many such items. Therefore, it is difficult to interpret scores on a scale that consists of items for which greater agreement always contributes to a higher score. If a person has a high score, does this indicate a high level of the trait, or does that score reflect (at least in part) a tendency to agree with items in general? Similarly, does a low score necessarily indicate a low level of the trait, or does that score reflect in part a tendency to disagree with items in general? In order to avoid this uncertainty, psychologists try to make roughly half of the items of a scale reverse-coded or negatively keyed items. In this way, agreeing with items sometimes contributes to a high score (in the case of regular items), but sometimes contributes to a low score (in the case of reverse-coded items). By having roughly equal numbers of regular and reverse-coded items, the tendency to agree or disagree with statements in general is balanced out, with the result that higher scores on the scale really do indicate higher levels of the trait, and lower scale scores really do indicate lower trait levels.

Strategies of Personality Inventory Construction

Now that you understand how personality inventories work, you might wonder how they are constructed in the first place. That is, how exactly do psychologists decide what items will be used when assessing a given personality trait? Is there one universal approach, or are there many different ways of constructing a personality inventory?

In some sense, the number of different ways of developing a personality questionnaire is very large, because every psychologist who constructs such questionnaires will do so a little bit differently from every other psychologist. But in a broader sense, we can say that there are three basic strategies or approaches to developing personality inventories, and that every psychologist uses one (or more) of these strategies. These three approaches are each known by various names, but here we will refer to them as the *empirical* approach, the *factor-analytic* approach, and the *rational* approach. The approaches differ in the ways that the items are generated and selected for inclusion in the inventory.

The Empirical Strategy

In the empirical strategy of constructing personality inventories, the psychologist begins by writing a large number of items that describe a very wide variety of actions, thoughts, and feelings, as well as (in many cases) items that ask for ratings on various characteristics.

The items may be administered in a true/false or yes/no format, or they may be administered in a multipoint scale (e.g., 1-to-5, 1-to-9) in which the individual indicates his or her level of agreement or disagreement with a statement. The psychologist then obtains self-reports (or observer reports) on this large pool of items from a large sample of individuals. But in addition, the psychologist also obtains some other information from these individuals, and it is this extra information that is used in deciding which items should be kept for the purpose of assessing the traits that are of interest to the psychologist. In fact, the idea of the empirical approach is that items should be selected "empirically"—that is, on the basis of observed evidence of the relations of those items with some other information that is believed to give an accurate indication of the individual's level of a given trait. Let us consider how this might be done.

Suppose, for example, that the psychologist would like to measure the trait of "femininity versus masculinity." For the purpose of measuring this trait, the psychologist who uses an empirical approach would want to choose items that are empirically related to some variable that should be a good indicator of femininity versus masculinity. You can probably think of several variables that should be strongly associated with femininity versus masculinity, and would therefore be a good basis for deciding which items were the better measures of this trait. For now, let us consider one such variable: The individual's own sex. We would expect that items that are empirically related to an individual's sex—that is, items that show a difference in responses between the average woman and the average man—would tend to be good indicators of an individual's level of femininity versus masculinity. Therefore, the psychologist who was using the empirical strategy could select the items that show the largest differences between the responses of women and the responses of men.

As another example, suppose that another trait of interest to the psychologist is "achievement orientation." If the sample of individuals being measured by the psychologist was from a college or high school, the psychologist might obtain information about the individuals' grade point averages, on the assumption that grade point average is a good indicator of achievement orientation. That is, the items measuring achievement orientation most effectively should be those that are empirically associated with grade point average. The psychologist would therefore select the items for which individuals' responses show the strongest correlations with grade point average.

These examples give some idea of how the empirical method works. Note that, in using this approach, psychologists are not concerned about the "content" of an item—in other words, they are not really interested in what kind of action, thought, or feeling is described by the item. For example, if responses to the item, "I like to eat apples," show a large difference between women and men (or a strong correlation with grade point average) then the psychologist will choose that item, even though it does not appear to have anything to do with femininity versus masculinity (or with achievement orientation). In other words, the empirical strategy is based solely on the observed, empirical links between the items and some variable that is assumed to be a good indicator of the trait.

To some extent, the fact that the empirical strategy may select items having no obvious relevance to a trait may be a strength of that approach. The potential advantage is that, if items are not obviously related to the trait they are intended to measure, it will be difficult for individuals to know how to adjust their responses in such a way as to give a desired impression—that is, it will be hard to "fake" responses. However, psychologists have raised some serious concerns about the use of the empirical strategy.

One criticism of the empirical method involves the samples of individuals from whom data are obtained: Specifically, an item selected on the basis of its observed associations with a given variable within a certain sample of individuals might not show such strong associations within every sample of individuals. Consider the example of selecting items to measure achievement orientation on the basis of their correlations with grade point average. Perhaps the items that show the strongest associations with grade point average in a sample of big-city high school students will not show the largest differences within a sample of small-town high school students. Or, the items that are most strongly correlated with grade point average in a sample of high school students might not be so strongly correlated with grade point average in a sample of college students. In addition to these concerns, it is also important that the sample whose data are used for selecting items be very large (generally, at least several hundred persons); otherwise, if the sample is small, then the selected items might have been related to the trait simply by chance, having had a "fluke" association with the trait. Thus, one concern about the empirical approach is that very different sets of items might be selected, depending on the nature and the size of the sample of individuals that is used as the source of the empirical data.

Another criticism of this approach involves the variables that are used as the basis for selecting items. For example, in the previous case involving achievement orientation, we used grade point average as an indicator of that trait, and used items' relations with grade point average as a basis for selecting the best items for measuring achievement orientation. But, even if we agree that grade point average tends to be a good indicator of achievement orientation, there are presumably several other variables that we could have used instead, and each of these might have been an equally good indicator. To take a couple of examples, we could have measured how many hours the individuals worked at paid jobs, or how many hours they spent practicing at sports or music, or how highly their friends rated their achievement orientation levels. Presumably, the items that were selected on the basis of relations with grade point average would not all be the same as those selected on the basis of relations with these other variables. And yet, how do we know which set of items would represent the "best" measures of achievement orientation? Thus, another concern about the empirical strategy is that very different sets of items can be selected, depending on the variable that is used as the indicator of the trait.

The preceding criticisms are potentially important ones, but there are ways that their impact can be reduced. First, if the items can be selected on the basis of empirical relations that are observed within several different samples of individuals, then it is more likely that the selected items really will produce a scale that is a valid measure of the trait. Also, if the items can be selected on the basis of their average or overall empirical relations with several different variables that are all good indicators of the trait, then it is also more likely that the selected items will make a valid scale. However, the use of these procedures may not be very practical, as it may be very difficult to obtain several different, large samples of individuals who can all be measured on several variables that are all good indicators of a given trait.

The Factor-Analytic Strategy

In the factor-analytic strategy of constructing personality inventories, the psychologist begins with a large and diverse pool of items, much as is done with the empirical strategy. Also as is done in the empirical approach, the factor-analytic approach involves administering these items to a large sample of individuals. But in the factor-analytic approach, the basis for selecting items is different: Rather than examining the items' relations with some outside variable that serves as an indicator of a given trait, as is done in the empirical approach, the psychologist who uses the factor-analytic method instead finds groups of related items, such that each group measures a different trait.

In Chapter 3, we will describe the technique of factor analysis in some detail. For now, it is enough to say that factor analysis provides a way of sorting groups of correlated items together into the same category (i.e., the same *factor*), while putting uncorrelated items into different categories (i.e., different factors). Because the items belonging to the same factor are correlated with each other, they tend to measure the same broad personality trait. When psychologists apply factor analysis to the construction of a personality inventory, they use the results to find out (a) what personality trait is being measured by each of the resulting factors, and (b) which items clearly belong to each factor, so that these items can be selected to make up the scales of the personality inventory. For example, imagine a very simple case in which the factor analysis shows only two factors, one of which contains items describing "risk-taking" behaviors, and the other of which contains items describing "energy level" behaviors. In the factor-analytic approach, the psychologist would select the items that clearly belong to the risk-taking factor and the items that clearly belong to the energy level factor, and would use those two sets of items to measure those two traits.

Notice that the factor-analytic strategy also differs from the empirical strategy in several other ways. In the empirical strategy, the psychologist starts out with a clear idea in mind as to which trait or traits are to be measured. In the factor-analytic strategy, however, the researcher does not necessarily have any specific plan as to which traits should be measured: Instead, the identity of these traits is revealed by the results of the factor analysis. This might be considered an advantage of this approach, insofar as the use of factor analysis will allow the psychologist to measure whatever are the major traits that are assessed by the items of the pool that has been administered to the individuals. But on the other hand, if the item pool does not contain a wide variety of items, then the product of the factor-analytic strategy will be an inventory that measures a rather limited set of traits. In addition, even if the factor analysis does produce a diverse set of traits, there is no guarantee that these traits will be the ideal traits to be measured for practical purposes. Depending on the way in which the inventory is to be used, it might be better to measure some completely different trait that is especially important in a given setting.

The Rational Strategy

In the rational strategy of constructing personality inventories, the first step is usually different from that of empirical and factor-analytic approaches. Instead of beginning with a large existing pool of items, the psychologist writes items specifically for the purpose of assessing each trait that is to be measured. This process of writing the items to measure each trait is conducted "rationally," in the sense that the psychologist tries to produce items that would rationally be considered relevant to the trait in question. In other words, the items are intended to describe actions, thoughts, or feelings that reveal a high level of the trait (or, for reverse-coded items, a low level of the trait), and to represent all the various aspects of the trait. The next step in the rational strategy is to figure out which of the items are the "best" ones, which ought to be kept in a final version of the scale measuring the trait. Sometimes, the psychologist might make these decisions by asking several experts—for example, graduate students or professors of personality psychology—to rate each item in terms of how well it appears to measure the trait, and then by keeping the items with the highest ratings overall. But usually, the psychologist will administer the items to a large sample of individuals, and then select the items that show the strongest correlations with the entire set of items overall—that is, the items that will produce the most reliable scale. (At first, this might sound very much like the empirical strategy, but note the crucial difference: The rational strategy involves choosing the items that are most strongly related to *each other*, whereas the empirical strategy involves choosing the items that are most strongly related to *some outside variable* that is supposed to be a good indicator of the trait.)

In addition to examining the items' correlations with each other, the psychologist will also consider breadth of content when selecting items. In some cases, the psychologist might decide to keep an item that shows a somewhat modest correlation with the other items, instead of an item that shows a higher correlation, if the former item captures some important aspect of the trait that is not well represented by the other items. But on the other hand, if items representing a certain aspect of the trait are found to have very low correlations with the remaining items, then this might suggest to the psychologist that these items are actually measuring a different trait entirely. In such a case, the items would be discarded, but the psychologist might then construct a new scale to measure this separate trait.

One potential limitation of the rational approach is that the resulting scales can only be as good as the sets of items that the psychologist had written to measure the traits: If some important aspects of a trait have been neglected, and other aspects over-emphasized, then these will probably be shortcomings of the final scale also. Another potential drawback is that the items of rationally constructed scales might be so clearly relevant to their intended traits that it might be easy for individuals to figure out what is being measured by the inventory, and to adjust (or "fake") their responses in such a way as to give a good impression. (We will discuss the issue of faking on personality inventories in Chapter 9, when we discuss the use of personality measures in personnel selection.)

One final note about the rational approach: Although, as described before, this strategy usually involves writing items "from scratch," it can also be applied to an existing item pool. In the latter case, the psychologist would consider all of the items in such a pool, and select those that seemed theoretically most relevant to the trait.

Comparisons of the Three Strategies

By now you are probably wondering which of these methods is most successful in producing good personality inventories. Beginning in the 1960s, psychologists conducted many studies that were intended to compare the three strategies, in terms of the validity and the reliability of the scales that those strategies produced. In some of these comparison studies, the rational strategy outperformed one or both of the other two strategies. For example, Jackson (1975) found that rationally constructed self-report scales—even those made by psychology students as a classroom exercise—showed higher correlations with observer reports on the same traits than did empirically constructed scales of published inventories. An earlier study by S. G. Ashton and Goldberg (1973) found similar results. Another comparison study by Knudson and Golding (1974) found that rationally constructed self-report scales showed higher validity than did factor-analytically constructed self-report scales, as judged in terms of correlations with observer reports on the same traits.

Several other investigations generally reported similar levels of reliability and validity for scales produced by all three strategies, and one review of this research (Burisch, 1984) suggested that there was little difference among the three approaches in their usefulness for constructing personality inventories. However, Burisch noted that the rational approach is generally much simpler and easier to implement that the other two approaches, because the rational approach does not require a large existing item pool; instead, the psychologist can simply write the items as needed for a given trait. Nowadays, most personality inventories are constructed mainly according to the rational strategy, but often in combination with some aspects of the other two strategies as well. For example, a psychologist might use the rational approach to generate the items for a given scale and to guide the selection of items for the final scale; however, he or she might also use factor analysis to make sure that the items intended to measure different traits really do belong to different factors, and he or she might use some empirical data, such as with observer ratings on a trait, as one of the bases for selecting items.

BOX 2-2
Some Widely Used Personality Inventories

When reading about personality research, you will often come across the names of several inventories that are widely used by psychologists. This box will give you some familiarity with these inventories; the details need not be memorized. Although all of these instruments are structured personality inventories, they differ in the response formats of their items (some are true/false, others use a five-point response scale, etc.) and in their length (from a few dozen to a few hundred items). (As a rule of thumb, it might take the average college student up to 10 minutes to respond carefully to 100 typical personality inventory items.)

The California Psychological Inventory (CPI)

The CPI was developed by Gough (1996) as a measure of various psychological characteristics that he found to be useful in predicting important outcome variables. This inventory contains over 400 items, which are grouped into 20 "basic" scales as well as various other scales that have been constructed more recently. The CPI was developed according to an empirical approach, and as noted before, this strategy has sometimes been found to produce

(continues)

scales less valid than those produced by the rational strategy. However, the CPI scales have frequently shown quite good validity in predicting important criterion variables (delinquent behavior, academic performance, etc.).

Incidentally, the construction of the CPI was guided in part by that of another inventory, called the Minnesota Multiphasic Personality Inventory (MMPI). The MMPI was also developed according to an empirical approach, but unlike the CPI, the MMPI was intended to measure characteristics associated with mental illness, rather than characteristics of normal variation.

The Hogan Personality Inventory (HPI)

The development of the HPI (Hogan & Hogan, 1995) was inspired in large part by the CPI, but Hogan's inventory is aimed more directly at the prediction of variables associated with job performance. The HPI contains slightly more than 200 items, which are grouped into many short scales that measure specific characteristics, and also into several longer scales that measure broader characteristics. This inventory has been widely used in predicting various aspects of job performance, and has shown very good criterion validity.

The 16 Personality Factors Questionnaire (16PF)

The 16PF (Conn & Rieke, 1994) was originally constructed in 1949 by Cattell, whose factor-analytic research suggested to him that a set of 16 traits would summarize personality characteristics. (As such, the 16PF is perhaps the only major inventory to have been developed using the factor-analytic approach. Although other psychologists have decided what traits to measure on the basis of factor analyses, they have usually used the rational approach when actually constructing the scales of their inventories.) Earlier versions of the 16PF were often criticized for the low internal-consistency reliabilities of their scales, but the scales have been improved in the most recent version of the 16PF (Conn & Rieke, 1994), which contains nearly 200 items. The 16 scales of this inventory can be combined into five broader factors

that assess more general personality characteristics. (Note, however, that one of the 16PF scales is actually not a self-report personality scale at all, but rather an intelligence test.) More recent research has found the 16PF scales to show considerable validity in predicting a variety of criterion variables in contexts such as school and the workplace.

The Eysenck Personality Questionnaire (EPQ) and Eysenck Personality Profiler (EPP)

A series of questionnaires of varying length was developed by Eysenck (Eysenck & Eysenck, 1975; Eysenck & Wilson, 1991) to measure the three personality characteristics that he believed were the basic dimensions of personality, each governed by its own structures in the brain and nervous system (see Chapter 5). Eysenck's scales are generally correlated strongly with scales of other inventories measuring similar traits, and have been widely used in studies of the biological basis of personality.

The Myers–Briggs Type Indicator (MBTI)

The MBTI (Myers & McCaulley, 1985) is loosely based on a theory of psychological "types" developed by the Swiss psychologist, Carl Jung. The MBTI consists of nearly 100 self-report items that each contain two statements; the respondent chooses which item best describes him or her. The MBTI assesses four characteristics. Unlike most other inventories, people do not obtain numerical scores for each characteristic, but instead are assigned to one pole or another of each characteristic. For example, instead of obtaining a certain score on the extraversion scale, an individual is declared as an "extravert" (E) if he or she answers most questions in the extraverted direction, or alternatively is declared as an "introvert" (I) if he or she answers most questions in the introverted direction. (Sometimes, a difference in response to one question could make the difference between being declared, say, an extravert as opposed to an introvert.) On the basis of this method of scoring, each person is assigned a "type" based on the combination of his or her scores on the four scales.

The MBTI is used very widely in business settings, for example, in seminars aimed at improving employees' self-understanding and understanding of each other. Moreover, some studies have shown some support for the construct validity of the MBTI (McCrae & Costa, 1989). However, one shortcoming of the MBTI is that it loses a great deal of precision by describing people in terms of only two levels of each characteristic rather than in terms of a more specific score on each characteristic. For example, consider a person who is slightly on the "extraverted" side of the boundary between extraverts and introverts: This person would actually be more similar to a slightly "introverted" person than to an extremely "extraverted" person. (In the same way, suppose that we had to describe everyone's height as being either "tall" or "short." A "tall" 5-foot-10 person would actually be much closer in height to a "short" 5-foot-6 person than to a "tall" 6-foot-6 person.)

The Temperament and Character Inventory (TCI)

The TCI was developed by Cloninger and colleagues (e.g., Cloninger, Przybeck, Svrakic, & Wetzel, 1994) to measure the basic dimensions of his biological model of temperament (described in Chapter 5), as well as additional dimensions of "character," whose biological bases are thought to be less direct. Several versions of the TCI have been used widely in research, particularly in studies of the biological basis of personality; the more recent versions generally contain between 200 and 300 items, and measure roughly 30 narrower personality traits that are grouped into seven scales representing the broader temperament and character variables. The TCI scales have generally shown good levels of reliability and validity, and have been widely used in studies of the biological basis of personality.

The Multidimensional Personality Questionnaire (MPQ)

The MPQ was constructed by Tellegen (in press) to assess a variety of traits of normal personality variation. This questionnaire contains nearly 300 items and measures 11 traits, which are classified into three groups intended to represent basic dimensions of personality. The MPQ scales have generally shown high levels of reliability and validity and have been widely used in studies of emotions, impulsivity, and imagination.

The Jackson Personality Inventory (JPI) and the Personality Research Form (PRF)

These two instruments (Jackson, 1984b, 1994) were originally developed during the 1960s by Jackson, who employed a rational strategy carried out using very large numbers of items and very large participant samples. Each of the resulting inventories contains 300 or more items, which are grouped into 15 scales (JPI) and 22 scales (PRF) measuring a wide variety of traits. Although the JPI and PRF scales are not usually grouped into broader scales representing broad personality factors, those scales span a very wide variety of personality characteristics, and some research suggests that the PRF and JPI in combination can assess all of the major dimensions of personality (e.g., Ashton, Jackson, Helmes, & Paunonen, 1998). The PRF and JPI scales have generally shown adequate reliability and very good criterion validity.

The Nonverbal Personality Questionnaire (NPQ)

The NPQ (Paunonen, Jackson, & Keinonen, 1990) differs from all of the other inventories considered here in that its items are cartoon sketches rather than written statements. Each item shows a stick figure drawing of a person performing some behavior, and the individual who responds to the inventory is asked to indicate how likely he or she would be to perform the kind of behavior shown in the drawing. The NPQ scales were developed to measure the same traits as those of the PRF, and have shown levels of reliability and validity approaching those of the original scales. Figure 2-1 shows two example items from the NPQ, which contains 136 items.

(continues)

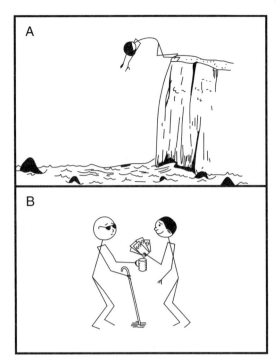

FIGURE 2-1. Example items from the Nonverbal Personality Questionnaire.

Note. The item in panel A assesses the trait of thrill-seeking; the item in panel B assesses the trait of nurturance (i.e., helpfulness). For each item, self-reports (or observer reports) are made using a scale from 1 (extremely unlikely to perform this kind of behavior) to 7 (extremely likely to perform this kind of behavior).
Source: Reproduced by permission of SIGMA Assessment Systems, Inc. P. O. Box, 610984, Port Huron, MI 48061-0984. See also Paunonen *et al.* (1990).

The Big Five Inventory (BFI)

The BFI (John, Donahue, & Kentle, 1991) was developed as a short measure of five important personality characteristics known as the "Big Five" (see Chapter 3; see also the following description of the "NEO" inventories). This inventory contains only 44 items, but given its brevity, it shows rather high levels of internal-consistency reliability and of content validity.

The NEO Personality Inventory—Revised (NEO-PI-R) and the NEO Five-Factor Inventory (NEO-FFI)

The NEO-PI-R (with its earlier version, the NEO-PI) and the NEO-FFI were developed to measure five major dimensions of personality (Costa & McCrae, 1985, 1992b). The NEO-PI-R is the longer inventory, with 240 items that are grouped into 30 scales measuring narrower personality traits, with those scales in turn grouped into the five scales measuring broader characteristics: Neuroticism (N), Extraversion (E), Openness to Experience (O), Agreeableness (A), and Conscientiousness (C). (See Chapter 3 for descriptions of the 30 scales.) The NEO-FFI is a shorter, 60-item inventory that measures the five broad dimensions only. The scales of both questionnaires have shown very good levels of reliability and validity, and have probably become the most widely used personality inventories in psychological research.

The HEXACO Personality Inventory Revised (HEXACO-PI-R)

The HEXACO Personality Inventory was constructed recently (Lee & Ashton, 2004, 2006a) to measure the six dimensions of personality that were found in personality research conducted in various cultures. The inventory has recently been revised; the long form of the HEXACO-PI-R contains 200 items, and the shorter form contains 100, with the items of each form being grouped into scales measuring narrower personality traits. These scales are in turn grouped into broader scales measuring the six dimensions called Honesty–Humility (H), Emotionality (E), Extraversion (X), Agreeableness (A), Conscientiousness (C), and Openness to Experience (O). (See Chapter 3 for descriptions of the scales.) Initial indications are that the HEXACO-PI-R scales show good levels of reliability and validity.

The International Personality Item Pool (IPIP)

The IPIP (Goldberg, 1999) is actually not a personality inventory, but rather a list of personality questionnaire items that has been developed on an ongoing basis since the early 1990s. (The IPIP Web site is found at http://ipip.ori.org.) By the year 2006, there were over 2000 different items in the IPIP, and these items are grouped together into short scales (generally about 10 items) to measure a variety of personality characteristics. In particular, Goldberg has provided lists of items that he has selected to measure each of the traits assessed by most of the published inventories listed above. Each scale can be administered separately or in combination with other scales, as desired by the researcher. Table 2-1 shows some example IPIP items. (Note that these items, unlike those of most personality questionnaires, generally omit the pronoun "I" at the beginning of each self-report statement.)

TABLE 2-1

Example Items from the International Personality Item Pool

Pay attention to details.
Get upset easily.
Feel other people's joy.
Do crazy things.
Keep in the background.
Am not interested in abstract ideas.
Am usually active and full of energy.
Try to impress others.
Like to take it easy.

These items can be used for self-reports or observer reports. The person who provides the reports is asked to indicate the accuracy of each statement on a scale from 1 (very inaccurate) to 5 (very accurate).
Source: http://ipip.ori.org/; see also Goldberg (1990).

Self- and Observer Reports on Personality Inventory Scales

Most of the inventories described in Box 2-2 were developed in self-report format only, but several of them have also been adapted for measurement using observer reports. For example, some investigations of the NEO-PI-R have used spouse reports, and some research with the HEXACO-PI in college settings has involved reports by friends. The use of observer reports is important, because it provides a way of verifying results obtained by self-report; moreover, the use of self- and observer reports in combination may produce measurements that are more accurate than can be obtained from either kind of report on its own.

Agreement between Self- and Observer Reports

One way in which the criterion validity of personality inventory scales is often judged is by examining the correlations between self-reports and observer reports for each trait. That is, for each scale, researchers obtain self-reports from a large sample of persons on that scale and also obtain reports of those same persons on that same scale from others who are well acquainted with them. (Of course, these reports must be made independently, so that the persons giving the self- and observer reports do not influence each other's responses.) The researchers can then calculate the extent to which people who have higher self-report scores for a given trait also tend to have higher observer report scores for that trait. In other words, the researchers try to determine how much agreement there is between people's self-reports and the reports of others who know them well.

The results of these investigations generally show fairly high levels of agreement between self-reports and observer reports, and therefore support the convergent validity of the personality inventory scales. For example, one recent study examined self- and observer reports on the HEXACO-PI scales, as obtained from over 300 college students who participated in pairs, where the two persons of each pair were well acquainted with each other. Correlations between self-reports and observer reports ranged from .55 to .65 for the six broad personality dimensions of that inventory (Lee & Ashton, 2006a). In another study of the same inventory, the self/observer correlations on these scales were even higher when the persons of each pair were spouses or close relatives, who presumably know each other very well (de Vries, Lee, & Ashton, in press). Similarly, for the five broad domains of the NEO-PI-R (Costa & McCrae, 1992b), correlations of self-reports with observer reports have averaged about .60 (for observer reports obtained from the participants' own spouses) or about .40 (for observer reports obtained from the friends or neighbors of the participants). (Note that, because these correlations involve the same scale, they support the *convergent* validity of each scale. When, instead, correlations are calculated between self-reports on one scale and observer reports on a different scale, the obtained values tend to be very small, thus supporting the *discriminant* validity of the scales.)

The levels of convergent validity as reported before can be considered to be fairly high. As you will recall from our discussion of the correlation coefficient, a correlation of .50 this means that for every 100 persons whose self-reports suggest an above-average level of the trait, about 75 will also have observer reports suggesting an above-average level of the trait, and only 25 will have observer reports suggesting a below-average level of the trait. This can be considered a good level of validity; in fact, we probably would not expect the correlations to be much higher than this, given that the two individuals who make the reports have such different perspectives—people are unlikely to see themselves in exactly the same way that others see them.

Why Do Self- and Observer Reports Tend to Agree?

In reading about these results, however, you might have some concerns about what they really mean. In the preceding paragraphs, the high correlations between self-reports and observer reports on a given personality inventory scale are described as evidence of convergent validity—that is, as evidence that the scale is really providing an accurate measurement of some personality trait. But let us consider some alternative possibilities. One alternative explanation is that the agreement between self- and observer reports might happen simply because people who know each other have developed a shared opinion about each other's personality, but an opinion that is not necessarily accurate. (For example, perhaps you and your friend have somehow decided that you are a wild, uninhibited person, even if your actual behavior is not really so wild and uninhibited. Or, perhaps you and your friend have somehow decided that your friend is a stubborn, obstinate person, even if your friend's actual behavior is not really so stubborn or obstinate.)

This explanation probably does not sound very likely, but it is a possible explanation, and many personality researchers have taken it seriously. One way in which this explanation can be tested is by examining how much agreement there is between two different observer reports of an individual's personality, where the observer reports are taken from two people who do not know each other, even though they both are well acquainted with the individual whose personality they describe. The logic of this approach is that, if these two people do not know each other, then any agreement between them in their assessment of the personality of their mutual acquaintance cannot be due to any discussion between them about that individual's personality.

One study used exactly this strategy (Funder, Kolar, & Blackman, 1995), comparing reports of college students' personalities as provided (a) by their friends from their hometowns and (b) by their friends from college (which was in a different town). In some cases, the hometown friend and the college friend had never met, thus satisfying the requirement described previously, but in other cases, those friends had met. This allowed Funder *et al.* to examine whether the observer reports obtained from two friends who had met each other were any more similar than the observer reports obtained from two friends who had never met. (Again, keep in mind that in every case, both of these friends were well acquainted with the mutual friend whose personality they were describing.)

The results of this study showed that there was a moderate degree of agreement between the observer reports obtained from "hometown friends" and from "college friends." The correlations between these two observer reports, as averaged across five broad personality characteristics, were about .30. On average, the results were the same regardless of whether or not the hometown friend and the college friend had ever met each other. Therefore, the agreement between those persons in their assessment of their mutual friend's personality could not be the result of any discussions about that individual's personality. Instead, these results suggest that the hometown friend and the college friend have simply observed similar behaviors on the part of their mutual friend.

Funder *et al.* (1995) also examined the links between self-reports and observer reports of personality. Interestingly, the correlations between the two observer reports were almost as high as the correlations between self-reports and observer reports: When averaged across the five broad characteristics, self-reports correlated about .35 with observer reports from the hometown friend, and about .45 with observer reports from the college friend. The fact that the correlations between the two observer reports are almost as high as the correlations of self-reports with observer reports is also important: It indicates that the agreement between the hometown friend and the college friend (i.e., about .30, as mentioned before) cannot be due to each friend having discussed the mutual friend's personality with that mutual friend.[4] Instead, again, the results indicate that the hometown friend and the college friend have both observed similar behaviors on the part of their mutual friend.

---

[4] If the correlation between observer reports were simply due to the mutual friend having discussed his or her personality with both the hometown friend and the college friend, then that correlation would be no higher than the product of the correlations between self-reports and the two observer reports. But the average correlation between the two observer reports (.30) was considerably higher than the product of the average correlations between self-reports and observer reports (.35 × .45 = .16).

The Validity of Self- and Observer Reports in Predicting Behavior

The substantial correlations between self-reports and observer reports on personality inventory scales provide some important evidence for the validity of those scales. However, it would also be useful to examine the validity of personality inventory scales in predicting actual behaviors or outcomes that are theoretically relevant to the traits measured by those scales. For example, if we have a personality inventory scale that is intended to measure the trait of talkativeness, we would expect not only that self- and observer reports of talkativeness would be correlated, but also that those reports would correlate with actual observations of how much people talk. Or, if a scale is intended to measure the trait of orderliness, we would expect not only that self- and observer reports of orderliness would be correlated, but also that those reports would correlate with actual observations of the orderliness of people's rooms, desks, etc.

When considering this issue of the validity of self- and observer reports on personality inventory scales in predicting trait-relevant behaviors and outcomes, another interesting question also comes to mind: Which kind of report is more accurate in predicting those criteria? That is, are self-reports more accurate indications of an individual's personality, or are observer reports (from close aquaintances) more accurate? Two investigations that examined self-reports and observer reports of personality as predictors of behaviors have allowed an examination of the validity of those reports, both in an absolute sense and in comparison with each other.

In one study (Kolar, Funder, & Colvin, 1996), 140 college students each participated in a series of videotaped interactions with others (e.g., meeting another person, participating in a debate) in the researchers' laboratory. In addition, the students' personality characteristics were assessed by self-report and also by reports from two close acquaintances. The researchers compared the validity of self- and observer reports of personality in predicting four different kinds of behaviors (called "nervous withdrawal," "domineeringness," "serious intelligence," and "heterosexuality"), as rated by several research assistants who watched the videotapes (without knowing the self- and peer report personality scores). The results showed that the personality self-reports had some validity for predicting behavior, with an average correlation of slightly under .30 across the four kinds of behavior. However, each of the observer reports was slightly better in predicting behavior; even the less accurate acquaintance averaged about .35, and in combination, the average of the two observer reports correlated over .40 with behavior. Thus, the results of the Kolar *et al.* study suggest that personality might be assessed somewhat more accurately by observer reports than by self-reports, at least when the observer reports are provided by rather close acquaintances.

Another interesting implication of the Kolar *et al.* (1996) study is that an individual's personality is likely to be assessed even more accurately by *averaging* his or her self-report with the observer reports provided by two or more persons who know him or her well. Taken individually, the self-report and each of the observer reports is fairly accurate, but by combining them into an overall average, we can obtain an even more accurate indication of the individual's personality. This is because each of the reports provides some accurate information that might not be provided by some of the remaining reports;

consequently, the averaged reports will give a better indication than any one report alone will give. (Recall the discussion of interrater reliability in Chapter 1.)

In a similar study (Borkenau, Riemann, Angleitner, & Spinath, 2001), 600 adults were videotaped as they participated in a variety of situations in the researchers' laboratory (telling a joke, introducing someone, singing a song, solving a complex problem, etc.). The personalities of the participants were assessed in terms of five personality character-istics, both by self-reports and by observer reports from two close acquaintances. The researchers' assistants (who did not know about the self- and observer report personality scores) then watched the videotapes and provided their own ratings of the participants' personalities, again in terms of the same five characteristics. The results showed that self-reports were modestly correlated with the video-based judgments, averaging slightly above .20 for the five characteristics. The observer reports (as averaged across the two acquaintances) showed somewhat higher correlations, averaging above .30. These results are therefore consistent with those of Kolar *et al.* (1996), suggesting that observer reports (specifically, observer reports from two or more close acquaintances) are likely to be more accurate indicators of personality than are self-reports.

In considering the results of these two studies, it should be kept in mind that the partici-pants' behaviors in these situations are unlikely to provide a completely accurate indication of their personalities in general. Presumably, personality would be more precisely revealed through observations of participants' behaviors in a wide variety of natural settings (i.e., outside the personality research laboratory) over a long period of time. If behaviors were observed in this way, thereby providing a more accurate criterion for judging the validity of self- and observer reports of personality, it is likely that both the self- and observer reports would show much higher levels of validity. Moreover, it is possible that this increase in correlations would be particularly large for self-reports, because an individual might be a better judge of his or her own behavior across a wide range of situations than would his or her acquaintances, who do not observe him or her in all situations.

BOX 2-3
Projective Tests

Although there are some differences among the *struc-tured* personality inventories described before, those instruments are all similar in the sense of providing a structured set of alternative responses to each item or stimulus (true/false, 1-to-5 scale, etc.). In sharp contrast to the previous inventories are instruments that use *unstructured* responses, which allow the individual to respond in his or her unique fashion—and often at great length—to each of the items or stimuli that are presented. These unstructured meas-ures of personality are generally known as *projective* tests. A projective test provides the individual

with some ambiguous stimulus—for example, a strangely shaped inkblot, a drawing of two or more people interacting in some uncertain way, or a para-graph that tells the beginning of a story. The indivi-dual is then asked to respond to this stimulus—for example, by describing what he or she sees in the inkblot, by explaining the situation depicted in the drawing, or by completing the story that begins with the paragraph. Usually, a series of such stimuli are presented to the individual, and when the entire test is completed, the psychologist can then attempt to assess the individual's personality by considering his or her responses to the stimuli.

One well-known projective test is the Rorschach inkblot test (Rorschach, 1921). The Rorschach

(continues)

contains a series of inkblot patterns; for each inkblot, the individual is asked to give an interpretation, by explaining what he or she sees in the pattern. The scoring of the Rorschach tends to differ from one psychologist to another—thereby limiting the reliability and validity of the test—but some efforts have been made to produce standard rules for scoring the test (Exner, 1974). The interpretation of Rorschach responses sometimes involves the content of those responses: For example, responses that describe violence or weapons are thought—not surprisingly—to indicate a hostile personality (Gleitman, 1986). However, many interpretations of Rorschach responses focus on what aspects of the pattern are interpreted, rather than on the specific content of the interpretation: For example, responses that discuss the colors of the inkblots are taken to suggest emotionality and impulsivity; responses that describe movement are thought to indicate imagination; responses that refer to the white space around the inkblot are seen as signs of rebelliousness and negativity (Gleitman, 1986).

Although the Rorschach inkblot test is still widely used by some clinical psychologists, the test suffers from serious shortcomings (Wood, Garb, Lilienfeld, & Nezworski, 2000). Many psychologically normal people appear to be pathological when compared with the normative data (i.e., the results obtained on samples of people from the general population), a problem that suggests some inaccuracy with those norms. The scoring of the Rorschach test is complex and painstaking, and levels of test–retest reliability and interrater reliability are frequently rather low. Although a few Rorschach scoring scales have shown moderate validity in predicting thought disorders (e.g., schizophrenia), most have not provided much additional validity in predicting clinical psychologists' diagnoses, beyond what is provided by the much simpler self-report measures. These limitations of the Rorschach inkblot test, and the impracticality of administering and scoring the test, have led most personality researchers to use structured methods of assessment instead.

Another well-known projective test is the Thematic Apperception Test (TAT; Murray, 1943). The stimuli used in the TAT are less abstract than those of the Rorschach, as the TAT stimuli typically involve either a picture of some people interacting or a paragraph that describes the beginning of a story. The individual who takes the TAT is asked to tell a story about the picture or to complete the story that has been introduced by the paragraph. Based on various features of the individual's responses, the psychologist can attempt to assess the individual's levels of various characteristics. To take a few examples, responses describing goal-setting suggest "need for achievement," responses describing conflict suggest "need for power," and responses describing friendship suggest "need for affiliation."

Some investigations do suggest at least modest correlations between TAT scores for these various "needs" and relevant criterion variables. Spangler (1992) reviewed over 100 previous investigations, and found average correlations of about .20 between TAT need for achievement scores and outcomes such as occupational success or school performance. However, there has been a lack of studies in which the TAT has been administered along with self- and observer reports of personality, and thus it is difficult to know the extent to which the TAT would add to the predictive validity of those other methods of assessing personality. In general, the TAT is not widely used in personality research, in large part because use of this test does not readily allow the researcher to assess large numbers of people on a wide variety of characteristics; testing time is long and scoring of the test is labor-intensive.

Thus, although there is some evidence to suggest that at least some projective tests may have adequate levels of validity, these instruments are not widely used in personality research. In contrast, structured methods of assessment—particularly self- and observer reports—can be used much more efficiently, in the sense that structured inventories allow many individuals to be assessed quickly on many traits, with good reliability and validity, and without any difficult judgments to make about the scoring of any given item.

====== ## *Summary and Conclusions*

Let us summarize briefly the main points of this chapter. First, the idea of a personality trait refers to differences among individuals in a tendency to behave, think, or feel in some conceptually related ways, across a variety of relevant situations and across some fairly long period of time. During the 1970s and 1980s, many researchers doubted the importance of personality traits, arguing that there was little consistency across situations in the differences among people's behaviors. However, when people's behaviors are considered across a wide variety of situations, by taking an overall average of each person's tendencies, the differences among people are found to be very important. This supports the idea of personality traits.

In measuring personality traits by self- or observer report inventories (i.e., questionnaires), researchers typically use one or more of three approaches, which are known as the empirical, the factor-analytic, and the rational strategies of inventory construction. Several widely used inventories are briefly reviewed in this chapter, and the use of "projective" tests is also discussed (see the boxes).

Many research studies have examined the validity of personality inventory scales by investigating the extent to which self-reports and observer reports agree for a given trait. These studies generally show fairly high levels of agreement between self-reports and reports from observer people who are well acquainted with the person being described. Further research indicates that this agreement is due to the fact that people can provide rather accurate descriptions of their own and others' personalities. Both self-reports and observer reports can predict behavior with moderate levels of validity, but observer reports may be slightly more accurate in predicting behavior, especially when those reports are based on the average of two or more persons.

Chapter 3

Personality Structure: Classifying Traits

Which Traits to Measure? Completeness without Redundancy   53

A Gentle Introduction to Factor Analysis   54

Factor Analysis of Personality Traits: How to Find a Representative Set of Traits?   59

  The Idea of the Lexical Approach   60

  The Early Use of the Lexical Approach   61

Lexical Studies in the English Language: The Big Five Personality Factors   62

  The Big Five   62

Personality Inventories and the Five-Factor Model   64

Lexical Studies in Many Languages: The HEXACO Personality Factors   66

  Different Languages, Same Six Factors   66

  The HEXACO Model of Personality Structure   70

What It All Means: A Few Dimensions, but Many Personalities   72

Summary and Conclusions   73

Which Traits to Measure? Completeness without Redundancy

Imagine that you are planning to do some research about personality. Perhaps you are interested in assessing the extent to which one's personality can predict job performance, or marital satisfaction, or political attitudes. Or perhaps you are interested in finding out how a certain brain chemical, or a certain kind of experience in childhood, can influence one's personality. Whatever research question you might have, you will need to decide which personality traits to measure. In some cases, you might have a specific interest in a particular personality trait, and so your decision is already made. But in other cases, you might be interested in personality *in general*, in which case your task is quite difficult: How can you choose a set of personality traits that will represent the whole domain of personality as broadly as possible?

In the absence of any real knowledge about which traits to select, you might simply choose a few traits that, in your opinion, seem to be interesting, important, and diverse.

In fact, this is exactly what many researchers have done in the past when investigating research questions or when constructing personality inventories. But this approach suffers from some serious problems. First, it is subjective, because the set of traits that strike you as interesting, important, and diverse might be quite a bit different from the set of traits that another researcher would select. If each researcher uses a different set of traits, it will be difficult for researchers to communicate with each other about their findings, or to compare and combine the results of different studies.

But suppose that this first problem could be overcome—suppose that you could somehow convince other researchers that your set of favorite traits was the best set to measure. How would *you* know that your set of traits was really complete or comprehensive? It seems likely that at least some important traits would be left out of your original set. To solve this second problem, you might try adding more traits to your set, to fill in any gaps that you noticed. But even if you added many more traits, you still might not be certain of having captured every important trait. Moreover, by adding these other traits, you would now have so many traits that measuring them reliably would take a very long time. And, with such a large set of traits, it seems likely that some traits in your set would be very similar to each other, and therefore somewhat redundant. Thus, in an attempt to ensure that you are measuring personality comprehensively—an attempt whose success would be uncertain—you would likely make the measurement of personality very inefficient, with much time now needed to measure a large set of traits, at least some of which would be redundant with each other.

Thus, when a researcher simply chooses his or her own favorite set of traits, the measurement of personality is incomplete and inefficient, and communication among researchers is difficult. These problems have led many psychologists to believe that a systematic approach is needed for deciding which personality traits to measure. Although these psychologists have often disagreed about the details of this approach, they have generally agreed that it will need to use the statistical technique known as *factor analysis*. This technique, which is described in the following section, allows researchers to reduce a very large number of related variables into a small number of unrelated groups of variables. Personality researchers can use factor analysis to classify a vast array of personality traits into a few basic groups of traits. By doing this, researchers can then measure some small collection of traits representing each group, so that all of the major aspects of personality are measured, but without redundancy.[1]

A Gentle Introduction to Factor Analysis

When a researcher has measured many variables that show some substantial correlations with each other, it may be useful to reduce the number of variables by categorizing them

---

[1] In addition, the results of factor analysis might teach us some interesting insights about personality characteristics. For example, if we find that certain traits tend to go together on the same factor, then this might help us to understand what those traits have in common, and might give us some clues about what causes those traits or why those traits are important. We will address these kinds of questions in the following chapters of this book.

into groups according to the correlations. However, when the number of variables is large and the pattern of correlations among them is complex, it is not easy to see which variables ought to be combined into a group. This is where the statistical technique of factor analysis is used. Factor analysis allows the researcher to reduce many specific traits into a few more general "factors" or groups of traits, each of which combines several of the specific traits.

Factor analysis can be used with many kinds of variables, and not just personality characteristics. Consider the following example of a factor analysis. Suppose that I have persuaded a few hundred of my fit, healthy young personality students to change into their gym clothes and to do a battery of physical tests. Here are the variables on which my student participants are to be measured:

1. vertical jump (height of jump from a crouching position)
2. 40-yard dash (time to sprint 40 yards, or 36.5 meters)
3. standing triple jump (distance of hop, step, jump from standing start)
4. 12-minute run (distance run in 12 minutes)
5. 2-kilometer row (time to row 2 kilometers, or 1.25 miles, on rowing machine)
6. 20-minute cycle (distance cycled in 20 minutes on standard exercise bike)
7. percent fast-twitch muscle fiber (from tissue sample taken from thigh)
8. percent body fat (measured by skin-fold callipers)

Now, suppose that I have measured my students on these variables. The correlations among the variables are shown in Table 3-1. (Note that all of these data are artificial. I have not really measured anyone for these variables, so these correlations are just "made up" for the purpose of this example. But the correlations are probably not too far from what would be found in real life.)

The correlation matrix in Table 3-1 shows how each variable correlated with each other variable. By looking for the name of one variable across the top, and for the other variable down the side, and then finding the cell where the column of one variable and the row of the other variable meet, you can see the correlation between those two variables. (If the cell is blank, just switch the two variables around; I have only filled in one half of the matrix, because the correlation of A with B is the same as the correlation of B with

TABLE 3-1

Correlations among Physical Fitness and Physiological Measurements

Variables	VJ	Dash	TJ	Run	Row	Cycle	Type	Fat
Vertical jump height (VJ)	1.00							
40-yard (36-meter) dash time (Dash)	−.52	1.00						
Standing triple jump distance (TJ)	.56	−.60	1.00					
12-minute run distance (Run)	.00	.00	.00	1.00				
2-kilometer (1.25-mile) rowing time (Row)	.00	.00	.00	−.54	1.00			
20-minute cycle distance (Cycle)	.00	.00	.00	.58	−.50	1.00		
Fast-twitch muscle fiber type percentage (Type)	.30	−.26	.22	−.29	.25	−.21	1.00	
Body fat percentage (Fat)	−.20	.28	−.24	−.21	.25	−.29	.00	1.00

These are hypothetical (imaginary) data.

A. I have put 1.00s in the diagonals because the correlation of each variable with itself is 1.00.)

Notice in Table 3-1 that there are fairly strong correlations among the first three variables. The vertical jump and standing triple jump show a strong positive correlation with each other, and the 40-yard dash time correlates negatively with both variables. Apparently, the ability to jump up and the ability to jump forwards are related to each other, and both are related to the ability to sprint quickly. Note that the correlations of the jumps with the 40-yard dash are negative, because people who *took a long time* to sprint 40 yards did not jump very high or very far.

Notice also that there are fairly strong correlations among the second three variables. The 12-minute run distance and the 20-minute cycle distance are positively correlated with each other, and negatively correlated with 2-kilometer rowing time. Apparently the ability to run a long distance and to cycle a long distance are related to each other, and both are related to the ability to row a long distance. Note that the correlations of the run and cycle distances with rowing times are negative, because people who *took a long time* to row 2 kilometers did not run or cycle very far.

With regard to these two groups of three variables, notice that the correlations across the two groups tend to be quite weak. The correlations of the vertical jump, the 40-yard sprint time, and the standing triple jump with the 12-minute run, the 2-kilometer row, and the 20-minute cycle are all about zero. This indicates that a person's performance on the first three tests does not give us any indication as to how that person will perform on the second three tests, and vice versa. (For example, the correlation of .00 between vertical jump and 12-minute run suggests that, among the people who are above average in vertical jump, 50% will be above average in the 12-minute run, but 50% will be below average.)

Now let us consider the last two variables. First, the fast-twitch muscle fiber percentage shows some modest correlations with the first three variables (positive with vertical jump, negative with 40-yard sprint time, and positive with standing triple jump), and also with the second three variables (negative with 12-minute run distance, positive with 2-kilometer row time, and negative with 20-minute cycle distance). These results indicate that people with a higher percentage of fast-twitch muscle tended to do relatively well in the first three events, but relatively poorly in the last three events.

Finally, the body fat percentage shows some modest correlations with all six variables (negative with vertical jump, positive with 40-yard sprint time, negative with standing triple jump, negative with 12-minute run distance, positive with 2-kilometer row time, and negative with 20-minute cycle distance). These results indicate the people with a higher percentage of body fat tended to do relatively poorly in all six events.

Now, let us see what happens when we factor analyze these correlations. According to the factor analysis, the correlations among the eight variables measured here indicate that those variables can be sorted into two groups, or factors.[2] Table 3-2 shows these two factors

---

[2] The mathematical calculations involved in factor analysis are fairly complex, and are beyond the scope of this course. You can learn how to do factor analysis in a course on measurement, but when you actually do factor analysis, you will use a computer, which is much faster. Doing factor analysis by hand is nowadays done only on small, simple variable sets, for the purpose of explaining how it is done.

TABLE 3-2
Loadings of Physical Fitness and Physiological
Measurements on Two Factors

	Factors	
Variables	**I**	**II**
Vertical jump height	.71	−.01
40-yard (36-meter) dash time	−.76	−.01
Standing triple jump distance	.77	.01
12-minute run distance	−.02	.77
2-kilometer (1.25-mile) rowing time	.01	−.70
20-minute cycle distance	.01	.74
Fast-twitch muscle fiber type percentage	.35	−.34
Body fat percentage	−.32	−.34

These are hypothetical (imaginary) data.

by indicating how strongly each variable belongs to each group—or, to use more technical terms, how much each variable "loads on" each "factor."

Look first at the column of numbers on the left for factor I. These numbers are called *factor loadings*, and they can range in size between −1 and +1, just like correlation coefficients. Notice that, for this column, the numbers beside vertical jump, 40-yard sprint time, and standing triple jump are quite large: Vertical jump has a "loading" of .71, 40-yard sprint time has a loading of −.76, and standing triple jump has a loading of .77. These large loadings indicate that these variables very clearly are part of the first factor. This factor apparently represents an overall jumping and sprinting ability, because the three jumping and sprinting variables have high loadings (the highest of any of the variables) on this factor. Notice that, unlike the loadings of the two jumping variables, the loading for 40-yard sprint time is negative; however, this makes sense, because a person who takes a long time to sprint 40 yards is slow, and would be unlikely to jump very high or very far.

Now look at the column of numbers on the right for factor II. Notice that, for this column, the numbers beside 12-minute run, 2-kilometer row time, and 20-minute cycle are quite large: 12-minute run has a loading of .77, 2-kilometer row time has a loading of −.70, and 20-minute cycle has a loading of .74. These large loadings indicate that these variables very clearly are part of the second factor. This factor apparently represents an overall long-distance racing ability, because the three long-distance variables—running, rowing, and cycling—have high loadings (the highest of any of the variables) on this factor. Notice that, unlike the loadings of running and cycling, the loading for 2-kilometer rowing time is negative; however, this makes sense, because a person who takes a long time to row 2 kilometers is unable to maintain a fast rowing pace, and would be unlikely to run or cycle a very long distance.

So, the factor analysis has revealed one factor that includes variables associated with sprinting and jumping ability, and another factor that includes variables associated with endurance or long-distance performance. It is important to understand that these are two separate, independent factors, and not two opposite poles of the same factor. If the sprinting/jumping variables and the long-distance variables had been opposite to each other—if they had been strongly negatively correlated—then they would have belonged to the *same* factor, but would have shown *opposite* loadings on it. Instead, each of these groups of variables defined its own factor. Notice that the sprinting and jumping variables all had loadings close to zero on the second factor, and that the long-distance variables all had loadings close to zero on the first factor. This indicates that each set of variables is unrelated to the factor that is defined by the other set of variables; that is, each set is neither positively nor negatively related to the other set.

There are two other variables that we have not yet considered. First, look at the loadings for percent fast-twitch muscle fiber. As you can see, this variable showed a modest-sized positive loading on the first factor (.35) and a modest-sized negative loading on the second factor (−.34). These results indicate that this variable does not fit neatly within either factor, but is instead partly within both factors. The positive loading on the first factor indicates that having a high percentage of fast-twitch muscle fibers is associated with good sprinting and jumping performances. However, the negative loading on the second factor indicates that having a high percentage of fast-twitch muscle fibers is associated with poor long-distance, endurance performances. (This makes sense given the function of fast-twitch muscle fiber: If you have taken a kinesiology class, you might be aware that these muscle fibers contract quickly and allow rapid, explosive movement, but become tired easily and do not enable sustained steady effort.)

Next look at the loadings for percent body fat. As you can see, this variable showed a modest-sized negative loading on both the first factor (−.32) and also the second factor (−.34). As was the case for the muscle fiber variable, above, these results indicate that percent body fat does not fit neatly within either factor, but is instead partly within both factors. But notice that the pattern is different, because percent body fat loads negatively on both the first and the second factors. These loadings indicate that high body fat percentage is associated both with poor sprinting and jumping performance and with poor long-distance, endurance performance. This makes sense, because having a lot of body fat means a lot of extra "dead" weight that will make it harder to sprint and jump explosively and harder to cover a long distance at a sustained speed.

Given the results described above, we can see that factor analysis allows us to summarize the relations among a large number of variables in terms of only a small number of groups, or factors. Whereas we began with eight variables in the previous case, we were able to show that these represented two major groups of variables, and we were able to understand the nature of each group by considering the identity of the variables within it. From now on, if I want to measure the physical abilities of my students, I could probably save some time by using just one sprinting or jumping test, and just one long-distance test, instead of the full battery of eight variables. Of course, if I were interested in every variable in its own sake, I would continue to use all eight. However, if I were trying to save time and effort, I could get a good overview of my students' physical abilities by using only two variables. For example, perhaps I could just measure the standing triple jump (which represents the "sprinting and jumping ability" factor) and the 12-minute run (which represents the "long-distance" factor).

In the example shown previously, the number of variables was fairly small, and the pattern of correlations among those variables was relatively simple. By looking at the matrix of correlations among the variables, you could probably see that the variables would fall into two main factors. But in most cases when psychologists use factor analysis, the results are not nearly so obvious: There are often many, many variables, and the pattern of correlations among them is very complex, with many medium-sized correlations and fewer correlations that are very large or very small. When this is the case, factor analysis can be of much help to the researcher, by taking an extremely complicated pattern of correlations among a large number of variables, and reducing those variables to a small number of factors.

Exactly how many factors there are in a given set of variables is not always easy to figure out. There are various rules that a researcher can use to decide how many factors there really are, but these rules do not always give the same result. One important way to figure out the true number of factors is to see which sets of factors can be found in many different studies, using different research participants or even different sets of variables measuring the same general kinds of characteristics. For example, you might find that the same set of three factors can be recovered consistently in many different studies, but that no single set of four factors is consistently found. If this were true, then you would decide that there were three, but not four, factors that underlie this domain of characteristics.

One important note about factor analysis: The factors that are produced by this technique should be thought of as *dimensions* along which people differ, and not as "types" of people. In the example before, people have different levels of the factor (or dimension) of sprinting and jumping ability, with a few people being very good at these abilities and a few others being very poor, but with most people somewhere in between. Similarly, for the other factor (or dimension) of long-distance racing ability, there are also a few people with very high levels, a few others with low very levels, and most others somewhere in between. That is, for *each* of these two dimensions, we can describe an individual in terms of some number (such as a standard score) that represents his or her *level* of that dimension.

Factor Analysis of Personality Traits: How to Find a Representative Set of Traits?

The use of factor analysis might seem like an ideal way to find a set of personality trait categories that would together account for all of the important personality traits. If we measure many people on a wide variety of personality traits, a factor analysis of those traits should reveal the major groups of traits. But we still face the problem of deciding which traits should be factor analyzed. This decision is a crucial step, because if there are some important aspects of personality that are not well represented in our list of traits, then factor analysis will probably fail to reveal any groups defined by those traits. Therefore, we need to select a set of traits in such a way that all of the important aspects of personality are sufficiently represented.

This brings us back to the problem that was discussed in the previous sections. Just as a researcher's list of a few favorite traits might miss some important aspects of personality, so too might a researcher's list of all of the important traits. (For example, consider the many self-report personality questionnaires that researchers have constructed: The scales of one researcher's questionnaire usually miss some of the traits that are measured by another researcher's questionnaire, and vice versa.) If a researcher simply tries to assemble a list of traits that represents the personality domain as a whole, it is difficult for anyone to judge whether or not this list really does cover all of the important aspects of personality. Another researcher might well generate a very different list of traits, and in fact it seems likely that every researcher would provide a somewhat different collection.

At this point, it might occur to you that these disagreements might be resolved by holding a big meeting of all personality researchers, who would collectively try to decide on the complete list of important traits. (For example, perhaps they could put together the scales measured by the personality questionnaires that have been developed by various researchers.) This would probably produce a more complete list than any lone researcher could produce, but there is no guarantee that the collective choices of these researchers would represent all aspects of personality. Instead, it is still possible that some important personality traits would be underrepresented in their list, if those researchers tended to neglect some aspects of personality in favor of other aspects. For example, researchers might be particularly interested in characteristics that are associated with good (or poor) mental health or with good (or poor) job performance. Consequently, they might tend to include many of those traits at the expense of other traits that are also interesting parts of personality but that are less strongly related to those criterion variables. Therefore, we might not feel much confidence in the results of a factor analysis of a list of traits that was generated according to the interests of personality researchers.

The Idea of the Lexical Approach

Given the difficulties described before, you might wonder how it would ever be possible to obtain a list of important personality traits, in which all aspects of personality are represented fairly. The solution that most researchers have adopted is one that takes much of the decision making out of their own hands, and instead uses an already existing list of traits. This existing list is simply the set of personality-descriptive adjectives that can be found in the dictionaries of any language.

The idea behind the use of the dictionary as a source of personality characteristics is based on the *lexical hypothesis*. The lexical hypothesis states that people will want to talk about the personality traits that they view as having important consequences in their lives. As a result, people will inevitably invent some words to describe people who have high or low levels of these important traits. Over long periods of time, words that describe important traits should become established in every language. Therefore, by considering the full list of personality-descriptive adjectives in a given language—in other words, a language's personality "lexicon"—we should be able to obtain a reasonably complete list of important personality traits. If we then do a factor analysis of the adjectives in this list, we should be able to find the major groups of personality traits. (Or, to be more precise, we should be able to find the major groups of the personality traits that people consider important enough to talk about.)

In the next section, we will discuss the results obtained using the lexical approach to finding the basic categories of personality traits. But first, let us consider how this approach is generally used. First, the researcher searches systematically throughout the dictionary of the language to be studied, in order to obtain a list of personality-descriptive adjectives. When going through the dictionary, the researcher tries to identify every word that is mainly used for the purpose of describing normal personality variation. (This is a boring job!) After obtaining such a list, the researcher excludes terms that are very rarely used (and hence not widely understood). The resulting list—usually several hundred adjectives in length—is then administered to a large sample of people who are willing to serve as the participants in the research study. Those people are asked to provide self-ratings on these adjectives, indicating the extent to each adjective describes their own personalities. (Or, sometimes, the participants are asked to provide observer ratings on the adjectives for some other person, generally someone whom they know well.) For example, the participant might be asked to rate how accurately a given adjective describes himself or herself, using a scale from, say, 1 (very inaccurate) to 5 (very accurate). When ratings have been obtained from several hundred participants, the researcher can then calculate the correlations among the adjectives, and conduct a factor analysis to find the major categories of personality traits.[3]

The Early Use of the Lexical Approach

As early as the nineteenth century, some psychologists understood the basic idea of the lexical approach: Galton (1884) noted that the various personality-descriptive words listed in the dictionary would overlap and blend into each other, with each word partly sharing its meaning with other words, and partly having some unique meaning of its own. But the first systematic attempts to list the personality lexicon of a given language were only made in the 1930s. Baumgarten (1933) undertook an inventory of German personality-related words, and Allport and Odbert (1936) did the same in the English language, using Webster's dictionary. The result of Allport and Odbert's work was a list of nearly 18,000

---

[3] There have been several criticisms of the use of the lexical hypothesis as a way of obtaining lists of personality traits. One objection is that some personality traits are too complex or too specific to a certain situational context to be summarized by single adjectives. Another criticism is that people do not understand the workings of personality, so it would be mistaken to assume that the adjectives people use would be adequate for finding the basic categories of personality traits. These objections, however, are based on a misunderstanding of the lexical hypothesis (Ashton & Lee, 2005a). First, the lexical hypothesis does not require that every imaginable personality trait should have its own word; instead, the idea is that people tend to talk about important traits, and therefore any major group of personality traits should be represented by many adjectives in any language. Second, the lexical hypothesis does not assume that people understand the causes of personality; it only assumes that people will notice and describe the basic, important features of personality.

English words that described people, of which about 4500 actually described people's personality traits.

The first researcher to do a factor analysis of ratings on personality-descriptive adjectives in the English language was Raymond Cattell (e.g., Cattell, 1947). Cattell did not analyze all 4500 terms, however. This full list would be too long for research participants to complete, but even more importantly, it was far too large a variable set to be factor analyzed during the 1940s. (In the days before computers, factor analysis had to be performed by hand, and the calculations are very complex and time-consuming.) To allow a study whose computations would be manageable, Cattell sorted through the adjectives, putting synonyms and antonyms together, and produced a set of 35 variables. He then asked research participants to provide observer ratings of their peers on those variables, and factor analyzed the responses.

Cattell (1947) reported that his data revealed 12 factors, which is a rather large number. However, when other researchers later reanalyzed Cattell's data, or when they collected new data from other research participants using the same variables, they were unable to recover those same 12 factors. This is probably because Cattell's method of using factor analysis—a technique that was still being refined at the time of his research—tended to produce more factors than really existed among the variables being analyzed. But although it was not possible to replicate Cattell's finding of 12 personality factors, some researchers did notice a striking similarity in the results of several studies in which Cattell's 35 adjective-based variables had been factor analyzed. These results showed a consistent set of only five personality factors (Tupes & Christal, 1961; later republished as Tupes & Christal, 1992).

Lexical Studies in the English Language: The Big Five Personality Factors

The Big Five

The summary of studies using Cattell's list of personality variables was conducted by two researchers—Ernest Tupes and Raymond Christal—who analyzed many different personality data sets. The consistent result from these data sets was that the 35 variables of Cattell's list could be classified in terms of a set of five factors. Soon after Tupes and Christal's research, these five groups of traits were also recovered in several new studies. This finding was an important one, because it suggested that the wide variety of personality characteristics—and hence the personalities of individuals—could be summarized reasonably well by a set of only five basic dimensions.

At this point, you are probably wondering about the nature of these five personality factors: Just what are they, exactly? Let us consider each of these "Big Five" dimensions in turn, in order of the number of personality traits that each factor subsumes. These factors and their defining traits are also listed in Table 3-3.

> *Extraversion.* The factor that has frequently been the largest is usually called Extraversion. This factor contrasts traits such as talkativeness, liveliness, and outgoingness versus shyness, quietness, and passivity.

TABLE 3-3

Examples of Adjectives That Have High Loadings on the Big Five Personality Factors as Obtained in Lexical Studies of Personality Structure in the English Language

Factor	Adjectives
Extraversion	Talkative, extraverted, sociable, assertive, enthusiastic, verbal versus withdrawn, silent, introverted, shy, reserved, inhibited
Agreeableness	Sympathetic, kind, warm, cooperative, sincere, compassionate versus cold, harsh, rude, rough, antagonistic, callous
Conscientiousness	Organized, systematic, efficient, precise, thorough, practical versus careless, sloppy, absent-minded, haphazard, disorderly, unreliable
Emotional Stability (versus Neuroticism)	Relaxed, unemotional, easy-going, unexcitable versus moody, jealous, possessive, anxious, touchy, high-strung
Intellect/Imagination[a]	Intellectual, complex, philosophical, innovative, unconventional versus simple, conventional, uninquisitive, unintelligent, shallow

Source: Hofstee, De Raad, and Goldberg (1992); Saucier and Goldberg (1996).

[a] Intellect/Imagination is sometimes known as Openness to Experience.

Agreeableness. The second factor, also very large, is known as Agreeableness. In the English-language studies discussed in this section, it contrasts traits such as kindness and gentleness with rudeness and harshness.

Conscientiousness. The third factor is called Conscientiousness. This factor includes traits such as organization, discipline, and thoroughness versus sloppiness, laziness, and unreliability.

Emotional Stability (versus Neuroticism). The fourth factor, which is usually considerably smaller than the first three, is known as Emotional Stability. This factor contains traits such as relaxedness versus moodiness, anxiety, and touchiness. You will often see this factor described in terms of its opposite pole, and referred to as Neuroticism. In other words, the opposite end of Emotional Stability is Neuroticism, which roughly means the same thing as emotional instability.

Intellect or Imagination. The fifth factor, which is consistently the smallest of the five, is known by various names, including Intellect and Imagination. This factor contains traits such as philosophicalness, complexity, and creativity versus shallowness and conventionality. The choice of name for this fifth factor was a difficult one for researchers; it was originally called Culture by Tupes and Christal, and many researchers now refer to this factor as Openness to Experience.

Now we return to the history of the Big Five factors. By the 1960s, these five personality dimensions had been found in several different studies, but nearly all of this research had been based on Cattell's 35 variables. (Recall that Cattell had obtained this list of 35 by taking the list of 4500 personality-descriptive words from Allport and Odbert's list, and then forming groups of roughly synonymous words.) Because Cattell's method had been quite subjective, some researchers wondered whether other personality factors, additional to the "Big Five," might be found if a larger, more complete list of personality-descriptive adjectives were administered to research participants.

The researcher who undertook this project was Warren Norman, a psychologist who had earlier used Cattell's variables in his own research. Norman and his assistants used the original list that Allport and Odbert had compiled during the 1930s, and added some new words from a more recent edition of the dictionary. Norman (1967) took the resulting list and reduced it to approximately 2800 terms that he considered to be descriptive of personality. Norman himself never conducted a factor analysis of these terms, but a colleague of his, Lewis Goldberg, did. Goldberg used about 1700 of these terms, excluding the ones whose meanings were unfamiliar to the university students who participated in his research.

When Goldberg performed his factor analyses during the 1970s and 1980s, computers were not yet powerful enough to analyze all 1700 adjectives separately. So, before conducting the factor analysis, he combined similar adjectives into 75 clusters that Norman had recommended. Goldberg (1990) factor analyzed the 75 clusters of adjectives, using responses from college students who provided self-ratings and observer ratings on the adjectives. The results were clear: Again, the Big Five factors—and only the Big Five factors—were found. Moreover, even when Goldberg rearranged the adjectives into other clusters, based on his own judgment, he again recovered the Big Five factors, and nothing else. These results were strong evidence in favor of the Big Five factors, because they showed that the emergence of these categories of personality traits did not depend on the variables that Cattell had used. Instead, the Big Five categories emerged even when different researchers assembled adjectives in different ways (see also Saucier & Goldberg, 1996).

Personality Inventories and the Five-Factor Model

By the 1980s, many researchers had begun to accept the Big Five factors as the major categories of personality traits. Among the psychologists who adopted the Big Five factors were Paul Costa and Robert McCrae. Costa and McCrae were interested in studying personality in relation to the aging process, but they wanted to develop a complete and efficient system for measuring personality. They conducted some analyses of questionnaire scales that Cattell had developed on the basis of his earlier lexical research, and then combined the results of those analyses with results from recent lexically based findings. Taken together, these results convinced Costa and McCrae that the Big Five framework was the best way to organize personality traits. To measure the factors of this "Five-Factor Model," Costa and McCrae (1985) constructed a questionnaire called the NEO Personality Inventory, and this instrument was soon being widely used in personality research. Its more recent versions, the NEO Personality Inventory–Revised and the shorter NEO Five-Factor Inventory (Costa & McCrae, 1992a; see Chapter 2), have become so popular that many psychologists are familiar with the Big Five factors chiefly through the high profile of those instruments, and are not even aware of the lexically based research that led to the discovery of those factors. These NEO questionnaires were used in a series of studies by Costa and McCrae during the 1980s and 1990s, in which they showed that nearly all of the scales of other personality inventories were related to one or more of the five factors

TABLE 3-4

Broad Personality Factors and Narrower Personality Traits Assessed by the NEO Personality Inventory Revised (NEO-PI-R)

Neuroticism	Agreeableness
Anxiety	Trust
Angry Hostility	Straightforwardness
Depression	Altruism
Self-Consciousness	Compliance
Impulsiveness	Modesty
Vulnerability	Tender-mindedness
Extraversion	**Conscientiousness**
Warmth	Competence
Gregariousness	Order
Assertiveness	Dutifulness
Activity	Achievement Striving
Excitement-Seeking	Self-Discipline
Positive Emotions	Deliberation
Openness to Experience	
Openness to Fantasy	
Openness to Aesthetics	
Openness to Feelings	
Openness to Actions	
Openness to Ideas	
Openness to Values	

The five headings refer to the five broad factors (i.e., dimensions, domains) assessed by the NEO-PI-R; the six names under each heading refer to the six narrower traits (i.e., facets) that form each of the broad factors.
Source: Costa and McCrae (1992b).

(e.g., Costa & McCrae, 1988a), and that the NEO scales themselves produced five factors even when administered (in translation) in other countries (e.g., McCrae & Costa, 1997; McCrae, Zonderman, Costa, Bond, & Paunonen, 1996).

For most purposes, the Five-Factor Model as assessed using the NEO inventories can be considered to be the same as the Big Five structure. As seen in Table 3-4, the characteristics that are measured within the five broad factors of the NEO Personality Inventory–Revised are generally very similar to those that defined the Big Five factors in lexical studies (see Table 3-3). But one difference involves the name of the Big Five Intellect or Imagination factor, which in the Five-Factor Model is instead labeled Openness to Experience. This alternative name emphasizes the characteristics that Costa and McCrae view as the central elements of this factor, such as a willingness to examine new ideas, to explore one's imagination, and to try new things. It also downplays the role of intellectual ability, which Costa and McCrae consider to be something different from a personality characteristic. Another minor difference involves the Agreeableness factor, within which Costa and

McCrae have included some traits—such as straightforwardness and modesty—that are only weakly related to the Big Five Agreeableness factor as found in lexical studies of personality structure.

Lexical Studies in Many Languages: The HEXACO Personality Factors

Different Languages, Same Six Factors

Now let us return to our discussion of the results of lexical studies of personality structure. As we have seen, the repeated emergence of the Big Five factors in English-language research led many psychologists to conclude that these five dimensions represented the major groups of human personality characteristics. But personality researchers wanted to find out whether or not these results would also occur when other languages were studied. By conducting lexical studies of personality structure in a variety of languages, psychologists could hope to learn whether or not there existed a universal set of basic groups of personality traits. One possibility was that the Big Five factors would be found in each language, in much the same form as in English. Another possibility was that one or more of the factors would fail to emerge in other languages; if so, this would suggest that those missing factors were not really among the main groups of personality traits. Still another possibility was that most other languages would contain one or more factors that were missing in the English-language results; if so, this would suggest that the English lexical studies had failed to identify some major aspects of personality variation.

Beginning in the late 1980s, lexical studies of personality structure were conducted in several languages, using methods similar to those of the English-language studies described in the previous section. However, unlike those English investigations, the studies conducted in other languages generally each used several hundred adjectives that could all be factor analyzed individually, rather than in clusters of synonyms as had been done in English. The reason for this change was that, at about this time, advances in computing power had made it feasible to factor analyze very large numbers of variables. By the beginning of the twenty-first century, lexical studies of personality structure had been conducted in several languages, including Dutch, French, German, Hungarian, Italian, Korean, and Polish. Interestingly, the results of these studies showed some striking similarities among these languages, but also some surprising differences from the earlier English-language studies (see Ashton, Lee, Perugini, *et al.*, 2004).

The main finding of these lexical studies was that a similar set of six personality factors was found in each of these diverse languages. The English translations of the adjectives that typically had high loadings on a given factor are shown, for all six factors, in Table 3-5. Now let us describe these factors.

> *Extraversion, Conscientiousness, and Intellect or Imagination.* Three of the factors obtained from the various languages were nearly identical in content—that is, in the overall meaning of the adjectives that defined the factors—to the Extraversion,

TABLE 3-5

Examples of English Translations of Adjectives That Typically Have High Loadings on the Six Factors Obtained in Lexical Studies of Personality Structure in Various Languages

Factor	Adjectives
Honesty–Humility	Sincere, honest, faithful/loyal, modest/unassuming, fair-minded versus sly, deceitful, greedy, pretentious, hypocritical, boastful, pompous
Emotionality	Emotional, oversensitive, sentimental, fearful, anxious, vulnerable versus brave, tough, independent, self-assured, stable
Extraversion	Outgoing, lively, extraverted, sociable, talkative, cheerful, active versus shy, passive, withdrawn, introverted, quiet, reserved
Agreeableness	Patient, tolerant, peaceful, mild, agreeable, lenient, gentle versus ill-tempered, quarrelsome, stubborn, choleric
Conscientiousness	Organized, disciplined, diligent, careful, thorough, precise versus sloppy, negligent, reckless, lazy, irresponsible, absent-minded
Intellect/Imagination/ Unconventionality[a]	Intellectual, creative, unconventional, innovative, ironic versus shallow, unimaginative, conventional

[a] Intellect/Imagination/Unconventionality is sometimes known as Openness to Experience.
Source: Ashton and Lee (in press); Ashton, Lee, Perugini, *et al.* (2004).

Conscientiousness, and Intellect or Imagination (a.k.a. Openness to Experience) factors of the Big Five (compare with Table 3-3). Note, however, that the adjectives of the latter factor tended to vary somewhat across different studies. In several cases, this factor included terms suggesting unconventionality, in addition to intellectual or imaginative tendencies.

Agreeableness. Each of the languages also revealed an Agreeableness factor (see Table 3-5) that was similar to the Big Five Agreeableness factor in some ways. For example, adjectives describing gentleness versus quarrelsomeness loaded on this factor in various languages. But this version of Agreeableness was in some ways different from the Big Five version, as we will discuss below.

Emotionality. Across the various languages, a factor called Emotionality (see Table 3-5) was recovered. Notice that in some ways, this factor is the same as the Big Five Emotional Stability factor, but is "flipped" to the opposite side of that Big Five factor—that is, to the Neuroticism side. For example, the Emotionality factor includes characteristics such as anxiety, which are also associated with Big Five Neuroticism (i.e., with Big Five Emotional Stability, as viewed from the opposite direction). But in other ways, this Emotionality factor obtained from many languages is different from the Big Five Neuroticism factor obtained in English.

Figure 3-1 illustrates the differences between, on the one hand, the original Big Five Agreeableness and Emotional Stability (versus Neuroticism) factors, and on the other hand, the Agreeableness and Emotionality factors observed in many languages. First, notice that the Big Five Emotional Stability (versus Neuroticism) factor contains traits such as patience versus irritability. Notice also that the Big Five Agreeableness factor contains traits such as sentimentality versus toughness. But in the lexical studies of many languages, the arrangement of traits within factors is different. Traits of patience versus irritability belong to the Agreeableness factor, and traits of sentimentality versus toughness belong to the Emotionality factor. (The name "Emotionality" is used instead of "Neuroticism" or "low Emotional Stability" for the factor observed in many languages.)

> *Honesty–Humility.* In addition to the differences involving the Agreeableness and
> Emotionality factors, there was another striking difference between the results
> obtained in various languages and those obtained in the earlier English studies.
> This surprising difference was the consistent finding of a factor that has been
> called Honesty–Humility. This factor includes traits such as sincerity, fairness,
> and modesty versus slyness, deceit, greed, and pretentiousness. In the earlier
> English-language studies, these traits were to some extent located within the
> Agreeableness factor, but they had fairly small loadings on that factor.

The finding of a set of six personality factors was an interesting result, but it raises the question of why the entire set of six factors did not emerge in the English language. After all, the English language does have many adjectives to describe a wide array of personality traits, and each of the six factors found in other languages appears to be described by many English adjectives. One possible explanation for the discrepancy is that the studies done in English involved the factor analysis of *clusters* of very similar adjectives, rather than on individual, separate adjectives. As you will recall from the previous section, computers were not fast enough or powerful enough, until quite recently, to factor analyze very large numbers of variables. So, at the time when the English-language studies were conducted, it was necessary to combine similar terms into clusters before performing the factor analysis. For example, Norman (1967) had identified many hundreds of personality terms, but because of limited computing power, he and Goldberg (e.g. Goldberg, 1990) had to condense those terms into 75 clusters of synonyms before performing any factor analyses. After the adjectives had been averaged together into the 75 clusters, then it was possible to do a factor analysis. But for the purpose of finding all of the major dimensions of personality, analyzing the clusters is not as powerful as analyzing the original adjectives themselves.

Recently, a new factor analysis has been performed using all 1700 of the English-language personality-descriptive adjectives that Goldberg and Norman had identified. With modern high-speed computers, it is now possible to analyze the adjectives separately. The results of these analyses, which were based on self-rating responses from college students, showed six factors that were nearly identical to those of the various other languages described previously (see Ashton, Lee, & Goldberg, 2004). Not surprisingly, there were very clear Extraversion, Conscientiousness, and Openness to Experience factors. But also, there were Agreeableness and "Emotionality" factors similar to those of the various other languages, not to the previous English-language factors: In this analysis, the Agreeableness factor included traits such as patience versus anger, and the "Emotionality" factor contained traits such as sentimentality versus toughness. In addition, there was a sixth

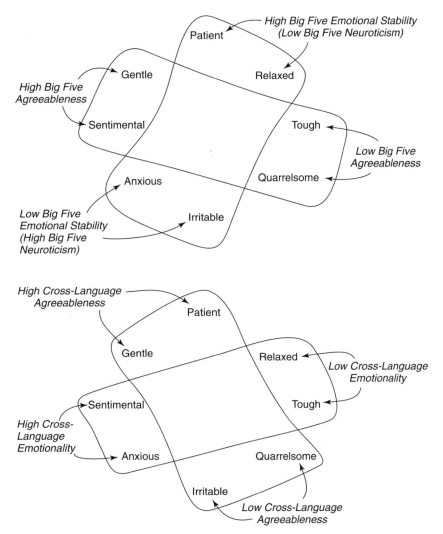

FIGURE 3-1. Graph showing similarities and differences between the Big Five Agreeableness and Emotional Stability (versus Neuroticism) factors (top panel) and the cross-language Agreeableness and Emotionality factors (bottom panel).

factor that corresponded to Honesty–Humility, containing (at its negative pole) traits such as slyness, deceit, and pretentiousness. So, these results indicated that there was little discrepancy between the results in English and those in other languages: The English language contained all six factors, but limited computing power had made it difficult to find them until very recently.

Since the publication of the English-language results, there have been further reanalyses of the results of lexical studies of personality structure as conducted in other languages.

BOX 3-1

Many Traits Are Blends of Two (or More) Factors

When researchers conduct a factor analysis of a set of variables, they use some mathematical procedures to make the results as simple and as easy to interpret as possible. One aspect of this is that the variables tend to be sorted rather neatly into the various factors: Most variables have strong loadings on only one factor, and most factors have strong loadings for a few variables only. But this ideal cannot be achieved completely, because some variables tend to be mixtures, or blends, of two or more factors. (Recall the example factor analysis shown at the beginning of this chapter: In that analysis, the variables "fast-twitch muscle fiber" and "body fat percentage" both showed medium-sized loadings on two factors.)

Let us consider a couple of examples, using the set of six factors described above. Some traits, such as self-confidence, usually have some loadings on the positive pole of the Extraversion factor and also on the negative pole of the Emotionality factor; sometimes the highest loading is on Extraversion, and sometimes on (low) Emotionality. This result suggests that self-confidence is a blend of high Extraversion and low Emotionality. As another example, consider the trait of generosity. This trait usually has some loadings on the positive poles of both Honesty–Humility and Agreeableness, sometimes showing its highest loading on one, and sometimes on the other. Thus, generosity appears to be a blend of Honesty–Humility and of Agreeableness.

The preceding examples are described with reference to the six factors observed across many languages, but similar cases can be observed for the loadings of traits within the Big Five framework. In fact, most research on the existence of traits that represent blends of two or more factors has been conducted using the Big Five factors (e.g., Hofstee, et al., 1992; Saucier, 1992).

In several investigations, the researchers were interested mainly in finding out whether or not the Big Five factors would be observed, and did not check to see whether or not the more recently discovered set of six factors would be observed. But in these languages—Croatian, Filipino, Greek, and Turkish—the same set of six factors is recovered as in the other languages described above (e.g., Ashton *et al.*, 2006; Lee & Ashton, 2006b; Lee, Ashton, & de Vries, 2005; Wasti, Lee, Ashton, & Somer, 2006). Thus, it is now clear that the personality-descriptive adjectives of many diverse languages can be classified into six broad categories, not just the five categories that had been observed in the early English-language studies.[4]

The HEXACO Model of Personality Structure

The set of six personality factors that has been observed in studies of many languages has been called the "HEXACO" structure. This label suggests both the number of factors (the Greek prefix "hexa" means six) and also their names: H is for Honesty–Humility, E is for Emotionality, X is for Extraversion, A is for Agreeableness, C is for Conscientiousness, and O is for Openness to Experience. (Note that the last factor is named as in the

---

[4] Researchers have also looked to see whether some set of more than six factors can be recovered across languages, but this search has so far not been successful. For example, when seven factors are examined, the "seventh" factor is usually different from one language to the next, without any single set of seven factors being observed in the majority of languages.

TABLE 3-6

Broad Personality Factors and Narrower Personality Traits Assessed by the HEXACO Personality Inventory–Revised (HEXACO-PI-R)

Honesty–Humility	Agreeableness
Sincerity	Forgiveness
Fairness	Gentleness
Greed-avoidance	Flexibility
Modesty	Patience
Emotionality	**Conscientiousness**
Fearfulness	Organization
Anxiety	Diligence
Dependence	Perfectionism
Sentimentality	Prudence
Extraversion	**Openness to Experience**
Social self-esteem	Aesthetic appreciation
Social boldness	Inquisitiveness
Sociability	Creativity
Liveliness	Unconventionality

The six headings refer to the six broad factors (i.e., dimensions, domains) assessed by the HEXACO-PI; the four names under each heading refer to the four narrower traits (i.e., facets) that form each of the broad factors. The Social self-esteem scale of the HEXACO-PI-R replaces the Expressiveness scale of the original HEXACO-PI.
Source: Lee and Ashton (2004, 2006a).

Five-Factor Model, rather than as in the original Big Five.) For the purpose of measuring these six factors, a questionnaire called the HEXACO Personality Inventory was developed (HEXACO-PI; Lee & Ashton, 2004, 2006a). The traits measured within the six broad factors of the revised version of this instrument are listed in Table 3-6.

As can be seen by comparing this table with Table 3-4, the Extraversion, Conscientiousness, and Openness to Experience factors of the HEXACO-PI-R are largely similar to the same-named factors of the NEO-PI-R. Some differences can be observed, however, in the remaining factors: HEXACO-PI-R Emotionality includes some traits associated with NEO-PI-R Neuroticism, but also some traits not included in Neuroticism. Also, HEXACO-PI-R Agreeableness includes traits associated with NEO-PI-R Agreeableness but also traits associated with low Neuroticism. Finally, HEXACO-PI-R Honesty–Humility includes some traits associated with NEO-PI-R Agreeableness, but also some traits not included in the NEO-PI-R version of Agreeableness.[5]

---

[5] Note that the traits measured by the NEO-PI-R and the HEXACO-PI-R were not meant to be a complete list of all personality traits associated with each factor. Instead, those traits were intended simply as a sampling of several characteristics within each of the factors, and presumably some other traits could have been selected as an alternative way of sampling the content of the factors.

Do these differences matter? Some investigations have examined whether or not the HEXACO framework can account for some personality traits that are not well accounted for by the Big Five or Five-Factor Model. The results of these studies (e.g., Lee, Ogunfowora, & Ashton, 2005) have suggested that several traits do not fit well within the Five-Factor Model, but do fit well within the HEXACO framework. For example, traits such as physical risk taking and femininity are strongly related to low Emotionality of the HEXACO model, but not to any combination of factors of the Five-Factor Model. Similarly, traits such as egotism, manipulativeness, and lack of integrity are strongly related to low Honesty–Humility of the HEXACO model, but less strongly to any combination of factors of the Five-Factor Model. These results suggest that the domain of personality characteristics is more thoroughly summarized by the HEXACO framework than by the Five-Factor Model.

But even though the HEXACO model has some advantages over the Big Five or Five-Factor Model in accommodating some personality characteristics, the five-dimensional framework is for many purposes a very good summary of personality characteristics. Since the 1980s, hundreds of researchers have measured the Big Five factors in their studies of personality, and those dimensions continue to be studied very widely. Therefore, it is worthwhile to study the content of both the Big Five factors and the HEXACO factors, and thus to understand the similarities and differences between the Five-Factor Model and the HEXACO model.

What It All Means: A Few Dimensions, but Many Personalities

Now that we have described the nature of the major categories of personality traits, it is worth reflecting for a moment on the significance of this knowledge. Essentially, the results of the lexical studies of personality structure tell us that human personality traits can be classified into six major groups. Therefore, if you could find an individual's overall level of the traits within each group, then these six levels would give you a pretty complete summary of his or her personality. Of course, some of the finer detail would certainly be lost, because any person would show differences among the traits that fall within the same category. (For example, you and I might both be fairly high in Extraversion, but I might be very outgoing and moderately lively, whereas you might be moderately outgoing and very lively.) But nevertheless, the six broad personality factors would together account for the important features of personality.

It might seem surprising that human personality traits can be summarized by only six groups and, by extension, that people's personalities can be described at least fairly thoroughly with only these six dimensions. At first, it might even seem preposterous that something as complicated as human personality can be reduced, even in rough outline, to only six characteristics. But remember that the finding of six personality factors does not mean there are only six "types" of people. To appreciate this point more fully, let us consider how many different "kinds" of people can be described with these six variables.

First, suppose that, for each factor, we can discriminate among five different levels of the factor. For example, let us say that for Agreeableness, we can divide people up into five levels, say, "very disagreeable," "disagreeable," "neutral," "agreeable," and "very agreeable." If we do this for each of the six factors, then we could describe $5 \times 5 \times 5 \times 5 \times 5 \times 5 = 15,625$ different kinds of people. And, if we could discriminate with a bit more precision, with seven levels for each factor, then we would be able to describe nearly 118,000 different kinds of people. So, it is possible to explain a great deal of the variety and complexity of human personality with only six basic factors. This is not to say that personality is *completely* accounted for by these factors—instead, the various specific traits within a given factor will provide us with important details about a person's personality—but we can go a long way toward describing someone's personality using only the six broad dimensions.

Another important implication of the results described in this chapter is that there is apparently some similarity across cultures in the nature of the major elements of personality. Recall the languages that were investigated in the lexical studies of personality structure described before: Even though some of these languages were closely related to each other (e.g., French with Italian, or Dutch with German), other languages were almost completely unrelated to each other (e.g., Hungarian, Korean, and English). Nevertheless, these languages all contained similar sets of personality-descriptive adjectives, and this indicates that people in very different cultures are describing the same major elements of personality. Across these diverse cultures, people talk about personality traits that can be classified within the same six groups, and this result suggests that these six factors represent the basic components of human personality variation. It will be interesting to examine the results of future research involving other languages: Perhaps future studies will recover the six personality dimensions, but it is possible that some languages will omit one or more categories, or that some languages will contain one or more additional categories not shared by the other languages.

Summary and Conclusions

We began this chapter with the problem of how to summarize the vast array of personality characteristics in terms of a few major dimensions. By finding the basic personality factors, researchers would be able to measure people's personalities thoroughly (i.e., without missing important characteristics) but without redundancy (i.e., without measuring many very similar characteristics). This in turn would make personality research much easier, and it would also give us a better understanding of the meaning of personality itself.

The process of identifying the major personality dimensions involves a statistical technique called factor analysis, which uses the correlations among variables to categorize them into groups called factors. One of the challenges in trying to find the basic factors of personality is to obtain a set of personality characteristics that represent all of the important aspects of personality. Researchers have accomplished this through the "lexical" approach, which involves identifying the familiar personality-descriptive adjectives of a language. By finding such a variable set, researchers can study the characteristics

BOX 3-2
Broad Factors versus Narrow Traits

The finding that so many personality traits can be classified into six broad categories is important, because it allows us to summarize people's personalities very efficiently, and it gives us some direction for future research about personality. But we should not get too carried away with this result, because it is important to remember that the broad factors are only summaries of many narrower traits that each have some unique aspect that is not shared with the others.

The importance of this fact can be seen when we use personality measurements to predict criterion variables. In many cases, the criteria that we want to predict are likely to be strongly related to some specific narrow trait, but not so strongly related to other narrow traits (even those that belong to the *same* factor as does the one that we expect to be a good predictor). As a result, that specific narrow trait would probably be a more valid predictor of the criterion than would the broad factor that combines this narrow trait with many other narrow traits that are less relevant to the criterion. That is, if one of the narrow traits within a factor is strongly relevant to a criterion variable, its validity will be weakened by combining it with other narrow traits that are less relevant to that criterion.

Consider the following example. Suppose that you are interested in predicting students' levels of academic performance. Presumably, measurements of students' levels of the Conscientiousness factor would be associated with the grade point averages obtained for the students. However, some traits within Conscientiousness, such as achievement motivation, seem likely to contribute especially strongly to academic performance, and might be very strongly associated with grade point average. In contrast, other traits within Conscientiousness, such as impulse control or neatness, seem less relevant to academic performance, and might be only weakly associated with grade point average. Therefore, if we want to predict students' grade point averages, we might be better off measuring students' levels of the narrow trait that seems most relevant to the criterion (in this case, achievement motivation) rather than the broad factor (in this case, Conscientiousness) that contains this trait (Paunonen & Ashton, 2001a,b).

So, despite the importance of the broad factors of personality, we should not forget that the narrow traits that make up those factors are themselves important. By measuring these specific aspects of personality, we can sometimes predict criterion variables more effectively than we could if we were to rely only on a half-dozen major factors.

that the speakers of that language have found to be useful and important for describing personality.

Factor analyses of the personality characteristics identified in lexical studies were first conducted in the English language. Researchers obtained self- or peer ratings of personality, using familiar personality-descriptive adjectives taken from the dictionary. When these adjective ratings were factor analyzed, the results indicated a set of five factors now known as the "Big Five." These factors are known as Extraversion, Agreeableness, Conscientiousness, Emotional Stability (versus Neuroticism), and Intellect/Imagination. The Big Five factors have become popular in personality research through the "NEO" questionnaires, which measure the characteristics of this "Five-Factor Model." In the Five-Factor Model, the Intellect/Imagination factor is called Openness to Experience.

More recently, lexical studies of personality structure have been conducted in many different languages, using much larger sets of adjectives than were used in the earlier research. These studies have recovered a set of six—not just five—factors. Three of the factors are similar to the Big Five Extraversion, Conscientiousness, and Intellect/ Imagination (or Openness to Experience) dimensions. Two other factors of the six (Agreeableness and Emotionality) are broadly similar to the Big Five Agreeableness and Emotional Stability factors, but differ in some noteworthy ways. Another of the six factors is called Honesty–Humility, and is only modestly related to the Big Five factors. This six-dimensional framework is called the "HEXACO" model, and there now exists a personality inventory to assess those six factors. Some personality characteristics that do not relate strongly to any combination of the Big Five factors show considerably stronger relations with the six HEXACO factors.

Since the 1990s, many researchers have measured personality using the Big Five framework, and today many researchers use either that framework or the newer HEXACO model. By assessing these sets of basic personality dimensions, researchers have been able to examine more efficiently some very interesting questions about personality. How do people's personalities change throughout the life span? How do brain structures and brain chemicals relate to personality? What are the genetic and environmental influences on personality? How did personality variation evolve and maintain itself across human history? How does personality influence important life outcomes? These fascinating questions will be the subjects of the next several chapters of this book.

Chapter 4

Developmental Change and Stability of Personality

Defining Change and Stability   77

Developmental Changes in Mean Levels of Personality Traits   79

Longitudinal Research Studies   79

Patterns of Life Span Change: Increasing Maturity?   80

Stability of Traits across the Years (and the Life Span)   82

Stability across a Period of Several Years during Adulthood   82

Stability across Longer Periods of Time during Adulthood   83

Stability during Adolescence and Young Adulthood   84

Personality in Childhood and Infancy: Measurement and Structure   86

Personality Structure during Childhood   86

Developmental Change in Personality Traits during Childhood   88

Stability of Traits during Childhood   89

Summary and Conclusions   90

Our next topic is that of personality development, and of the change and stability in personality throughout the life span. In this chapter we will consider the ways in which the typical person tends to change in personality while progressing through different stages of life. We will also examine the extent to which people's levels of personality characteristics—relative to other people of their own age cohort—tend to be stable across long periods of time. In a separate section, we will investigate these same questions in relation to children's personalities, whose measurement poses some special challenges for the researcher.

Defining Change and Stability

As explained in Chapter 2, the idea of a personality trait is that people differ in their tendencies to show a pattern of related behaviors, thoughts, and feelings. An important part of this idea is that the differences among people are rather stable across fairly long periods of time. That is, personality traits are relatively enduring dispositions, not temporary states. If we say that Cathy is a more talkative person than most, we are saying that, over the long run, Cathy tends to talk more than most people do; we are not merely saying that Cathy has been more talkative today (or even this week, or this month) than most other people have been.

But the idea of a trait does not require that an individual's tendencies remain equally strong or weak throughout his or her entire life span. Instead, one can imagine that trait levels could gradually change quite substantially across the years, or even that trait levels might be changed rather suddenly by some major event. In this way, it is conceivable that Cathy might have had a consistent, relatively enduring tendency to be somewhat less talkative than average during her 20s, but that she had a consistent, relatively enduring tendency to be rather more talkative than average during her 40s. But does this actually happen? Do people show important changes throughout their life span in their levels of personality traits?

In an important sense, this question about personality change combines two rather different questions. One question is whether people in general tend to show consistent changes across their lives in some personality trait—in other words, do people typically show similar patterns of development in personality trait levels? For example, consider a trait such as excitement seeking. Perhaps you would expect people to increase in their desire for thrills and excitement as they reach adolescence or early adulthood, but then to show gradually declining levels in middle and old age. Thus, one question about change in personality trait levels involves the typical "path" that is followed by people as they progress through the various stages of development in their lives. In other words, if we take a large group of people who were born at roughly the same time, will we see important changes in the group's average level of a given personality trait, as we observe these people at various points throughout their lives?

The other question about personality change is whether people tend to remain stable in their levels of some personality trait, in comparison with other people of the same age cohort. That is, in a large group of people of roughly the same age, will the individuals' relative levels of a trait remain consistent across time? Consider again the example of the trait of excitement seeking: Perhaps nearly everyone shows some increase in sensation seeking as they reach adolescence or young adulthood, and perhaps nearly everyone shows some decrease as they approach middle age. But suppose that we want to compare people of roughly the same age as they progress through these periods of their lives: Will the adolescents who were the highest in excitement seeking (relative to their peers) usually become the middle-aged adults who are highest in excitement seeking (again relative to their peers)? Perhaps even if everyone becomes less of a "thrill seeker" as they go through their 20s and 30s, the differences among people of the same age might remain roughly the same. Or, alternatively, perhaps many people tend to "switch places" during this long interval, with some of the less excitement-oriented adolescents now being among the most excitement-oriented middle-aged adults. More generally, the question is this: If we take a large group of people of roughly similar age, will we see a high level of long-term stability in their relative standings on a given personality trait, as would be shown by high correlations between trait levels even when measured many years apart?[1]

In the following sections, we will address both of the above questions. First, we will examine whether or not people in general tend to show similar developmental changes in their levels of personality traits, by comparing the average levels of those traits for persons of a given age cohort at different points in their life span. Then, we will examine whether or not there is considerable stability across the years in the relative standings of people from the same age cohort on personality traits, by finding the correlations between levels of a trait at intervals many years apart. In addressing these questions, we will focus our attention on adulthood and to some extent on adolescence. In a later section of this chapter, however, we will also examine personality during childhood and infancy.

Developmental Changes in Mean Levels of Personality Traits

Longitudinal Research Studies

The main strategy by which researchers have investigated the possibility of developmental changes in personality trait levels has been to use what is called a *longitudinal* research design. What this means, in the case of a personality study, is that researchers have assessed the personality trait levels of some group of persons (usually of similar ages) on two or more occasions, often many years or even decades apart. By finding the average level of a given trait across all members of the group, and then comparing the average levels as observed at the different time periods, the researchers can then detect any systematic changes in personality across those segments of the life span.

Many studies of this kind have now been undertaken, using self-reports or observer reports on various personality characteristics. Across these different studies, the ages of participants have varied widely. In some investigations, the participants were adolescents when first studied; in other investigations, the participants were already rather elderly when first studied. These studies have also differed in the time intervals between personality assessments. In some investigations, the participants were assessed again a few years later; in other investigations, the participants were assessed again a few *decades* later.

---

[1] One way to understand the difference between the two questions is to consider changes in height. If we ask whether people's height changes much across the life span, the answer is obviously yes, in the important sense that children generally grow so much taller. But if we ask whether people's height remains stable or consistent in relation to that of other people of the same age, the answer might also be yes (at least to some extent). It is likely that the tallest children will tend to be taller-than-average adults, even though sometimes a tall child will be "overtaken" in height by a shorter child who happens to have a later or greater "growth spurt" at some point during adolescence.

Patterns of Life Span Change: Increasing Maturity?

A more recent review of longitudinal personality research, as based on the results of over 90 different studies, has allowed some fairly clear conclusions to be drawn about the patterns of developmental change in personality across the life course (Roberts, Walton, & Viechtbauer, 2006). By combining the results from these many investigations, Roberts *et al.* were able to examine the overall pattern of personality development across the entire life span, not just across a period of several years. Roberts *et al.* organized the results of their review largely in terms of the Big Five personality factors, although they considered two aspects of Extraversion, one involving sociability and liveliness, and the other involving assertiveness or social boldness.

Did the levels of these personality dimensions show any important developmental changes? For some characteristics, there was a rather clear and steady pattern of change across the life course (see Figure 4-1). Average levels of Conscientiousness, Emotional Stability, and (especially) the assertive aspects of Extraversion tended to increase during adolescence, during young adulthood, and during early middle age; the latter two traits stopped increasing during later middle age. These differences were substantial in size, as the average 60-year-old would be roughly one standard deviation unit higher than the average 15-year-old in these characteristics. A somewhat similar pattern was observed for Big Five Agreeableness, but the increases were considerably smaller, except for a moderate increase during middle age (particularly during one's 50s).

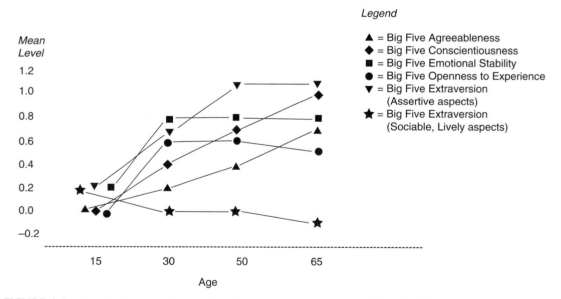

FIGURE 4-1. Mean level changes in personality characteristics across several periods of the life span.
Source: Roberts *et al.* (2006). Mean levels are given in standard deviation units, using a mean of 0.0 for early adolescence.

For other characteristics, the pattern was different (see Figure 4-1). Average levels of the sociable and lively aspects of Extraversion showed a slight decrease during young adulthood (during one's 20s), and a further slight decrease toward the end of middle age (during one's 60s). Also, average levels of Openness to Experience showed some moderate increases between adolescence and young adulthood (up to the early 20s), with an overall increase of about half of a standard deviation, but then remained stable throughout adulthood before showing a modest decline during late middle age (during one's 60s).[2]

Overall, the results of these longitudinal studies of change in personality suggest that in some important ways, most people can be said to develop greater maturity as they grow older—not only as they make the transition from adolescence to adulthood, but throughout much of their adult life course as well. For example, the finding that people gradually increase in Conscientiousness and in Emotional Stability between adolescence and middle age indicates that people develop better impulse control and generally become "steadier" or more stable in their behavior. But on the other hand, there does not seem to be any strong trend for people to pursue what might be called their personal growth, as most people do not show increases in Openness to Experience or in the sociable and lively aspects of Extraversion.

The observed changes in mean levels of personality characteristics across the life span raise the question of why those developmental trends occur. One possibility is that the changes are due to biological processes of maturation: It may be that people are genetically inclined to show changes in the levels of certain hormones or neurotransmitters, which in turn lead to influences on personality characteristics. Another possibility (which may operate in addition to the first one) is that the important events and the changes in social roles that most people experience during their lives tend to have an influence on their personalities. For example, it may be that the demands of working for a living and of being married and raising a family are themselves a cause of changes in the levels of some characteristics, such as Conscientiousness or Emotional Stability. In this way, changes in personality between late adolescence and adulthood might reflect the greater sense of purpose or direction in life that many people develop after having become fully integrated into the adult world. Similarly, it may be that the exposure to different people and ideas while a young adult—particularly if one is a college student—tends to increase one's level of Openness to Experience. And it is also possible that the slight decreases during later

---

[2] Because the review by Roberts *et al.* focused on the broad Big Five characteristics, the trends for more specific personality traits were not examined. But some studies suggest that developmental changes may be especially pronounced for some traits. As was hinted earlier in this chapter, there is some evidence, for example, that levels of excitement-seeking traits tend to be much higher during late adolescence or early young adulthood than during later adulthood, with a potential decline of close to a full standard deviation unit during the late 20s or 30s (see, e.g., McCrae *et al.*, 2005). This is probably consistent with your own observations, as you have probably noticed that most people in their 30s are generally less interested in being "wild" and in "partying" than are most people in their teens or early 20s.

middle age in the sociable and lively aspects of Extraversion, and in Openness to Experience, might reflect the decreases in physical vitality and health that some people experience during this period of their lives.

Stability of Traits across the Years (and the Life Span)

Stability across a Period of Several Years during Adulthood

As discussed earlier in this chapter, one important aspect of the idea of a personality trait is that individual differences show some stability over fairly long periods of time. In other words, when we say that people differ in their levels of some personality trait, we are describing differences in an enduring disposition, not just in a temporary state. Consistent with the idea of a trait, several large-scale investigations have shown that there are strong correlations between measurements of people's personality trait levels taken at time intervals several years apart.

For example, Costa and McCrae (1988b) studied a sample of nearly 1000 adults, whose ages at the beginning of the investigation spanned a very wide range, from 25 to 84 years. Costa and McCrae obtained self-reports of these adults' personality characteristics on two occasions, 6 years apart. The results showed very strong relations between the level of a given personality trait at the first occasion and the level of the same trait at the second occasion, with correlations averaging over .70 across the various traits measured by Costa and McCrae. These correlations are very high: As you will recall from our earlier discussion of the correlation coefficient, a value of .70 in this study would mean that a person who is above-average on a given trait on the first occasion would have an 85% chance of being above-average on the second occasion also. This in itself suggests a great deal of stability across these years, but it is especially impressive when one considers the fact that when personality measurements are taken only a few *weeks* apart, correlations are only slightly higher (typically in the .80s; Costa & McCrae, 1992a): In other words, people's levels of personality traits showed almost as much stability across a period of several years as they would across a period of several weeks.

A second study by the same researchers obtained similar results, but this time using observer report data. In this investigation, Costa and McCrae (1992c) obtained observer reports of about 90 adults whose ages ranged from 31 to 57 at the beginning of the study; the reports were provided at two periods, 7 years apart, by close friends of these adults (that is, each participant was rated on two occasions by the same friend). The results were similar to those of the earlier study of self-reports, as the correlations between measures of the same trait across the two occasions again averaged in the .70s. This suggests that personality traits show a high level of stability across a period of several years, regardless of whether the traits were measured by self- or observer report.

One interesting aspect of the results obtained by Costa and McCrae (1988b, 1992c) in both of their investigations was that the stability of personality traits did not depend very much on *which* trait was being considered. Although you might expect that some characteristics would be nearly constant and that some other characteristics would show a fair

TABLE 4-1
**Stability of Personality Trait Levels across a
Nine-Year Period**

NEO-PI-R scale (1994)	HEXACO-PI scale (2003)	Correlation
Order	Organization	.71
Angry Hostility	Patience	−.64
Anxiety	Anxiety	.63
Assertiveness	Social Boldness	.69
Openness to Aesthetics	Aesthetic Appreciation	.71
Modesty	Modesty	.55

Results based on self-reports from 655 adults. NEO-PI-R was administered in 1994; HEXACO-PI was administered in 2003. Angry Hostility and Patience are opposite in meaning, so correlation between those scales is expected to be negative.
Source: Data examined in Ashton and Lee (2005b) using Goldberg's Oregon sample (see Goldberg, 1999).

amount of fluctuation across the years, the results instead showed very similar levels of stability for a wide variety of traits. There was no consistent pattern of higher stability for some traits and lower stability for other traits.

The preceding studies show that adults' personality trait levels show very high stability across a period of several years, at least when the same inventories are used to measure personality at both time intervals. However, similar results are also obtained when the same traits are measured by the scales of different personality inventories. For example, Ashton and Lee (2005b) examined the relations between scales from two personality inventories—the NEO-PI-R and the HEXACO-PI (see Chapters 2 and 3)—that were administered 9 years apart to a sample of over 600 adults. Despite the use of different inventories and despite this 9-year interval, the respondents' self-reported levels of personality traits were very stable in this sample (see Table 4-1). For several diverse traits (e.g., organization, patience, anxiety, social boldness, aesthetic appreciation, and modesty), the correlations between the two measures of the same trait were generally in the .60s. Given that the reliabilities of the scales measuring these traits were typically about .75, this again indicates a high level of stability. Interestingly, the level of stability was similar regardless of the age of the participants at the time when the first inventory was administered: The correlations across the 9-year period were similar for respondents who were in their 30s, in their 60s, or in between.

Stability across Longer Periods of Time during Adulthood

The results summarized above indicate a high level of stability over periods of several years. But they also raise another interesting question: How stable would personality trait levels remain across much longer segments of the life span? Does personality remain stable over periods of, say, 20 years or 40 years? Keep in mind that, even if personality did change substantially over these *very* long periods, this would not really contradict the idea of a trait. Although traits are viewed as enduring dispositions, it is possible that the strengths of those dispositions would change gradually over the life span: In this way, there would be hardly any noticeable change in an individual's personality over a period of a few years, but nevertheless the individual's personality might show some clear differences across periods of a few decades.

Some idea of the stability of personality across longer periods of the life span can be gained by considering an investigation by Costa and McCrae (1992c), who administered self-report personality questionnaires to participants at several points across a period of 24 years. The results showed that the stability of personality across the entire 24-year period, based on the average correlation for the various traits, was very high, at .65. This level of stability was only slightly lower than that observed across a 12-year period, for which the average correlation for the various traits was .70. This result suggests that the stability of personality declines only modestly when longer time intervals are considered. Note that a correlation of .65 means that, if a person has a higher-than-average level of a given trait at a given time, then there is more than an 80% chance that he or she will also have a higher-than-average level of that trait 24 years later. This is much higher than the 50% that would be observed if personality were completely unstable across this time period. On the basis of similar results, Costa and McCrae have estimated that the stability of personality across a 50-year interval—say, between the ages of 30 and 80—would probably be about .60.

Stability during Adolescence and Young Adulthood

All of the preceding results suggest that there is a fairly high degree of stability in personality, even across very long periods of time. However, those results are all based on samples of people who were at least 25 to 30 years old at the beginning of the investigations, and therefore had already emerged from young adulthood. But is the long-term stability of personality traits equally strong for young adults or adolescents? Or, instead, is there a greater degree of personality change during those earlier periods of the life span, such that individuals' relative levels of a trait might be more likely to shift?

These questions have been investigated in several studies that have measured the personality trait levels of high school or college students and have then measured those individuals again several years or even several decades later. One such study was conducted by Robins, Fraley, Roberts, and Trzesniewski (2001), who obtained self-reports from 270 American students at the beginning of their college career and on their graduation 4 years later. They found that the correlations between levels of a given trait averaged about .60 across this 4-year period. This value is certainly high enough to suggest that traits are rather stable during the college years, but it is also somewhat lower than that observed for older adults. This suggests that personality is undergoing some change during the college-age years, before entering a period of greater consistency later on in adulthood. Another investigation of personality stability during young adulthood was that of Roberts, Caspi, and Moffitt (2001), who examined the personalities over 900 New Zealand young adults who provided self-reports at age 18 and at age 26. Across this 8-year period, the correlations between levels of a given trait averaged about .55. Thus, these results are broadly similar to those of the Robins *et al.* study.

Similar results have been observed when personality trait levels have been measured during high school or college, and then measured again during middle age. For example, Finn (1986) found that personality trait levels assessed by self-report *in college students* were correlated .35, on average, with levels of the same traits when assessed in the same individuals 30 years later. In comparison, levels of the same traits measured originally *in 40-year-olds* were correlated about .55, on average, with levels of the same traits 30 years later. These results also suggest that personality traits are somewhat less stable during the period of early adulthood than during later adulthood.

When personality is examined still earlier in the life span, at the beginning and end of the teenage years, the levels of stability tend to be somewhat lower than in early adulthood. A study by McCrae *et al.* (2002) examined self-reports of the Big Five personality traits as provided by 230 American adolescents at two time intervals 4 years apart, when the participants were 12 and 16 years old. The correlations between levels of the same trait across this 4-year interval were generally about .40, although one of the dimensions, Conscientiousness, showed a correlation of about .50. These results suggest that personality is somewhat stable during adolescence, but that it is less stable than during early adulthood (i.e., college-age years) or (especially) older adulthood.[3,4]

Let us summarize all of the preceding results about the stability of personality traits. First, when measured on occasions that are several years apart, personality traits generally show high correlations across those occasions. This indicates that differences among people are, in fact, very stable over these time periods, and are consistent with the idea of a personality trait. Also, when measured across much longer periods of time, such as 20 years or more, the levels of stability are lower, suggesting that there are some changes in personality across the life span. However, these changes tend to be smaller after young adulthood than during the earlier periods of the life span, when personality tends to undergo somewhat larger changes.

---

[3] The adolescents of the McCrae *et al.* (2002) study were selected as part of a search for "gifted" students, so the results might not be typical of those for adolescents in general. On the other hand, the status of these students as "gifted" suggests that they were probably able to read and understand the personality inventory very well even at the age of 12. Therefore, it is unlikely that any lack of comprehension of the items can explain the somewhat modest level of stability that was observed in this study.

[4] The levels of stability in the studies described in this section are somewhat higher than the levels of those observed in some earlier studies (see review by Roberts & DelVecchio, 2000). However, many of those earlier investigations were based on personality inventories whose scales are likely to be less reliable and less valid than those used in the studies described above.

Personality in Childhood and Infancy: Measurement and Structure

So far in this chapter, our examination of personality change and stability has focused chiefly on adulthood and on adolescence, without considering personality development during childhood or infancy. This is largely because the study of personality during the early years of the life span can present several major challenges to the researcher.

One difficulty is that of obtaining accurate personality descriptions from children. For example, it appears to be only after about the age of 10 years that most children begin to describe themselves and others in terms of personality traits. Prior to that age, many children tend simply to give overall evaluations of themselves and others (i.e., as good or bad) rather than to give descriptions that differentiate between specific traits. A second difficulty is that the self-report personality inventories that are used with adults generally demand a level of reading comprehension that is not reached until adolescence. As a result, these inventories are unlikely to be useful for making comparisons of mean levels of a personality trait between childhood and adulthood. Finally, a third difficulty emerges when assessing the personality of very young children (or especially of infants), because many of the behaviors and situations in which personality is assessed are not really observed in those children. For example, children who have not yet passed the toddler stage may not yet have well-developed language skills or the complex social interactions that can be observed even in young school-aged children.

Of course, the study of personality in children is still of much interest in spite of the preceding challenges. Investigations of personality change and stability can still be informative, as long as we keep in mind the difficulty of making meaningful comparisons of personality between childhood (especially infancy) and adulthood. In the following sections, we will examine the patterns of change and stability during the early periods of life. But first, let us consider a related question about personality during childhood—specifically, what are the major dimensions of personality during this phase of the life span?

Personality Structure during Childhood

In the earlier sections of this chapter, we discussed the issues of personality change and stability across various stages of adulthood and adolescence. However, we did not examine the topic of personality structure at these various periods of the life span. There are two rather simple reasons why this is not really necessary: First, we can use the same personality characteristics to describe differences among the adults (and among the adolescents) of any age group. Second, the correlations among those various personality characteristics are rather similar within any given age group, with the result that personality structure— that is, the number and the meaning of the major dimensions or factors of personality— remains pretty much the same across those parts of the life span. Thus, models of the major personality dimensions, such as the Big Five framework or the HEXACO framework, can be used to summarize personality throughout adolescence and the whole of adulthood.

But if we consider children—especially very young children—it is possible that personality structure could be somewhat different. First, some of the personality traits that describe adults or adolescents might not be applicable to young children. For example, it might not be meaningful to compare 3-year-old children in terms of how philosophical, or how self-conscious, or how pretentious, or how casual they are. Also, it is possible that some of the personality traits that can be applied to children might show patterns of correlations different from those observed within adult samples. For example, traits such as irritability, shyness, and sentimentality are roughly uncorrelated with each other in samples of adults, but are these traits also uncorrelated in children? Perhaps those traits might have positive correlations with each other during childhood, if there are very strong differences among children in how emotionally reactive they tend to be. Or, perhaps some of these traits would be negatively correlated during the childhood years.

The preceding concerns are reasonable, but the evidence so far suggests that at least during much of childhood, personality structure is similar to that observed during adulthood. For example, factor analyses of teachers' ratings of children's personalities, as assessed using the adjective descriptions developed by Cattell (see Chapter 3), have produced the Big Five factors (Digman & Takemoto-Chock, 1981). These factors have also been obtained in several other analyses of personality characteristics in childhood (see review by Shiner & Caspi, 2003), although the Openness to Experience dimension does not always emerge as strongly as the others (e.g., Halverson *et al.*, 2003). More recently, factor analyses of descriptions of child personality as provided by parents (or other guardians) have also produced meaningful dimensions. Lahey *et al.* (2004) found a set of factors that showed similar content to those of several of the HEXACO dimensions: One factor was defined by ill-temper and stubbornness (similar to low Agreeableness), a second factor by lack of energy and of social confidence (similar to low Extraversion), a third factor by disorganization and inattention (similar to low Conscientiousness), a fourth factor by lying and theft (similar to low Honesty–Humility), and a fifth factor by fearfulness and dependence (similar to Emotionality).[5]

The structure of personality among very young children or among infants is somewhat less clear. When parents or other observers provide ratings of the personality or the "temperament" traits of infants or of toddlers (e.g., Caspi, Roberts, & Shiner, 2005; Rothbart & Bates, 1998),[6] the resulting factors usually include dimensions representing activity

---

[5] When six factors were examined, the last-named factor divided into two parts. Lahey *et al.* did not obtain a factor similar to Openness to Experience, probably because of the lack of Openness-related variables in their analysis.

[6] Some researchers use the terms "temperament" and "personality" to refer to two different concepts. According to this view, temperament characteristics are basic emotional tendencies (such as being fearful, impulsive, or energetic), whereas personality characteristics are more complex patterns of behavior that occur only in social contexts (such as being stubborn, hardworking, or unconventional). In this book, we will use the term "personality" to include both kinds of characteristics. However, we will sometimes use the term temperament when researchers have used this term in describing young children (in this chapter) or in discussing the biological basis of personality (in Chapter 5).

level, irritability, fearfulness, positive emotions, attention span or persistence, soothability, and "rhythmicity" (i.e., preferring a clear daily rhythm or routine). Several of these dimensions resemble those obtained in studies of adult personality, such as Extraversion, Conscientiousness, Emotionality, and Agreeableness. But the correspondence is not perfect, because there is no counterpart of Openness to Experience or of Honesty–Humility in these early childhood factors. As noted earlier, some personality traits are difficult to assess at such an early stage of the life span, and some personality traits might not yet exist at that age. Conversely, the activity level, soothability, and rhythmicity factors do not emerge as separate factors later in the life span. It appears that at least some of these characteristics tend to join other factors during later periods of the life span; for example, during adulthood, activity level tends to be associated with Extraversion and with Conscientiousness.

Developmental Change in Personality Traits during Childhood

When considering the development of personality during childhood, one interesting issue is that of personality change during these formative years. That is, for any given personality characteristic, do children typically tend to show increasing, decreasing, or stable levels? One study by Lamb, Chuang, Wessels, Broberg, and Hwang (2002) addressed this question by examining the personalities of about 100 Swedish children at various time intervals during a 13-year period. The first personality assessments were made when the children were 2 years old, and further assessments were made at ages 3, 6, 8, and 15. All of the assessments were obtained using mothers' reports of their children's personalities in terms of the Big Five personality factors.

The results of the Lamb *et al.* (2002) study showed that for most children, personality trait levels changed in similar ways during childhood. Across the duration of the study, the typical child became lower in Extraversion, higher in Agreeableness, and higher in Conscientiousness. These differences were moderately large, being roughly one standard deviation unit in size. In addition, the children typically became somewhat lower in Emotional Stability between the ages of 3 and 6 (i.e., during the period when they began school), and most became somewhat lower in Openness to Experience between the ages of 8 and 15 (i.e., during the period when they reached adolescence).

It is interesting to speculate on the possible reasons for these patterns of developmental changes. For example, Lamb *et al.* (2002) suggested that the demands imposed by the educational system tended to make children become more conscientious throughout their childhoods, and perhaps a similar suggestion could be offered for Agreeableness. However, these results are based on only one investigation, and future research will be needed to find out whether the results will apply to children in general. The interpretation of these findings is complicated by the fact that the personality trait scales had low reliabilities during the early periods, especially Extraversion and Openness to Experience. This low reliability might reflect one of the difficulties in examining developmental change in children's personality: Because children's personalities are expressed in terms of different behaviors as they grow older, it might not be possible to assess personality by using reports of the same behaviors at different ages.

Stability of Traits during Childhood

Now let us turn to the question of whether there is personality trait stability throughout childhood: Do children who have high levels of a given characteristic at one age (relative to their same-age peers) tend to maintain those high levels at some later age (again, relative to their same-age peers)? This question was also examined in the study by Lamb *et al.* (2002), who measured children's personalities at five intervals beginning at the age of 2 years and ending at the age of 15. Lamb *et al.* found that personality was rather stable between adjacent intervals (i.e., between 2 and 3 years old, between 3 and 6, between 6 and 8, and between 8 and 15), with most correlations above .50 for each of the Big Five factors. (This means that, of the children who had an "above-average" level of a trait at one point, more than 75% would have an above-average level at the next assessment time also.) However, over the much longer period between the beginning and the end of the study—a total interval of 13 years—the children's personalities were less stable, with correlations only about .20 for each of the Big Five factors. (This means that, of the children who had an "above-average" level of a trait at age 2, about 60% would have an above-average level at age 15. This is not very much higher than the 50% that would be expected if the traits showed no stability at all.)

BOX 4-1
The Development of Self-Esteem across the Life Span

The trait of self-esteem—that is, one's overall evaluation of oneself—is related to personality factors such as Extraversion and Emotional Stability. However, the pattern of changes across the life span in self-esteem levels is somewhat different from that of those broader factors.

Many studies have examined the development of self-esteem across the life span, with self-esteem being measured by self-report measures in children as young as 10 years of age and in elderly adults as old as 80 years of age. Taken together, the results of these studies show some important changes in people's average levels of self-esteem at different points in the life course (e.g., Robins & Trzesniewski, 2005). Most people tend to have fairly high self-esteem during childhood, but this level tends to drop sharply during adolescence. Even after this decline, most people still have mainly positive feelings about themselves, but those feelings are much more "mixed" than is the case in childhood. Levels of self-esteem tend to remain at this moderate level during young adulthood, but then rise during middle age to reach rather high levels by the age of 65. However, self-esteem levels tend to drop again during old age, to a similar extent to that seen during adolescence.

Why do these changes occur? High self-esteem during childhood might reflect some overly optimistic self-perceptions, which are then deflated by increased criticism from peers and from adults during late childhood and adolescence. In particular, social relationships during adolescence can pose especially strong challenges to the sense of self-worth. During adulthood, increases in one's status presumably help to increase one's self-esteem, but during old age, awareness of one's own limitations tend to become much stronger, with a resulting decline in self-esteem. (See discussion by Robins & Trzesniewski, 2005.)

With regard to the stability of individual differences in self-esteem, the results are similar to those observed for other aspects of personality (Robins & Trzesniewski, 2005). That is, the differences among persons in the tendency to feel good about oneself tend to be stable across time: People who have higher self-esteem than do their peers of the same age will usually continue to have higher levels, even though their absolute levels of self-esteem will tend to change throughout the various stages of life.

These results probably underestimate the true level of stability in personality trait levels, because the personality assessments of very young children were not very reliable. Nevertheless, there does appear to be some considerable shifting in the relative levels of personality characteristics between toddlerhood and adolescence; for example, a toddler who is relatively talkative (or anxious, or cautious, etc.) might become an adolescent who is relatively quiet (or calm, or impulsive, etc.). Interestingly, the results of the Lamb *et al.* (2002) study suggest that the changes are rather gradual, as personality was generally fairly stable across each of the shorter intervals (a few years each) within that study. The reasons for these changes will need to be explored in future research. For example, do children's early experiences with their peers and their teachers, as encountered in elementary school, have an important influence on the development of their personalities? Or, do the differences in development result mainly from genetic influences that may become stronger at different points during childhood? We will examine these questions about the genetic and environmental influences on personality a bit later in this book, in Chapter 6.

Summary and Conclusions

In this chapter we considered the patterns of developmental change and stability in personality characteristics, and the main points can be summarized as follows. First, let us recall the developmental trends in mean levels of personality characteristics. Findings from many previous studies suggest that most people develop steadier, more mature personalities as they progress from adolescence through late middle age, becoming higher in Conscientiousness and in Emotional Stability. In contrast, changes in aspects of personality involving what might be called "personal growth", such as Openness to Experience or the sociable and lively aspects of Extraversion, are much smaller.

With regard to the stability of individual differences among adults of the same age cohort, there are generally very strong correlations between levels of any given personality trait at two intervals several years apart. When much longer intervals of two or more decades are considered, these stability correlations become lower, but remain fairly high. In general, individual differences in personality characteristics are more stable after young adulthood (during and after the 30s) than during adolescence or young adulthood.

The study of personality during childhood presents some serious challenges to the researcher. This is particularly true of the earliest years, when the range of behaviors in which children express their personalities is much less varied than it is during later childhood, adolescence, or adulthood. For the same reason, comparisons between personality in early childhood and personality in later periods are difficult to undertake. Research thus far suggests that among children, the structure of personality—that is, the nature of the major personality dimensions—may be similar to what is observed among adults, but this is not yet clear, especially for the early years. Little research has been conducted thus far to determine the typical changes in levels of personality characteristics as children develop, but one study has suggested modest decreases in Extraversion and modest increases in Agreeableness and Conscientiousness during childhood. Results from the same study suggest that children's personalities, in the sense of individual differences among children of the same age cohort, are fairly stable across a period of a few years, but show only weak stability across the entire span of childhood. However, our knowledge of personality in childhood remains limited and uncertain, and will be improved as the results of future investigations become known.

Chapter 5

Biological Bases of Personality

Early Ideas: The Four "Humors" and Personality 93
Neurotransmitters 96
   Cloninger's Theory 97
Brain Structures 99
   Gray's Theory 99
   Eysenck's Theory 101
   Comparing Gray's and Eysenck's
     Dimensions 102

Empirical Evidence and the Theories of
   Gray and Eysenck 103
   Zuckerman's Model 105
Hormones 106
   Testosterone 107
   Cortisol 108
   Oxytocin 109
Summary and Conclusions 111

More than 2000 years ago, the philosophers of ancient Greece suspected that personality was influenced by various fluids in the body. Today, researchers have made systematic efforts to find the biological basis of personality, by studying substances such as neurotransmitters and hormones and also by studying the workings of the brain itself. In this chapter, we will take a quick look at the very early ideas about the bodily origins of personality. We will then examine the recent theories that have been proposed to explain how personality variation might be influenced by various substances and brain structures, and we will discuss some of the research that has attempted to evaluate and to refine those theories.

Early Ideas: The Four "Humors" and Personality

As noted before, ancient Greek thinkers believed that one's personality, or temperament, depended on the strengths of various fluids, or "humors," in one's body. According to the

Greek physicians Galen and Hippocrates, there were four main humors, each of which was responsible for a particular pattern of personality (and also of susceptibility to disease). One of these humors was blood, an excess of which was thought to produce a very cheerful ("sanguine") temperament. Another was black bile, which in excess was believed to cause a depressive ("melancholic") temperament. An excess of the humor called yellow bile was considered responsible for an angry ("choleric") temperament. And an excess of the remaining humor, phlegm, was seen as the basis of a calm ("phlegmatic") temperament. There is no evidence that any of these ideas is accurate, and in fact the ancient Greeks themselves did not try to do any empirical research to find out whether the levels of these bodily humors were in fact related to personality characteristics.

Nevertheless, the idea of the four humors or temperaments remained popular during medieval times, and was influential even in the modern era. One researcher who tried to interpret his own observations in terms of the four temperaments was the famous Russian psychologist and physiologist, Ivan Pavlov. Although Pavlov is famous chiefly for his discovery of classical conditioning, he was also interested in temperament. In observing the dogs of his laboratory, Pavlov suggested that there were four basic kinds of temperaments in those dogs, and he believed that there were parallels between dogs and people. According to Pavlov, the four kinds of dogs' temperaments were as follows:

Weak: inhibited, anxious, easily upset (similar to melancholic);
Strong unbalanced: excitable, hyperactive, irritable (similar to choleric);
Strong balanced slow: calm, consistent, not easily aroused (similar to phlegmatic);
Strong balanced mobile: lively, fast, eager (similar to sanguine).

Pavlov did not try to study these four temperament types in people, but in recent decades some researchers have done so, developing self-report questionnaire scales for this purpose (Strelau, Angleitner, Bantelmann, & Ruch, 1990). In general, the results suggest that there is some similarity between the characteristics of Pavlov's temperament dimensions and the characteristics associated with the four humors (Ruch, 1992). However, these results do not provide any indication as to what might be the biological *cause* of these personality differences. But as we will see later in this chapter, other researchers have proposed some possible biological bases for personality dimensions, and have even conducted experiments to test those hypotheses.

Now that we have considered some of the early history of ideas regarding the biological bases of personality, we can next consider some of the more recent theories and investigations that have dealt with the same topic. In the remainder of this chapter, we will review research on the potential biological causes of personality characteristics, with attention to neurotransmitters, brain structures, and hormones.

BOX 5-1
Physique and Personality

Some early proposals of a biological basis for personality were based on the idea that an individual's physique, or body type, could be related to his or her personality characteristics. In 1925, a German psychiatrist, Ernst Kretschmer, suggested that there were three basic types of physiques: pyknic (fat), athletic (muscular), and asthenic (thin). On the basis of his clinical observations, Kretschmer (1925) suggested that manic-depressive patients tended to have pyknic physiques, and that schizophrenic patients tended to have asthenic physiques. However, Kretschmer did not conduct any research to find out whether or not these observations were accurate, and later research did not support his suggestions (Cabot, 1938).

Nevertheless, some of Kretschmer's ideas were adopted by an American researcher, William Sheldon, who suggested that each person's physique could be described as a combination of the three basic types suggested by Kretschmer. Sheldon (1940) referred to the three physiques as "somatotypes," and used different names for each: endomorph (fat), mesomorph (muscular), and ectomorph (thin). (These names referred to different layers of cells in the human embryo; according to Sheldon, the endomorphic physique emphasized the digestive system, the mesomorphic physique emphasized the circulatory system, and the ectomorphic physique emphasized the skin and the nervous system.) In Sheldon's proposal, an endomorphic physique was associated with traits such as cheerfulness, sociability, relaxedness, love of comfort and luxury, and indulgence in food and drink. The mesomorphic physique, by contrast, was associated with traits such as dominance, activity level, assertiveness, and adventurousness. Finally, the ectomorphic physique was associated with traits such as nervousness, shyness, sensitivity, and intellectuality.

Sheldon did conduct some research to examine the links between somatotype and personality, and he found some extremely strong relations. For example, Sheldon (1942) reported correlations of about .80 between endomorphic physical characteristics and the personality characteristics that were supposed to be associated with endomorphy; similarly strong relations were observed for the other body types and their presumed personality characteristics. These values are amazingly strong, and would suggest that the link between somatotype and personality is almost perfect. However, there was a major problem with Sheldon's research: It was Sheldon himself who assessed the personality characteristics of his research participants, after having first observed the body types of those persons. This leaves the possibility that Sheldon's ratings of the participants' personalities might have been influenced by his knowledge of their body type. When this bias is removed, by conducting studies in which the assessments of body type and personality are made by different raters, the relations are much weaker, with correlations only in the .20s (Child, 1950).

Thus, it appears that there are some links between body type and personality, but that these relations are quite modest in size. However, there has been very little recent research on this topic, and it will be interesting to see the results of future studies that might examine the relations of various physical characteristics (height, bone mass, muscle mass, fat mass, etc.) with the major personality dimensions. Such studies might also be able to examine the questions of why such relations (even very weak relations) might exist. For example, if muscular persons tend to be slightly more dominant and assertive, on average, than are less muscular persons, what could be the source of this difference? Is there some substance in the body (perhaps testosterone?) that influences both muscularity and dominance? Or, is it simply that muscular persons find that their attempts to be dominant and assertive tend to be successful, which leads those persons to develop a dominant and assertive style of behavior? Or, then again, do persons with dominant personalities tend to develop muscular physiques as a result of dietary and exercise habits? These are interesting questions, but again, the links between personality and body type appear thus far to be rather weak.

Neurotransmitters

Much modern research on the biological basis of personality has focused on substances known as *neurotransmitters*. These biochemical substances are involved in the communication among nerve cells, or *neurons*. Specifically, neurotransmitters can act in such a way as to speed up the communication of messages from one neuron to the next, or they can act in such a way as to slow down that communication. Because this sending of messages—the "firing" of neurons—is the basis of our emotions, our thoughts, and our behaviors, the levels of the substances that influence these messages might be very important in influencing one's personality.

Let us consider for a moment how the neurotransmitters work. First, imagine two neurons, one of which sends (or transmits) messages to the other (see Figure 5-1). The messages are sent as electrical impulses that travel down a very long, thin segment, called an *axon*, of the sending (or transmitting) neuron. When these impulses reach the end of the axon (called the axon terminal), they then cause some molecules of the neurotransmitter substance to be released from the axon terminal and into the space, called the *synapse*, between the two neurons. These neurotransmitter molecules are then absorbed by the receiving neuron at a segment called the *dendrite*. Depending on which neurotransmitter is involved, these molecules can either encourage the receiving neuron to send an electrical impulse to the next neuron in the chain, or to discourage the receiving neuron from sending that message.

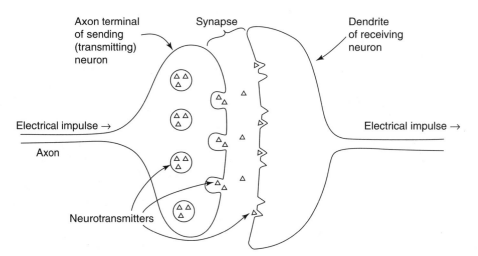

FIGURE 5-1. The role of neurotransmitters in nerve cell communication. An electrical impulse travels through the axon of the sending (transmitting) neuron, stimulating the release of neurotransmitter chemicals into the space between the two neurons (the synapse). The neurotransmitters are then absorbed by the receiving neuron, and make that neuron either more likely or less likely to send an electrical impulse to the next neuron.

TABLE 5-1

Summary of Cloninger's Theory of Neurotransmitters and Personality

Neurotransmitter	Function of neurotransmitter	Personality dimension
Dopamine	Facilitates response to pleasurable, exciting stimuli	Novelty Seeking (excitability, impulsiveness, extravagance, disorderliness)
Serotonin	Inhibits response to harmful, unpleasant stimuli	Harm Avoidance (worry/pessimism, fear, shyness, fatigability)
Norepinephrine	Inhibits response to stimuli that have previously been associated with pleasure	Reward Dependence (sentimentality, warm communication, dependence)

Source: Cloninger (1987), Cloninger *et al.* (1993). According to Cloninger's theory, high levels of dopamine are associated with high levels of novelty seeking, high levels of serotonin are associated with low levels of harm avoidance, and high levels of norepinephrine are associated with low levels of reward dependence.

Cloninger's Theory

In discussing the role of neurotransmitters in personality variation, we will focus on three neurotransmitters that are active in the brain and the spinal cord—the areas known as the *central nervous system*. (Other neurotransmitters are active in the *peripheral nervous system*, which extends throughout all of the remaining parts of the body.) We will discuss these neurotransmitters—dopamine, serotonin, and norepinephrine—in the context of a theory proposed by Robert Cloninger (e.g., Cloninger, 1987; Cloninger, Svrakic, & Przybeck, 1993) regarding the relations between neurotransmitters and personality dimensions (see Table 5-1).[1]

Dopamine and Novelty Seeking

Dopamine is a neurotransmitter that facilitates the transmission of signals of reward. In other words, dopamine helps your neurons to send messages in response to things that feel pleasurable or exciting. Cloninger has suggested that this neurotransmitter is therefore implicated in personality characteristics related to one's response to pleasure and excitement. According to Cloninger, individuals whose dopamine system is very active will tend to have high levels of a personality dimension that he calls "Novelty Seeking"—the tendency to seek pleasure and excitement. This dimension is seen in traits that Cloninger calls *exploratory excitability, impulsiveness, extravagance*, and *disorderliness*. Conversely, individuals whose dopamine system is very inactive will tend to be low in Novelty Seeking; that is, they will not be particularly motivated to find fun and variety.

---

[1] Note that the personality dimensions described by Cloninger do not match those discussed in Chapter 3, such as the Big Five or HEXACO dimensions; instead, Cloninger's dimensions generally represent combinations of two or more of those factors.

When the dopamine system is either extremely underactivated or extremely overactivated, there can be some important effects on levels of Novelty Seeking-related traits. For example, persons who suffer from Parkinson's disease have an extremely inactive dopamine system, and these individuals display a marked lack of interest in new things, in fun activities, or in their environment more generally (and, even more strikingly, display very slow, uncoordinated movements). At the opposite end, persons who use cocaine feel extremely aroused and stimulated while under the influence of that drug, which increases dopamine activity and novelty-seeking behavior.

Serotonin and Harm Avoidance

Serotonin is a neurotransmitter that inhibits the transmission of signals of punishment. In other words, serotonin tends to prevent your neurons from sending messages in response to things that feel harmful or unpleasant. Cloninger has suggested that this neurotransmitter is therefore implicated in personality characteristics related to one's response to pain and anxiety. According to Cloninger, individuals whose serotonin system is very *inactive* will tend to have high levels of a personality dimension that he calls "Harm Avoidance"—the tendency to avoid pain and anxiety. This dimension is seen in traits that Cloninger calls *worry/pessimism, fear of uncertainty, shyness with strangers*, and *fatigability*. Conversely, individuals whose serotonin system is very active will tend to be low in Harm Avoidance; that is, they will not be particularly motivated to avoid pain and anxiety (at least, not as much as other people are).

The links between the serotonin system and Harm Avoidance can be seen in the effects of antidepressant drugs such as Prozac and Paxil. These drugs act to keep serotonin molecules in action, allowing those molecules to continue inhibiting the transmission of punishment signals. As a result, persons who take these drugs tend to experience a reduction in negative emotions such as anxiety and depression (as well as irritability and anger, which are not themselves included among Cloninger's Harm Avoidance-related traits). The long-term effects of those drugs are not known, however.

Norepinephine and Reward Dependence

Norepinephrine, also known as noradrenaline, is a neurotransmitter that inhibits the transmission of signals of *conditioned* reward—that is, of signals responding to stimuli that in the past have been associated with reward. Cloninger has suggested that this neurotransmitter is therefore implicated in personality characteristics related to one's response to people and things that have tended to be associated with pleasure. According to Cloninger, individuals whose norepinephrine system is very *inactive* will tend to have high levels of a personality dimension that he calls "Reward Dependence"—the tendency to develop strong sentimental attachments. This dimension is seen in traits that Cloninger calls *sentimentality, warm communication*, and *dependence*. Conversely, individuals whose norepinephrine system is very active will tend to be low in Reward Dependence; that is, they will tend not to develop strong sentimental attachments.

Empirical Tests of Cloninger's Theory

In recent years there have been several investigations aimed at testing Cloninger's model of the relations between neurotransmitters and personality. Typically, the strategy used in these studies has been to identify people who have different alleles (varieties) of a gene that influences the activity of one of the neurotransmitters. The people who have one of the alleles are then compared with the people who have a different allele, to see whether or not there are any differences in the average levels of personality traits that Cloninger has hypothesized to be influenced by these neurotransmitters. According to Cloninger's model, people having different alleles of a gene that regulates a given neurotransmitter should differ in their levels of the personality traits that are hypothesized to be influenced by that neurotransmitter.

So far, the results of these studies have been mixed. Sometimes, the results are consistent with Cloninger's model, but sometimes they are not. One study (Comings *et al.*, 2000) examined a large number of genes, including seven that influence dopamine, twelve that influence serotonin, and nine that influence norepinephrine. The results showed that each set of genes tended to be related to more than one of Cloninger's personality dimensions. Overall, Reward Dependence was more strongly related to norepinephrine genes than to the other genes; to a lesser extent, a parallel result was found for Harm Avoidance and serotonin genes. However, Novelty Seeking was not more strongly related to dopamine genes than to other genes. This pattern of results is partly consistent with Cloninger's model, but the correspondences are not nearly as neat as one might have hoped. Nevertheless, Cloninger's theory remains an elegant and pioneering attempt to understand the links between neurotransmitter activity and personality.

Brain Structures

In addition to the study of neurotransmitters, another way to learn about the biological basis of personality is to examine various structures within the brain. Some researchers have suggested that personality might be influenced by the extent to which the brain performs certain functions, each of which would involve some complex interaction among different regions of the brain.

Gray's Theory

One influential theory of the relation between brain structures and personality variation has been the *reinforcement sensitivity theory* of Jeffrey Gray, who conducted much research on the biological basis of animal behavior. Gray (e.g., 1981, 1987) suggested that certain regions of the brain work together as mechanisms or systems that underlie personality. According to Gray, differences among people in the activity of these systems are the basis of important personality dimensions. Two of the systems identified by Gray on the basis of his research are called the Behavioral Activation System and the Behavioral Inhibition System. As you will see from the following descriptions, these two systems are conceptually very similar to two of Cloninger's dimensions as described before.

The Behavioral Activation System

The Behavioral Activation System, as described by Gray, involves regions of the brain that are responsible for receiving signals from the nervous system which indicate that rewards are being experienced (or that rewards are about to be experienced). This system can be called a "go" system, as it encourages the pursuit of rewards, by transmitting signals within the brain to communicate the pleasurable and exciting nature of those rewards. In Gray's model, people differ in the extent to which their Behavioral Activation System, or go system, is sensitive to reward stimuli: The stronger or more sensitive one's go system is, the more one tends to pursue rewards. As a result, people differ in their tendency to be impulsive and to seek pleasure and excitement. This trait of impulsivity, as described by Gray, is therefore similar conceptually to the Novelty Seeking dimension as described by Cloninger (whose work was influenced by that of Gray). The difference between the perspectives of Gray and Cloninger is that Gray focuses more on the role of brain structures in governing these traits, whereas Cloninger focuses more on the role of neurotransmitters (in this case, dopamine). Note, however, that the correlations between scales measuring the Behavioral Activation System and Novelty Seeking are only modest in size (see Carver & White, 1994; Zelenski & Larsen, 1999).

The Behavioral Inhibition System

The Behavioral Inhibition System, as described by Gray, involves regions of the brain that are responsible for receiving signals from the nervous system which indicate that punishments are being experienced (or may soon be experienced). This system can be called a "stop" system, as it encourages the avoidance of punishments, by transmitting signals within the brain to communicate the painful and frightening nature of those rewards. In Gray's model, people differ in the extent to which their Behavioral Inhibition System, or stop system, is sensitive to punishment stimuli: The stronger or more sensitive one's stop system is, the more one tends to avoid punishments. As a result, people differ in their tendency to be anxious and to avoid pain and danger. This trait of anxiety, as described by Gray, is therefore similar conceptually to the Harm Avoidance dimension described by Cloninger, partly on the basis of Gray's earlier work. (Scales measuring the Behavioral Inhibition System and Harm Avoidance are fairly strongly correlated with each other; see Carver & White, 1994; Zelenski & Larsen, 1999.) As was the case for the go system above, the difference between the perspectives of Gray and Cloninger is that Gray focuses more on the role of brain structures in governing these traits, whereas Cloninger focuses more on the role of neurotransmitters (in this case, serotonin).

The Fight-or-Flight System

In addition to the "go" and "stop" systems described above, Gray also suggested a third system that is also responsible for an important dimension of personality. The third system proposed by Gray is referred to as a "Fight-or-Flight" system, and involves regions of the brain that are responsible for motivating extreme reactions—fighting and/or fleeing—in response to extremely threatening situations. According to Gray, people differ in the extent to which their "Fight-or-Flight" system is sensitive to these extremely threatening situations: The stronger or more sensitive one's Fight-or-Flight system is, the more ready one is to fight or to flee when an emergency situation arises. (Be careful, because this can be confusing: This third system is *not* a dimension of fighting *versus* fleeing, but rather a dimension of *being ready to fight or to flee* in response to extreme dangers.) As a result, people differ in their tendency to show extreme reactions, such as responding aggressively or leaving hurriedly, when confronted with situations that appear potentially threatening. It is possible that low levels of this fight-or-flight system might have some link with Cloninger's third dimension, Reward Dependence, which involved traits such as sentimentality, dependence, and warmth. Some researchers have suggested that the latter traits represent a response to threat that is an alternative to fight-or-flight (see Taylor *et al.*, 2000), but there is not yet any empirical evidence that traits associated with fight-or-flight are negatively related to traits associated with Reward Dependence.

Eysenck's Theory

The theory proposed by Gray was in some ways a modification of an earlier theory by Hans Eysenck. During World War II, Eysenck worked in clinical psychology at military hospitals in England. Based on his observations of individual differences in the personalities of the soldiers whom he treated, he proposed a theory involving two major dimensions of personality, called Extraversion and Neuroticism (Eysenck, 1947). Later, Eysenck added a third dimension, which he called Psychoticism (S. B. G. Eysenck & H. J. Eysenck, 1968; Eysenck, 1970), and modified somewhat his ideas regarding the earlier two dimensions. A summary of Eysenck's theory in its revised form is given below.

Extraversion

Eysenck's observations led him to believe that one of the fundamental differences among people involved the strength of their reactions to stimulation of their senses—in other words, in the arousability of their brains. According to Eysenck, some people are very sensitive to stimuli, and as a result, these people tend to feel uncomfortable with strong sensations, and instead prefer a low level of stimulation. In contrast, Eysenck said, some people are much less sensitive to stimuli, and as a result, these people tended to feel bored by a low level of stimulation, and instead prefer to experience strong sensations. This dimension of differences was described by Eysenck as Extraversion versus Introversion. At one extreme, very extraverted people tend to seek stimulation, and therefore enjoy bright colors, loud noises, and other sensations; these extraverts enjoy meeting and interacting with lots of people, for example, at parties. At the other extreme, introverted people tend to avoid stimulation, and therefore prefer quieter surroundings; these introverts would prefer to be alone or with a few others rather than to attend parties or other large social gatherings.

Eysenck believed that individual differences in Extraversion were governed by a brain mechanism that he called the ascending reticular activating system (ARAS). In Eysenck's model, this system is located in the brain stem, where the spinal cord meets the brain itself. Together, the ARAS works as a kind of filter that regulates the amount of stimulation that is admitted to the brain from the nervous system, which receives stimulation from the environment. To the extent that one's ARAS admits little stimulation, one feels under-aroused and thus seeks stimulation, producing an extraverted personality. Conversely, to the extent that one's ARAS admits a great deal of stimulation, one feels overaroused and thus avoids stimulation, producing an introverted personality.

Neuroticism

Eysenck's research also suggested to him that another fundamental difference among people involved the strength of their reactions to stressful stimuli. Eysenck observed that some people are very sensitive to stress, and therefore tend to experience fear and anxiety. At the opposite pole, Eysenck noticed, some people are much less sensitive to stress, and therefore experience rather little fear and anxiety. This dimension of differences was described by Eysenck as Neuroticism (versus Emotional Stability). At one extreme, very neurotic people feel a great deal of worry and nervousness in response to life's problems; at the other extreme, emotionally stable people feel little of the negative emotions that are caused by life's stresses.

Eysenck believed that individual differences in Neuroticism were governed by segments of the brain belonging to what is called the limbic system. One of the functions of the brain's limbic system is to regulate responses to stress. To the extent that one's limbic system tends to be overwhelmed by stressful stimuli, one tends to have a neurotic personality; conversely, to the extent that one's limbic system is able to handle those stresses, one tends to have a stable personality.

Psychoticism

Finally, Eysenck also suggested a third major dimension of personality, which he called Psychoticism. According to Eysenck, this dimension included traits such as aggressiveness, manipulation, tough-mindedness, risk taking, irresponsibility, and impulsivity versus their opposites.[2] He suggested that high levels of Psychoticism were associated with criminal behavior, but also with various mental illnesses (including manic-depressiveness and schizophrenia) and even with creativity. As far as the biological basis of the Psychoticism dimension is concerned, Eysenck suggested that persons high in Psychoticism tended to have high levels of the hormone called testosterone (see later in this chapter for a discussion of hormones) and low levels of a substance called monoamine oxidase (MAO), which influences the levels of neutotransmitters.

Comparing Gray's and Eysenck's Dimensions

In reading the descriptions of the dimensions proposed by Gray and Eysenck, you might have noticed some strong similarities between them. It was previously believed that the

---

[2] Eysenck here used "impulsivity" in the sense of poor control of impulses. This is different from Gray's use of "impulsivity" as spontaneity or novelty-seeking.

relations between these dimensions were somewhat complicated. Gray (e.g., 1987) had suggested that the Eysenck's Extraversion was a blend of high Impulsivity and low Anxiety, and that Eysenck's Neuroticism was a blend of high Impulsivity and high Anxiety. But more recent research (Carver & White, 1994; Zelenski & Larsen, 1999) has suggested that the relations, although not particularly strong, might actually be rather simple: Gray's Behavioral Activation System (i.e., Impulsivity, or the go system) is related to Eysenck's Extraversion, and Gray's Behavioral Inhibition System (i.e., Anxiety, or the stop system) is related to Eysenck's Neuroticism. With regard to the third dimension, some researchers have suggested that Gray's "fight-or-flight" is similar to Eysenck's Psychoticism, but this similarity is more difficult to examine, given the lack of detail about the traits associated with Gray's third dimension.[3]

Empirical Evidence and the Theories of Gray and Eysenck

Many research studies have been conducted to test the theories of Gray and of Eysenck. Of these studies, a few have been intended to compare the relative accuracy of the two theories, but the results have not been conclusive (Rusting & Larsen, 1999). Many more investigations have been focused on investigating Eysenck's idea that the Extraversion versus Introversion dimension reflects individual differences in the arousability of the brain. Two of these investigations—one rather simple, and the other more complex—are described next.

One classic study (S. B. G. Eysenck & H. J. Eysenck, 1967) was based on the "lemon juice test," in which the researchers dropped small amounts of lemon juice onto the tongues of the research participants, and then measured the amounts of saliva that each participant produced in response. According to Eysenck's theory, the stimulation produced by the lemon juice would tend to be perceived more strongly by introverted participants than by extraverted participants, and therefore would elicit (on average) more salivation from the introverts than from the extraverts. This is indeed what was found: The participants who were more introverted (as measured by Eysenck's questionnaire) tended to produce the greatest amounts of saliva in response to the lemon juice.

In another study, Geen (1984) identified persons who had above-average levels or below-average levels of Extraversion, on the basis of their self-report questionnaire

---

[3] In addition to the three-dimensional models of Gray and Eysenck, another set of three biologically-based dimensions has been proposed by Tellegen (1985). Tellegen's dimensions, which are assessed by the Multidimensional Personality Questionnaire (see Chapter 2), are known as Positive Emotionality, Negative Emotionality, and Constraint. Positive Emotionality is similar to Eysenck's Extraversion and to Gray's Behavioral Activation System. Negative Emotionality is similar to Eysenck's Neuroticism and Gray's Behavioral Inhibition System. Constraint is less clearly related to the third dimensions of Eysenck's and Gray's systems, but has some aspects in common with the low pole of Eysenck's Psychoticism.

responses. He then assigned these "extraverts" and "introverts" to complete a learning task while being exposed to noises, and he measured the heart rates of the participants as they performed the task. In this study, some of the participants were allowed to choose the loudness of the noise. According to Eysenck's theory, the more extraverted participants would tend to choose the louder noises, because those persons would prefer the higher level of stimulation provided by loud noise; in contrast, introverted persons would prefer a lower level of stimulation, and hence a quieter noise. Geen's results confirmed this expectation. Moreover, when exposed to their preferred levels of noise, the extraverts and introverts had similar heart rates, which suggested that the quieter noises were as stimulating for introverts as the louder noises were for extraverts.

But there is more to Geen's (1984) study: Some participants did not get to choose the loudness of the noise to which they were exposed while performing the word-learning task; instead, a given loudness level was assigned to them. Some participants were assigned the louder noises (i.e., the levels typically chosen by extraverted persons), and some were assigned the quieter noises (i.e., the levels typically chosen by introverted persons). Note that some of the participants who were assigned loud noises were extraverts, and that some were introverts; similarly, the participants who were assigned quiet noises also represented a mix of extraverts and introverts. Geen measured the participants' heart rates as they performed the task under the noise conditions that they were assigned. According to Eysenck's theory, one would expect that introverts (but not extraverts) would have high heart rates when exposed to loud noises (as a result of feeling overstimulated by the noise), whereas extraverts (but not introverts) would have low heart rates (as a result of feeling understimulated by the noise).

The results found by Geen (1984) were consistent with this hypothesis. When loud noise levels were assigned, introverted participants had high heart rates, whereas extraverts had heart rates similar to those of participants who had chosen their own noise levels. In contrast, when quiet noise levels were assigned, extraverted participants had low heart rates, whereas introverts had heart rates similar to those of participants who had chosen their own noise levels. Thus, these results suggest that introverts do tend to prefer a lower level of stimulation than do extraverts, and that introverts do tend to react more strongly to a given level of stimulation than do extraverts.

Geen's (1984) study also investigated levels of skin conductance—that is, how well the skin can conduct small amounts of electricity. (The presence of sweat on the skin increases skin conductance, and therefore higher skin conductance suggests more sweating. Because sweating tends to indicate arousal, Geen used skin conductance in assessing how strongly aroused participants were in response to the noise.) The results for skin conductance were parallel to those for heart rate, with introverts showing high skin conductance when noises were loud, and with extraverts showing low skin conductance when noises were quiet. In addition to heart rate and skin conductance, Geen also measured how many trials participants needed to perform the learning task successfully. He found that extraverts performed better than introverts under loud noise conditions (suggesting that the introverts were too highly aroused to perform well), and that introverts performed better than extraverts under quiet noise conditions (suggesting that the extraverts were not aroused highly enough to perform well).

Thus, the results of some laboratory experiments are broadly consistent with Eysenck's theory of the biological basis of Extraversion. However, many other studies have examined the links between Extraversion and the arousal levels of various segments of the brain, and those studies have produced rather complex patterns of results that are only partly consistent with Eysenck's theory (e.g., Zuckerman, 2005). A really clear understanding of the brain structures that underlie personality is yet to be achieved.

Zuckerman's Model

One recent attempt to describe the biological bases of personality characteristics has been that of Marvin Zuckerman (e.g., Zuckerman, Kuhlman, & Camac, 1988; Zuckerman, Kuhlman, Thornquist, & Kiers, 1991; Zuckerman, Kuhlman, Joireman, Teta, & Kraft, 1993; Zuckerman, 2005). In developing his model of the biological bases of personality, Zuckerman did not begin with a theory in which each dimension of personality would be linked directly to a single brain structure or a single neurotransmitter. Instead, Zuckerman and his colleagues conducted factor analyses of a few dozen personality questionnaire scales. Those analyses were based on scales measuring traits that, in Zuckerman's view, would be good candidates to represent basic dimensions of personality or temperament in humans and in other animals. (But recall the problem discussed in Chapter 3: When researchers select sets of personality traits to examine the structure of personality characteristics, some aspects of personality might be over- or underrepresented.)

The results of these analyses (see Zuckerman *et al.*, 1988, 1991, 1993) showed three factors that were similar to Eysenck's Extraversion, Neuroticism, and Psychoticism dimensions. Alternatively, Zuckerman and colleagues also suggested that the scales could also be summarized in terms of five factors: In this five-dimensional model, Extraversion was divided into an Activity factor and a Sociability factor, and Psychoticism was divided into an "Impulsive Sensation-Seeking" factor and an Aggression factor, the latter of which was also somewhat related to Neuroticism. Some researchers suggested that these five factors could be understood as being combinations of various Big Five factors (Costa & McCrae, 1992a), although the Openness to Experience (or Intellect/ Imagination) factor might not be well represented in the "alternative five" factors (see Zuckerman *et al.*, 1993). But in any case, Zuckerman (e.g., 2005) has suggested that each of the personality dimensions is caused by its own set of complex interactions among brain structures, neurotransmitters, and hormones, and not by any single brain structure or neurotransmitter or hormone. The results of various studies conducted so far—for example, the investigations of neurotransmitter-regulating genes on personality, as described before in the section on Cloninger's theory—suggest that the causal bases of personality are indeed likely to be complex. The challenge for future research will be to understand the details of the direct and indirect links between biological variables and personality variables.

BOX 5-2
Some Biological Bases
for Conscientiousness?

Some research on the biological basis of personality has been conducted without being based on any theories involving several personality dimensions. For example, let us consider some investigations that might reveal the biological bases of the personality dimension of Conscientiousness.

First, there are many studies that have tried to identify some biological origins of attention-deficit/hyperactivity disorder (ADHD). The symptoms of this disorder—which we will discuss in more detail in Chapter 8—include inattention, poor impulse control, disorganization, and lack of persistence, and these symptoms correspond closely to the traits that define low levels of Conscientiousness (see Chapter 3). Some of the investigations of ADHD have made use of machines that take pictures of the brain, using a technique called functional magnetic resonance imaging (fMRI). (Functional magnetic resonance imaging measures the activity of various areas of the brain by producing images that show how much glucose is consumed in those brain areas, as glucose is the main "fuel" used by the brain.) Those studies have suggested that adults diagnosed with ADHD show less activity in the areas of the brain that control attention (Zametkin et al., 1990), with the difference between ADHD and non-ADHD adults being more than half of a standard deviation unit in size. Other areas of the brain are also involved in ADHD, and the overall picture is very complex, but these studies suggest that ADHD symptoms— and hence, low levels of Conscientiousness—are

associated with reduced activity (i.e., glucose consumption) in regions of the brain responsible for attention. In addition, other studies using fMRI have found that these same areas of the brain tend to be smaller in volume for ADHD-diagnosed people than for people without ADHD (Castellanos et al., 1996).

Traits related to Conscientiousness, particularly achievement motivation, may also be related to the levels of uric acid in the blood. Some researchers have suggested that uric acid, which has a chemical structure similar to that of caffeine, may act as a stimulant for the brain, thereby facilitating work output. In some studies conducted around 1970 (e.g., Kasl, Brooks, & Rodgers, 1970a, 1970b), blood levels of uric acid (i.e., "serum urate" levels) were measured in samples of high school and college students, and were found to be correlated positively with indicators of achievement, such as grade point average and performance in extracurricular activities. These uric acid levels were only weakly related to scores on tests of mental ability, which suggests that uric acid is related to achievements through effort or motivation to achieve, rather than through ability or aptitude. The possibility of a link between uric acid and achievement was first noted after it was discovered that the disease called *gout* showed a high level of prevalence among persons who had made great achievements in various fields. (Gout involves bouts of sharp pain in the joints, especially the big toe, caused by uric acid crystals that form when blood levels of uric acid are too high.) Further investigations will be needed to find out whether or not uric acid levels actually influence achievement motivation and other Conscientiousness-related traits.

Hormones

Hormones are biological chemicals that are produced in glands of one part of the body, but then transmitted to other parts of the body where those chemicals have their effects. Some hormones have effects on the activity of neurons, and thus may influence behavior and personality. Next, we will discuss the possible associations of several hormones— specifically, testosterone, cortisol, and oxytocin—with various personality characteristics.

Testosterone

Testosterone is a hormone that is responsible for many of the physical characteristics of men. During the gestation of the fetus, testosterone triggers the development of the male reproductive organs. During puberty, testosterone triggers the development of male secondary sex characteristics, such as hair growth, deepening of the voice, and increased muscle mass. Women do naturally have some testosterone, but men's levels are typically at least 10 times higher. Testosterone is secreted mainly by the testes in men and mainly by the ovaries in women.

Many research studies have examined the question of whether individual differences among men (or among women) in testosterone levels might be related to individual differences in their behaviors. Before we begin reviewing this research, however, there are a couple of important points to note.

First, even though testosterone levels tend to be higher in some individuals than in others, those levels can be influenced by events. Such events include competitive situations, as testosterone levels tend to increase after a victory and to decline after a defeat. One interesting example of this was observed by Bernhardt, Dabbs, Fielden, and Lutter (1998), who found that soccer fans' testosterone levels tended to rise after their team had won a game, but tended to fall after their team had lost. As another example, testosterone levels tend to rise (both for men and for women) after sexual activity (Dabbs & Mohammed, 1992).

Second, it is not only the current levels of testosterone that may influence an individual's behavior, but also the levels of androgens (i.e., testosterone and related hormones) during early periods of development. For example, a study of girls who were exposed prenatally to high levels of testosterone indicated that those girls tended to prefer playing with toys that are usually preferred by boys rather than by girls (Berenbaum & Hines, 1992). (In the same study, boys who were exposed to these higher androgen levels did not show any especially heightened preference for boy-typical toys.) In another study, higher levels of aggression were found in the children—both boys and girls—of mothers who had undergone medical treatments involving synthetic testosterone-like hormones during pregnancy (Reinisch, 1981).

But now back to the original question: How do testosterone levels relate to behavior? In other words, do men (or women) with higher levels of testosterone behave differently from men (or women) with lower levels? Much of the research in this area has been conducted by James Dabbs and his colleagues, who have found a variety of interesting correlates of testosterone. In one study (Dabbs, Hargrove, & Heusel, 1996), the researchers measured testosterone levels in the saliva of 240 members of 12 college fraternities, and also obtained descriptions of these various fraternities. (The descriptions were obtained from a variety of sources, including ratings by fraternity officers and by university officials; in addition, the researchers also made ratings of the fraternity members' characteristics, based on fraternity photographs and on interactions with the fraternity members.) Dabbs and colleagues found that the fraternities with higher average levels of testosterone were rated as being wilder, more unruly, and more rambunctious. In contrast, the fraternities with lower average testosterone levels were better behaved and more socially responsible, with better academic achievement and more friendly and pleasant behaviors, including more smiling.

In another investigation, Dabbs, Carr, Frady, and Riad (1995) studied nearly 700 prison inmates, measuring their salivary testosterone levels and examining records of their criminal offences and prison rule violations. Dabbs and colleagues found that, on average, prisoners who had committed crimes of a violent or sexual nature had higher average testosterone levels than did prisoners who had committed drug offences, theft, or burglary. In addition, higher testosterone levels were also associated with more frequent rule breaking in prison, especially infractions that involved confrontations with others.

Although both of the previously mentioned studies involved individual differences among men, generally similar relations between testosterone and behavior tend to be observed among women (e.g., Dabbs, Alford, & Fielden, 1998). This relates to an important point regarding the links between testosterone and personality more generally: Even though men and women differ very greatly in their testosterone levels—with even low-testosterone men having much higher levels than do high-testosterone women—the differences between men and women in personality (and other psychological characteristics) are much smaller, with considerable overlap between the male and female distributions. (Even in the most extreme case, for the variable of sexual attraction to women versus sexual attraction to men, there is some overlap: At least a few percent of the persons of each sex feel more sexual attraction to members of their own sex than to members of the other sex.)

This means that, despite the potentially important role of testosterone in influencing personality and behavior, it is clearly not the only cause at work. For example, given that the difference between men and women in the personality trait of dominance is much less than one standard deviation unit in size (e.g., Jackson, 1984b), it is clear that some variables other than testosterone are influencing dominance levels. (If testosterone were the only influence, then virtually all men would be higher in dominance than virtually all women, given the extremely large difference between men and women in testosterone levels. But the difference in dominance is not nearly so large.) Examples such as this remind us that the links between biology and personality are not likely to be reducible to the action of a single substance, or a single anatomical region.

Before leaving our discussion of testosterone levels, we should briefly consider individual differences that result artificially, from the use of anabolic steroids (a form of synthetic testosterone). Many athletes and bodybuilders have taken steroids as a way of increasing strength or muscularity, but these substances have other effects, both physical (such as shrinking the testicles or enlarging the clitoris) and psychological. In one study (Pope & Katz, 1994), steroid users showed higher levels of mood-related problems, including manic and aggressive symptoms. Similar findings were observed in an experiment (Pope, Kouri, & Hudson, 2000) in which some men were administered testosterone, and in which other men were not.

Cortisol

Cortisol is a hormone that is released by the adrenal cortex, which is found on the perimeter of the adrenal glands, which in turn are located just above the kidneys. The release of cortisol is triggered by physical or psychological stress. The function of cortisol is to prepare the body for action in response to stress, and among its effects are an increase in blood pressure, an increase in blood sugar, and a suppression of the immune system. As with testosterone, researchers have been interested in examining whether individual differences in cortisol levels are associated with personality differences. In the case of cortisol, researchers have primarily examined traits involving emotional reactivity.

One study by Loney, Butler, Lima, Counts, and Eckel (2006) investigated cortisol levels (as measured from saliva samples) of about 100 adolescent boys and girls. These adolescents had been selected for this investigation on the basis of having very high levels or very low levels of "callous-unemotional" personality traits, as rated by their parents. Loney *et al.* found that, among the boys, higher levels of callous-unemotional traits were associated with low cortisol levels; however, there was no such relation between these traits and cortisol among the girls. In contrast, testosterone (which was also measured from the saliva samples) was not associated with callous-unemotional traits in either boys or girls. The results of this study suggest that cortisol levels might be an indicator (at least in males) of an individual's overall emotional reactivity, and that persons having a tendency to release little cortisol will tend to be somewhat emotionally insensitive. (Keep in mind, however, that an individual's cortisol levels at a given time will reflect not only his or her general tendency to release cortisol, but also the amount of stress being experienced at that time.)

Interestingly, an earlier study (Rosenblitt, Soler, Johnson, & Quadagno, 2001) showed a similar pattern of results for the trait of sensation seeking, which includes a variety of risk-taking tendencies. In a sample of college students, there was a tendency for men having high sensation-seeking levels to have low cortisol levels, but this tendency was not observed among women. Also, sensation-seeking levels were not associated with testosterone levels, in either sex.

Oxytocin

Oxytocin is a hormone that is produced in the hypothalamus and released by the pituitary gland. (Both of these glands are located just below the brain, behind the eyes.) In women (and in female mammals more generally), oxytocin is released when giving birth, when breast-feeding, and when experiencing orgasm. The psychological effects of oxytocin appear to be associated with emotional bonding, such as that between a mother and her child or between a wife and her husband. Note, however, that men also have oxytocin, and that it may play a similar role in facilitating a man's emotional attachments with his children and with his wife. Because of the role of oxytocin in promoting close attachments with others, researchers have examined whether individual differences in the levels of this hormone are related to personality characteristics.

One interesting study by Zak, Kurzban, and Matzner (2005) measured hormone levels in the blood samples taken from university students who participated in a "trust game" involving money. Zak *et al.* found that students who were more trusting of others—that is, students who were willing to let another person make decisions about how to divide some money—had higher levels of oxytocin than did students who were less trusting. In addition, Zak *et al.* also found that students who were more trustworthy—that is, students who divided the money equally—had higher levels of oxytocin than did students who were less trusting. Although the levels of several hormones were measured, only oxytocin was associated with trusting and trustworthy behavior. These results are consistent with the role of oxytocin in establishing attachments between persons, as the levels of this hormone may contribute to cooperative relationships by facilitating the tendencies to be trusting and to be trustworthy.

BOX 5-3
Is Personality Related to Blood Type, Handwriting Style, or Astrological Sign?

Blood Type

The possibility of a link between personality and blood type has often been discussed in popular books, particularly in countries of eastern Asia. Several decades ago, Furukawa (1930) reported that persons with certain blood types as described by the ABO system tended to have higher levels of certain personality characteristics. In the following decades, several studies reported links between personality and blood type, although the results tended to be inconsistent. More recently, however, several investigations (Cramer & Imaike, 2002; Rogers & Glendon, 2003; Wu, Lindsted, & Lee, 2005) have failed to find any significant differences between persons having different blood types (i.e., types O, A, B, and AB) in their average self-reported levels of personality characteristics, such as the Big Five dimensions. Thus, the current evidence suggests that there are no strong relations between personality and blood type.

Handwriting Style

Possible relations between personality and handwriting style have also received much attention, and in fact "graphology" (the analysis of handwriting) has been used widely as a method of personnel selection by employers in many countries, particularly France and Israel (Edwards & Armitage, 1992). Recently, some efforts have been made to investigate any relations between personality characteristics and

features of handwriting. In these studies (e.g., Furnham, Chamorro-Premuzic, & Callahan, 2003; Tett & Palmer, 1997), large samples of participants have had their personalities assessed by self-report questionnaires and have also provided handwriting samples. The handwriting samples have then been evaluated in terms of various features (overall size, size of loops, roundedness versus pointedness, positions and angles of T-crosses, etc.), as judged by individuals who do not know the personality trait levels of the participants. The handwriting features were reliably measured in these studies, as there was a high level of agreement among judges as to the features of a given individual's handwriting. However, there were few significant correlations between those features and any personality characteristics, and those relations often involved features that graphologists had not predicted to be related to personality. Thus, the evidence so far suggests that personality is not strongly related to handwriting features.

Astrological Sign

The popularity of horoscopes and of astrology is well-known, and one feature of astrology is the idea that persons born at different times of the year will tend to have different personalities, because of the supposed influence of heavenly bodies on these characteristics. Probably the largest systematic investigation of the relations between personality and astrological sign was that of Dahlstrom, Hopkins, Dahlstrom, Jackson, and Cumella (1996), who examined the personality characteristics (as assessed by self-report questionnaire) of over 2000 adults whose dates of birth were also recorded. The results showed that there was no relation between astrological sign and any of the diverse personality characteristics that were assessed. That is, persons having a given astrological sign did not show any significant differences in their average levels of any traits in comparison with persons having any other astrological sign. These results suggest that there are not any strong links between personality and astrological sign. Dahlstrom *et al.* also examined possible links between personality and the day of the week on which persons were born, and also between personality and the year of birth as given in the Chinese calendar (year of the tiger, year of the snake, etc.). However, the personality characteristics were unrelated both to the day of the week on which persons were born and also to the Chinese year in which persons were born.

Summary and Conclusions

Let us now make a brief overview of the main points of this chapter. First, the idea of a biological basis for personality is very old. Even in the days of ancient Greece, some thinkers speculated that personality might be governed by the amounts of various substances in the body. In modern times, scientists have tried to develop more systematic theories about the biological bases of personality, and to test those theories empirically.

One such attempt to understand the biological origins of personality variation has been that of Cloninger, who proposed that three of the brain's neurotransmitters were involved in influencing three important aspects of personality. In Cloninger's model, dopamine promotes Novelty-Seeking, serotonin inhibits Harm-Avoidance, and norepinephrine inhibits Reward Dependence. Empirical tests of this model have shown some support for Cloninger's theory, but the results have been rather mixed.

Other efforts to determine the biological bases of personality have focused on various structures or regions of the brain. Gray's theory involves dimensions of Impulsivity (roughly similar to novelty-seeking) and Anxiety (similar to harm-avoidance), which are thought to be governed by a Behavioral Activation ("go") System and a Behavioral Inhibition ("stop") System that each involves its own distinct structures within the brain. An earlier theory by Eysenck was also based on individual differences in the activity of various structures in the brain, and the two original dimensions in Eysenck's theory were similar to the dimensions that were later elaborated by Gray. In Eysenck's system, an Extraversion factor is attributable to individual differences in how easily the brain is stimulated, and a Neuroticism factor is attributable to individual differences in how readily the brain can handle stressful situations. A third dimension was included in both Gray's theory ("Fight-or-Flight") and Eysenck's theory (Psychoticism), but it is not clear how similar those dimensions are to each other or to Cloninger's Reward Dependence dimension. Empirical tests of the theories of Eysenck and Gray, particularly the aspects of Eysenck's theory concerning Extraversion, have supported some aspects of those theories. More recently, Zuckerman has suggested that the biological bases of personality are likely to be much more complex than might be indicated by the models of Cloninger or Gray or Eysenck.

Other recent research has examined the role of hormones in personality. Among the most widely studied hormones have been testosterone, cortisol, and oxytocin. In general, testosterone has been associated with disinhibited behavior, cortisol with reactions to stress, and oxytocin with emotional bonding. However, the links between hormones and personality characteristics have not yet been clearly established.

In reading this chapter, you will have noticed that there has already been a great deal of theory and research on the biological bases of personality. But perhaps the most important challenge for future research will be to figure out the complex ways in which each of the major dimensions of personality (see Chapter 3) are influenced by those various biological bases. For example, what exactly are the biological variables that influence levels of, say, Agreeableness or Openness to Experience, and how do those variables exert their effects on those dimensions? Now that personality psychologists have identified the major broad factors of personality, research into the biological causes of personality can aim at explaining *how* each of those factors is influenced by the action of various substances and structures.

Chapter 6

Genetic and Environmental Influences on Personality

The Question: Nature versus Nurture   114

Examining the Similarity of Relatives   114

Separating Heredity and Environment   116

Examining the Similarity of Identical Twins Raised Apart   116

Examining the Similarity of Other Relatives Raised Apart   116

Additive and Nonadditive Heritability   117

Comparing the Similarity of Different Kinds of Relatives   119

Examining the Similarity of Adoptive Relatives: Common and Unique Environment   120

The Answers   121

Similarities between Relatives   121

Strong Genetic Influences (Both Additive and Nonadditive), with Weak Common Environment Influence   122

Assumptions Underlying Heritability Studies in General   124

Are Relatives' Personalities Really Measured Independently?   124

Is There Really No Assortative Mating for Personality?   127

Assumptions Underlying Twin-Based Heritability Studies in Particular   128

Are Twins' Early Environments Really Separate?   128

Are Twins' Adoptive Households Really Very Different?   129

Are Identical Twins Really Treated Differently by Others?   131

Effects of the Unique Environment on Personality? Parental Treatment, Peer Groups, and Birth Order   132

Parental Treatment and Peer Groups   132

Birth Order   133

Summary and Conclusions   134

Appendix: Difficulties in Separating the Effects of Heredity and Environment   135

Genotype–Environment Interactions   135

Genotype–Environment Correlations: Passive, Reactive, and Active   137

The Question: Nature versus Nurture

One of the crucial questions of personality psychology is that of "nature versus nurture": the extent to which personality variation is caused by heredity or by the environment. In other words, do people have different personalities because they inherit different genes from their biological parents, or because they have different experiences during development? This chapter will address that important question, by first describing how researchers have attempted to answer it, and then describing various aspects of the results that they have obtained. As you will see, the methods for answering this question are rather complex, but in some ways the results have been much less so.

When considering this question of nature versus nurture,[1] it is important to keep in mind that we are asking about the origins of the *variability* or *differences* among persons in certain personality traits, and not of the absolute levels of those traits. Consider an analogy with the physical trait of height: We might ask what proportion of the variability in height among adults is due to hereditary differences, and what proportion is due to environmental differences. But it would not make sense to ask what proportion of a given individual's height is due to heredity or due to environment. For example, we cannot meaningfully say that $x\%$ of my height is due to my genes, and the other $y\%$ is due to my environment; instead, *all* of my height results from a combination of my genes and my environment acting together. My height (and I) can only exist because my genes and my environment are both operating. But because people *differ* from each other in height, we can try to figure out whether this variation is chiefly due to the *different* genes that people inherit, or chiefly due to the *different* environments that people experience.

Examining the Similarity of Relatives

When researchers try to assess the relative importance of heredity and environment in accounting for individual differences, the first step is to figure out how similar are the personalities of people who are related to each other. But this is only the first step, because even if we find that relatives tend to be more similar than different in personality, we do not know *why* they are similar. Maybe the similarity is due to the fact that relatives are biologically related, and therefore have more genes in common than do unrelated persons. Or, maybe the similarity is due to the fact that relatives have lived together over a period of many years, and have had many features of their home environment in common. To find out whether any similarities among relatives are due to heredity or to the environment, we need to find a way to separate these two kinds of effects.

---

[1] In a sense, the expression "nature versus nurture" does not correspond exactly to the contrast between heredity and environment. This is because environmental influences on personality include not only family experiences, but also a variety of other influences that are experienced outside the family. These experiences outside the family are not really "nurture" in the sense of the way a child is raised.

One solution used by personality researchers has been to study two different kinds of relatives: Biological relatives who have not lived in the same household (i.e., because of adoption), and adoptive relatives who are biologically unrelated. In this way, researchers can figure out the relative strength of heredity and environment in influencing the personality similarity of relatives. Another solution is to study different kinds of biological relatives that have different degrees of relatedness, even if the relatives have lived together; we will examine this approach a bit later on in this chapter.

To see how personality researchers can calculate the relative influence of heredity and environment, let us consider first how those researchers can calculate how similar relatives tend to be on a given trait. First, the researchers identify large numbers of pairs of a certain kind of relative from a large number of families. For example, they might find many pairs of brothers, or many mother–daughter pairs, or many opposite-sex twin pairs. Then, the researchers measure the personalities of all of the people of the type of relative pair that is to be studied. The most common method of measurement has been to use self-report questionnaires, but observer report questionnaires are also used in some studies. (It is important that the reports be obtained independently; that is, the relatives should not discuss their responses with each other.)

Next, the researchers calculate how much variance there is altogether in the trait of interest, across all of the people being studied. Finally, they calculate what proportion of that variance is *within* families (i.e., due to differences between the two members of each pair) and what proportion is *between* families (i.e., differences among the pairs, where the score for each pair is the average of the two relatives who are its members). You can see why they do this: If the relatives within each pair tend to be very similar to each other, then the proportion of total variance that is due to within-family differences will be very small, and the proportion of total variance that is due to between-family differences will be very large. In contrast, if the relatives within each pair tend to be quite different from each other, then the proportion of total variance that is due to within-family differences will be much larger, and the proportion of total variance that is due to between-family differences will be much smaller. (The mathematical formulas used for calculating these proportions are based on the technique called analysis of variance, or ANOVA. This technique corrects for the fact that there are many pairs but only two persons within each pair.)

To figure out how similar the relatives tend to be on the trait in question, researchers calculate the proportion of variance due to between-family differences. (Again, when most of the variation is between the families, this means that differences within families tend to be small, which also means that relatives are similar.) This value is called an *intraclass correlation coefficient*, and although it is calculated in a way different from that of the usual correlation coefficient, it has similar properties and can be thought of as the correlation between the relatives on the trait. If relatives tend to be much more similar to each other than to unrelated persons, then the correlation will be high, perhaps above .50. If relatives tend only to be modestly more similar to each other than to unrelated persons, then the correlation will be low, perhaps not much above zero.

The preceding paragraphs have described how researchers can calculate how similar relatives tend to be on a given trait. But now let us return to the issue of figuring out whether that similarity is due to heredity or due to the environment. To separate the effects of heredity and environment, one approach is to compare relatives who either have their heredity in common but not their environment, or have their environment in common but not their heredity.

Separating Heredity and Environment

Examining the Similarity of Identical Twins Raised Apart

One way to estimate the hereditary, or genetic, influence on a trait is to evaluate the similarity between biological relatives who have not lived in the same household. In some cases, this has been achieved by studying a very special kind of pair of relatives; specifically, identical twins who were adopted into two different families. If the adoptions take place shortly after birth, before the siblings have had any common experiences in growing up, then we can assume that the similarities between the siblings are due to their genetic similarity rather than due to any environmental similarity.[2]

Now, suppose that we find large numbers of these raised-apart identical twins after they have grown up, and that we measure their personalities. If we find that the correlation between identical twins raised apart for a given trait is .60, then this suggests that the identical twins raised apart tend to be more similar to each other than to unrelated persons, and in fact quite a lot more similar. This value of .60 means that 60% of the variance among people in this trait is due to the variance among people in their genes or heredity. Another, equivalent way to state this is that the genetic similarity between identical twins makes them 60% less different from each other than from people in general.

One useful feature of investigations involving identical twins is that their genetic makeup is truly identical. Even when we consider the genes that differ from one person to the next, fully 100% of the genes of one identical twin are the same as those of the other identical twin of that pair. Therefore, if we find that the correlation between identical twins raised apart for a given trait is .60, we know that this value tells us the full influence of genes on the trait, because this is the amount of similarity that results when all genes are in common.

Examining the Similarity of Other Relatives Raised Apart

The situation is slightly different when we consider relatives who are not identical twins. Suppose that, instead of studying identical twins raised apart, we instead studied pairs of relatives who were fraternal twins raised apart, or nontwin siblings raised apart, or a

---

[2] Actually, this assumption might not be completely accurate, for reasons that you might already have realized. But let us accept this assumption for the time being, and then examine some possible problems a little later on in this chapter.

biological parent and an adopted-away child.[3,4] The important difference here is that the members of these other pairs of relatives—fraternal twins, nontwin siblings, and parent–child pairs—each have, on average, only 50% of their genes in common.[5] Therefore, when we find some similarity in a given trait between these kinds of relatives, we are witnessing the effects of only 50% of the genes. This means that, if we want to know the full effect of genetic influence on the trait, we need to take into account the fact that only half of the genes were involved. The way that researchers do this is straightforward: They double the amount of similarity that is observed between these relatives on the trait in question. For example, suppose that the correlation between fraternal twins on a given trait is found to be .20, indicating that these fraternal twins tend to be a bit more similar to each other than to people in general. This degree of similarity, however, reflects the effects of only the 50% of genes that siblings have in common. To estimate the full proportion of variance in this trait that is due to heredity, we must multiply the value of .20 by two, which gives .40, or 40% due to heredity.

Additive and Nonadditive Heritability

If the previous logic makes sense to you, you will probably expect that when researchers actually do study the similarities between relatives on various traits, they should obtain similar estimates of genetic influence, or "heritability," regardless of whether they study identical twins or other kinds of relatives. According to the logic explained before, the similarity of identical twins should be twice as great as that of fraternal twins (or nontwin siblings, or parent/child pairs). So, if we double the correlation obtained between those latter kinds of relatives, we should get the same result as we do for identical twins, right? Well, the result usually turns out to be somewhat different. In fact, even when we double

---

[3] You might have wondered whether similarities or differences among relatives might seem exaggerated or underestimated depending on whether or not they are of the same sex and age. Researchers control for sex and age differences by calculating people's personality trait scores relative to other persons of the same sex and age.

[4] Identical twins are twins who developed after a single fertilized egg cell divided into two separate embryos. Fraternal twins are twins who developed after two different egg cells were fertilized. Identical twins are therefore called *monozygotic (MZ)* twins, and fraternal twins are therefore called *dizygotic (DZ)* twins. Note that fraternal twins are no more genetically similar to each other than nontwin siblings are.

[5] Actually, all human beings have the vast majority of their genes in common with each other. But when we talk about the degree of genetic similarity between two persons, we ignore those genes completely, and focus only on the small fraction of genes (still a large number!) that differ from one person to the next. When studying the effects of heredity on personality, we consider only the genes that do vary from one person to the next, because only these genes can cause personality differences among people. In this sense, it is meaningful to say that two siblings have 50% of their genes in common (or that two unrelated persons have 0% of their genes in common), because we are intentionally putting aside all the genes that everyone has in common.

the correlation obtained for, say, fraternal twins, the result is usually less than that obtained for identical twins. Why does this happen?

The reason for this finding involves the different ways in which genes can influence a trait when acting in combination. Sometimes, the combined effects of two or more genes on personality are very simple, with each gene contributing separately to making one's level of the trait a bit higher or lower. In such a case, there are *additive genetic effects*, because the combined effect of the genes can be estimated simply by adding together their separate effects. For example, suppose that a particular *allele* (i.e., a particular version of a gene) tends to cause higher levels of a trait, and that a person has one out of a possible two copies of this allele. In this case, his or her expected level of the trait would be about halfway between what would be expected if he or she had neither allele and what would be expected if he or she had both alleles.

Sometimes, however, the combined effects of two or more genes are more complex, with the combined effects being different from what you would expect based on adding the separate effects of the genes. In such a case, there are *nonadditive genetic effects* (also called *multiplicative genetic effects*). For example, suppose that if a person has two very rare genes, a and b, then he or she ends up with a higher level of a given trait, but that this happens only if he or she has *both* of those genes. If, instead, the person has genes A and b, or genes a and B, or (like most people) genes A and B, then he or she will not end up with a higher level of the trait—not even partway higher. In this case, the influence of genes a and b is not additive; instead, the effects depend on the presence or absence of the other gene.[6]

What does this difference between additive and nonadditive genetic influences have to do with the heritability studies comparing identical twins versus other kinds of relatives? Notice that if two individuals have all of their genes in common, they will always have the same combinations of genes. Therefore, any effects on a trait caused by nonadditive genetic effects will affect both identical twins in the same way. But, notice that if two individuals have only half of their genes in common, they will have the same combinations of genes less than half of the time. If it is a combination of two genes, the two fraternal twins would have the same combination about one-quarter of the time; if three genes, then one-eighth of the time; if four, then one-sixteenth. Therefore, when nonadditive genetic influences on a trait are important, identical twins will be considerably more than twice as similar as fraternal twins (or any other 50% genetically similar relatives) will be. This means that even if we double the obtained similarity between these relatives, we will obtain an estimate of heritability (or genetic influence) that is less than that obtained for identical twins.

So, which is the "right" number to consider—the heritability based on identical twins, or the heritability based on other kinds of relatives? It depends on your purpose. If you

---

[6] When the genes in question are at different places (i.e., different *loci*), the nonadditive effect is known as *epistasis*. When the genes in question are different versions (i.e., different alleles) of a gene that is at the same place (i.e., the same *locus*), this nonadditive effect refers to *recessive* versus *dominant* genes.

want to know the full effect of genetic influence on a trait, both additive and nonadditive, then the estimate based on identical twins is the most useful. Because this estimate includes both sources of genetic influence, researchers refer to this as "broad-sense" heritability. On the other hand, if you want to know how much a given trait runs in families—the extent to which nontwin relatives, such as siblings, or parents and children, will be similar on a trait—then the estimate based on relatives other than identical twins is the most useful. This estimate is chiefly due to additive heritability, and so is known among researchers as "narrow-sense" heritability.[7]

Comparing the Similarity of Different Kinds of Relatives

You might have noticed that all of the preceding methods involved studying people who had been adopted at a very early age. One practical disadvantage of this method is that it can be somewhat difficult to find large numbers of biological relatives—whether identical twins, fraternal twins, regular siblings, or parents and children—who have been adopted into different families. But there is a way to estimate the influence of heredity on a trait without having to rely only on people who have been adopted. This method is to compare pairs of relatives who are from the same households, but to determine how much *more* similar certain kinds of relatives tend to be, and to examine this in relation to their degree of genetic similarity.

One example of this strategy involves comparing the similarity between identical twins raised together with the similarity between fraternal twins raised together. This is done by first calculating the similarity of identical twins raised together, then calculating the similarity of fraternal twins raised together, and finally calculating how much more similar the identical twins are in comparison with the fraternal twins. (Note that, in order to make meaningful comparisons with identical twins, who are always of the same sex, these analyses use fraternal twins who are also of the same sex.) Because, in both cases, we are considering the similarity between relatives raised together, we can assume that the effects of growing up in the same household should affect both kinds of twins equally. Therefore, any "extra" similarity of identical twins, beyond that of fraternal twins, should be due to the additional genetic similarity of identical twins, beyond that of fraternal twins.[8]

Let us see how this would work. Suppose we study a large number of *identical* twin pairs (where in every case the twins of a given pair have been raised together), and we

---

[7] As mentioned before, researchers can measure the effect of additive genetic influences by using estimates of heritability that are obtained from studies of relatives other than identical twins. To measure the effect of nonadditive genetic influences, researchers can subtract the estimates based on relatives other than identical twins (raised apart) from the estimates based on identical twins (raised apart). The reason why this method works is that the estimates based on identical twins are "*broad-sense*" estimates (which include both additive and nonadditive effects), whereas the estimates based on other relatives are "*narrow-sense*" estimates (which include additive effects only).

[8] Again, you might have some doubts about this assumption. We will discuss this a bit later on in the chapter.

find that the proportion of between-family variance—that is, the correlation between identical twins—is .70. Suppose we also study a large number of *fraternal* twin pairs (where again in every case the twins of a given pair have been raised together), and we find that the proportion of between-family variance—that is, the correlation between fraternal twins—is .40. Now, the difference between the correlations for identical twins (.70) and fraternal twins (.40) is .30. This difference is due to the "extra" genetic similarity of identical twins (who are 100% genetically similar) beyond that of fraternal twins (who are 50% genetically similar). Therefore, the difference results from $100 - 50 = 50\%$ extra genetic similarity. To estimate the full impact of heredity on the trait, we therefore need to double the difference between the correlations for the two types of twins: .30 times 2 is .60, so this would give an estimate of 60% genetic influence on the trait. Note that the estimates of heritability obtained by this method will be broad-sense heritability estimates, because the similarity of the identical twins will be due to both additive and (especially) non-additive influences.

Examining the Similarity of Adoptive Relatives: Common and Unique Environment

Now that we have described some research strategies that allow us to estimate the influence of heredity on personality traits, let us briefly consider a research strategy that allows us to estimate the influence of the environment on personality traits. At first, you might wonder why this is needed at all: If we find using the preceding research strategies that, say, 60% of the variance in a trait is due to genetic influence, then the remaining 40% must be due to environmental influence. Or, if 25% is genetic, then 75% must be environmental. But these estimates conceal an important distinction between two very different kinds of environmental influence. One kind of environmental influence tends to make relatives *more* similar to each other, and the other kind tends to make relatives *less* similar to each other.

Consider two siblings growing up in the same family and household. Both siblings experience many of the same features of their environment: They will both grow up in a high-income household, or both in a low-income household; they will both be raised in a household with few books, or both in a household with many books; they will both be raised by religious parents, or both by nonreligious parents; they will both be raised by harsh parents, or both by gentle parents. As a result, we might expect that siblings would tend to develop similar levels of some personality traits, and we might even expect that they would tend to develop trait levels similar to those of the parents who raise them. To the extent that this is true, we would expect that even biologically *unrelated* persons would show some similarity in their personality traits after having lived in the same household (This similarity might be greater for two siblings than for a parent and child, because the two siblings are both raised by the same parents.) Researchers refer to these environmental influences as *shared* or *common*, for the simple reason that these are aspects of the environment that relatives share or have in common with each other. These are also called *between-family* environmental influences, because they differ between families (i.e., from one family to the next).

A simple way to test for the influence of the shared, or common, environment on a trait is to measure the similarity between biologically unrelated persons from the same household. For example, researchers might study biologically unrelated siblings raised in the same family, or an adopting parent and an adopted child. The correlations between the levels of the trait for these kinds of relatives will tell us the extent to which personality is influenced by being raised in the same household. Genetic influences will not be responsible for these similarities, because the persons being studied are not biologically related.

The other kind of environmental influence includes many different features of the environment that differ even for individuals from the same household. For example, two siblings (even two twins) may have different friends, who might influence their personalities in different directions. Or, two siblings might be treated differently by their parents, which might lead the siblings to differ in terms of some personality traits. These environmental influences are called *nonshared* or *unique*, because by definition they are not shared, but are instead unique to each person, even when those persons belong to the same family. These are also called *within-family* environmental influences, because they differ within families (i.e., from one family member to the next).

To estimate the total effect of the nonshared or unique environment, researchers do not have any direct method of calculation that is comparable to those used for estimating the effects of heredity or of the common environment. Instead, the effects of the unique environment must be estimated by figuring out how much variance in a trait is "left over" after those other sources have been estimated: For example, if 50% of variation in a trait is due to genetic influences (additive and nonadditive together), and if 10% if due to common environment influences, then this leaves 40% to be accounted for by unique environment influences.

On the other hand, researchers can estimate the effect of *any particular kind* of unique environment influence by measuring the extent to which siblings who have differed in some feature of their environment also differ in a given trait. For example, researchers can try to measure how differently siblings were treated by their parents, and then correlate these differences between siblings in parental treatment with differences between siblings in a given personality trait. This result would indicate how much the differences between siblings in treatment by their parents are later reflected in personality differences. Similarly, researchers can try to measure how different were the groups of friends that the siblings had (i.e., the siblings' peer groups), and then correlate these differences between siblings in their peer groups with differences between siblings in a given personality trait. This result would indicate how much differences in peer groups are later reflected in personality differences.

The Answers

Similarities between Relatives

As you have now noticed, the methods for calculating the relative influence of heredity and environment on personality variation can be a bit complicated. But the results that researchers have actually obtained when conducting investigations of the genetic and environmental influences on personality variation—at least when based on self-report measures of personality—have been rather consistent across different investigations and across different personality traits.

Table 6-1 shows the correlations that have typically been found between the personality trait levels of various kinds of relatives (see reviews by Bouchard & Loehlin, 2001; Loehlin, 2005; Plomin & Caspi, 1999). Because the results have generally been similar regardless of which personality trait is considered, the results are not reported separately by trait. The correlations between trait levels for these different kinds of relatives have allowed researchers to estimate the relative effects of heredity and environment on personality, using the methods of calculation described earlier in this chapter. For the purposes of this book, it will not be necessary to do these calculations ourselves; instead, we will summarize the results as computed and reported in the original research studies (see Table 6-2).

Strong Genetic Influences (Both Additive and Nonadditive), with Weak Common Environment Influence

One interesting result of the investigations of genetic and environmental effects on personality has been the finding that heredity does have a substantial influence. In many different studies, using the various strategies described before, the genetic influence on personality variation among adults has been fairly strong, typically accounting for nearly 50% of the variance in personality traits. This result has been similar across personality traits, so that the impact of heredity appears to be comparable regardless of which trait is studied. Of this genetic influence, about two-thirds (i.e., about 30% of the total variance) is due to additive genetic variation, and about one-third (i.e., about 15% of the total variance) is due to nonadditive genetic variation. In other words, the "broad-sense" heritability (which includes both additive and nonadditive influences) is considerably larger than the "narrow-sense" heritability (which includes additive influences only).

In contrast to the strong genetic effects on personality variation in adults, the effects of the common environment have been relatively quite weak, typically accounting for only 5 or 10% of the variance in personality traits. Again, this result is similar across traits, and does not depend on which trait is considered.[9] The remainder of the variance in personality traits is accounted for by differences in the unique environment—the specific sources of which we will discuss further in a moment—and in error of measurement (i.e., the "unreliable" portion of variance in the measurements of a given trait). Error of measurement might typically account for nearly 20% of the total variance, leaving about 25% to be accounted for by the unique environment.

---

[9] There are, however, some other psychological characteristics—specifically, some religious beliefs and political attitudes—that do show a stronger influence of the common environment. We will discuss these findings in Chapter 11.

TABLE 6-1

Typical Correlations of Personality Trait Levels between Relatives of Various Kinds

Type of relative	Correlation
Identical twins raised together	.45
Identical twins raised apart	.45
Fraternal twins raised together	.20
Nontwin biological siblings raised together	.20
Parent and biological child (together)	.10–.15
Parent and biological child (apart)	.10–.15
Adoptive siblings	.00–.05
Adoptive parent and child	.00–.05

All values are approximate, being averaged across different traits and different samples of persons.
Sources: Bouchard and Loehlin (2001); Plomin and Caspi (1999); Loehlin (2005).

TABLE 6-2

Summary of Genetic and Environmental Influences on Personality Trait Levels

Source of influence	Percentage
Genetic	Almost 50%
Additive genetic	About 30%
Nonadditive genetic	About 15%
Environmental	About 30%
Common environment	About 5 or 10%
Unique environment	About 25%
Error of measurement	Almost 20%

All values are approximate, being averaged across different traits and different samples of persons.
Sources: Bouchard and Loehlin (2001); Plomin and Caspi (1999); Loehlin (2005).

When first discovered, the preceding results were very surprising to many people, including personality researchers. Most people probably would have expected a stronger role for the influence of the common environment, which instead seems to have very little impact on people's personality trait levels. Instead, genetic variation is apparently a much stronger source of differences among people in personality. Some of this genetic variation is additive, which means that biological relatives tend to show at least some similarity in personality (although even this similarity tends to be modest, because even siblings or parents and children have only 50% of their genes in common). And some of the genetic variation is nonadditive, meaning that although identical twins will tend to be particularly similar, other kinds of relatives will be considerably less so. To sum up, the evidence so far suggests that relatives are only modestly similar in personality, and that this similarity is not due to having lived together in the same household and same family, but instead is mainly due to shared genes.

Assumptions Underlying Heritability Studies in General

In describing the methods and results of investigations of the heritability of personality, we have been making some important assumptions. Let us now consider some of the most important assumptions on which heritability studies are based. First, we will consider the assumption (1) that each participant's personality is measured independently, that is, without being influenced by the personality of his or her relatives. Then, we will consider the assumption (2) that there is little or no "assortative mating" for personality—in other words, that parents do not tend to be more similar to each other in personality than two people picked at random would tend to be.

Are Relatives' Personalities Really Measured Independently?

As mentioned earlier in this chapter, one of the assumptions on which heritability studies are based is that the personalities of relatives can be assessed independently. If, instead, measurements of one individual's personality might influence the measurements of his or her relative's personality, then this could either inflate or deflate the similarity between those relatives, and thereby distort the results of the heritability study.

But how could this problem of nonindependent measurements happen? Consider, for example, two siblings (or two twins) who complete a self-report personality inventory. It is possible that, when responding to the questions of that inventory, the siblings would tend to compare themselves not to people in general but instead to each other, and thus to give answers that emphasize differences between them. For example, suppose that two brothers both tend to be rather anxious or nervous, but that one is more so than the other. In responding to self-report items about worry and anxiety, the somewhat less anxious brother might be contrasting his tendencies with those of his brother, and would thereby underestimate his own anxiety level, which would end up causing the researchers to overestimate the difference between himself and his brother. A similar process could also influence the other brother's self-reports, causing him to overestimate his anxiety level and thus again to lead the researchers to overestimate the difference between brothers.

The same lack of independence could occur when an individual's personality is assessed through observer reports. In the example before, suppose that the mother of the two brothers is the one who provides reports of each brother's personality. When describing each brother's personality, she might be considering not how each brother compares with all other boys, but rather how each brother compares with the other. If she thinks of one brother as "the nervous one" and the other as "the calm one," then she might tend to overestimate the anxiety level of the first, and underestimate the anxiety level of the second. As a result, the researchers would conclude that the brothers are less similar in personality than might really be the case.

This tendency to emphasize differences between related persons is called a *contrast effect*, but it is not clear how much these effects really do occur in personality assessments. Nevertheless, it is possible that contrast effects could be stronger for some kinds of relatives than for others. For example, perhaps the relatives of two twins will be less likely to emphasize contrasts between them if the twins are identical rather than fraternal. But it is also possible that contrast effects are not observed at all for some kinds of relatives, or even that instead there is a tendency to emphasize similarities between relatives. Suppose, for example, that two sisters consider themselves to be similar in personality. If the two sisters actually do differ somewhat in a given trait, such as creativity, then perhaps the more-creative sister will underestimate her own level of creativity, and perhaps the less-creative sister will overestimate her own level of creativity, thereby leading the researcher to conclude that the sisters are more similar than they really are. And again, this effect might also be seen in observer reports of the personalities of relatives; for example, if the father of these two sisters tended to see them as being similar to each other, then this might also influence his reports of each sister's level of creativity (or of any other trait), in such a way as to cause researchers to overestimate that similarity. This tendency to emphasize similarities between related persons is called an *assimilation effect*.

How can researchers overcome the potential problems that could be caused by the nonindependence of personality assessments? One solution is that the researchers could assess an individual's personality by obtaining reports from someone who knows that individual well, but who does not know that individual's relative(s) very well. The problem of contrast effects (or assimilation effects) is unlikely to occur if the personality assessments are provided by someone who is not a family member and who is not well acquainted with anyone in the family other than the individual to be assessed.

One study whose methods were fairly close to those of the strategy just described was an investigation of identical and fraternal twins in Germany by Riemann, Angleitner, and Strelau (1997). In this study, each participant provided self-reports on a personality questionnaire, but each participant was also assessed using observer reports from two persons who knew that participant well, but who in most cases did not know the participant's twin well. Were the results different depending on the use of self- or observer reports? No, for both sources of personality data the results indicated substantial similarity for identical twins and modest similarity for fraternal twins. (Specifically, identical twin correlations were about .50 for most traits in self-report, and about .40 in observer reports, whereas fraternal twin correlations were about .25 for most traits in self-report, and about .20 in observer report.) The greater similarity of identical twins relative to fraternal twins, as observed for both kinds of personality reports, suggests that the personality characteristics were substantially heritable.

One additional result of the Riemann *et al.* (1997) study, although not directly related to the problem of contrast and assimilation effects, is also very interesting. When the researchers tried to obtain a more accurate estimate of each individual's personality, by averaging the self-reports with the observer reports, they obtained heritability estimates of about .70, which is higher than has been observed in previous studies based on self-reports alone. This suggests that previous estimates of the heritability of personality might have been underestimated somewhat, as a result of the imperfect accuracy of self-report assessments (see Chapter 2 for a discussion of the validity of self- and observer reports).

Another study that also attempted to overcome the problems of contrast and assimilation effects was an investigation by Borkenau, Riemann, Angleitner, and Spinath (2001) of participants from the same sample of German twins. In this study, personality was assessed not only using self-reports and observer reports, but also by direct observations made by the experimenters and by students who watched videos of the participants' behaviors. That is, the participants took part in a variety of activities while being observed and being video-recorded by the experimenters. These observations and video recordings allowed the experimenters to make further assessments of the participants' personalities. When making the personality assessments, each experimenter (and each person who later watched the video) was assigned to observe only one member of any twin pair, so that contrast and assimilation effects would not occur.

The results of the Borkenau *et al.* (2001) study suggested that twins—whether fraternal or identical—were more similar to each other in personality when assessed by experimenters or by video "judges" than when assessed by self-report or observer report; however, this effect was stronger for fraternal twins than for identical twins, thus suggesting that contrast effects are larger in fraternal twins. One important consequence of this result was that fraternal twins were *more than* half as similar to each other as were identical twins, and therefore it did appear that there was some effect of the common environment on personality, perhaps as much as .25. (The effect of heredity was estimated at about .40.) The common environment effect was much higher than in previous studies, and it will be interesting to see if the result is replicated in future studies; if so, it would suggest that earlier investigations had underestimated the effect of the common environment.

Before leaving this section, one other important point should be made about contrast effects and assimilation effects. Even though we have been describing these effects as occurring simply in people's style of responding to personality inventories, it is also possible that these effects could genuinely influence people's personalities. That is, for some characteristics, two siblings (whether twins or not) might really become more different from each other, or they might really become more similar to each other. For example, you can imagine that two twins might diverge in such a way that one becomes "dominant" and the other "submissive"; or, those twins might converge in such a way that both develop higher (or lower) levels of some traits, such as organization or creativity or any others.

To the extent that these true contrast and assimilation effects do occur, however, it would be difficult to assess them. For example, if contrast effects occur for twins, then twins raised apart could actually be more similar than twins raised together. But then again, if shared environment influences outweigh any contrast effects, than twins raised together would be still more similar than twins raised apart, in spite of those true contrast effects.

This is a complicated issue of personality measurement, and one that researchers will address in future studies.

Is There Really No Assortative Mating for Personality?

Another assumption on which heritability studies are based is that the parents of the individuals being studied are no more similar to each other in the characteristic of interest than are any two people chosen at random. That is, researchers assume that there is no *assortative mating* for the characteristic, or in other words, that there is no tendency for parents to be similar in their levels of the trait. For example, if researchers study the heritability of Agreeableness by comparing the personalities of many pairs of fraternal and identical twins, the researchers assume that their mothers' and fathers' levels of Agreeableness are nearly uncorrelated—put another way, that there is no tendency for the more agreeable mothers to be married to the more agreeable fathers.

Why is this assumption made? Consider what would happen if, at the opposite extreme, mothers' and fathers' levels of a trait were perfectly correlated. If this trait were strongly influenced by some genes that happened to be shared by the mother and father, then all of the children of any pair of parents would tend to inherit similar genetic tendencies from both parents. Therefore, those children (even if regular siblings or fraternal twins) would have more than 50% of their genes in common with each other. As a result, they would end up being more similar in this trait than would be the case if no assortative mating occurred. Consequently, if researchers estimated the heritability of the trait by studying fraternal twins or nontwin siblings raised apart, those researchers would *overestimate* the heritability if they used the usual method. (The usual method is to double the correlation, but if the siblings have more than 50% of their genes in common, then this will overestimate the heritability.) Or, if researchers estimated the heritability of the trait by comparing the similarity of identical twins with that of fraternal twins, those researchers would *underestimate* the heritability if they used the usual method. (The usual method is to double the *difference* between the identical-twin and fraternal-twin correlations; however, if fraternal twins have more than 50% of their genes in common, then this difference will represent the effects of less than 50% of genes, and doubling the difference will underestimate the heritability.)

How accurate is the assumption of no assortative mating? Researchers have studied the extent to which spouses are similar in personality characteristics, but let us save the precise results of those studies until Chapter 9. For now, it is enough to say that the obtained results do not show particularly high levels of assortative mating; that is, in most families, the parents are not so similar in any personality characteristic that this similarity would cause any important distortion of the results of heritability studies. However, the situation is rather different for some other characteristics, such as beliefs, attitudes, and abilities, and we will discuss the implications of this in later chapters that deal with those topics.

Assumptions Underlying Twin-Based Heritability Studies in Particular

Now let us consider some assumptions that underlie heritability studies involving twins in particular. First, we will discuss objections to two assumptions related to the study of twins raised apart, including (1) that these twins would share some features of their early environment, and also (2) that the twins might be placed into adopting households that are different in important ways from households in general. Then we will discuss an objection to an assumption related to the study of twins raised together, specifically, (3) that identical twins raised together might tend to receive more similar treatment than would fraternal twins (or regular siblings) raised together.

Are Twins' Early Environments Really Separate?

With regard to twins raised apart, you might have wondered whether these twins really have been raised apart for the entire duration of their development. If instead the twins have spent some considerable part of their childhood together before being separated, then this leaves open the possibility that the similarity of the twins' personalities (or any other characteristics) might be due to this common experience rather than to the common genetic background of the twins. In most heritability studies that have been based on twins raised apart, the typical age at which the twins were separated is very young; for example, in one large study, the average age at separation was only 5 months (Bouchard, Lykken, McGue, Segal, & Tellegen, 1990). Thus, although the twins in these studies have usually been separated at a very young age, the fact that they were together for at least a few months means that we cannot automatically rule out the possibility of the shared environment making a contribution to their similarity.

To address the problem that twins raised apart have usually spent at least some time raised together, researchers have done some additional analyses of their data. One way that researchers have tried to find out whether the early time spent together might have increased the similarity of twins raised apart has been to compare the similarity of twins who were separated very early with the similarity of twins who were separated somewhat later. To the extent that the later-separated twins were more similar, this would suggest that the early environment shared by the twins had tended to make them similar to each other. However, the results of analyses using this approach have not shown any substantially greater similarity for the twins who were separated at somewhat later ages, relative to the twins who were separated even earlier (e.g., Bouchard *et al.*, 1990). Thus, this result suggests that the similarity between twins raised apart is not attributable, in any substantial part, to the early time spent together by those twins.

But we are not finished yet with the problem that twins raised apart have actually spent some time together. This is because of the fact that, even if we compare twins who have been separated at birth, we have not in fact eliminated the influence of the common environment on those twins. Can you figure out why this is so? The reason is that the twins would have experienced a common environment during their development in the uterus (i.e., the womb) of their mother. Because the twins experienced the same uterine (womb) environment, and because their womb environment may have differed in many ways from that experienced by other twins developing in the wombs of other mothers, some of the similarity of the twins might be attributable to their experience of a common womb environment. For example, suppose that the mother's level of various nutrients (or various toxins, or various stresses) was different from that of other mothers. These differences might have influenced the development of the twin fetuses of that mother in similar ways, and in ways that would then lead both twins, after being born, to develop personalities different from those of twins who had shared the womb environment of a different mother. As a result, the observed similarities between twins raised apart would be attributable in some part to the common environment that they shared prior to being born.

You might also have noticed that the womb environment could also be the source of some unique environment influences, to the extent that the twins might not receive exactly the same levels of nutrients, of toxins, etc., from the mother's bloodstream. Both kinds of influence can also apply to nontwin siblings. Siblings who are not twins have also developed within the womb of the same mother, and any features of their mother's womb environment that are *consistent across pregnancies* will represent features of the *common environment* experienced by the siblings. (For example, if a mother smokes during both pregnancies, then both siblings will be exposed to the same smoking-related toxins.) But any features of the mother's womb environment that *change across pregnancies* will represent features of the *unique environment* experienced by the siblings. (For example, if a mother's diet during her first pregnancy differs from that during her second, or if a mother's experience of stress during her first pregnancy differs from that during her second, then the siblings will have been exposed to different womb environments.) In this way, the features of the womb environment can constitute aspects both of the common environment and also of the unique environment.

What is the actual effect of the womb environment on personality? Is the similarity of twins (or of nontwin siblings) raised apart actually due in some degree to the common environment experienced in the same mother's womb? Unfortunately, this question has not yet been addressed in heritability studies involving personality traits, and so it is quite possible that some fraction of the "heritable" influences on personality are instead attributable to the common womb environment experienced by twins. As we will see in Chapter 10 of this book, the contribution of the common womb environment has already been examined in studies of variation in mental abilities. The results of those investigations suggest that the womb environment is responsible for some of that variation.

Are Twins' Adoptive Households Really Very Different?

As described before, investigations of the heritability of personality characteristics have found very little influence of the common or shared environment. Many of those investigations are based on comparisons of siblings who are biologically unrelated but who were raised in the same family because of adoption. But there is a potential problem here: What if the households that adopt children tend to be rather similar to each other in most ways? For example, if adopting parents in general tend to have fairly high levels of income or education, or to be rather gentle and attentive in their parenting styles, then the relative lack of variation among adopting households would tend to limit the effect of the common environment on personality. In other words, even if personality could be substantially influenced by some aspects of the shared environment—such as socioeconomic status or parenting style—we might never see these influences in a sample of families that are all fairly similar in those respects. We would only notice these influences if the sample of adopting families had a really wide range on these variables, by including families of very low income and educational levels and of very harsh and distant parenting styles. But because of the screening process that is involved in placing children to be adopted (and also because of the characteristics of people who wish to adopt), it may be that these latter families would only rarely adopt children.

Researchers have addressed this concern by checking to see how much variation there really is among adopting households in a variety of characteristics, including socioeconomic status and parenting styles. The results suggest that although adoptive families are rarely very low in socioeconomic status or in the overall quality of parenting, there still does remain a great deal of variation among adoptive households in these variables. In an adoption study conducted in Colorado, the researchers found that the adoptive families tended to be somewhat above average in socioeconomic status and in quality of parenting, but that there was nevertheless almost as much variation in these characteristics among adoptive families as there is among families in the general population (Plomin & DeFries, 1985). According to these results, it seems unlikely that the effects of the shared environment have been greatly underestimated by the use of adoption studies. Instead, the apparently weak influence of the shared environment on personality characteristics is probably genuine. Nevertheless, these results do not rule out the possibility that being raised in an extremely unfavorable environment could have lasting influences on personality. It might be the case, for example, that the effects of household environments could become stronger as one moves from more favorable to less favorable environments. Therefore, even if a very good environment and an average environment would lead to similar outcomes, it is possible that an average environment and a very bad environment could lead to very different outcomes.

A related concern about studies based on adoptive families is the possibility that those families may be selected in such a way as to be similar to the biological parents of the children who are to be adopted. For example, perhaps children whose biological parents were from a high socioeconomic status background would tend to be placed into adoptive families having the same background. This is called *selective placement*, and if it were to happen, then it could distort the results of heritability studies in various ways. For example, it could make it appear as though the characteristics of the adopted children were caused by the environment of their adoptive families, even if those characteristics were really caused by genes inherited from biological parents. Or, it could make it appear as though the similarities between identical twins raised apart (but adopted into similar households) were due to genetic similarities, even if the similar household environments were responsible. However, the evidence from adoption studies suggests that there is very little selective placement: On average, the biological parents of an adopted child are only very slightly more similar to the adoptive parents than to parents in the general population (Plomin & DeFries, 1985). Therefore, it is unlikely that selective placement has had any important effect on the results of heritability studies.

Are Identical Twins Really Treated Differently by Others?

In some heritability studies, researchers estimate the heritability of a trait by comparing the similarity of identical twins with the similarity of fraternal twins. In those investigations, it is assumed that the greater similarity of identical twins is due to their greater genetic similarity, and not due to any greater similarity of their environments. This is called the *equal environments assumption*, but what if this assumption is false? Could it be, instead, that identical twins become very similar to each other because they experience environments that are especially similar? Perhaps the parents of identical twins tend to treat those twins more similarly than they would treat fraternal twins or regular siblings, for example, by dressing them in the same sets of clothes, enrolling them in the same activities, or giving them the same birthday presents. And perhaps the extremely similar physical appearance of identical twins leads them to be treated in a very similar way by people in general, including teachers or classmates. As a result of this very similar treatment, perhaps identical twins would become more similar in personality than would be caused by their genetic similarity alone.

Researchers have examined this possibility in two different ways. One way has been to find out whether the similarity of identical twins depends on how similarly their parents have treated them. That is, do identical twins whose parents have tried to treat them in very similar ways end up being more similar than do identical twins whose parents have tried to treat them differently? This question was examined by Loehlin and Nichols (1976), who studied a large sample of over 300 identical twin pairs in Texas. They found that the similarity of identical twins' personalities was only very slightly related to how similar their experiences had been, in terms of being dressed alike, playing together, or being treated similarly by parents or teachers. Because this similarity of treatment had little effect on the similarity of personality for identical twins, it appears that the greater personality similarity of identical twins, compared with fraternal twins, cannot be attributed to the similar treatment of identical twins.

Another way to examine the possibility that similar treatment might make identical twins more similar than fraternal twins involves an unusual comparison. Specifically, which kinds of twins are more similar: Identical twins whose parents mistakenly believe them to be fraternal twins, or fraternal twins whose parents mistakenly believe them to be identical twins? Answering this question allows us to determine whether the personality similarity between twins depends more on their *actual* genetic similarity (as measured by biological tests of their status as identical or fraternal twins) or on their *perceived* genetic similarity (as indicated by their parents' belief as to their status as identical or fraternal twins)? If actual genetic similarity is the better predictor of personality similarity, then similar treatment is not the source of much of the twins' similarity; but, if perceived genetic similarity is a better predictor, then similar treatment is responsible for much of that similarity. When researchers have examined this question, they have found that similarity of personality (and other) characteristics is greater for identical twins whose parents mistakenly believed them to be fraternal than for fraternal twins whose parents mistakenly believed them to be identical (e.g., Scarr & Carter-Saltzman, 1979). Therefore, these results also indicate that the similarity of identical twins is not due to similar treatment of those twins.

Effects of the Unique Environment on Personality? Parental Treatment, Peer Groups, and Birth Order

Now let us consider some environmental influences on personality. To the extent that the variation in the unique environment contributes to personality variation, which specific features of the unique environment are important? People have suggested several possible sources of unique environment influence on personality, and a few of these have been investigated empirically. Here we will explore some of the most prominent of these possible unique environment influences on personality: Parental treatment, peer groups, and birth order.

Parental Treatment and Peer Groups

A study by Loehlin (1997) attempted to determine whether or not differences in personality within twin pairs would be related to differences in parental treatment and to differences in friends. To examine these questions, Loehlin had about 800 pairs of twins (both identical and fraternal) provide self-reports on several variables, including (a) various personality characteristics, as well as (b) any differences between twins in the same family in the way their parents had treated them, and (c) any differences between twins of the same family in their peer groups (i.e., the fraction of friends of one twin who were not friends of the other).

Loehlin (1997) found that the size of the difference between two twins' personalities (across various traits) was positively, but weakly, correlated with both the amount of difference in parental treatment and the degree of difference in their friendship groups. That is, when two twins had different personalities, they had a slight tendency also to report different treatment by their parents, and to report having different groups of friends. Again, these tendencies were rather weak, with correlations only about .15, but they suggest that these aspects of the unique environment—different treatment by parents and different peer groups—might have at least some small influence on differences between twins (or other siblings) in personality. (On the other hand, it is possible that the influence runs in the opposite direction: Perhaps twins with more different personalities are likely to be treated more differently by their parents, and likely to have fewer friends in common.)

The preceding findings regarding the effects of one's group of friends on one's personality are important given the increased recent interest in the effects of the peer environment on personality. A researcher named Judith Rich Harris suggested that the peer groups to which one belongs during childhood and adolescence are crucial to personality development (Harris, 1995, 1998). As seen in terms of many variables, such as the prevailing accent, clothing, and music of a given time and place, the influence of one's peer group is obviously strong. Similarly, peer groups also influence norms regarding drug use, sexual activity, delinquency, and other behaviors, so that there can be large differences between communities (or cultures, or generations) in the prevalence of these behaviors. However, in terms of *individual differences* in levels of personality characteristics among people from the same time and place, the evidence from Loehlin's study suggests that which particular group of friends one has can exert only a modest influence.

Birth Order

Another aspect of the unique environment that received a great deal of research attention beginning in the mid-1990s is that of birth order. The idea that siblings having different birth order positions—first-born, middle-born, last-born, or "only" child—might develop different personalities has been around for a long time. In the early twentieth century, a theorist named Alfred Adler suggested that first-born children would tend to be insecure, after having experienced the trauma of being "dethroned" from their favored position by the arrival of a younger sibling. Adler also suggested that last-born children would, by virtue of being the "baby" of the family, tend to be rather spoiled. He suggested that middle-born children would be better adjusted, because their experiences of dethronement and of spoiling would be less strong than those of their other siblings.

More recently, a researcher named Frank Sulloway argued that first-born and later-born siblings would tend to develop different personalities. Sulloway (1995, 1996) believed that differences would emerge in several aspects of personality, as described in terms of the Big Five framework: For example, he believed that the later-born siblings would have higher levels of Agreeableness and lower levels of Conscientiousness than would the earlier-born siblings. However, he suggested that the largest differences would be found in the Openness to Experience factor, where later-born siblings would be expected to have higher levels than would first-born siblings. Sulloway believed that younger siblings would need to develop a more creative, unconventional, risk-taking personality in order to find areas in which they could excel and thereby impress their parents. This diversity of interests was necessary for younger siblings, Sulloway suggested, in order to avoid direct competition with their older siblings, who would (during childhood) tend to be smarter and stronger by virtue of their age.

Sulloway (1995, 1996) supported these arguments with a wide range of historical evidence, including the records of the votes and decisions made by first-born and later-born politicians and judges, and the theories and writings of first-born and later-born scientists and intellectuals. However, there has also been much criticism of this evidence (Townsend, 2000), and several empirical tests of the theories have shown mixed results. Studies in which first- and later-born siblings are directly compared with reference to each other (e.g., by asking which sibling is more rebellious) generally do find that the later-born siblings tend to be rated as having higher levels of traits related to Openness to Experience

---

BOX 6-1
Identifying Specific Genes
That Influence Personality:
Molecular Genetic Studies

As noted in Chapter 5, some studies have examined the role of specific genes in influencing personality. In these investigations, the researchers have identified different alleles (i.e., different gene "versions" at the same place, or locus) that influence the levels of some neurotransmitter substance. The researchers have then compared the personalities of people who have different alleles (and therefore, different levels of the neurotransmitter) to find out whether those people differ in their levels of characteristics thought to be influenced by that neurotransmitter. (A similar approach could also be taken by studying genes that influence hormone levels or activity levels of brain structures.) The results of some studies have suggested, for example, that a gene called DRD4 may influence levels of dopamine (Benjamin *et al.*, 1996), which in turn influence levels of the trait of

novelty seeking. Similarly, the results of other studies have suggested that a gene called 5-HTTLPR may influence levels of serotonin (Lesch *et al.*, 1996), which in turn influence levels of the trait of harm avoidance.

However, the findings involving these genes have been inconsistent across studies, and this may be due in part to the fact that any single gene is likely to have only a weak effect on personality (Plomin & Caspi, 1999). The genetic influences on any given personality characteristic are likely to be attributable to the overall effects of many different genes. Some genes are likely to contribute in an independent, additive fashion, whereas others are likely to have complex interactions with each other. Moreover, the genes that influence trait levels strongly in one population (i.e., in one country, or in one ethnic group) might not be the same genes that influence levels of the same trait in some other population. For these reasons, it may be difficult for researchers to find specific genes that reliably have strong effects on personality.

(Paulhus, Trapnell, & Chen, 1999). But on the other hand, studies in which the personalities of first- and later-born siblings are measured by self- and peer report questionnaires have generally found very weak results, with virtually no difference between them on the Openness to Experience factor (Jefferson, Herbst, & McCrae, 1998). These latter results, which represent the most direct way of assessing the size of the personality differences between siblings, suggest that the effects of birth order on personality are quite small. It may be that the effects observed in some studies of birth order and personality have capitalized on "contrast effects" (as described earlier in this chapter) that are especially strong when personality reports ask the respondent to make direct comparisons between siblings.

Summary and Conclusions

In this chapter, we have examined the methods used by researchers to measure the extent to which differences among people's personalities are due to genetic (hereditary) differences and due to environmental differences. Let us briefly review the main points.

First, psychologists use several methods to examine the heritability of a trait—that is, the extent to which variation in the trait is due to genetic variation. These methods generally involve determining the extent to which relatives have similar levels of a personality trait. The researchers try to separate the effects of heredity and environment in several ways, such as by comparing relatives who have been raised apart (e.g., twins adopted into different households), or by comparing relatives who have more genes in common with relatives who have fewer genes in common (e.g., identical twins versus fraternal twins). Research on the heritability of personality is based on many assumptions, which researchers have attempted to verify; some of the questions associated with these assumptions are complex and have not yet been fully resolved, but the basic results obtained in heritability studies are probably fairly accurate.

The results of heritability studies suggest that there are fairly strong genetic influences on personality characteristics, regardless of which characteristics are considered. These genetic influences are partly "additive" (whereby the trait tends to "run in families," tending to be similar for relatives) and partly "nonadditive" (whereby the trait tends to be similar only for identical twins, and otherwise tends not to run in families). In contrast, personality differences are only weakly influenced by the common environment—that is, by the features of the household that are shared among siblings. Instead, environmental effects on personality chiefly involve the unique environment—that is, experiences that are different for each sibling of the same family. Some research has examined the possibility that birth order and peer relationships may be important aspects of the unique environment, but thus far the relations between these variables and personality have not been very strong.

Appendix: Difficulties in Separating the Effects of Heredity and Environment

As described in this chapter, researchers have devised some creative and useful ways of separating the influences of genetic variation and environmental variation on individual differences in personality variation. But in some sense these effects cannot be so easily divided, because it is possible that genetic and environmental influences can combine in complex ways, or that genetic and environmental influences can "go together" in some circumstances. These interactions and correlations between heredity and environment add some interesting complications to the study of genetic and environmental influences on personality, and this Appendix gives a brief summary of these genotype–environment interactions and correlations.

Genotype–Environment Interactions

In the previous sections, we have described the role of genetic and environmental variation as if each aspect contributed independently to personality variation. For example, we have assumed that a given environmental situation would tend to influence everyone in the same way. This might well be the case for many aspects of the environment: It might well be the case that poor nutrition would make all children grow up to be shorter than they would otherwise be, or that exercise would make all adults leaner than they would otherwise be. In some cases, however, the situation might be more complicated than this: It is possible that the same environment will influence people's levels of a given characteristic in different ways, depending on their genetic characteristics (i.e., their genotype). This is known as *genotype–environment interaction*.

It is not hard to imagine plausible examples of genotype–environment interactions. Suppose that two children grow up in a household in which one of the parents is very overprotective. If one child has a genetically based inclination to enjoy being protected, then he or she may accept and encourage the parent's overprotectiveness, and thus grow up to be a rather risk-averse, dependent person. However, if the other child has a genetically based inclination to dislike being protected, then he or she may try to escape from the parent's overprotectiveness, and grow up to be a daring, independent person. Or, consider another example, in which a parent is very domineering. A child with a genetic tendency to be somewhat submissive might grow up to be very submissive as a result of consistently accepting domination by the parent. However, a child with a genetic tendency to be somewhat rebellious might grow up to be very rebellious as a result of consistently resisting domination by the parent. Of course, genotype–environment interactions can involve aspects of the environment other than those provided by parents: For example, children with different genetic tendencies might react very differently to the same opportunities for playing sports, for playing a musical instrument, or for playing video games. Similarly, children with different genetic inclinations could react very differently to the influence of "delinquent" peers: One child might be very easily influenced, but another might not be.

Genotype–environment interactions can influence the estimates of genetic influence that are obtained from heritability studies. Because these interactions will make people different from each other whenever those people differ *either* genetically *or* in their environments, any such interaction will tend to make all relatives less similar to each other than would be the case if that interaction did not exist. As a result, estimates of heritability based on correlations between relatives (e.g., siblings or twins raised apart) will tend to be lower when genotype–environment interactions are operating on a characteristic. However, heritability estimates based on *differences between* the correlations between relatives (e.g., identical twins relative to fraternal twins) will not be affected, because both correlations will be lowered by the interactions.

This raises the question of how important these genotype–environment interactions actually are. Do these interactions have strong influences on many characteristics? The methods used to study these questions are very complex, but the research on this topic suggests that genotype–environment interactions are usually not very strong (e.g., Plomin, DeFries, & Fulker, 1988). One example of a genotype–environment interaction that was observed in an adoption study involved the personality characteristic of Neuroticism (Plomin *et al.*, 1988). For adopted children whose biological mothers were high in Neuroticism, the level of Neuroticism of the adoptive mothers did not influence children's levels of behavioral problems (which tended to be high regardless of the mother's Neuroticism level). In contrast, for adopted children whose biological mothers were low in Neuroticism, the level of Neuroticism of the adoptive mothers did influence children's levels of behavioral problems (which tended to be high only when the adoptive mother was high in Neuroticism). This example is evidence of a genotype–environment interaction on personality, but for the most part, strong influences of this kind appear to be relatively uncommon.

Genotype–Environment Correlations: Passive, Reactive, and Active

As described above, a genotype–environment interaction occurs whenever the same environment has different influences on people's characteristics depending on the genetic differences among those people. But genotype–environment interactions are not the only way in which the effects of heredity and environment can combine in complex ways to influence individual differences in characteristics. Another phenomenon involves the tendency for people with different genetic tendencies to experience different environments, which then in turn have different influences on the characteristics of those people. In other words, your genetic tendencies might actually cause you to be exposed to some kinds of environments more than other kinds, and the differences between those environments might then influence the development of your personality characteristics. This is known as *genotype–environment correlation*.

Genotype–environment correlations can occur in three different ways. One kind of genotype–environment correlation happens when the environment experienced by children is influenced by their parents' genetic predispositions, which are also inherited by those children. For example, suppose that two parents have a genetic tendency to be very athletic. As a result, those parents might be enthusiastic sports participants, and might thereby raise their child in a very sports-oriented home environment. In this way, the child inherits both a genetic tendency to be athletic as well as an environment that tends to encourage athletic ability. This kind of situation is called a *passive genotype–environment correlation*, because the children inherit this combination of genes and environment "passively," not as a result of their own behavior.

A different kind of genotype–environment correlation happens when children experience different environments depending on other people's reactions to the children's different genetic tendencies. Let us consider athletic ability as an example once again. Suppose that a child inherits a genetic tendency to be very athletic. The adults who interact with the child—including his or her parents, teachers, and coaches—might then react to his or her natural talent by providing the child with additional opportunities for playing and practicing sports. This highly sports-oriented environment might then contribute, along with the child's natural athletic talent, to the development of a very high level of athletic ability. This kind of situation is called a *reactive genotype–environment correlation* (sometimes also called an *evocative genotype–environment correlation*), because other people's reactions to the child's genetic tendencies end up influencing the environment that the child experiences.

Finally, another kind of genotype–environment correlation happens when children themselves seek out a particular kind of environment as a function of their own genetic tendencies. Continuing with our athletic ability example, consider a child who inherits a genetic predisposition to be highly athletic. As a result of his or her talent, this child might find sports participation to be very satisfying, and he or she might therefore seek many opportunities to play and practise various sports. This very sports-oriented environment might then cause the child's athletic ability to develop still further, beyond even what his or her genes alone would have caused. This kind of genotype–environment correlation is called an *active genotype–environment correlation*, because the child actively chooses environments as a function of his or her genetic predispositions.

When considering genotype–environment correlations, it is important to keep in mind that these correlations could be either positive or negative. In the preceding examples, we have described situations in which the genotype and environment are correlated positively, but it could work the other way around. Consider the example of the reactive genotype–environment correlation that was mentioned above. It is possible that a child with a genetic tendency to be high in athletic ability would cause his parents and other adults to react by providing a very sports-oriented environment; thus, the genes for athletic ability and the environment for developing that ability would be positively correlated. But imagine that a child has a genetic tendency to be low in athletic ability. It is possible that this could also lead the child's parents to provide a sports-oriented environment, as a way of improving the child's athletic ability. If this were to happen frequently enough, then the genes for athletic ability and the environment for developing that ability would be negatively correlated, because genes for *low* ability are causing an environment that develops *higher* ability. If this example seems a bit unlikely, consider another trait: Parents whose child is genetically inclined to have low ability in math or in reading might try to develop his or her ability by providing extra exposure to math or reading experiences.

The possibility of genotype–environment correlations leaves us with the question of whether these influences actually have an important influence on individual differences in various characteristics. Researchers who study the genetic and environmental influences on characteristics (e.g., Plomin *et al.*, 1988) have figured out some ingenious ways of answering this question. As far as passive genotype–environment correlations are concerned, these effects will—if the correlations are positive—tend to make the variation in characteristics greater in nonadopted children than in adopted children. Why should this be true? When a child is raised by his or her biological parents, there is the possibility that the parents' genetic tendencies will influence *both* the child's genetic tendencies *and* the environment that the children experience. As a consequence, the child could develop more extreme levels of the characteristics: When the child receives the genes *and* the environment that produce high levels of the characteristic, the child will tend to develop a very high level; conversely, when the child receives the genes *and* the environment that produce low levels of the characteristic, the child will tend to develop a very low level.

Thus, genotype–environment correlations could produce greater differences among children in their levels of various characteristics. But note that this would only happen when children are raised by their biological parents. When, instead, children are raised by adoptive parents, the environment created by those parents would not be influenced by the genes of the biological parents, so there would be no special tendency for the genetic and environmental influences on the characteristic to be similar. As a result, there would not be as many cases of adopted children developing extremely high or extremely low levels of the characteristic, and variation would be smaller than for children raised by their biological parents.

To what extent do children raised by biological parents show more variation in levels of a characteristic than do children raised by adoptive parents? Results so far suggest that there is not much extra variation among nonadopted children than among adopted children, thus suggesting that passive genotype–environment correlations are rather weak. In some cases, slightly higher amounts of variation have been observed for nonadopted children, compared with adopted children, when scores on tests of mental abilities are considered; however, this has not been observed for personality characteristics.

To examine whether reactive genotype–environment correlations are important, researchers have tried to figure out whether the child's genetic tendencies influence the environment provided by the parents. This can be achieved in a very inventive way—by finding out whether the characteristics of a child's *biological* parents tend to be associated with features of the environment provided by a child's *adoptive* parents. Why is this approach used? If the biological parents have genetic predispositions to behave in certain ways, then these predispositions will tend to be inherited by their children. If the children's behavior then influences the way they are treated by their adoptive parents, we will be able to detect some link between the biological parents' characteristics and the environment produced by the adoptive parents. (Notice that, if we tried simply to compare the adopted children's characteristics with the environments provided by their adoptive parents, then this might be due to an effect of the environment on the child, not the other way around. By considering the child's biological parents, we avoid this problem.)

Are there any correlations between biological parents' characteristics and features of the environment created by adoptive parents? Some studies have reported such results (see Plomin *et al.*, 1988): For example, if a child's biological parents have high levels of activity and impulsivity, and low levels of depressiveness, then the child's adoptive parents tend to have a slightly more "responsive" style of interacting with the child. Presumably, the child inherits these rather upbeat characteristics from his or her biological parents, and then these characteristics tend to encourage a more engaging style of parenting by the adoptive parents. However, the strength of these relations as observed by Plomin *et al.* was rather weak, suggesting that the influence of reactive genotype–environment correlations is not very strong.

To sum up, the study of genetic and environmental influences on personality is made more complicated by the difficulty in separating the effects of genes and environment. Rather than only acting additively and independently, the genetic and environmental influences may interact with each other and may be correlated with each other. Thus far, however, research findings have not shown especially strong effects of these genotype–environment interactions and genotype–environment correlations on individual differences in personality trait levels.

Chapter 7

The Evolutionary Function of Personality

The Idea of Evolution by Natural Selection 142

Why Are We Not All the Same? Fluctuating Optimum and Frequency Dependence 144

Several Reasons Why Variation Does Not Go Away 144

Fluctuating Optimum: Ideal Levels of a Characteristic Vary across Places and Times 145

Frequency Dependence: The Advantages of Doing What Others Are Not Doing 146

The Operation of the Fluctuating Optimum and Frequency Dependence: Genetic and Developmental Routes 147

Adaptive Trade-offs between High and Low Levels of the HEXACO Personality Factors 148

Honesty–Humility 148

Agreeableness 149

Emotionality 149

Summary for Honesty–Humility, Agreeableness, and Emotionality: Altruism versus Aggression 150

Extraversion 151

Conscientiousness 151

Openness to Experience 152

Summary for Extraversion, Conscientiousness, and Openness to Experience: Engagement in Areas of Endeavor 152

The Operation of the Fluctuating Optimum and Frequency Dependence: Some Examples 153

Honesty–Humility and Agreeableness 153

Emotionality 156

Extraversion 157

Conscientiousness 158

Openness to Experience 158

Summary and Conclusions 160

Like the human body, human behavior has been influenced by the process of evolution by natural selection. In this chapter, we will begin with a brief summary of how evolution works, and then turn to the question of how personality variation has evolved. In doing so, we will consider the ways by which evolution can act to preserve the differences among people in personality, and we will examine the advantages and disadvantages—from an evolutionary standpoint—that are associated with high and low levels of each personality dimension.

The Idea of Evolution by Natural Selection

One of the cornerstones of modern biology is the concept of evolution by natural selection, as discovered by Charles Darwin (Darwin, 1859).[1] Briefly, the idea of evolution by natural selection can be summarized as follows:

a. individuals differ in various characteristics;
b. these characteristics are to some extent transmitted directly—through reproduction itself—from parents to offspring; and
c. some characteristics are associated with greater numbers of surviving offspring (i.e., with *reproductive success*); therefore,
d. across generations, those characteristics will become more widespread among the individuals of the population.

Because of (d), there will sometimes emerge large differences between two populations of individuals that were originally a single population, but that have been divided or separated for a long period of time. For example, suppose that one group of individuals has moved out of its original range to a different region, and later becomes permanently isolated from the individuals who stayed behind. As a result of being separated and of needing to adapt to different environments, the two groups may then change in very different ways as the generations pass. After a very long time, the two groups might become so different from each other that they would no longer be able to interbreed, even if they were to be reunited in the same location. At this point, two different "species" would have emerged from the single, original species that had once existed.

Now, to understand how evolution by natural selection can apply to human characteristics, let us consider each of the preceding four steps in turn, focusing on variation among people.

Individual Differences among People. First of all, it is obvious that for many characteristics, there are important individual differences among humans: We vary in physical characteristics such as our heights, body builds, limb length ratios, body compositions, colors of skin and hair and eyes, and blood types, and we vary in psychological characteristics such as our shyness, impulsiveness, and aggressiveness.

Inheritance of Characteristics. Next is the question of whether or not these characteristics are transmitted from parents to offspring. The answer, as reviewed in Chapter 6, is that to an important extent, those characteristics are indeed transmitted via heredity. For an array of psychological (and physical) traits, the variation that exists within a population is typically due about 30% to additive ("narrow sense") genetic variation. In other words, for many traits, about one-third of the variability that exists in a population is due to genetic differences

---

[1] Actually, the principle of evolution by natural selection was also discovered independently by another biologist, Alfred Russel Wallace. However, Darwin provided a much more detailed and thorough explanation of this theory.

that are passed directly from parents to offspring. Given that variation in traits is often rather large, this means the amount of variation due to heredity can be rather important.[2]

Characteristics Associated with Reproductive Success. The next issue is whether or not the variation in some characteristics can be associated with survival and, ultimately, with reproductive success. That is, are some levels of a trait better, or more "adaptive," from the point of view of increasing one's likelihood of having surviving offspring? On the one hand, it is clear that some varieties of a trait are indeed more adaptive and others less so; for example, some alleles (i.e., versions) of some genes are associated with fatal childhood diseases. But on the other hand, it is not so obvious as to whether or not the different varieties, or levels, of characteristics that show *normal* variation—that is, variation among basically healthy individuals—are also associated with different levels of reproductive success. This is a very big and very tricky question, and we will discuss it in detail in the next section; for the moment, however, let us assume that reproductive success does sometimes depend in part on the characteristics one inherits.[3,4]

Changes across Generations in Levels of Characteristics. The final issue is whether or not population-level differences can emerge as a result of the accumulated action of evolution over many generations. That is, suppose that two groups of

---

[2] In case you are wondering where these variations actually come from, they emerge as a result of genetic mutations—that is, as a result of changes in the genes that carry the instructions to produce the many features of our bodies. For example, some random change in the genetic code might lead to a new variety of eye color emerging, or a different proportion in the lengths of limbs, or various other characteristics, both physical and psychological. Although these "mistakes" in the genetic code are often disastrous for an individual's chances of survival and reproduction, they sometimes produce characteristics that actually improve those chances.

[3] Note that variation in characteristics might influence reproductive success in two distinct ways. First, one's level of a characteristic might improve (or undermine) one's reproductive success by making one more (or less) able to deal with the natural environment, for example, by getting food or by avoiding predators. Alternatively, it might instead operate by making one better able to obtain a mate (whether directly, by being more attractive to mates, or indirectly, by defeating one's rivals in confrontations). Darwin referred to the environment-related mechanism as natural selection, and to mating-related mechanism as sexual selection. For the sake of simplicity, we will use the term "natural selection" to refer to both of them together.

[4] By the way, it is important to understand that the idea of evolution by natural selection does *not* suggest that people (or any other organisms) are consciously trying to improve their reproductive success. The idea instead is that people (or other organisms) inherit physical and psychological characteristics that have tended to promote reproductive success, within the environments in which their evolution occurred. For example, human evolution has not necessarily selected individuals who have a drive to want as many children as possible, but it has tended to select individuals who are interested in sexual intercourse and who are motivated to care for their offspring. These latter drives have tended to lead to reproductive success in most environments that our ancestors inhabited, even though this may no longer be the case in modern societies.

people inhabit different environments, with the possibility that the characteristics associated with reproductive success will differ from one environment to the next. Will those groups eventually end up having (on average) different levels of those characteristics, as a result of natural selection? This is also a hard question to answer, and it depends in part on the way that evolution by natural selection actually operates: As we will see in the following section, there are some ways in which evolution might tend to produce differences between groups, but other ways in which it might keep those groups almost the same.

Why Are We Not All the Same? Fluctuating Optimum and Frequency Dependence

Several Reasons Why Variation Does Not Go Away

For many characteristics, the forces of selection tend to eliminate all variation, by favoring a single solution that is apparently the "best" that can be easily achieved. For example, virtually every healthy human is born with two eyes, two ears, two arms, and two legs. This is presumably because having two of these organs simply worked much better for the ancestors of all modern humans, in terms of facilitating survival and reproduction, than did having one or three of those organs.

But there are also many characteristics for which the forces of selection have apparently preserved a great deal of variation. In addition to the obvious physical differences between men and women, there is also a great deal of variation among people of the same sex (and the same age) in basic physical characteristics such as height and body build, as well as in the psychological characteristics that are the topic of this book. But the existence of so much variation in these various traits raises the question of *how* that variation has been maintained over the course of human evolution: Why has it not been eliminated? Why is there not a single "ideal" level for each trait—such as height, body build, or any personality trait—for every adult of a given sex and age?

There are several possible reasons why variation has been maintained in many characteristics (see also Buss & Greiling, 1999, for a detailed discussion that includes some additional reasons not examined here). One possibility is that the variation is simply unimportant, in the sense that it has no consequences for survival and reproduction. A related possibility is that new mutations do cause variation away from an ideal level of a trait, but that natural selection cannot remove these mutations quickly enough to eliminate variation in the trait. However, both of these explanations seem unlikely to account for the very wide variation in many traits.

Another potential reason for the maintenance of variation in many traits across long periods of evolutionary time is perhaps a surprising one: The importance of variation in combating infections by parasites. This might not seem to be an obvious reason, but some researchers have pointed out that parasitic infections—which can be very damaging to an individual's health, and thus can have a serious negative impact on reproductive success—tend to spread less quickly when the individuals of a species are different from each other in various ways. That is, when each individual's body is slightly different, these variations make it more difficult for parasites to invade those bodies successfully. According to this idea, variation among individuals might persist across long periods of time simply because individuals who were too nearly identical to each other would tend to die out due to the easy spread of parasites among them, whereas the more divergent individuals would tend to survive. This idea has much support, and it may explain the reason why sexual reproduction originally involved: One of the advantages of sex (in contrast to asexual reproduction) is that it produces offspring who are slightly different from each other and from their parents. But with regard to variation among people in physical and psychological characteristics, it seems unlikely that defence against parasites is the sole reason why this trait variation persists. As noted before, it seems intuitively more likely that the very large individual differences in many traits might sometimes be associated with individual differences in reproductive success.

Fluctuating Optimum: Ideal Levels of a Characteristic Vary across Places and Times

So, if a characteristic is important to survival and reproduction, why would variation in that characteristic be maintained across long periods of time? Why would one "ideal" level of the trait not simply defeat all the others? Researchers have proposed two main reasons, which are likely to operate in combination.

One reason is that the ideal level of the characteristic might differ depending on environmental conditions that change from one time and place to another. If the ideal level varies from one generation or from one region to the next, then variation in the characteristic would always be maintained. Depending on when and where a group of people was living, the people with "high" levels might have better reproductive success, or the people with "low" levels might have better reproductive success. If a group of people moved from one place to another, the ideal level of any given trait would probably shift somewhat, according to changes in various features of the environment, such as the climate or vegetation. Or, if they stayed in the same place for a long enough period of time, the ideal level of the same characteristic would also be likely to shift somewhat, again according to any changes in features of the environment. As a result of this *fluctuating optimum* level of the characteristic, the variation in the characteristic would tend to be maintained even over very long periods of time.[5] The average level of the trait would gradually shift up or down within a given population, in response to the features of its current environment, but the amount of *variation* in those levels would not be reduced very much.

---

[5] Actually, for the trait variation to persist across generations, some conditions might need to be met, such as migration of some individuals between different regions, and the occasional emergence of new mutations. But we will assume that these conditions are at least sometimes met.

As a possible example of the way in which the fluctuating optimum could operate, consider the characteristic of "parental investment." Suppose that there are some partly heritable differences among the individuals of a given animal species, such that some individuals tend to have many offspring (but give little parental care to those offspring), whereas other individuals tend to have few offspring (but give much parental care to those offspring). During times when there is abundant food, the individuals who have many offspring (but who give little parental care) will probably have better "reproductive success," because those many offspring are likely to survive even without any help from their parents, and will therefore become more numerous than the offspring of other individuals. But in times when food shortages occur, the individuals who have few offspring (but who give much parental care) will probably have better "reproductive success," because those few offspring have a good chance of surviving due to their parents' assistance, while the offspring of other individuals may nearly all die. Depending on changes across times and across places in the abundance of food, either high or low parental investment may be favored, with the result that the population of the species would tend not to become uniformly high or low with regard to this characteristic.[6] We will consider some more examples later in the chapter.

Frequency Dependence: The Advantages of Doing What Others Are Not Doing

Along with the "fluctuating optimum" reason described before, a second reason why the variation in a characteristic would persist is that there might never be a *single* ideal level of a characteristic, but rather an ideal *balance* of different levels of a characteristic. Suppose that nearly everyone had a high level of a characteristic. If so, perhaps the few people who had a low level of that characteristic would be more successful. Conversely, if nearly everyone had a low level of a trait, then perhaps the few people who had a high level of that trait would be more successful. As a result of this process, which is similar to one that biologists call *frequency-dependent selection*, we might see a rough balance in the population between people who have higher and lower levels of the characteristic.[7]

As a possible example of the way in which frequency dependence could operate, consider the characteristic of color. Suppose that there are partly heritable differences among the males of a given bird species in the color of their feathers, and that the females of this species prefer to mate with males who have a rare color. If so, then a lone blue male among a group of many green males would be more likely to reproduce successfully, and blue

---

[6] Note, of course, that over very long periods of time, there might be an overall trend in one direction or another, with the possible result that the species *would* show a major increase or decrease in its level of a trait.

[7] Specifically, this is *negative* frequency dependent selection, because individuals having a given level of a trait become less successful when there are more of these individuals in the population. If, instead, the individuals having that level of the trait become more successful when there are more individuals with that same level, then this is *positive* frequency-dependent selection. Positive frequency-dependent selection eliminates trait variation.

males would become more frequent in the next generation. But over the generations, the advantage of being blue would decrease, because this color would no longer be so rare, and hence would no longer be so attractive to females. Eventually, when blue males became as common as green males, there would be no advantage at all, and the two colors would balance each other out. (Note that if one color had an advantage in some other way, such as for avoiding predators, then the "balance" would not be 50-50, but would instead favor a higher proportion of that color.)

The Operation of the Fluctuating Optimum and Frequency Dependence: Genetic and Developmental Routes

When we think about the role of frequency dependence and of the fluctuating optimum, it is useful to keep in mind two different ways in which both of those mechanisms preserve trait variation. One way is by favoring the reproductive success of individuals who have a *genetic inclination to have a particular level of the trait*. Sometimes, individuals who are genetically inclined to have high levels of a trait will be favored, and sometimes, individuals who are genetically inclined to have low levels of a trait will be favored. But over the long run, the mechanisms of the fluctuating optimum and of frequency dependence tend to produce roughly equal levels of reproductive success for individuals whose genes tend to produce very different levels of the trait. As a result, heritable variation in the trait is maintained.

A second way by which these mechanisms can operate (and one that can occur alongside the first) is by favoring the reproductive success of individuals *whose genetic inclination is more flexible, allowing the development of* either *a high* or *a low level of the trait*, depending on experiences early in life. That is, some individuals have genes that allow either a fairly high or a fairly low level of the trait to be developed, depending on experiences during development that indicate the optimal level of the trait in the current environment. In many environments, these individuals would be able to adapt successfully by developing a level of the trait that is suitable for that environment. (For example, suppose that in a given species of animals, individuals who have heavy fur are more likely to survive and reproduce in cold climates, but that individuals who have lighter fur are more likely to survive and reproduce in hot climates. If some individuals inherit genes that allow them to develop *either* heavier fur *or* lighter fur, depending on the temperatures that they experience while developing, then those individuals would be likely to survive and reproduce successfully in either type of climate.) The reproductive success of these individuals would then mean a preservation of their genes, which allow an individual to develop a different level of the trait in response to cues from his or her environment.[8]

---

[8] However, these individuals would probably not be able to develop quite as high or quite as low a level of the trait as would individuals whose genetic inclinations are to be high only or to be low only. As a result, in more extreme environments, the more developmentally flexible individuals would not be quite as successful as the more specialized individuals (see Wilson, 1994).

≡≡≡ ## *Adaptive Trade-offs between High and Low Levels of the HEXACO Personality Factors*

A little later on in this chapter, we will consider how the mechanisms of the fluctuating optimum and of frequency dependence could maintain variation in each of the major dimensions of personality (see also Ashton & Lee, 2001, 2007). But first, we should consider the more basic question of what costs and benefits might be associated with high or low levels of each dimension. In other words, what are the "trade-offs" involved for each personality factor, as judged in terms of how a high or a low level might influence one's chances of survival and reproductive success? These advantages and disadvantages are discussed below (and summarized in Table 7-1) for each of the six "HEXACO" factors as described in Chapter 3. Keep in mind, however, that this discussion does not necessarily apply to the situation that currently exists in modern societies. Instead, it is meant to apply to the situations that existed in the prehistoric and historic environments in which evolution by natural selection would have operated on our ancestors.

Honesty–Humility

The traits that belong to the Honesty–Humility factor include sincerity, fairness, modesty, and lack of greed (see Table 3-6). A common element of these traits seems to be a tendency not to exploit or take advantage of others: For example, a sincere person tends to avoid manipulating or deceiving others, a fair person tends to avoid cheating or stealing from

TABLE 7-1
Summary of Theoretical Interpretations of HEXACO Personality Factors

Factor	Interpretation	Benefits of high levels?	Costs of high levels?
Honesty–Humility	Reciprocal altruism (fairness)	Gains from cooperation (mutual help and nonaggression)	Loss of potential gains that would result from exploitation of others
Agreeableness (versus Anger)	Reciprocal altruism (tolerance)	Gains from cooperation (mutual help and nonaggression)	Losses due to being exploited by others
Emotionality	Kin altruism	Survival of kin (especially offspring); personal survival (especially as favors kin survival)	Loss of potential gains associated with risks to self and kin
Extraversion	Engagement in social endeavors	Social gains (i.e., friends, mates, allies)	Energy and time; risks from social environment
Conscientiousness	Engagement in task-related endeavors	Material gains (i.e., improved use of resources), reduced risks	Energy and time
Openness to Experience	Engagement in idea-related endeavors	Material and social gains (i.e., resulting from discovery)	Energy and time; risks from social and natural environment

Sources: Ashton and Lee (2001), Ashton, Lee, and Paunonen (2002), Lee and Ashton (2004), Ashton and Lee (2007).

others, a modest person tends not to feel entitled to exploit others, and a person who is not greedy tends not to feel tempted to gain at others' expense.

As explained in this way, the potential costs and benefits of having high or low levels of Honesty–Humility might be imagined (see Table 7-1). A person with a very high level of Honesty–Humility would be unwilling to exploit others even if he or she could surely get away with doing so; therefore, such a person would forgo any of the gains that might be had by taking advantage of others. But, on the other hand, a person high in Honesty–Humility would not create any victims, and therefore would avoid the risk of retaliation (including withdrawal of future cooperation) by those victims. At the opposite end of the dimension, a person with a very low level of Honesty–Humility would sometimes gain by exploiting others, but would sometimes lose the potential gains from future cooperation with others, because those exploited persons would be likely to retaliate by ending their cooperation.

Agreeableness

The traits that belong to the Agreeableness factor include forgiveness, gentleness, flexibility, and patience (see Table 3-6). A common element of these traits seems to be a tendency to continue cooperating (or to resume cooperating) with others who might have exploited one in some way: For example, a forgiving person tends not to hold a grudge for past injustices, a gentle person tends not to retaliate harshly, a flexible person tends to cooperate despite some degree of unfairness, and a patient person tends not to become angry at the first sign of exploitation.

As explained in this way, the potential costs and benefits of having high or low levels of Agreeableness might be imagined (see Table 7-1). A person with a very high level of Agreeableness would be likely to continue cooperating with others even when it is likely that he or she is being exploited; therefore, such a person would incur some costs due to being taken advantage of by others. But, on the other hand, a person high in Agreeableness would gain from future cooperation with someone who might not *really* have been trying to exploit him or her (it is not always obvious, after all), or who might usually be cooperative rather than exploitative. At the opposite end of the dimension, a person with a very low level of Agreeableness would sometimes gain by avoiding being exploited by others, but would sometimes lose some potential gains that would have been obtained by cooperating with others who usually are rather cooperative.

Emotionality

The traits that belong to the Emotionality factor include fearfulness, anxiety, dependence, and sentimentality. A common element of these traits seems to be a tendency to promote the survival of oneself and one's kin: For example, a fearful person tends to avoid physical dangers, an anxious person tends to worry about potential harms, a dependent person tends to seek help and support in times of need, and a sentimental person tends to feel a sense of empathy and attachment toward one's family and friends. As explained in this way, the potential costs and benefits of having high or low levels of Emotionality might be imagined (see Table 7-1). A person with a very high level of Emotionality would gain in several ways: By avoiding harm to oneself and one's kin, by gaining help for oneself and one's kin, and by being motivated to help one's kin. But, on the other hand, a person high in Emotionality would also lose out on potential gains from any endeavors that involve some threats to the well-being of oneself or one's kin. A person with a very low level of Emotionality (and his or her kin) would be more likely to experience death or serious injury, but would potentially enjoy greater gains as a result of confronting various dangers.

Summary for Honesty–Humility, Agreeableness, and Emotionality: Altruism versus Aggression

Notice that each of the three characteristics described above is thought to involve some trade-off between behavior that is altruistic (or nonaggressive) and behavior that is non-altruistic (or aggressive). In other words, higher levels of these three dimensions are associated with the tendency to help other individuals (or to avoid harming them), as opposed to the tendency to harm other individuals (or to avoid helping them).

In the cases of Honesty–Humility and Agreeableness, the form of altruism that is involved is called *reciprocal altruism* (e.g., Trivers, 1971), because the benefit to the altruistic individual comes from the *reciprocation* of that altruism by the other individual. Although reciprocal altruism can be beneficial for both individuals, it can break down. As described above, a person low in Honesty–Humility will try to exploit the other person. Similarly, a person low in Agreeableness will be too quick to decide that the other person is trying to exploit him or her (see also Perugini, Gallucci, Presaghi, & Ercolani, 2003).

In the case of Emotionality, the form of altruism that is involved is called *kin altruism* (e.g., Hamilton, 1964), because the benefit to the altruistic individual comes from the fact that the other individual is likely to be his or her kin. When those kin are one's own children, then the benefit to one's own reproductive success is obvious. But note that there can also be benefits to an altruistic individual even when he or she helps kin who are *not* his or her own children: Whenever one helps *any* genetic relative to improve his or her chances of survival and reproduction, this might *indirectly* improve one's own reproductive success, because the children of that relative will also carry one's own genes.

According to these explanations, an individual who tends to be very altruistic would be expected to have high levels of Honesty–Humility, of Agreeableness, and of Emotionality; conversely, a person who tends to be very aggressive would be expected to have low levels of all three of those dimensions. Some evidence suggests that this is indeed the case: In lexical studies of personality structure, adjectives suggesting an overall altruistic tendency (*sympathetic, softhearted*, etc.) tend to divide their loadings across these factors, and questionnaire scales assessing altruistic (versus aggressive) tendencies show moderate correlations with each of the three dimensions (Lee & Ashton, 2006a).

BOX 7-1

Sex Differences in Personality Traits: The Emotionality Factor

For most personality traits, there are only small differences between the average man and the average woman. But some moderately large differences are observed for traits within the Emotionality factor: More than 70% of women (but less than 30% of men) have an above-average level of Emotionality; conversely, more than 70% of men (but less than 30% of women) have a below-average level of Emotionality. This sex difference in the Emotionality factor might be explained by the interpretation of Emotionality as a dimension that influences kin altruism (Ashton & Lee, 2007).

There are several reasons why we might expect kin altruistic tendencies to be stronger on average in women than in men. Consider the case of parenting:

Having a child imposes a heavier biological cost on women than on men, because it is women who undergo pregnancy, childbirth, and lactation. Also, a woman can be certain as to which children are her biological children and which children are not, whereas this is not always the case for a man. And throughout the human evolutionary past, the survival of a child has depended more heavily on the survival of its mother than of its father.

Several researchers have explained sex differences in Emotionality-related personality traits in terms of kin altruism and "investment" in one's children. For example, fearfulness of physical dangers (Campbell, 1999) and willingness to ask others for help (Taylor et al., 2000) are likely to improve the chances of personal and offspring survival, and feelings of emotional attachment and empathy are likely to motivate one to care for one's children. All of these tendencies belong to the Emotionality factor of personality.

Extraversion

The traits that belong to the Extraversion factor include social self-esteem, social boldness, sociability, and liveliness. A common element of these traits seems to be a tendency to engage actively in *social* endeavors: For example, a person with high social self-esteem feels that he or she is popular, a socially bold person tends to lead others and to state opinions, a sociable person tends to make friends and to interact frequently with them, and a lively person tends to exhibit cheerfulness and enthusiasm. As explained in this way, the potential costs and benefits of having high or low levels of Extraversion might be imagined (see Table 7-1). A person with a very high level of Extraversion would tend to gain and hold the attention of other people, and would thereby have an advantage in gaining friends and allies, and also in attracting a desirable mate (or mates). But on the other hand, a person with a high level of Extraversion would also expend a great deal of energy by engaging actively in social endeavors, and might also be the target of some hostility from other people, who might dislike that person's attention-drawing behavior or resent the attention being paid by others to that person.

Conscientiousness

The traits that belong to the Conscientiousness factor include organization, diligence, perfectionism, and prudence (or caution). A common element of these traits seems to be a tendency to engage actively in *task-related* endeavors: For example, an organized person tends to arrange his or her physical surroundings, a diligent person tends to work hard and long, a perfectionistic person pays thorough attention to details, and a prudent person thinks through options carefully. As explained in this way, the potential costs and benefits of having high or low levels of Conscientiousness might be imagined (see Table 7-1). A person with a very high level of Conscientiousness would tend to perform many important tasks efficiently and accurately, and would thereby potentially gain material advantages. (In earlier times, "material advantages" would mean a better food supply, better clothing and shelter, and better safety from impending dangers; nowadays, material advantages would mean making money and staying healthy.) But, on the other hand, a person with a high level of Conscientiousness would also expend a great deal of energy by engaging actively in task-related endeavors, and these endeavors might not always yield worthwhile rewards.

Openness to Experience

The traits that belong to the Openness to Experience factor include aesthetic appreciation, inquisitiveness, creativity, and unconventionality. A common element of these traits seems to be a tendency to engage actively in *idea-related* endeavors: For example, an aesthetically appreciative person tends to contemplate artistic or natural beauty, an inquisitive person tends to search for understanding of the human or natural world, a creative person tends to generate new ideas and new solutions, and an unconventional person tends to be receptive to people and ideas that are new or strange. As explained in this way, the potential costs and benefits of having high or low levels of Openness to Experience might be imagined (see Table 7-1). A person with a very high level of Openness to Experience would tend to discover, learn, and invent new things that would then be useful in social or task-related endeavors. But, on the other hand, a person with a high level of Openness to Experience would also expend a great deal of energy by engaging actively in idea-related endeavors. Moreover, these endeavors might also involve some risks, to the extent that one's new ideas and discoveries are in fact mistaken or dangerous, or tend to elicit hostility from more conventional persons.

Summary for Extraversion, Conscientiousness, and Openness to Experience: Engagement in Areas of Endeavor

Thus, the three personality dimensions of this second set described above are all associated with some contrast between high and low levels of engagement, but each within its own area of endeavor. That is, higher levels of each of these three dimensions are associated with being, in some sense, more "activated" or "involved." There is not yet any biological evidence to show whether or not this is in fact the case, but it will be interesting to see the results of future research studies that examine the biological bases of the Extraversion, Conscientiousness, and Openness to Experience factors. Presumably, such investigations could test the idea that each of these three dimensions involves a greater intensity of some kind, such as (perhaps) the energy consumption of the body or brain.

BOX 7-2
Adaptive Trade-offs from the Perspective of the Big Five Personality Dimensions

The discussions given above and in Table 7-1 regarding the adaptive trade-offs of personality variation were described in terms of the six HEXACO personality dimensions. However, these trade-offs can also be considered from the perspective of the Big Five personality dimensions, as has recently been done by Nettle (2006). (For further interesting discussions, see also Buss, 1996; Hogan, 1996; MacDonald, 1995, 1998.)

Recall from Chapter 3 that the Big Five factors of Extraversion, Conscientiousness, and Openness to Experience (or Intellect/Imagination) are very similar to the same-named factors of the HEXACO model. Therefore, interpretations of the costs and benefits for any of these factors should be applicable regardless of which model is considered. In general, the discussion of these factors as given by Nettle (2006) is similar to that given in this chapter (see also Ashton & Lee, 2001, 2007; Ashton et al., 2002). But some of the potential costs and benefits suggested by Nettle for these factors are different from those

discussed in this chapter. For example, Nettle suggested that high levels of Openness to Experience tend to be attractive to potential mates, but that high Openness is also associated with increased risk of some mental disorders, particularly schizophrenia and other delusional disorders.

With regard to the Big Five Agreeableness factor, Nettle's (2006) interpretation is similar to the interpretations that are given in this chapter (and in Ashton & Lee, 2001, 2007) for the HEXACO Agreeableness and Honesty–Humility factors. For Big Five Neuroticism (i.e., low Emotional Stability), Nettle suggested that high levels have some benefits, such as avoidance of dangers as well as competitive success, but also some costs, such as the illnesses and relationship problems caused by excessive stress. The suggestion that Neuroticism is associated with avoidance of dangers is consistent with the interpretation of Emotionality as given here; however, most evidence suggests that Neuroticism is associated with less, not more, competitive success (e.g., Judge, Higgins, Thoresen, & Barrick, 1999). Nevertheless, the interpretations proposed by Nettle provide some interesting hypotheses regarding the costs and benefits of the Big Five personality factors.

The Operation of the Fluctuating Optimum and Frequency Dependence: Some Examples

On the basis of the preceding interpretations, it is possible to speculate on ways in which the mechanisms of the fluctuating optimum or of frequency dependence might maintain variation in the major personality factors. Let us consider some of the more likely possibilities, considering each of the dimensions in turn.

Honesty–Humility and Agreeableness

First, let us consider how frequency dependence might maintain variation in the factors of Honesty–Humility and Agreeableness. To start, try to imagine a society in which everyone had very high levels of Honesty–Humility and of Agreeableness. This sounds too good to be true, and it probably is. To understand why, imagine what would happen if a few people low in Honesty–Humility were suddenly to appear (whether by being born, or by moving in, or by "going bad"). Those persons would be easily able to make important gains by exploiting other people, because other people's high levels of Agreeableness (and Honesty–Humility) would leave them as very soft targets—as "suckers." That is, the low Honesty–Humility people might have an important advantage in gaining material resources and social status.

As a result of this intrusion of persons low in Honesty–Humility, two things would happen. First, the advantages gained by those low Honesty–Humility individuals would tend to give them greater "fitness" (in the evolutionary sense of achieving greater reproductive success). Therefore, the proportion of low Honesty–Humility people within the society would tend to increase over the generations. Second, now that some people are exploiting others, there would likely be some advantage to being low in Agreeableness, because this would make one less susceptible to being exploited by the low Honesty–Humility people. Therefore, as a result of the fitness advantage for low Agreeableness persons, levels of Agreeableness would also become lower over the generations.

Notice, however, that these trends toward lower Honesty–Humility and lower Agreeableness would not continue forever. At some point, when there were many people low in Honesty–Humility, the lower levels of that dimension would no longer be advantageous. This would happen for two reasons: First, there would be too much "competition" among the many low Honesty–Humility people in trying to take advantage of others—that is, there would not be enough "victims" to support them. Also, the lower levels of Agreeableness in the society would mean that there would be fewer people who would be easily exploited. As a result, persons low in Honesty–Humility would no longer have higher levels of fitness than would persons high in Honesty–Humility. Instead, high Honesty–Humility persons would be able to gain benefits from cooperating with others, and those benefits would be just as good as those gained by low Honesty–Humility persons from exploiting others. In this way, a balance would be reached between low and high levels of Honesty–Humility.

At the same time, there would no longer be any fitness advantage for low Agreeableness people over high Agreeableness people. That is, even though low Agreeableness would tend to prevent one from being exploited by others, it would also tend to prevent one from cooperating with others. At some point, there would be a balance between the gains from cooperating with others and costs of occasionally being exploited by others. In this way, a balance would also be reached between low and high levels of Agreeableness.

Notice that this process would also work in the opposite direction: If we had started with a society in which everyone was very low in Honesty–Humility and in Agreeableness, then a few persons high in Honesty–Humility would gain a fitness advantage by cooperating with each other. This would then lead to fitness advantages for persons high in Agreeableness, because the increasing numbers of people high in Honesty–Humility would mean more opportunities for cooperation and fewer risks of being exploited. But the levels of Honesty–Humility and Agreeableness would not be able to increase forever: As described before, a society with very high levels of Honesty–Humility and Agreeableness would not be able to last for very long.

According to the preceding scenarios, frequency dependence will likely prevent the levels of Honesty–Humility or of Agreeableness from becoming extremely high or extremely low within any given society. But this does not mean that the overall level of each of these characteristics must be the same across all times and places. Instead, the fluctuating optimum mechanism might also operate, with the result that higher or lower average levels might be favored. Let us consider some examples.

Some researchers (e.g., Cohen, 1996; Cohen, Nisbett, Bowdle, & Schwarz, 1996; Nisbett, 1993) have suggested that societies whose economies were traditionally based on raising livestock (such as sheep or cattle) tend to be more violent than do societies whose economies were traditionally based on raising crops (such as wheat, corn, rice, or potatoes). Why would this be the case? As discussed by Cohen and by Nisbett, there exists a much greater opportunity for major thefts within a livestock-based, "herding" society than within a crop-based, "farming" society. Because sheep and cattle are very mobile, it is relatively easy for a would-be thief to round up large numbers of those animals and to take them away. In contrast, because crops are not mobile, it is very difficult for a would-be thief to take large quantities of those crops; in fact, it would be too much work to try to harvest the crops and then to carry them away. As a result of this situation, there exists a much greater temptation to commit theft within a herding society than within a farming society, as well as a much greater motivation to retaliate against thieves and to intimidate or deter potential thieves. (After all, the prospect of having all one's cattle or sheep taken away is extremely serious in a herding society.)

This hypothesis was developed in an effort to explain the widespread observation that herding societies place an emphasis on revenge and on retaliation even for minor insults; historically, such societies tend to have more numerous (and deadlier) "feuds" between families, and even today tend to have higher rates of homicide related to personal confrontations and arguments (e.g., Cohen, 1996; Cohen *et al.*, 1996; Nisbett, 1993). Again, the origin of these tendencies is thought to be the serious threat of theft that exists in a herding society: In order to protect one's livestock, it is important to demonstrate to others that one can and will defend oneself, and therefore one is more likely to fight when insulted or offended in some way. In contrast, such tendencies would be counterproductive within a farming society: Given that there is little risk of one's livelihood being stolen, there is little need to demonstrate a willingness to retaliate against exploitation. Instead, a more tolerant, cooperative attitude tends to be more successful within a farming-based society.

Another example of how there may exist a fluctuating optimum level of traits related to Agreeableness and Honesty–Humility is provided by hunter-gatherer societies. A study by Cashdan (1980) investigated the amount of cooperative behavior observed in different bands of the Bushman (or San) people, who inhabit the Kalahari desert of southwestern Africa. Some of the Bushman bands live primarily by hunting various game animals, especially antelope, whereas other Bushman bands live primarily by gathering edible plant foods, especially mongongo nuts. This is an important difference, because the way in which food is obtained has important implications for the consistency of the food supply. For bands that live mainly by gathering, the food supply tends to be rather stable from one day or week to the next: Each day, every family can collect enough nuts for itself, and there is no need to try to get any more. But for bands that live mainly by hunting, the food supply is much more variable: Some days, a given family might not be successful in catching any game, but on other days, that family might kill an animal far too big to be eaten before the meat becomes rotten. As a result of this difference in the stability of the food supply, there exists a greater need for cooperation—that is, for mutual sharing— within the hunting bands than within the gathering bands. Because the members of the gathering bands can each look after their own food supplies, there is little need to develop a strong readiness to share with others. But because the members of the hunting bands will sometimes have too much food, and sometimes too little, a readiness to share becomes very important: The hunter who was successful yesterday shares the meat from his kill with the hunter who was unsuccessful, but tomorrow the roles may well be reversed.

Emotionality

Variation in the Emotionality dimension is also likely to be maintained in part by fluctuating optimum levels of its defining traits. Consider the implications of high levels of Emotionality in different environments. First, suppose that in one environment, there are some dangers that may threaten oneself and one's kin, but that it is possible to avoid these dangers, and that there are few gains to be made by confronting those dangers (or by allowing one's kin to confront them). In this environment, an individual who is high in Emotionality—that is, someone who tends to be deeply concerned about the well-being of one's kin (and about one's own security)—is likely to improve the chances of survival of one's kin. But now consider a different environment, in which there are either (a) few dangers of any kind, or (b) dangers that cannot be avoided, or (c) dangers that also present the possibility of great potential gains. In any of these cases, a high level of Emotionality is unlikely to improve the chances of survival of one's kin very much; in fact, high Emotionality could actually reduce those chances, by leading one to avoid risks that could yield important gains.

A couple of hypothetical (and not very likely) examples may help to illustrate the preceding contrasts. Imagine some people living in some prehistoric environments in which there are very poisonous snakes that frequently bite (and kill) people. But suppose that in one area, the chances of deadly snakebites can be minimized by staying far away (and by keeping one's children far away) from certain species of trees that those snakes inhabit—species of trees that do not, in any case, provide anything useful to people. In this environment, a high level of Emotionality would tend to keep one and one's kin away from those trees (and hence from the snakes), and would improve the chances that one and one's kin would survive. Therefore, levels of Emotionality would tend to increase over the generations within this environment.

Now suppose that in another area, the species of tree that is inhabited by the deadly snakes is the same species that provides some fruits or nuts that are an important supplement to the people's diet. In this environment, a high level of Emotionality would not necessarily improve the chances of survival for oneself or one's kin, because the avoidance of those trees would mean a somewhat lower food intake and hence reduced strength and health. Or alternatively, suppose that in yet another area, the snakes are distributed throughout the entire environment, and are almost undetectable. (You were warned that this example was not very likely.) In such an environment, a high level of Emotionality would not contribute to the chances for survival of oneself or one's kin, because no amount of fearfulness or of care for one's kin would reduce the chances of deadly snakebites; in fact, high Emotionality might distract from gaining food or from other important tasks. Therefore, in either of these two latter environments, levels of Emotionality would tend to decrease over the generations.

In reality, of course, the environments of different geographical areas would probably not differ so sharply in the avoidability of their dangers or in the benefits associated with confronting those dangers. Moreover, the environment of any one area would tend to change across the long time periods of many generations. But the preceding example can show how the features of an environment might tend to favor higher or lower levels of Emotionality. In any case, perhaps a more plausible example can be taken from some research by a cultural anthropologist (Gilmore, 1990). According to Gilmore, the men of the Pacific island of Truk tend to value toughness a great deal, whereas this is not so much the case for the men of the Pacific island of Tahiti. Gilmore noted that the men of Truk traditionally had to make a living by fishing in deep, open, shark-infested waters far from their home island, and that bravery and toughness were therefore considered to be important traits. In contrast, Gilmore noted, the men of Tahiti had traditionally been able to make a living by fishing in the safe waters of their own lagoons (and by doing other nonrisky work), and that there was therefore no special demand for low-Emotionality traits such as bravery and toughness.

Extraversion

Frequency dependence may also play an important role in maintaining individual differences in Extraversion over the long term (see Ashton *et al.*, 2002). Consider a society in which people are all very introverted: An extraverted person would tend to attract a great deal of social attention, and would likely be a popular choice as a friend, an ally, and a mate. Thus, extraverts would potentially have high reproductive success when dispersed among large numbers of introverted persons. But over the generations, the proportion of extraverted individuals would increase, and as a result of the decreased uniqueness of extraverted people, the social attractiveness of any one extraverted person would no longer be so great. At some point, the benefits enjoyed by extraverts in terms of their ability to attract positive social attention could become rather small, and even small enough to be outweighed by the costs of the greater energy and risks involved in being an extravert. The result would be that extraverts would no longer tend to have higher reproductive success than introverts, and the overall level of this dimension would reach a balance within the population.[9]

---

[9] Likewise, if a population started out with a very high proportion of extraverted persons, then introverts might enjoy better reproductive success as a result of the intense competition among extraverts.

As was the case for Agreeableness and Honesty–Humility, it is plausible that variation in Extraversion is also preserved by fluctuating optimum levels of this dimension across different environments. In fact, there seem to be some differences across cultures in the typical level of Extraversion. For example, there is a widespread perception that people from northern European countries (e.g., Finland, Iceland) are less extraverted on average than are people from southern European countries (e.g., Greece, Spain), and that people from East Asian countries tend to be less extraverted on average than are people of other countries. Even if these perceptions are assumed to be accurate, it is not clear what features of the environment might be responsible for those differences. Is there something about, say, the length of the winter season at northern latitudes, or the growing of rice as opposed to other crops, that makes a society more introverted? These are interesting questions to be addressed in future research.

Conscientiousness

The fluctuating optimum mechanism may also serve to preserve variation in levels of Conscientiousness. Specifically, in a time and place in which being organized and hard-working tend to pay off in terms of gaining the resources needed to survive and reproduce, high Conscientiousness will be favored. However, in a time and place in which those characteristics are not needed for survival and reproduction, low Conscientiousness will be favored, because energy invested in task-related efforts will be wasted.

A possible example of this has been suggested by Flynn (1991), who suggested that nineteenth-century Chinese-American immigrants tended to be more hardworking than did Irish-American immigrants of the same period. Flynn suggested that agriculture in the areas of southern China from which the Chinese had emigrated had demanded very intense work, because it was based on the cultivation of a rice crop that demanded careful year-round attention and (if grown successfully) could produce a useful surplus for storage. In contrast, according to Flynn, agriculture in Ireland had not demanded so much work, because it was based on a potato crop that required little attention during most of the year, and could not in any case produce a useful surplus because of the tendency for potatoes to rot.

It is not known whether or not Flynn's hypothesis is correct, but it gives an interesting example of the way in which the fluctuating optimum might operate. Note that, if the economic activities of southern China or of Ireland were to change from the patterns of the late nineteenth century, then there might be a resulting change in the levels of Conscientiousness-related characteristics of the people of those areas. Certainly, Ireland in the early twenty-first century—like southern China—has seen rapid economic growth and modernization, so it is likely that the difference observed by Flynn would not be so prominent today.

Openness to Experience

The influence of fluctuating optimum levels of a trait might be important in relation to aspects of the Openness to Experience dimension. Some researchers have suggested that the tendency to explore and to seek new and different surroundings is likely to be more adaptive in some environments than in others. Chen, Burton, Greenberger, and Dmitrieva (1999) proposed that these novelty-seeking characteristics would be beneficial for people who lived as nomadic hunters, because such traits would encourage those people to keep moving in search of better hunting grounds. In contrast, Chen *et al.* suggested high levels of novelty seeking would not be suitable for sedentary farmers, because such traits would distract those people from the day-to-day routine of tending their crops and animals. Chen *et al.* also proposed that high novelty seeking would be especially important for people who were undertaking long-distance migrations, because these traits would again facilitate the search for better places to live.[10]

Chen *et al.* (1999) tested their hypotheses, by comparing a variety of human ethnic groups in terms of the frequencies of alleles of a gene that regulates levels of the neurotransmitter dopamine, which is thought to be implicated in novelty-seeking traits (see Chapter 5). Consistent with their hypotheses, Chen *et al.* found high levels of the high-dopamine (and hence, high novelty seeking) alleles in nomadic South American Indian hunters, but low levels of these alleles in Chinese people (who were descended from many generations of farmers in China). Another finding reported by Chen *et al.* was that South American Indian farmers had intermediate levels of those alleles. This result was also consistent with the hypotheses, because these farmers' ancestors had undertaken a long-distance migration relatively recently. (You might already know that the native people of the Americas are believed to have migrated from Siberia during the last ice age, perhaps not much more than 12,000 years ago.) Thus, according to Chen *et al.*, these South American Indian farmers would have been expected to be higher in the novelty-seeking-related gene than the Chinese farmers, although not as high as the South American Indian hunters.

Other recent research has compared the levels of Openness to Experience in groups of people who inhabit areas that would be expected to differ in the optimal level of this dimension. Camperio Ciani, Capiluppi, Veronese, and Sartori (2007) obtained personality self-reports from people who live on small islands off the coast of Italy and from people who live on the mainland of Italy. The main finding reported by Camperio Ciani *et al.* was that the islanders tended to be lower in Openness to Experience than were the mainlanders. In addition, the researchers also found that people whose ancestors had stayed on the islands for many generations tended to be lower in Openness to Experience than were people who had recently moved away from the islands. Camperio Ciani *et al.* suggested that life on the islands tends to be somewhat repetitive, and that people who are less interested in exploration or in variety are more likely to stay on the islands rather than to move away.

---

[10] Chen *et al.* (1999) were referring to migrations of the kind that people used to do before the modern age, by traveling on foot or perhaps on horseback or in small boats. Nowadays, when long-distance moves are usually done by airplane or at least by an ocean liner, the importance of novelty-seeking characteristics is probably smaller.

Summary and Conclusions

In this chapter, we began with an overview of the process of evolution by natural selection, and then proceeded to the question of why the variation among people in their levels of personality characteristics has persisted across evolutionary time. Two main reasons why this variation has not disappeared were described in some detail: First, the ideal levels of characteristics tend to vary across different times and places (the "fluctuating optimum"); and second, when most people have a high level of a characteristic, there may be advantages to having a low level, and vice versa ("frequency-dependence").

Each of the major dimensions of personality can be discussed in terms of the likely advantages and disadvantages associated with higher or lower levels. These trade-offs can be summarized as follows. For Honesty–Humility, high levels allow gains from cooperation, whereas low levels may provide gains by exploiting others. For Agreeableness, high levels allow gains from cooperation, whereas low levels may prevent losses that would result from being exploited by others. For Emotionality, high levels reduce risks of harm to one's kin (both directly and by avoiding harm to oneself), but low levels allow potential

---

BOX 7-3
Cross-Generational and Cross-National Differences in Mean Levels of Personality Traits

As described in this chapter, the mechanisms of frequency dependence and the fluctuating optimum have different implications for variation across times and places in the mean levels of personality traits. Frequency dependence tends to make the mean levels similar, whereas the fluctuating optimum tends to make the mean levels different according to the conditions in a given time and place.

Perhaps we could get some idea of the relative influence of these mechanisms by examining how much variation there is between generations and between countries in the average levels of various personality traits. If the differences are large, then the fluctuating optimum would appear to be the stronger influence, but if the differences are small, then frequency dependence would appear to be stronger.

One complication in making these comparisons, however, involves the self-report questionnaire scales that are often used in measuring personality. When people provide self-reports on the items of these scales, their responses are likely based to some

extent on comparisons between him or her and the other members of his or her society. But if people tend to judge their own personalities by comparing themselves with the personalities of the people around them, then this would tend to conceal any differences between generations or between countries. For example, in a country of very quiet people, the average person might *not* describe himself or herself as being particularly quiet, because he or she seems average within that society; the same pattern would be observed in a country of very noisy people. As a result, there might appear to be no difference between the two countries when self-report questionnaire scales are considered, even though an outside observer would notice that the people of one country were much quieter than the people of the other country.

Another complication involving comparisons of the mean levels of personality traits across generations or across countries is due to people's "styles" of responding to personality questionnaire scales. If there are differences between generations or between countries in the tendency to give socially desirable responses to self-report (or observer report) statements, then this might give the appearance of differences in personality even if these do not really exist.

(continues)

For example, if people in one country tend to give less socially desirable responses than do people in other countries—independently of any real differences in behavior—then the people of that country will appear to be different in personality from the people of other countries, even though there might not be any real difference. One example of this has been observed already: McCrae, Yik, Trapnell, Bond, and Paulhus (1998) found that Chinese immigrants to Canada tended to give less socially desirable self-reports and observer reports than did Canadian-born people of Chinese ancestry.

Keeping these warnings in mind, it is still interesting to note the findings so far regarding differences in mean personality trait levels between age cohorts and between countries. Evidence from self-report (and observer report) personality questionnaires suggests that differences between countries in the average levels of various personality characteristics tend to be rather small. Even when countries with the highest and lowest levels of various traits are considered, the differences are usually not much more than one standard deviation unit in size (see McCrae, 2002, p. 112). Moreover, the differences that are observed tend *not* to correspond to commonly

held perceptions or stereotypes of national differences in personality (McCrae & Terracciano, 2006). One broad pattern of findings is that persons from Western countries tend to have higher levels of Extraversion, on average, than do people from Asian or African countries; however, there is some evidence that when people from the latter countries immigrate to the West, their average levels of Extraversion tend to increase (McCrae *et al.*, 1998).

With regard to differences between generations, self-report data from the United States suggest that people became considerably more anxious and more extraverted between the 1960s and 1990s. Increases of nearly one standard deviation unit have been reported for these characteristics (Twenge, 2000, 2001), although data from the Jackson Personality Inventory (Jackson, 1994) suggest much smaller increases.

Results such as those described here have given some useful information about cross-generational and cross-cultural differences in mean levels of personality characteristics. Future research will likely be aimed at obtaining other kinds of personality data—such as direct observations or "biodata"—as a way of testing the validity of findings based on self- and observer reports.

BOX 7-4
How "Old" Are Personality Characteristics? Evidence from Studies of Animal Personality

Some of the trade-offs between high and low levels of various personality characteristics are probably very old in their evolutionary history. For most of the major dimensions of personality, fluctuating optimum levels and frequency dependence have likely operated for many thousands of generations, and perhaps even before humans had evolved into their modern form. Some support for this suggestion comes from research on the personalities of the great apes (chimpanzees, bonobos, gorillas, and orangutans), with whom humans shared a common ancestral species perhaps about 13 million years ago. Several studies have assessed apes' personalities using human observers' ratings of many individual apes of a given species.

Those investigations have shown that apes' personalities can be rated with high levels of interobserver reliability, and that the factor structure of apes' personality characteristics is roughly similar to that of human beings (e.g., King & Figueredo, 1997; Weiss, King, & Perkins, 2006). But some other research suggests that human personality dimensions can also be reliably assessed among dogs (Gosling, Kwan, & John, 2003)—a result that is unlikely to surprise many dog owners—and this would suggest an extremely old history for personality characteristics, given that the common ancestral species of dogs and humans existed tens of millions of years ago. However, it is not at all clear that nonhuman animals can be meaningfully described in terms of every personality dimension. To take just one example, some aspects of the Openness to Experience dimension (e.g., intellectual curiosity) might not really describe individual differences in nonhuman species.

gains associated with those risks. For Extraversion, Conscientiousness, and Openness to Experience, high levels may produce social or material gains from "investing" one's time and energy in social, task-related, or idea-related endeavors, respectively; however, low levels avoid the energy costs and (in some cases) the risks associated with those endeavors.

Finally, we examined how the fluctuating optimum and frequency dependence could operate in maintaining the wide variation that is observed among people in each of the preceding dimensions. Social scientists have already documented several cases in which the typical levels of some traits may be very different across place and time. However, our understanding of this area is still sketchy, and much more systematic research will be needed to improve our knowledge of it.

Chapter 8

Personality Disorders

The Idea of a Personality Disorder   163
The DSM-IV Personality Disorders   165
   Schizoid   165
   Schizotypal   165
   Paranoid   166
   Antisocial   166
   Borderline   166
   Histrionic   167
   Narcissistic   167
   Avoidant   167
   Dependent   167
   Obsessive-Compulsive   168
Classifying the DSM-IV Personality
   Disorders: Clusters A, B, and C   168
Disorders Considered for Inclusion in
   DSM-IV but Rejected   169
   Depressive   169
   Passive-Aggressive (Negativistic)   170

Self-Defeating   170
Sadistic   170
Other Personality-Related Disorders Not
   Included as DSM-IV Personality
   Disorders   171
   Attention-Deficit/Hyperactivity Disorder   171
   Separation Anxiety Disorder   172
   Oppositional Defiant Disorder   172
   Specific Phobias   173
   Summary   174
Problems with the Concept of Personality
   Disorders   174
Alternative Systems for Personality
   Disorder Diagnosis   176
Origins of Personality Disorders:
   Development, Biological Bases,
   Heredity and Environment, and
   Evolutionary Function   178
Summary and Conclusions   179

The Idea of a Personality Disorder

In previous chapters, we have described personality variation as if all levels of all personality characteristics were about equally adaptive. From an evolutionary perspective, this is probably fairly accurate, because the persistence of personality variation suggests that both higher levels and lower levels of any given characteristic have been equally successful overall. That is, from the perspective of survival and reproduction, the costs and benefits associated with a particular level of a certain trait have tended to balance each other out over the long run.

But in another important sense, the different levels of personality characteristics are far from being equally adaptive. If we consider the influence of an individual's personality on his or her own sense of well-being—or on the well-being of persons who interact with that individual—then some personalities clearly seem better than others, and some personalities seem downright harmful. This is certainly the view held by people who work in mental health settings, such as psychiatrists and clinical psychologists, who consider some personality characteristics as being maladaptive enough to be called *personality disorders*. Mental health professionals view personality disorders as stable and enduring patterns of thought, feeling, and behavior—that is, as personality traits—that emerge in adolescence or early adulthood, that deviate from the norms of one's culture, that are pervasive and inflexible across many aspects of one's life, and that lead to distress or impairment (American Psychiatric Association, 1994). The last of these aspects of personality disorder is especially important, insofar as a "disorder" of personality must involve some negative consequences for the functioning and the happiness of the individual or of others around him or her.

In this chapter, we will describe the various personality disorders that are currently diagnosed by psychiatrists and clinical psychologists. After describing the features of each disorder, we will describe some related conditions that are not officially classified as personality disorders, but nevertheless share most of the important features of personality disorders. Finally, we will discuss some of the difficulties associated with the definition and diagnosis of personality disorders, and describe some alternative approaches to the classification of personality-related problems.

We will begin by describing the 10 personality disorders that are included in the reference book that is used by psychiatrists and clinical psychologists—the *Diagnostic and Statistical Manual of Mental Disorders*, Volume IV (DSM-IV; American Psychiatric Association, 1994). These 10 disorders (see Table 8-1) are classified into three groups or clusters according to the similarity of their symptoms. We will describe these clusters later in the chapter, but as we will also note, there are some problems with these groupings.

But even before we begin describing the disorders, one note of caution: When reading about these disorders, you may notice that some of the descriptions are reminiscent of your own personality or of the personalities of people you know well. But keep in mind that this will be true of virtually everyone, because most of the disorders involve characteristics that are found to varying extents in most people. It is only when these tendencies are especially extreme, and interfere with the person's functioning, that a personality disorder would be diagnosed. For most disorders, only about 1 or 2% of the population would be diagnosed as having the disorder, and even for the most common disorders the rate would be about 4% (Mattia & Zimmerman, 2001). In total, less than 15% of the population would be diagnosed as having one or more of the 10 disorders listed in the DSM-IV. To be diagnosed with a personality disorder, one would need to be diagnosed with several of the specific symptoms—usually most of the symptoms—that are associated with that disorder.

TABLE 8-1
Brief Descriptions of the DSM-IV Personality Disorders

Cluster and disorder	Description
Cluster A ("odd, eccentric")	
Schizoid	Extreme detachment and lack of interest in social or personal relationships
Schizotypal	Discomfort in close relationships, combined with eccentric behaviors and thoughts
Paranoid	Extreme distrust and suspiciousness of others
Cluster B ("dramatic, emotional, erratic")	
Antisocial	Disregard for and violation of the rights of others
Borderline	Extreme impulsivity and instability of relationships, self-image, and emotions
Histrionic	Excessive attention seeking and exaggerated expression of emotions
Narcissistic	Excessive sense of self-importance and entitlement
Cluster C ("anxious, fearful")	
Avoidant	Extreme shyness, low self-esteem, and fear of rejection
Dependent	Excessive need to be taken care of, with submissive and clinging behavior
Obsessive-compulsive	Excessive preoccupation with order, perfection, and control

Source: American Psychiatric Association (1994).

The DSM-IV Personality Disorders

Schizoid

Schizoid personality disorder involves an extreme degree of detachment from social relationships and a very limited expression of emotions in interpersonal settings (American Psychiatric Association, 1994). Schizoid individuals are not interested in family relationships, friendships, or sexual relationships, and instead prefer almost always to be alone. This social isolation is accompanied by emotional detachment, as the schizoid person expresses no affection for others and is indifferent to their praise or criticism. Even in the nonsocial settings that are preferred by the schizoid individual, he or she feels little joy or pleasure.

Schizotypal

Like the schizoid personality disorder described above, the schizotypal personality disorder also involves detachment from social relationships. But schizotypal personality disorder also involves an extreme discomfort with such relationships, and a pattern of odd thinking and eccentric behaviors (American Psychiatric Association, 1994). For example, the schizotypal individual may have unusual "ideas of reference," whereby he or she perceives a special personal meaning in everyday events or objects (such as billboard signs, television commercials, etc.). Similarly, schizotypal persons tend to be highly superstitious or fascinated with the paranormal, and may even have bizarre perceptual experiences, such as "seeing" what is happening somewhere far away. The overall behavior and appearance of the schizotypal person is generally considered by others to be extremely odd, peculiar, or eccentric.

Paranoid

The paranoid personality disorder shares many features with the schizoid and schizotypal disorders, but is characterized by an especially strong suspiciousness of others' motives and by a sense of being persecuted (American Psychiatric Association, 1994). Paranoid individuals suspect without good reason that others are trying to harm, deceive, or exploit them, and tend to dwell on doubts about the loyalty of those around them (this often includes suspicions about a spouse's possible sexual infidelity). They are quick to take offence or to feel insulted even in response to actions or comments that may be entirely innocent, and tend to hold grudges against those perceived as causing harm.

Antisocial

The hallmark of the antisocial personality disorder is a tendency to disregard and to violate the rights of others (American Psychiatric Association, 1994). Antisocial individuals are very deceitful, repeatedly lying to others and "conning" them for personal gain, and feel no remorse for the harm their actions have caused to others.[1] The antisocial person tends to be aggressive (e.g., committing assaults and getting into fights), to be irresponsible (e.g., failing to hold a job or to pay debts), and to be impulsive and reckless (e.g., often putting others at risk).

Borderline

Borderline personality disorder involves extreme instability in one's own self-image and in one's relationships with others, along with extreme impulsivity in various contexts (American Psychiatric Association, 1994).[2] The borderline individual has intense and unstable "love/hate" relationships with others, and tends to worry frantically about the possibility of being abandoned. There is a pattern of impulsive behavior—including drug and alcohol abuse, eating binges, spending sprees, or sexual escapades—and also of self-harming behaviors, including self-mutilation or suicide attempts. The borderline person tends to be extremely moody and temperamental, and has little sense of personal identity or of meaning in life.

---

[1] By the way, many people use the word *antisocial* to describe people who are unsociable, but psychologists instead use antisocial to describe people who harm others.
[2] The name *borderline* refers to the earlier idea among psychiatrists that this disorder was close to the boundary with disorders in which the individual suffers from delusions or hallucinations.

Histrionic

The histrionic personality disorder is characterized by an exaggerated display of emotions and by excessive attention seeking (American Psychiatric Association, 1994). Histrionic individuals have an intense need to be the center of attention, feeling uncomfortable when not the focus of others' attention. They use their physical appearance to draw attention, and have a seductive, sexually provocative style. Histronic persons also have an overly dramatic, exaggerated style of expressing their emotions, but those emotions are shallow and rapidly changing. They tend to be suggestible or easily influenced by others, and tend to consider casual acquaintanceships as being much closer relationships than is actually the case.

Narcissistic

The narcissistic personality disorder involves "grandiosity"—a tendency to consider oneself as a superior individual who deserves the admiration of others—and a selfish lack of concern for others' needs (American Psychiatric Association, 1994).[3] Narcissistic persons see themselves as being entitled to special treatment and admiration, and generally have an arrogant style, often exploiting others and failing to appreciate others' needs. The narcissistic person tends to fantasize about having high status and to envy those who are highly successful.

Avoidant

The avoidant personality disorder is defined by social inhibition and shyness, by feelings of inadequacy, and by oversensitivity to possible negative evaluation (American Psychiatric Association, 1994). Avoidant persons have such strong fears of criticism, disapproval, or rejection that their social interactions are severely restricted: They are unwilling to participate socially unless certain of being liked, and tend to avoid work activities that involve interpersonal contact. In general, there is a sense of low self-esteem and of inferiority along with an extreme sensitivity to embarrassment, criticism, and rejection.

Avoidant personality disorder shares the symptom of lack of social contact with schizoid and schizotypal disorders, but the reasons for that lack of contact are very different: The avoidant person wants social contact but is afraid of rejection, whereas the schizoid or schizotypal person is completely indifferent to such contact.

Dependent

The dependent personality disorder is characterized by an excessive need to be taken care of and by submissive, clinging behavior and fears of separation (American Psychiatric

---

[3] The name of this disorder comes from Narcissus, a figure in Greek mythology who fell in love with his own image as reflected by a pool of water.

Association, 1994). Dependent individuals require a great deal of advice and reassurance even in making everyday decisions, and lack the confidence to undertake projects on their own. They need other people to take responsibility for important features of their lives, and feel unable to take care of themselves when alone. Dependent persons often go to great lengths to maintain the support and nurturance of others—for example, by volunteering to do unpleasant tasks, or by avoiding any expression of disagreement. If a close relationship ends for some reason, the dependent person may desperately seek a new one.

Obsessive-Compulsive

The main features of obsessive-compulsive personality disorder involve preoccupation with orderliness, perfection, and control (American Psychiatric Association, 1994). The obsessive-compulsive person tends to be so preoccupied with details (e.g., lists, schedules) that the entire point of an activity is lost. Similarly, obsessive-compulsive individuals may be so concerned with attaining perfection and following specific rules that they fail to complete their tasks or projects, and fail to delegate any tasks to others. An obsessive-compulsive person tends to put work ahead of personal relationships, and to be highly stubborn and inflexible. There is a tendency to hoard money unnecessarily (rather than spend it) and to hoard objects unnecessarily (rather than discard them).

Note that obsessive-compulsive personality disorder is not the same as the condition known simply as obsessive-compulsive disorder; the latter condition involves repeated behaviors such as hand washing, counting, or tapping, and is not classified as a personality disorder. (The two conditions, however, tend to be related.)

Classifying the DSM-IV Personality Disorders: Clusters A, B, and C

The DSM-IV personality disorders are usually classified into three groups or "clusters." This categorization is not based on results of factor analytic studies, but rather on clinicians' views of the similarities of content among some of the disorders. (As we will discuss later in this chapter, the dimensions that emerge when personality disorder symptoms are factor analyzed are apparently somewhat different.) The three DSM-IV clusters of personality disorders are called cluster A ("odd and eccentric"), cluster B ("dramatic and erratic"), and cluster C ("anxious and fearful"). The disorders that have been categorized within each cluster are listed below (see also Table 8-1).

Cluster A contains the schizoid, schizotypal, and paranoid personality disorders. The disorders classified within this cluster are described as the odd or eccentric disorders, because the behavior of persons diagnosed with these disorders seems strange or unusual.

Cluster B contains the antisocial, borderline, histrionic, and narcissistic personality disorders. The disorders classified within this cluster are described as the dramatic and erratic disorders, because the behavior of persons diagnosed with these disorders seems impulsive and unstable.

Cluster C contains the avoidant, dependent, and obsessive-compulsive personality disorders. The disorders classified within this cluster are described as the anxious and fearful disorders, because the behavior of persons diagnosed with these disorders seems nervous and worried.

Disorders Considered for Inclusion in DSM-IV but Rejected

In addition to the 10 personality disorders that have been recognized in the DSM-IV (American Psychiatric Association, 1994), there are several other personality disorders that have been considered for inclusion. Two of these—the depressive personality disorder and the passive-aggressive (or negativistic) personality disorder—are recently proposed disorders that are described in an appendix to the DSM-IV. These proposed disorders might be incorporated in future editions of the DSM, depending on how much support emerges for the clinical usefulness of these disorders. Similarly, two other disorders—the self-defeating personality disorder and the sadistic personality disorders—had been included in the appendix to the edition of the DSM immediately before DSM-IV (see American Psychiatric Association, 1987). However, these proposed disorders were excluded from the DSM-IV partly because of social or political concerns that we will discuss later. Let us now examine the nature of all four proposed disorders (see also Table 8-2).

Depressive

The proposed depressive personality disorder involves a pervasive pattern of depressive thoughts and behaviors (American Psychiatric Association, 1994). The depressive individual is usually in a dejected, gloomy, unhappy mood, and is inclined to feel pessimism and anxiety as well as remorse and guilt. Depressive persons generally feel a sense of

TABLE 8-2
Brief Descriptions of Disorders Considered for Inclusion as Personality Disorders

Disorder	Description
Depressive	Chronic unhappiness, low self-esteem, and pessimism
Passive-aggressive (negativistic)	Excessively negative attitudes and passive resistance to others' requests
Sadistic	Cruelty and fascination with violence
Self-defeating	Undermines own happiness and repeatedly enters harmful situations and relationships

Source: American Psychiatric Association (1987, 1994). Depressive and passive-aggressive (negativistic) personality disorders were included in an Appendix to the DSM-IV; sadistic and self-defeating personality disorders were included in DSM-III but excluded from DSM-IV.

worthlessness and low self-esteem, and tend to be very critical of themselves and of others.

Passive-Aggressive (Negativistic)

The proposed passive-aggressive personality disorder (also known as negativistic personality disorder) is defined by a widespread pattern of negativistic attitudes and passive resistance to demands for adequate performance (American Psychiatric Association, 1994).[4] The passive-aggressive person will often fail to carry out routine tasks, but without directly refusing to perform those duties. Passive-aggressive individuals are unreasonably critical of authority and resentful of those who seem more fortunate. There are exaggerated complaints of being mistreated and misunderstood, and a generally argumentative disposition.

Self-Defeating

The proposed self-defeating personality disorder was characterized by a widespread pattern of self-defeating behavior, such as frequently avoiding or undermining pleasurable experiences, entering relationships or situations in which one will suffer, and preventing others from helping (American Psychiatric Association, 1987). The self-defeating individual chooses unrewarding relationships and situations even when there are obviously better options available, and rejects any help from other people. Self-defeating persons generally avoid opportunities for pleasure or success, and tend to make unnecessary self-sacrifices.

Self-defeating personality disorder was excluded from the DSM-IV partly because of concerns that its inclusion might lead to a tendency to blame the victims of domestic abuse for their circumstances, by diagnosing them with this disorder rather than blaming the abusive partner.

Sadistic

The proposed sadistic personality disorder was defined by a widespread pattern of cruel, demeaning, and aggressive behavior (American Psychiatric Association, 1987). The sadistic individual uses cruelty, violence, and intimidation to establish dominance within relationships. Sadistic persons generally enjoy observing the suffering of people (or of animals), and enjoy humiliating or mistreating others. There is often a fascination with weapons, torture, and combat.

Sadistic personality disorder was excluded from the DSM-IV partly because of concerns that its inclusion might lead to the use of the diagnosis of this disorder as an excuse for domestic violence, which might allow abusive partners to avoid prosecution.

---

[4] Actually, a somewhat different version of passive-aggressive personality disorder had also been included in previous versions of the DSM (American Psychiatric Association, 1987).

Other Personality-Related Disorders Not Included as DSM-IV Personality Disorders

In addition to the list of 10 personality disorders, the DSM-IV contains a wide array of other psychiatric disorders. (In fact, the list of personality disorders is only a small part of the DSM-IV book.) But some of the disorders listed in other parts of the DSM-IV —that is, in parts other than the personality disorders section—are very clearly disorders of personality, just as much as the disorders that are officially classified as personality disorders. Many disorders are classified elsewhere in the DSM-IV because they are diagnosed during childhood; as you will recall, personality disorders are defined in such a way that they must be first diagnosed during adulthood or adolescence. And, some disorders are classified elsewhere in the DSM-IV because they are viewed as "anxiety disorders" rather than as "personality disorders." (The reasons why the DSM-IV is organized in this way are rather complicated, but are not based closely on the actual relations among the disorders.) Next, we describe four of these personality-related disorders that are not classified as personality disorders (see also Table 8-3): Attention-deficit/hyperactivity disorder, separation anxiety disorder, oppositional defiant disorder, and specific phobias.

Attention-Deficit/Hyperactivity Disorder

You have probably heard a great deal about attention-deficit/hyperactivity disorder (ADHD): Not only is it widely diagnosed among children and adolescents—with a prevalence rate estimated at about 4% (Burd, Klug, Coumbe, & Kerbeshian, 2003) or 6% (Neuman *et al.*, 2005)—but there is also much controversy about the various drugs that have been used to treat ADHD. ADHD is listed in the DSM-IV, but not as a personality disorder; instead, it is found in the category of "Disorders First Diagnosed in Childhood." However, the symptoms that characterize ADHD involve inattentiveness, poor impulse control, and lack of persistence (American Psychiatric Association, 1994), which are generally considered as personality characteristics.

The specific features of ADHD are divided into three groups that correspond to symptoms of inattention, hyperactivity, and impulsivity. Inattention involves distractibility,

---

TABLE 8-3
Brief Descriptions of Four DSM-IV Disorders That Are Listed in Categories other than That of the Personality Disorders

Disorder	Description
Attention-deficit/hyperactivity disorder	Extreme inattention, impulsivity, and hyperactivity
Separation anxiety	Excessive anxiety and fear about separation from attachment figure
Oppositional defiant disorder	Extreme hostility, defiance, anger, and disobedience
Specific phobia	Excessive fear of some object or situation (blood, animals, heights, etc.)

Source: American Psychiatric Association (1994).

forgetfulness, disorganization, lack of persistence, failure to listen or follow instructions, and a tendency to make careless mistakes and to misplace or lose objects. Hyperactivity involves squirming and fidgeting, inappropriate running or climbing and inability to remain seated, and excessive talking and noisiness. Impulsivity involves difficulty in waiting one's turn, blurting out answers prematurely, and interrupting others' conversations and intruding on others' activities.

As you can see, the defining features of ADHD reflect almost perfectly the traits associated with the low pole of the Conscientiousness factor, as described in Chapter 3 (see also Box 5-2). Note that although the specific features of ADHD frequently differ between children and adults, the traits associated with ADHD can (and often do) characterize adults; indeed, ADHD is often diagnosed in adults as well as in children. Given the content of the ADHD symptoms, it seems that ADHD is very clearly a disorder of personality, even though it is not officially classified as a personality disorder.

Separation Anxiety Disorder

Another of the DSM-IV "Disorders First Diagnosed in Childhood" is separation anxiety disorder, and this is also a term that is likely to be familiar to you. Separation anxiety disorder, as diagnosed in children (up to the age of 18), is characterized by feelings of anxiety or even panic in the child when separated (or when about to be separated) from an attachment figure—usually a parent—for any length of time (American Psychiatric Association, 1994). Associated with this anxiety during actual separation is an obsessive ongoing concern with the possibility of being lost or kidnapped or of some tragedy befalling the attachment figure.

Specific features of separation anxiety include excessive distress when separated (or when anticipating separation) from home or attachment figures, as well as persistent worry about the possible harm to or loss of one's attachment figures. This fear of separation also involves a reluctance to go to school or other places where the attachment figure will not be present (especially on overnight trips), or to remain at home when the attachment figure is away.

Some of the specific features of separation anxiety disorder do not apply to adults, because an adult's relationships with attachment figures are not the same as those of a child. However, the tendency to feel anxiety and fear on being away from one's close relatives or spouse (and the tendency to worry obsessively about possible loss of those persons) can be found in adults as well as in children. In fact, some researchers have studied separation anxiety in adulthood, and have developed self-report questionnaire scales to measure this disorder (Manicavasagar, Silove, Wagner, & Drobny, 2003). Notice that the defining features of separation anxiety disorder are very similar to the traits associated with the high pole of the Emotionality factor, as described in Chapter 3 (see Tables 3-5 and 3-6). Thus, like ADHD described before, separation anxiety disorder can also be considered a disorder of personality, even though it is not officially classified as a personality disorder.

Oppositional Defiant Disorder

Also among the DSM-IV "Disorders First Diagnosed in Childhood" is oppositional defiant disorder, another diagnosis that you might also have heard about in the popular media.

Oppositional defiant disorder involves a pattern of negativistic, hostile, and defiant behavior observed in children (American Psychiatric Association, 1994). The specific features of oppositional defiant disorder include a tendency to be ill-tempered, argumentative, and spiteful, along with a tendency to defy adults' requests and rules, to annoy others intentionally, and to blame others for one's own misdeeds.

These features obviously apply also to adults, perhaps even more than is the case for ADHD or for separation anxiety disorder. However, oppositional defiant disorder is not included as one of the personality disorders diagnosed in adults. Nevertheless, the defining traits of oppositional defiant disorder—its quick-temperedness, argumentativeness, irritability, and obstinacy—are essentially the same traits that define the low pole of the Agreeableness factor as described in Chapter 3 (see Tables 3-5 and 3-6). As we saw for ADHD and separation anxiety disorder, oppositional defiant disorder is obviously a disorder of personality despite being excluded from the official list of personality disorders.[5]

Specific Phobias

Also among the disorders listed in the DSM-IV are specific phobias—intense fears of particular situations, such as those involving heights, storms, snakes, spiders, blood, injections, or many others (American Psychiatric Association, 1994). However, these disorders are not included within the Personality Disorders section of the DSM-IV, but rather within a separate section for anxiety disorders. In order to be diagnosed as having a specific phobia (also known as a simple phobia), an individual must experience intense fear and anxiety when the situation is present or anticipated. In addition, diagnosis of a specific phobia requires that the individual himself or herself recognizes his or her fear to be excessive and unreasonable, and that the fear is strong enough to cause disruption to the individual's routine, work, or relationships.

Although specific phobias are not included within the category of personality disorders, there seems to be little to distinguish them from those disorders. Fears of these various situations can be considered as personality traits, insofar as people in general show widely differing degrees of fear in response to those situations (e.g., Cutshall & Watson, 2004). (For example, almost everyone has at least some fear of heights, but people differ greatly in how much of this fear they experience, with only a small fraction of people being extremely or excessively afraid of heights.) Moreover, fear of any particular situation can be considered as a very narrow personality trait, but those fears tend to be correlated substantially with each other, thus indicating a broader trait of overall fearfulness (Cutshall & Watson, 2004).[6]

---

[5] Another disorder diagnosed in childhood is called conduct disorder, but this disorder is essentially the childhood version of antisocial personality disorder, and therefore we will not consider it separately.

[6] Another DSM-IV anxiety disorder, social phobia, is also similar in these ways to a personality disorder, but because its symptoms are very similar to those of avoidant personality disorder, we will not consider it separately.

Summary

As discussed above, several of the disorders listed in the DSM-IV guide are not included as personality disorders, but rather as disorders first diagnosed in childhood or as anxiety disorders. Although this categorization may have some convenience for the psychiatrists and clinical psychologists who aim to help people who have these disorders, it might also have the unfortunate side effect of restricting our understanding of personality-related problems to the set of disorders that are included in the DSM list of personality disorders. By considering not only the disorders that are listed officially as personality disorders, but also the various other disorders listed earlier in this chapter—including attention-deficit/hyperactivity disorder, separation anxiety disorder, oppositional-defiant disorder, and specific phobias—researchers can gain a better understanding of personality-related problems and, ultimately, of how those problems might be treated.

Problems with the Concept of Personality Disorders

The system of personality disorders described in the DSM-IV has been a convenient guide for mental health professionals, but there have been some serious criticisms of this system. Let us consider several difficulties that have been particularly prominent.

1. *Symptoms of a given disorder do not necessarily "go together."* One problem with the various personality disorders of the DSM-IV classification is that, for several disorders, there are some symptoms that do not really show much tendency to co-occur. In other words, for several disorders, there are some symptoms that are just about unrelated to each other, insofar as a person with one symptom is no more likely than anyone else to have another symptom. One example of this involves obsessive-compulsive personality disorder, for which some symptoms, such as rule following and tidiness, are not correlated with other symptoms, such as stubbornness and obstinacy.

2. *Two disorders may have overlapping symptoms, and may tend to be diagnosed together.* Not only do the symptoms of a given disorder not necessarily "hang together" in the sense of being likely to co-occur, but there are some symptoms that tend to co-occur despite being listed in different personality disorders. For example, the conning and deceitful behavior that characterize antisocial personality disorder tend to be observed in the same persons who also show the grandiosity and sense of entitlement that characterize narcissistic personality disorder. As a result of this problem, many persons are diagnosed with two or more personality disorders at the same time. For example, this "comorbidity" (i.e., joint occurrence of two or more disorders) is frequently observed for several pairs of personality disorders, including schizoid and schizotypal, or avoidant and dependent, or histrionic and borderline. The substantial overlap in the symptoms associated with the various disorders thus tends to make the system inefficient; it

would be better instead to develop a system in which the various disorders showed little or no overlap in their symptoms.

3. *"Clusters" of disorders do not match factor analysis results.* A related shortcoming of the DSM system is that the three "clusters" do not necessarily correspond to the factors that are obtained when personality disorder symptoms are factor analyzed. As we will discuss later, factor analyses of personality disorder symptoms have usually produced dimensions quite different from the clusters that have been proposed to summarize the DSM disorders.

4. *A personality disorder should be seen as a continuum, not as a category.* One problem with the DSM approach to disorders has been that it conceptualizes disorders as categories: Either you have the disorder, or you do not have it, depending on whether you are observed to show a certain number of the features of the disorder. Most researchers believe instead that having a personality disorder is a matter of degree, so that some people may have slight indications of a disorder, whereas other people may have a severe case.

5. *Disorders with a clear personality basis are excluded if the symptoms of those disorders are observed in children.* As we discussed before, some disorders— including attention-deficit/hyperactivity disorder, oppositional defiant disorder, separation anxiety disorder, and specific phobias—have several features that are identical to personality traits, and can be observed in adults as well as in children. However, the DSM system of personality disorder does not allow the inclusion of any disorder that can first be diagnosed during childhood; instead, those disorders are listed in a separate section of the DSM. These rules therefore exclude several disorders that are clearly personality based.

6. *Some disorders have origins in sexist stereotypes.* One issue associated with the DSM system of disorders has been the concern that the descriptions of some disorders are based on sexist stereotypes rather than on objective clinical evidence. We already discussed one aspect of the debate regarding sexism when we considered the proposed self-defeating and sadistic personality disorders; in these cases, concerns that the inclusion of these disorders would serve to excuse spousal assault were partly responsible for the decision to exclude those disorders from the DSM. But concerns have also been raised with regard to some of the existing disorders, and perhaps the clearest example of this involves the histrionic personality disorder. It has been argued that some of the symptoms of that disorder, including emotional expressiveness, seductiveness, and suggestibility, are simply exaggerations of characteristics that tend to be viewed as "feminine." (The name "histrionic" derives from a Greek word meaning "uterus"; this disorder was originally thought to result from a "wandering" of the uterus away from the body.) According to this criticism, it would have been equally meaningful to have included a disorder whose symptoms were stereotypically "masculine" characteristics, but the men who developed the list of disorders were not inclined to notice those symptoms. (One could perhaps imagine a "testrionic" personality disorder, defined by features such as exaggerated toughness, denial of emotions, and need for power.)

Alternative Systems for Personality Disorder Diagnosis

In light of the problems discussed above, several researchers have attempted to develop alternative systems for diagnosing personality disorders. These efforts share several important features. First, they are based on the view that the symptoms associated with personality disorders represent extreme levels of personality traits that show a wide range of normal variation among people in general. Also, they are intended to produce a list of problematic personality features, so that those features can be considered separately—not just as parts of disorders that might represent strange mixtures of unrelated features. In addition, they are meant to allow investigation of how these problematic aspects of personality are correlated and thereby form broader factors of disordered personality. In the following section, we will discuss two of the main research programs that have been aimed at the development of alternative systems for diagnosing disorders of personality, and then we will examine the similarities between those two programs.

One of the attempts to construct an improved system of organizing the symptoms associated with personality disorders has been that of John Livesley and his colleagues (e.g., Livesley & Jackson, in press). Livesley began by compiling a comprehensive list of behaviors and descriptions that most clearly characterize the various personality disorders of the DSM system. (In generating this list, he asked many experts on personality disorders to choose the behaviors and characteristics that, in their view, were most clearly associated with each disorder.) He then assessed this very large array of characteristics in samples of psychiatric patients and of people in general, and identified a set of 18 variables that could summarize all of those characteristics. As seen in the left column of Table 8-4, these 18 variables represent virtually the full array of symptoms included in the personality disorders of the DSM system. However, the system developed by Livesley has the important advantage that it allows each variable to be represented separately, rather than being combined into one or more disorders along with other variables that might be nearly unrelated to it. In addition, each of these problematic personality characteristics can be assessed in a dimensional way, so that each person can be located on a continuum ranging from very high to very low, rather than simply designating each person as either "having" or "not having" a given disorder.

The advantages of Livesley's system are shared with those of another research program aimed at developing a better organizing framework for personality disorders, as conducted by Lee Anna Clark and her colleagues. Clark (e.g., 1993) began by listing the various symptoms associated with each DSM personality disorder and with some other DSM disorders that involve anxiety and depression. She then identified "clusters" of these symptoms by asking experts on personality disorders to indicate which symptoms frequently co-occurred, in the sense of being observed in the same persons. On the basis of these ratings, Clark obtained a set of 22 symptom clusters (which she later reduced to 15), each of which could be reliably measured in patients and in the general population. (See the right column of Table 8-4 for a list of these 15 variables.)

As can be seen in Table 8-4, the systems developed by Livesley and by Clark are very similar to each other. Many of the variables of one system have direct counterparts in the other system: For example, Livesley's "self-harming behaviors" variable corresponds closely to Clark's "self-harm" variable; similarly, Livesley's "suspiciousness" matches

TABLE 8-4

Two Systems of Personality Traits Relevant to Personality Disorders

Livesley system	Clark system
Restricted expression	Detachment
Social avoidance	
Intimacy problems	
Identity problems (low self-esteem)	(low) Positive temperament
Anxiousness	Negative temperament
Self-harming behaviors	Self-harm
Cognitive distortions	Eccentric perceptions
Affective lability (mood swings)	Aggression
Suspiciousness	Mistrust
Callousness	Manipulativeness
Oppositionality	
Rejection (of others)	
Conduct problems	Disinhibition
Stimulus seeking	Impulsivity
Compulsivity	Workaholism
	Propriety
Narcissism	Exhibition
	Entitlement
Submissiveness	Dependency
Insecure attachment	

Source: Clark *et al.* (1996). Traits of one column are correlated with traits listed on the same line of the other column; if the same line of the other column is blank, see the next trait listed above the blank space.

Clark's "mistrust", whereas Livesley's "social avoidance" closely resembles Clark's "detachment," and Livesley's "conduct problems" is very similar to Clark's "disinhibition."

As mentioned before, the systems developed by Livesley and by Clark both have the advantage of allowing each of these problematic personality characteristics to be assessed separately, instead of being combined together into awkward groupings. But it is still important to know which of these aspects of personality pathology tend to occur together, because this might give clinicians and researchers some insight into causes that are common to several problems. This in turn might suggest some ways of treating those related problems. For this reason, Livesley and Clark have both examined the relations among the variables of their systems, in order to find a few major groupings of variables (Clark, Livesley, Schroeder, & Irish, 1996; see also Clark & Livesley, 2002). They together administered self-report measures of the variables represented in each system to a sample of over 200 persons, and then conducted a factor analysis of those variables.

The results of this analysis showed a set of five factors. The first factor was defined by scales involving anxiety and self-harm, and thus resembled a "Negative Affect" factor, similar to Big Five Neuroticism (or low Emotional Stability). A second factor was defined by variables related to detachment and social avoidance versus positive emotions and exhibitionism; this dimension therefore represents an Introversion versus Extraversion dimension. A third factor was defined by scales related to rejection of other persons, callousness, and aggression, and thus corresponds to the low pole of Big Five Agreeableness. Another factor was defined by variables involving impulsivity and uninhibited, sensation-seeking tendencies versus compulsive, workaholic tendencies; this dimension thus represents low versus high levels of Big Five Conscientiousness. Finally, the remaining factor was defined by scales related to submissiveness and dependence. Some scales that loaded on this factor also loaded on the first factor, which suggests that this remaining factor might also represent low levels of Emotional Stability, but emphasizing somewhat the dependent and submissive aspects of that dimension rather than the anxious and self-damaging aspects.

The main implication of the results obtained by Clark *et al.* (1996) is that the wide array of personality disorder symptoms can be summarized in terms of only a few basic dimensions. Moreover, these dimensions of personality disorders correspond fairly closely to the factors observed in analyses of personality characteristics more generally. As described above, four of the factors defined by personality disorder variables corresponded fairly closely to the "low" poles of the Big Five Emotional Stability, Extraversion, Agreeableness, and Conscientiousness, and a fifth factor also appeared to be relevant to low Emotional Stability.

Interestingly, none of the factors observed by Clark *et al.* (1996) were similar in content to Openness to Experience. Some researchers have suggested, however, that personality disorder symptoms such as those associated with schizotypal personality disorder are related to high levels of Openness to Experience, which involves a high level of fantasy-proneness (Widiger, Costa, & McCrae, 2002).

As a caution, it should be kept in mind that the particular set of variables included in the systems of Clark and of Livesley might not be representative of the full array of personality disorder-related variables, and that their factor analysis results might not be a perfectly accurate summary of this domain (recall the discussion related to this point in Chapter 3). However, those results do suggest that the structure of characteristics related to personality disorders (and several other disorders that also have a basis in personality) is not so much different from the structure of personality characteristics more generally (see also Krueger, 2005; Widiger, 2003).

Origins of Personality Disorders: Development, Biological Bases, Heredity and Environment, and Evolutionary Function

As discussed before, personality-related disorders can be understood, to a large extent, in terms of the same personality traits that all people exhibit to differing degrees. That is, most personality disorder symptoms correspond to extreme levels of various personality traits—levels that cause problems for the individual and for others. There are a few personality disorder symptoms that are exceptions; for example, self-harming behaviors (associated with borderline personality disorder) and perceptual distortions (associated with schizotypal personality disorder) seem to be expressed only in a small percentage of people. But for the most part, personality disorders represent maladaptive levels of the same personality dimensions that differentiate people in general. As a consequence of this fact, any questions that we might have about the nature of personality disorders will have essentially the same answers as do questions about the nature of personality more generally. For example, the developmental origins, the biological bases, the genetic and environmental origins, and the evolutionary adaptive functions of personality disorders can be understood simply by referring to the results for normal variation in personality characteristics, as summarized in Chapters 4, 5, 6, and 7.

Summary and Conclusions

In this chapter, we have surveyed the topic of personality disorders, beginning with an explanation of the concept of personality disorder itself. According to the DSM-IV (American Psychiatric Association, 1994), an individual may have a personality disorder when he or she exhibits patterns of behavior that deviate from the norms of his or her culture, that are pervasive and inflexible across many aspects of his or her life, and that lead to distress or impairment. To be considered personality disorders, these patterns of behavior must emerge in adolescence or in adulthood; problematic behaviors that emerge during childhood are classified in a different section of the DSM-IV.

The DSM-IV currently lists 10 personality disorders, which are grouped into three "clusters." Within cluster A (the "odd, eccentric" disorders) are the schizoid, schizotypal, and paranoid personality disorders. Cluster B (the "dramatic, erratic" disorders) contains the borderline, histrionic, narcissistic, and antisocial personality disorders. Within cluster C (the "anxious, fearful" disorders) are the avoidant, dependent, and obsessive-compulsive personality disorders. In addition to these 10, there are some additional disorders that have been considered for inclusion in the DSM-IV list, but have been excluded. These are the depressive, negativistic (passive-aggressive), sadistic, and self-defeating disorders. Also, several other disorders listed in the DSM-IV are not classified as personality disorders, but clearly involve personality; these include attention-deficit/hyperactivity disorder, separation anxiety disorder, oppositional defiant disorder, and various specific phobias.

Many researchers believe that the DSM-IV system has serious shortcomings. For example, the symptoms of a given disorder often do not appear together, whereas the symptoms of different disorders often do. Moreover, the grouping of personality disorders into clusters does not closely match observed results. Also, although the DSM-IV treats disorders as categories (i.e., a person is diagnosed as either having or not having a given disorder), the evidence indicates that these disorders are dimensions rather than categories. Also, the exclusion of disorders that begin in childhood is problematic, and some disorders appear to be based more in inaccurate stereotypes than in actual combinations of behaviors.

Some researchers have been working on alternative systems for assessing and classifying personality-related problems. These systems generally show that personality disorder symptoms can be classified into factors similar to those described in Chapter 3 of·this book.

Chapter 9

Personality and Life Outcomes

Does Personality Predict Features of One's Life Story? 181

Relationships and Marriage 182

Are Spouses Similar in Personality? 182

Marital Satisfaction 183

Attachment Styles 185

Parenting Styles 186

Peer Relationships: Friendships and Status 186

Health-Related Outcomes 187

Substance Use 188

Longevity 189

Heart Disease (and "Type A" Personality) 192

Academic Performance 193

Job Performance 194

How to Assess Job Performance? 195

The Role of Conscientiousness 195

Specific Traits: The Case of Proactivity 196

Integrity Tests 197

The Problem of Faking 198

Law-Abidingness versus Criminality 200

The Role of Self-Control 200

Primary and Secondary Psychopathy 201

Life Satisfaction 203

Summary and Conclusions 205

Does Personality Predict Features of One's Life Story?

Does personality matter? For both the scientist and the layperson, one of the most interesting issues in personality psychology is the extent to which personality characteristics can influence important features of people's life stories. Intuitively, it seems likely that a person's levels of various personality characteristics would make some life outcomes more likely or less likely to occur. That is, most people would probably expect that an individual's personality could influence a variety of important "results" in his or her life, such as marital satisfaction (one's own or that of one's spouse), friendships and popularity with peers, achievement at school and work, health and longevity, law-abidingness, or overall life satisfaction.

But is this actually true? It is clear that many life outcomes will be influenced heavily by situations and circumstances that can arise almost at random. For example, even if personality might influence health or wealth, there are many illnesses and many financial difficulties that can afflict people regardless of their personality. So, how much—if at all—does personality relate to these various life outcomes? In this chapter, we will discuss the research that personality psychologists have undertaken in their efforts to answer this question.

Relationships and Marriage

Romantic relationships are obviously an important aspect of most people's lives, and the role of personality in those relationships is a fascinating topic. Here we will consider two fundamental questions about personality and relationships: First, do spouses tend to be similar or dissimilar in their personality characteristics? Second, in what ways are the personality characteristics of spouses associated with the satisfaction they have with the marriage? (The same questions also apply to romantic partners other than spouses and romantic relationships other than marriage, but for the sake of brevity we can use "spouse" and "marriage.")

Several investigations of the personalities of dating and married couples have generally yielded similar results. In this chapter, we will focus on one study (Watson *et al.*, 2004) whose findings are rather typical of those obtained in these investigations. This particular investigation is of much interest, because it was based on a fairly large sample of participants—nearly 300 recently married couples—who were measured using self- and spouse reports on a very wide variety of characteristics. By comparing the characteristics of the husbands and wives of their sample, Watson and colleagues were able to examine the similarity (or dissimilarity) of spouses, as well as the relations between the characteristics of spouses and their marital satisfaction. Note that the couples all participated in the research project at the investigators' laboratory, and that each spouse was seated alone at a separate desk when completing the various questionnaires, in order to ensure that the responses—both self-reports and spouse reports—were independent and frank.

Are Spouses Similar in Personality?

First, to find out whether spouses tend to be alike or opposite in personality, Watson *et al.* (2004) calculated correlations between spouses on each of the wide variety of characteristics. For example, consider a personality dimension such as Extraversion. Watson *et al.* examined whether husbands who had high self-report scores on Extraversion tended to be married to wives who also had high self-report scores on this trait, by calculating the correlation between the self-report scores of husbands and of wives. (In other words, the correlation was calculated as if "husband Extraversion" and "wife Extraversion" were two variables being measured on the same person.) In addition to calculating correlations based on self-report data, Watson *et al.* repeated their analyses using, for each couple, each spouse's reports of the other spouse's personality. By calculating these correlations for each characteristic (using the Big Five personality factors), Watson *et al.* were able to find out the ways in which spouses tended to be similar or dissimilar to each other. That is, a large positive correlation for a given trait would indicate strong similarity, and a strong negative correlation would indicate strong dissimilarity.

At this point, you might want to try to guess at the results: Do you expect that spouses would tend to have personalities that are similar ("like marries like") or dissimilar ("opposites attract")? Well, for the Big Five personality characteristics, the answer appears to be neither: Instead, a wife's personality is correlated *approximately zero* with her husband's personality, across all of these broad dimensions of personality. The strongest relations involved Extraversion, which showed a small negative correlation between spaces (about −.15), suggesting a slight tendency for extraverted women to be married to introverted men, and vice versa. (Again, however, this tendency was slight, and it has not been observed in other studies of the personalities of spouses.) The finding that wives' and husbands' personalities are roughly uncorrelated is consistent with what has been observed in several previous investigations based on large samples, although some studies have showed some modest positive correlations for some dimensions. But the general pattern of results in the Watson *et al.* study, and in most other investigations, tells us that the personality of one spouse gives virtually no clue as to the personality of the other spouse: Husbands and wives tend to be neither similar nor different in the major dimensions of personality.[1]

Marital Satisfaction

As described above, spouses tend to be neither similar nor dissimilar to each other in personality characteristics. But there remains the important question of how these variables are related to marital satisfaction. Can we predict one's level of marital satisfaction from the personality of one's spouse? From one's own personality? From the similarity (or difference) between oneself and one's spouse?

Several studies have examined the links between psychological characteristics and marital satisfaction. One of these was the investigation described earlier in this chapter, where Watson *et al.* (2004) assessed the marital satisfaction of each spouse using items that asked about happiness with the marriage, about sexual satisfaction, and about the level of conflict in the marriage. (Remember that, for every couple, each spouse made these ratings without knowing what the other spouse's ratings were; this was also true for all of the personality characteristics and other variables that were assessed.) Another such study was that of Botwin, Buss, and Shackelford (1997), which used generally similar methods. Below, we will focus our discussion mainly on the Watson *et al.* investigation, but we will also mention the similarities and the (few) differences in results between the two studies.

---

[1] This is not the end of the story, however. Watson *et al.* also examined some other psychological characteristics, including mental abilities, religiosity, and political attitudes. In Chapters 10 and 11, we will examine the question of whether or not spouses were similar in these other important variables.

Watson *et al.* (2004) first considered how one's marital satisfaction was related to *one's own* characteristics. It might seem a bit strange to examine how a person's own personality relates to his or her own marital satisfaction, but there are reasons to expect that the relations could be fairly strong. For example, some characteristics might lead a person to feel satisfied even with a marriage that most people would find somewhat unhappy; other characteristics might cause someone to feel dissatisfied even with a marriage that most people would envy. In addition, some characteristics might elicit "positive" behaviors from one's spouse, and thereby enhance the quality of the marriage, or elicit "negative" behaviors that would undermine the quality of the marriage.

The results of Watson *et al.* (2004) showed that, for both husbands and wives, an individual's marital satisfaction was related to his or her own levels of the Big Five Agreeableness and Emotional Stability factors, with positive correlations in the .30s and .40s. The other Big Five factors were weakly associated with marital satisfaction, as were intelligence, religiosity, and political attitudes. Interestingly, these results are very similar to those obtained by Botwin *et al.* (1997), who also found that an individual's levels of Big Five Agreeableness and Emotional Stability were the best predictors of his or her own level of marital satisfaction. These findings indicate that an agreeable, stable person is likely to be more satisfied with his or her marriage than is a disagreeable, unstable person. But why is this? Are agreeable, stable people simply more easily satisfied with their marriages, or do they develop marriages that really are "better"?

One way to answer this question is to find out whether or not people who have agreeable, stable personalities tend to have spouses who report a high level of marital satisfaction. If these personality characteristics really do contribute to the quality of a marriage, then they should be correlated with the spouse's level of marital satisfaction; if instead these characteristics are associated only with a tendency to be more easily satisfied with one's marriage, then they should be uncorrelated with the spouse's level of marital satisfaction. Fortunately, Watson *et al.* (2004) did examine the relations between the personality characteristics of one spouse and the level of marital satisfaction of the other spouse. Their results were actually quite similar to those obtained in the analyses of one's own marital satisfaction, as the variables with the strongest links to one's spouse's marital satisfaction were again the Big Five Agreeableness and Emotional Stability factors. That is, individuals whose spouses had agreeable, stable personalities tended to be more satisfied with their marriages than were individuals whose spouses had disagreeable, unstable personalities. Thus, this result suggests that agreeable, stable people really do develop better marriages, beyond any tendency those people might have to be satisfied with a marriage independently of its "real" quality. A similar finding was obtained by Botwin *et al.* (1997), whose results also showed a relation between one's marital satisfaction and one's spouse's levels of Big Five Agreeableness and Emotional Stability. However, Botwin *et al.* found that marital satisfaction was also positively correlated (for both husbands and wives) with the spouse's levels of Big Five Openness to Experience.

In retrospect, the finding that Big Five Agreeableness and Emotional Stability are related to one's own and to one's spouse's marital satisfaction might seem rather obvious: It is not hard to imagine how a high level of these characteristics would make a marriage happier, or how a low level would make a marriage less happy. But then again, one might just as easily have expected that high levels of Extraversion or Conscientiousness would also be associated with happier marriages, yet the relations are apparently much weaker for those characteristics.[2]

Finally, Watson *et al.* (2004) also considered the extent to which marital satisfaction was related to similarity (or dissimilarity) between spouses. It is possible that marital satisfaction might depend not only on one's own personality and on one's spouse's personality considered separately, but also on the combination of the two. For example, perhaps it is not just each spouse's level of a given characteristic that is important, but also *the similarity (or difference) between* the spouses on that characteristic. One might expect that spouses would feel greater marital satisfaction to the extent that they are similar in some characteristics, or to the extent that they are different in some characteristics. Watson *et al.* examined this by finding the correlation between individuals' levels of marital satisfaction and the absolute value of the difference between the individual and his or her spouse in a given characteristic (after statistically controlling for each spouse's own level of that characteristic). In this way, the researchers could answer the question of whether a larger difference between spouses on any characteristic—not just each spouse's own level of a characteristic—would be associated with higher or lower levels of marital satisfaction.

The results of this analysis were rather straightforward: Neither similarity nor dissimilarity between spouses was associated with higher levels of marital satisfaction. For husbands and for wives, marital satisfaction was not substantially related to being more similar to one's spouse, or to being more different from one's spouse, on any of the personality characteristics. These results suggest that regardless of whether two people are similar or different in personality, their chances of having a happy marriage are about the same. What appears to be more important are the characteristics of each spouse *individually*, as people who are more agreeable and more stable tend to be more satisfied with their marriages and to have spouses who are more satisfied also.

Attachment Styles

As described above, several investigations have examined whether or not spouses tend to be similar in personality and whether or not personality predicts marital satisfaction. But there remains the question of how personality relates to *attachment styles*—that is, the ways in which people act, think, and feel in the specific context of their romantic relationships. Research on these relationship-related tendencies has shown two main dimensions of attachment styles (Bartholomew & Horowitz, 1991; Brennan, Clark, & Shaver, 1998). First, people differ in their levels of *anxious attachment*, which is the tendency to worry about the loss of a partner's love. Also, people differ in their levels of *avoidant attachment*, which is the tendency to feel uncomfortable being emotionally close to one's partner. These

---

[2] The Honesty–Humility factor was not assessed in the studies by Watson *et al.* (2004) or by Botwin *et al.* (1997), so it is not known how this dimension relates to marital satisfaction. Intuitively, it seems plausible that one's spouse's tendency to be sincere and modest (as opposed to deceitful and conceited) would be associated with higher levels of marital satisfaction, but this possibility has not yet been tested.

two dimensions are roughly uncorrelated with each other; thus, a person who has a high level of one attachment style is equally likely to have a high or a low level of the other. (When a person has low levels of both anxious and avoidant styles, he or she can be said to have a *secure attachment* style.)

Of course, a person's levels of these tendencies would vary a great deal, depending on one's partner and on the quality of the relationship with that partner. However, people tend to differ from one another in their *typical* attachment style, as observed in romantic relationships in general. This raises the question of how personality is related to attachment style, and one recent investigation (Noftle & Shaver, 2006) has attempted to answer that question, using self-report scales measuring the Big Five personality characteristics and the two attachment style dimensions. In a series of two studies, Noftle and Shaver found that anxious attachment was associated with low Emotional Stability (correlations in the −.40s and −.50s) and to some extent with low Conscientiousness (correlations in the −.20s and −.30s). In contrast, avoidant attachment was only weakly related to the Big Five dimensions, being modestly associated with low Extraversion and low Conscientiousness (correlations in the −.20s). It is possible that some characteristics not directly assessed by the Big Five, such as independence, would correlate more strongly with avoidant attachment. (Interestingly, Noftle and Shaver also reported that persons with an avoidant attachment style tended to report a poorer quality of relationship with their current partner. Relationship quality was only weakly related to the personality characteristics.)

Parenting Styles

In the field of developmental psychology, there has been much research on the ways in which parents raise their children. It is thus somewhat surprising that only a very few studies have examined the relations between parents' personality characteristics and their style of raising their children. One recent investigation in Finland (Metsäpelto & Pulkkinen, 2003), however, obtained self-reports from mothers and fathers on the Big Five personality characteristics and also (3 years later) on parenting styles. The parenting styles examined by Metsäpelto and Pulkkinen included nurturance (i.e., being affectionate and supportive), restrictiveness (i.e., demanding obedience and being punitive), and knowledge (i.e., of the child's activities, friends, and whereabouts). The results showed that parents who were higher in Openness to Experience and in Extraversion reported having a more nurturing, and also less restrictive, style of parenting than did those who were lower in those dimensions. (Parental knowledge was only very weakly associated with personality.)

More investigations will be needed to understand how parents' personalities relate to their parenting styles, but it seems likely that personality could be heavily involved. For example, it seems almost obvious that a tendency to be easily angered would have important consequences for the way that parents raise their children, or that a tendency to prefer order and structure would also be expressed in one's style of parenting.

Peer Relationships: Friendships and Status

Recently, researchers have begun to study systematically the relations of personality characteristics with social relationships, whether in childhood, adolescence, or adulthood.

Some studies have examined these questions by investigating the behaviors of children who differ in the extent to which they are liked and disliked by their peers. One large-scale review of such studies (Newcomb, Bukowski, & Pattee, 1993) organized the results in such a way as to show the behavioral differences between children who were classified into one of five groups: Specifically, Newcomb *et al.* compared "average" children with children who are identified either as *popular* (i.e., liked by many other children, disliked by few other children), *rejected* (i.e., disliked by many, liked by few), *neglected* (i.e., liked by few, disliked by few), or *controversial* (i.e., liked by many, disliked by many).

Newcomb *et al.* (1993) found that, across these many studies, popular children tended to be low in aggression and high in sociability, whereas rejected children showed an opposite pattern, being high in aggression and low in sociability. Children in the neglected category tended to be low in both aggression and sociability, but children in the controversial category were opposite, tending to be high in both aggression and sociability. These results suggest that sociability is associated with being liked, and that aggression is associated with being disliked. (However, these results on their own do not necessarily indicate that these characteristics are the *cause* of other children's liking and disliking, as opposed to being the *consequence* of being liked or disliked by other children.)

One recent study examined the links between personality and social status within samples of young adult college students (Anderson, John, Keltner, & Kring, 2001). Anderson *et al.* obtained self-reports on the Big Five personality factors from students in a fraternity, in a sorority, and in a mixed-sex dormitory. In addition, the researchers also assessed the social status of each student in these groups, by obtaining peer (observer) ratings of each student's prominence, influence, and respect within the group. In all three samples, Anderson *et al.* found that Extraversion was positively related to social status, with a correlation of about .40 both among men and among women. Interestingly, similarly strong relations were found—but only among men—for Emotional Stability and for physical attractiveness. The authors suggested that the "toughness" associated with Emotional Stability is admired by men more than by women, and that physical attractiveness—which is usually associated with positive perceptions by others—might elicit mixed reactions among women more than among men. (That is, a woman's attractiveness might be a source of some antagonism from other women.) The other "Big Five" personality characteristics were unrelated to social status, but the authors suggested that different results might be observed in groups that are not purely "social" in their purpose. For example, one hypothesis is that Conscientiousness would be related to social status in groups of workers. More generally, it should be remembered that the Anderson *et al.* study examined social status, but not other socially relevant variables; it is quite possible that important variables such as friendship quality would be positively related to Agreeableness or to Honesty–Humility, for example.

Health-Related Outcomes

An important goal for researchers in health psychology and personality psychology is to identify individual difference characteristics that are associated with mortality, with illness, and with behaviors that put one's health at risk. Many such investigations have now been conducted, and some clear patterns of results have emerged.

Substance Use

First, let us consider personality characteristics that might predict the use of substances such as tobacco products, alcohol, and various illegal drugs. One obvious hypothesis is that traits related to the Conscientiousness dimension, such as self-discipline and impulse control, would predict how well a person *would resist temptations* to smoke, to get drunk, and use other kinds of drugs. An additional hypothesis is that traits suggesting low Emotional Stability, such as anxiety, moodiness, and irritability, would predict how much a person *would be tempted* to use these drugs as a way of temporarily controlling these negative emotions.

The links between personality and substance use were recently examined in a large-scale study by Elkins, King, McGue, and Iacono (2006). Those researchers obtained self-reports on various personality traits from about 1000 17-year-olds, roughly evenly divided between the sexes. In addition, Elkins *et al.* also interviewed the participants to determine the extent of their use of tobacco, alcohol, and illicit drugs. These interviews were conducted both at the time of the personality assessment (i.e., when the participants were 17 years old) and again 3 years later (i.e., when the participants were now 20 years old). On the basis of the interviews, some participants were identified as having nicotine dependence, some as having an alcohol use disorder, and some as having a drug use disorder. By the time the participants were 20 years old, about 30% were diagnosed as nicotine-dependent, about 30% were diagnosed with an alcohol disorder, and almost 20% were diagnosed with a drug use disorder. (Some participants, of course, could have two or even all three of these disorders, so the majority of participants had no disorders at all.) For each disorder, almost half of the diagnoses had occurred at the time of the first interview.

How did personality relate to these substance use disorders? The results were similar for all three kinds of disorders: In each case, the participants who had been diagnosed with substance use disorders were about half or two-thirds of a standard deviation unit lower in Conscientiousness-related traits than were those who were not diagnosed. In addition, substance use disorders were also associated with traits involving low Emotional Stability (such as irritability, anxiety, and moodiness), but the relations were somewhat weaker than for Conscientiousness. Other personality traits generally showed rather weak relations with personality disorder symptoms.[3]

One interesting feature of the results obtained by Elkins *et al.* (2006) was that, even among 17-year-olds who did not have a substance use disorder, the personality characteristics described above showed some differences between those who continued to have no

---

[3] A few studies have found that traits related to Extraversion are associated, to a modest extent, with greater alcohol consumption (e.g., Walton & Roberts, 2004). However, the results of Elkins *et al.* (2006) did not show any difference in Extraversion between participants with alcohol disorders and participants without alcohol disorders. One possible reason for the discrepancy between these results, as suggested by the findings of Walton and Roberts, is that the link between Extraversion and alcohol consumption may become weaker at higher levels of alcohol consumption. That is, nondrinkers may be considerably less extraverted than are moderate drinkers, but moderate drinkers may be only very slightly less extraverted than are heavy drinkers.

substance use disorder 3 years later and those who did develop such a disorder during that interval. This suggests that personality was actually predictive of substance use problems, and not merely a consequence of these problems.

The results of the Elkins *et al.* (2006) are consistent with those obtained in a review of earlier studies that had investigated the relations between Conscientiousness-related traits and health-related behaviors. Bogg and Roberts (2004) reviewed dozens of earlier investigations that together involved tens of thousands of participants. They found that traits belonging to the Conscientiousness factor, especially self-control, were correlated negatively with excessive alcohol use and with illegal drug use (both correlations about $-.25$) and, to a lesser extent, with tobacco use (correlation about $-.15$). Thus, the finding of moderate negative relations between Conscientiousness and substance use appears to be very consistent.

The relations between personality characteristics and substance use raise the question of how personality might be associated with success in quitting—that is, in ceasing the use of tobacco, alcohol, or other drugs. One study of over 1600 elderly Americans (Terracciano & Costa, 2004) found that, on average, those who had never smoked (about 50% of the sample) were more than half of a standard deviation unit higher in Conscientiousness (and in Emotional Stability) than were those who were still smokers (about 7% of the sample). The remaining participants—those who had quit smoking—had levels of these personality characteristics that were about halfway in between those of the other two groups. Similarly, a much smaller study of about 70 alcohol-dependent patients (Bottlender & Soyka, 2005) found that most had emerged successfully from a 1-year treatment program, but that those who had relapsed tended to be lower in Conscientiousness (and in Emotional Stability) than those whose treatment had succeeded. Results such as these suggest that the high levels of self-control that are associated with Conscientiousness and Emotional Stability may contribute to success in quitting smoking or in quitting drinking.

Longevity

Given that substance use problems are harmful to one's health, the finding that personality is related to substance use raises the possibility that personality would also be related to health and even to longevity. That is, if some personality characteristics are associated with avoidance of substance abuse—or with engaging in health-promoting behaviors more generally—then persons with high levels of those characteristics might, on average, tend to be healthier and more long-lived than persons with lower levels. One obvious challenge in testing this hypothesis, however, is that a very long time is needed to conduct investigations: It would be necessary to measure personality in healthy young people, and then wait several decades in order to observe whether personality was predictive of health problems and of early mortality. Fortunately, some researchers have been able to address this question by identifying older adults who had participated in studies of personality decades earlier, during their childhood or adolescence. Using these "archival" data, the researchers have examined the relation between personality characteristics and later health outcomes.

One investigation of the relations between personality and longevity (Friedman *et al.*, 1993) used personality data that were obtained in a very early study of gifted children in

California (Terman, 1925). Terman's study was designed to examine the characteristics of children who obtained very high scores on intelligence tests, and involved the assessment of those children in terms of personality and other characteristics. Ratings of the personality characteristics of the children were provided by their teachers during the 1921–1922 school year, when the children were about 11 years old. In 1986, over 60 years later, Friedman and colleagues were able to obtain records of which participants had died and which were still alive. These records—obtained from about 1200 persons—allowed the researchers to examine how childhood personality was related to longevity.

The results obtained by Friedman *et al.* (1993) showed that childhood personality was indeed related to longevity. In particular, two groups of characteristics were predictive of the mortality rates. First, a group of traits that Friedman *et al.* called "conscientiousness" or "social dependability" was associated with longer life spans.[4] This relation was moderately strong: When the researchers compared persons who were low in dependability (i.e., in the bottom quarter of the sample) with persons who were high in dependability (i.e., in the top quarter of the sample), they found that the low-dependability persons had about a 35% greater chance of dying before the age of 70 than did the high-dependability persons. Also, a group of traits involving cheerfulness and optimism was associated with longevity, but in the negative direction: Persons high in cheerfulness had about a 35% higher chance of dying before the age of 70 than did persons low in cheerfulness. (Note, however, that even among the persons who were low in dependability or high in cheerfulness, most were still alive at the age of 70.) A variety of other personality traits were unrelated to longevity.

Friedman *et al.* (1993) examined possible reasons why these traits would be related to longevity. With regard to dependability, Friedman *et al.* suggested that perhaps the more dependable persons would be less likely to engage in an array of health-damaging behaviors, such as smoking, heavy drinking, overeating, or careless risk taking. In a later study, Friedman *et al.* (1995) investigated these possibilities, by obtaining information from the participants (or from their surviving relatives) about the drinking habits, smoking history, and body weight of the participants. The results showed that low dependability was associated with smoking and drinking (although not with obesity), and that smoking and drinking were associated with earlier death. However, these relations were not strong enough to explain the link between dependability and longevity. In other words, the tendency for dependable persons to live longer could only be explained in small part by their lower likelihood of smoking or of heavy drinking. This leaves open the question of why dependability is associated with longevity, but Friedman *et al.* suggested that dependable persons might have been better able to handle life's stresses, by virtue of being better prepared, or might have developed better networks of social support with their spouses, relatives, and

---

[4] Actually, this group of traits is not the same as Conscientiousness as described in earlier chapters, but is instead more like a blend of Conscientiousness, Agreeableness, and Honesty–Humility. When the personality scales were constructed, in the early 1920s, researchers had not yet identified the major dimensions of personality, so the scales were not constructed in such a way as to correspond directly to each of those dimensions individually.

friends. Also, it is possible that dependable persons took better care of their health in many subtle ways other than merely by not smoking or not drinking to excess.[5]

As for the link between cheerfulness and earlier death, the same team of researchers also examined possible explanations for this result (Martin *et al.*, 2002). The relations of cheerfulness with smoking and heavy drinking were fairly weak, and therefore the relation between cheerfulness and earlier mortality was not attributable in any important part to these behaviors. A possible remaining explanation (Friedman *et al.*, 1993) is that perhaps cheerful persons tend to be overly optimistic about their health prospects, and therefore tend to neglect any health problems that might be developing. However, it was not possible to test this hypothesis using the data that were available from these participants. The reasons for the link between cheerfulness and mortality are of some interest, because intuitively it might seem more likely that cheerful people would live longer.[6] Future studies will be able to examine this question in more detail.

In fact, some further data on the relation between childhood personality and longevity are currently being collected, and results will become available during the next few decades. One large-scale project (Hampson, Goldberg, Vogt, & Dubanoski, 2006) has been examining the health-related outcomes of about 1000 persons in Hawaii. These participants were born during the 1950s, and their personalities had been rated by their elementary schoolteachers during a research project conducted mainly during the early 1960s. (Unlike the participants whose longevity was examined by Friedman *et al.* (1993), the participants of this Hawaiian investigation represented a wide range of intellectual ability, rather than only the very high levels.) When Hampson *et al.* began obtaining health-related information from these participants during 1999–2000, nearly all were still alive. As a result, it has not yet been possible to study the relations between personality and longevity in this sample, but the links between personality and some health-related behaviors and outcomes have been examined. Thus far, the relations between personality and various health-related outcomes—including smoking, drinking, obesity, and self-rated health—have been rather weak (Hampson *et al.*, 2006). But in light of the results obtained by Friedman *et al.* (1993), it seems likely that some of the personality characteristics will

---

[5] Also considered by Friedman *et al.* (1995) was the possibility that persons having higher levels of dependability would be especially unlikely to die of certain specific causes. The more common causes of death that could be examined in this study were cancer, heart disease, and injuries. The results showed that, for each of these causes of death, the high-dependability persons were less likely to have died by age 70 than were the low-dependability persons. Thus, the difference in death rates for persons with different levels of dependability was not attributable to any single, particular cause of death.

[6] The results of one small-scale investigation do suggest that cheerfulness might be *positively* related to longevity. Danner, Snowdon, and Friesen (2001) examined the handwritten autobiographies of 180 Roman Catholic nuns, as written when the nuns were applying to their convent, at about 22 years of age. Danner *et al.* found that the nuns whose autobiographies showed more positive emotional content—presumably reflecting an upbeat and cheerful disposition—tended to live longer: Over three-quarters of those who were above average in positive emotions lived to be at least 85 years old, whereas only half of those who were below average in positive emotions lived to that age.

ultimately be associated with longevity. It will be interesting to see whether or not the findings obtained by Friedman *et al.* for traits related to dependability and cheerfulness will also be observed in the Hawaiian study.

Heart Disease (and "Type A" Personality)

Heart disease is one of the leading causes of death in modern societies, and the idea that personality may be implicated in heart disease has a long history (see Smith & Ruiz, 2002). In the early twentieth century, the Canadian physician, William Osler, suggested that persons who have a keen and ambitious disposition, and seem always to be moving at full speed, were more likely to be afflicted with heart disease (Osler, 1910). About half a century later, a more fully developed variant of this idea was proposed by Friedman and Rosenman (1959), who identified a set of several characteristics as potential risk factors for heart-related illnesses. These characteristics—including competitiveness, impatience, excessive job involvement, hostility, and time urgency—were collectively described as the "Type A" behavior pattern, which contrasted with the opposite pattern, known as "Type B." (Note, however, that people do not divide neatly into two "types" on these characteristics. As with other aspects of personality, most people have intermediate levels, with fewer people having very high or very low levels.)

By the 1980s, several studies had shown that Type A characteristics—as typically assessed through structured interviews between physician and patient—were associated with increased probability of heart disease, equivalent to a correlation coefficient of about .20 (e.g., Cooper, Detre, & Weiss, 1981; Miller, Smith, Turner, Guijarro, & Hallet, 1996).[7] However, it was primarily the *hostility* aspect of the Type A syndrome—not the various other characteristics—that was responsible for the relation with heart disease. In addition, some recent research has indicated that heart disease is also associated with the personality characteristic of dominance, perhaps even more strongly than with hostility (e.g., Houston, Babyak, Chesney, Black, & Ragland, 1997; Whiteman, Deary, & Fowkes, 2000).

This raises the question of *why* a personality characterized by "hostile dominance" would be at higher risk of heart disease (see, e.g., Smith & Spiro, 2002). One possibility is simply that the biological causes of hostility and dominance also influence heart disease risk, but the mechanism by which this would occur is not known. It is also possible that hostile, dominant people have poorer health habits, but this might not entirely account for the link with heart disease. Still another possible reason is that hostile, dominant people tend to create more stress for themselves by getting into conflicts with others, and also tend to receive less stress-reducing social support from others. Currently, the most widely accepted hypothesis is that persons who are high in hostility and dominance have greater physiological reactions to stress than do other persons, with greater increases in blood pressure, heart rate, and levels of stress-related hormones and neurotransmitters. These reactions in turn tend to damage the blood vessels, thereby increasing the risk of heart disease.

---

[7] The value of .20 may seem small, but it is actually comparable in size to that yielded by other well-known predictors of heart disease, such as cholesterol levels, high blood pressure, and so on.

Academic Performance

Among the important outcome variables that might be predicted by personality are those involving effectiveness, achievement, or performance: What are the personality character-istics of a high-performing worker, or of a high-performing student? Of course, one's personality characteristics are unlikely to be the only determinants of performance. For example, one's level of raw ability is likely to be an important contributor to performance, as is one's interest in specific courses of study or specific job tasks. But it still seems plausible that general behavioral tendencies—that is, personality characteristics—would also predict performance at school or on the job. Many investigations of the links between personality and performance have now been conducted, and reviews of these studies show some fairly consistent results. We will discuss these below, beginning with the prediction of academic performance, followed by the prediction of job performance.

Across several studies of personality and academic performance, a consistent finding has been a moderate positive correlation between traits associated with the Conscientious-ness factor and school grades or marks, whether in a single course or as averaged across several courses. This result is hardly surprising, because the characteristics that make up the Conscientiousness factor—traits such as self-discipline, organization, and diligence—seem likely to contribute to academic performance through greater effort, efficiency, and attention to detail, both in completing course work and also in studying for examinations. But one interesting result of these studies is that it is the more directly work-related aspects of Conscientiousness—particularly the trait of achievement motivation—that is the best predictor of academic achievement.

One example of the relation between achievement motivation and academic perfor-mance was found by Paunonen and Ashton (2001b), who obtained self-reports on personal-ity scales from over 700 university students who were enrolled in the same psychology course. Of the 20 personality characteristics assessed in that study, the one that showed the strongest relation with course grades was—as expected—a scale measuring achievement motivation, which correlated about .25 with that criterion variable. In addition to achievement motivation, other Conscientiousness-related traits also correlated posi-tively with course grades. However, the relations obtained by these other aspects of Conscientiousnsess—that is, traits such as planning, orderliness, and impulse control—were much weaker than that obtained by achievement motivation. Even when all of these traits (including achievement motivation) were combined into a broad Conscientiousness factor, they correlated about .20 with course grades, a value somewhat less than that shown by achievement motivation alone. This result suggests that it is the tendency to be a hard worker in particular—and not so much the tendency to be "conscientious" in other respects—that is the important personality basis of academic performance.

A similar example was reported by Lounsbury, Sundstrom, Loveland, and Gibson (2003), in a smaller sample of 175 university students enrolled in psychology courses: A self-report measure of "work drive" (similar to achievement motivation) correlated almost .30 with grades in a psychology course. A separate measure of Conscientiousness showed a somewhat weaker relation (nearly .20) with course grades, thus suggesting again that it is achievement motivation in particular, rather than "conscientious" traits in general, that is the best predictor of course grades. Interestingly, the study by Lounsbury *et al.* also included a mental ability test, which was substantially correlated (about .40) with course grades but uncorrelated with "work drive." This indicates that even though students having high levels of mental ability did not necessarily have high levels of work drive (and vice versa), the students who did have high levels of both characteristics tended to obtain the highest grades. When examined in combination, mental ability and work drive together correlated about .50 with course performance.

In considering the preceding results, it is important to keep in mind that Conscientiousness—as a broad combination of several more specific, mutually correlated traits—does still correlate positively with academic performance. In fact, when academic performance is considered in terms of a "grade point average" across many courses, rather than in terms of grades in a single course only, the relations between Conscientiousness and academic performance become somewhat higher, about .25 (Noftle & Robins, 2006) or even above .30 (Brackett & Mayer, 2003).

Broad personality factors other than Conscientiousness have not shown such consistent relations with academic performance. One plausible hypothesis would be that traits associated with the Openness to Experience factor—specifically, those involving intellectual curiosity—would be predictive of course grades, because intellectually curious persons might find academic work to be more interesting and engaging than would less curious persons. There is some support for this hypothesis: For example, in the study by Paunonen and Ashton (2001b) described before, the personality trait of intellectual curiosity correlated about .20 with course grades. But interestingly, the broad Openness to Experience factor correlated approximately zero with course grades. This is because other traits within this factor—including aesthetic sensitivity, independent-mindedness, and preference for change—were unrelated (or even slightly *negatively* related) to course performance, despite being positively related to intellectual curiosity. In other words, even though intellectual curiosity and several other traits "go together" as part of the broad Openness to Experience factor, it is only intellectual curiosity that facilitates academic performance.

Moreover, it is not clear even that intellectual curiosity would predict academic performance in all courses: Perhaps grades in an accounting course or in an administration course would not be associated with a generally inquisitive personality. This raises the interesting question of whether academic performance might relate differently to personality, depending on the subject matter of the course. For example, one might expect performance in a literature course and in a physical science course to be associated with rather different personality characteristics. However, this possibility remains to be examined in future research.

Job Performance

In comparison with the number of studies examining personality and academic performance, there have been many more studies of the relations between personality and job performance. In fact, since the early 1990s, several reviews of this research have been published (e.g., Tett, Jackson, & Rothstein, 1991), summarizing the results obtained in dozens of previous investigations. But before we discuss those results, we should briefly address the question of how job performance is measured.

How to Assess Job Performance?

In contrast to the situation in school settings—where course grades provide a ready indicator of performance—it is not always obvious how to assess job performance. One approach is to use some objective records of productivity. To take a few examples, one could count the number of customers served by a cashier, the number of pieces produced by a machine operator, the number of scientific articles produced by a university professor, and the number (or dollar value) of houses sold by a real estate agent. (Similarly, one could also keep track of the number of *counterproductive* actions, such as latenesses, days absent, rule violations, safety violations, lost merchandise, and even thefts and violent acts.) The objectivity of using such records is an advantage, but is not easily applied to some jobs; for example, it is not clear how a productivity "count" could be used to evaluate the performance of a nurse or a personnel manager or an engineer.

Another approach to the assessment of job performance is to obtain supervisors' evaluations—or sometimes even co-worker evaluations—of employee performance, using a rating scale (e.g., from 0 to 10), a ranking system (e.g., from best employee to worst employee), or some combination thereof. This method has the advantage of being widely applicable across jobs, although it does depend on the more subjective judgment of the persons who assess job performance. But in any case, studies of the relations between personality and job performance have shown relatively little difference between the results obtained on the basis of objective "counts" or of subjective ratings (Nathan & Alexander, 1988; Ones & Viswesvaran, & Schmidt, 1993), or have shown some tendency for the subjective ratings to be more easily predicted (Barrick & Mount, 1991; Tett *et al.*, 1991).

The Role of Conscientiousness

Now let us consider what those results have shown, first from the perspective of the broad dimensions of personality. When findings are averaged across studies that have reported the correlations between employees' personality self-reports and measures of their job performance, the most consistent finding is that the Conscientiousness dimension is positively correlated with job performance (e.g., Hurtz & Donovan, 2000; see also Barrick & Mount, 1991; Tett *et al.*, 1991). This is exactly what one would expect, given that the personality traits belonging to the Conscientiousness factor are the same traits that describe one's style of working, for example, being organized, disciplined, thorough, careful, and diligent. However, the strength of the relations between Conscientiousness and job performance is rather modest, typically about .20 (Hurtz & Donovan, 2000), even when corrections are made for the less-than-perfect reliability of job performance measures.

The validity of Conscientiousness in predicting job performance, although not very strong, appears to be rather general across a variety of occupations. In contrast, some other dimensions of personality are related to performance in some particular categories of occupations or in some aspects of any given job. For example, Big Five Agreeableness shows modest positive correlations with performance in customer service jobs, and Extraversion and Emotional Stability both show modest positive correlations with performance in sales and managerial jobs (Hurtz & Donovan, 2000). Similarly, Agreeableness is related to getting along with co-workers, Extraversion is related to showing leadership on the job, and Emotional Stability is related to better management of job stress (Hogan & Holland, 2003). But in general, it is the Conscientiousness factor of the Big Five that is the best predictor, *across* occupations, of *overall* job performance.

The finding that Conscientiousness shows positive correlations with job performance leads to the suggestion that Conscientiousness might also lead to higher levels of income and of occupational status. That is, if people who have high levels of job performance tend on average to receive more raises and promotions (or tend on average to be more successful as self-employed persons), then we might expect that people who have higher levels of Conscientiousness would tend to earn higher incomes and higher levels of job status. This is in fact what has been observed: Judge *et al.* (1999) examined archival data based on people whose personalities had been assessed (by a combination of self-reports, parent reports, and teacher reports) when they were of high school age. When the personality data of these participants were compared with their income and occupational status during their 40s and 50s, the results showed that Conscientiousness levels were correlated above .40 with both variables. Thus, the findings of Judge *et al.* suggest that the influence of Conscientiousness on job performance does tend to translate into higher levels of income and occupational status.

Specific Traits: The Case of Proactivity

But as noted for academic performance, above, the broad dimensions of personality do not necessarily tell the whole story. Instead, it is possible that more specific, narrowly defined personality traits could be better indicators of job performance, whether for occupations in general or for particular kinds of occupations. One study that supports this view was reported by Crant (1995), who examined a personality trait that he called *proactivity*. As described by Crant, proactivity involves a tendency to identify opportunities and to act on them, to take the initiative, and to persevere when taking on challenging tasks. (In this sense, proactivity is much like achievement motivation, but with an extra element of "seizing the opportunity.")

Crant (1995) obtained self-reports on scales measuring proactivity and the Big Five personality factors from a sample of about 130 real estate agents, and also obtained records of those agents' productivity, as measured by each agent's number of house listings, number of sales, and dollar value of sales. The choice of real estate agents as the employee group seems appropriate, given that a proactive personality would seem to be an important characteristic for employees in a sales-related job that involves considerable independence. The results showed that proactivity was correlated modestly (almost .25) with productivity levels, whereas none of the Big Five factors showed any noteworthy correlations with that criterion, even though proactivity was correlated positively with Big Five Extraversion and Conscientiousness. Thus, the results obtained by Crant suggest that better validity can sometimes be achieved by considering not only broad personality dimensions, but also some specific personality traits that are chosen for their likely relevance to performance in a certain kind of job.

Integrity Tests

Some moderately strong relations with job performance have also been obtained for instruments that are called *integrity tests*. Integrity tests are self-report questionnaires that are intended to assess a potential (or current) employee's level of honesty and dependability, and thus to predict his or her tendency to refrain from counterproductive behavior (rule breaking, theft, loafing, etc.), as well as his or her likely level of overall job performance. These instruments were used by employers as a means of selecting employees as early as the 1950s, but became widely used during the 1980s, by which time it was already estimated that 5000 employers were using these tests in the United States (Sackett & Harris, 1984).

Integrity tests are usually divided into two main types: *Overt* and *personality-based* tests. Overt integrity tests ask the job applicant to indicate whether he or she has committed various dishonest acts, such as stealing from previous employers, shoplifting, and various other criminal activities and counterproductive workplace behaviors. In addition, overt integrity tests often ask the respondent to indicate his or her attitudes and opinions about such acts. Personality-based integrity tests, by contrast, are more similar in content to typical self-report personality inventories. In principle, these tests may be somewhat more "subtle" in the sense that respondents might not know that the employer is attempting to assess integrity. However, the items of these personality-based tests are often obviously meant to assess socially desirable or undesirable characteristics.

Studies of the relations between integrity test scores and job performance have generally produced similar results for both overt tests and personality-based tests. These results, as shown in reviews of many previous investigations, suggest that integrity test scores show correlations in the .30s with overall job performance (Ones *et al.*, 1993), when the imperfect reliability of job performance measures is taken into account. This finding of rather strong validity for integrity tests suggests that those tests are among the best known predictors of job performance, outperforming measures of the Big Five personality characteristics and almost matching the validity of mental ability tests (as we will discuss in Chapter 10).

One question that is raised by these results is that of why integrity tests show better validity than do measures of the Big Five personality characteristics. Scores on integrity tests are correlated with some of the Big Five factors, particularly Conscientiousness. However, in comparison with Conscientiousness scales, integrity tests provide more direct measures of certain personality characteristics—such as trustworthiness and dependability—that are very highly valued by employers as qualities of good employees (Michigan Department of Education, 1989). These characteristics apparently represent a mixture of Conscientiousness and of Honesty–Humility (see Chapter 3), a dimension that is not fully represented in the Big Five framework (Lee, Ashton, & de Vries, 2005; Marcus, Lee, & Ashton, 2007).

The Problem of Faking

When reading the previous section, you might have been surprised to learn that integrity tests (or other measures of personality) could show even a modest level of validity for predicting job performance. Many people find it almost difficult to believe that these instruments can predict job performance, because it seems very likely that job applicants would "fake" their self-report responses in such a way as to make a good impression on a prospective employer. In particular, it can seem rather strange that people would readily admit, for example, to having stolen from a previous employer or to being an irresponsible or lazy or deceitful person.

Apparently, people do tend to "fake" to some extent—or at least to be rather generous in giving themselves the "benefit of the doubt"—when taking integrity tests or personality inventories in personnel selection settings. One study tried to assess the extent of faking (also called "response distortion") by comparing the self-report personality scores of two groups of people (Rosse, Stecher, Miller, & Levin, 1998). One group consisted of current employees, who knew that their responses were being obtained for research purposes only, and would not be seen by their employers. The other group consisted of job applicants who were applying for jobs similar to those of the current employees; these job applicants knew that their responses could be used by the employer to decide which applicants to hire. Note that there is no particular reason that there would be any systematic differences, on average, between the employees and the applicants. Therefore, if the applicants showed much higher scores on socially desirable characteristics, this would suggest some degree of faking. This is exactly what Rosse *et al.* found: Across a variety of socially desirable characteristics, the self-report scores of the job applicants were, on average, nearly one standard deviation unit higher than were the self-report scores of the current employees. This suggests a fairly strong degree of response distortion among the applicants.

Despite this response distortion among job applicants, however, the validity of integrity tests and personality inventories in predicting job performance suggests that the *differences* among people in their scores are still meaningful, and give a fairly accurate reflection of their *relative* levels of integrity and related traits. Presumably, though, the validity of these instruments would be improved if faking could be entirely prevented. Several methods for reducing or detecting faking by job applicants are currently being used or investigated.

For example, one method is to include some items that ask about moral lapses that presumably *everyone* has committed; persons who claim *not* to have performed these behaviors are then identified as having faked their responses. Scores on "faking scales" consisting of these items can be used to disqualify applicants or to "correct" their scores on the other scales, in order to estimate their real levels of various traits. The effectiveness of these faking scales is a matter of some dispute, however (Goffin & Christiansen, 2003). It is possible, for example, that some people who see themselves as good persons might claim (sincerely but not accurately) that they have not committed any of these very common but undesirable acts. In one study, persons who had high scores on a scale designed to detect faking were actually *more* honest than persons with lower scores, as assessed by observing which persons would return extra money when they were "accidentally" overpaid (Cunningham, Wong, & Barbee, 1994).

BOX 9-1
Personality and Occupational Choice

In addition to job performance, there are other important career-related variables that might be predicted by personality. For example, later in this chapter we will briefly note the relations between personality dimensions and job satisfaction. But another interesting variable is that of *job choice*: Does personality predict the kind of occupation or career that one chooses?

Ideally, it would be interesting to measure the personality trait levels of a very large sample of young people, and then conduct a follow-up study many years later to identify differences in personality between people who entered into different types of occupations or careers. Thus far, there have not been any systematic, large-scale comparisons of this kind.

However, there has been a great deal of research on the relations between personality characteristics and the major dimensions of *occupational interests* or *vocational interests*. These interests are assessed by self-report questionnaire scales whose items ask respondents about their levels of interest in various work activities, school subjects, and recreational activities. Much of the research on the topic of vocational interests has suggested that these interests (and their matching occupations) can be summarized by a set of six main dimensions (e.g., Holland, 1966; Campbell & Holland, 1972):

Realistic: practical, manual, mechanical occupations, often done outdoors (e.g., carpenter, mechanic, truck driver, farmer);
Investigative: logical, mathematical, scientific occupations (e.g., physical, biological, or social scientist);
Artistic: creative, aesthetic occupations (e.g., musician, visual artist, interior designer, writer);
Social: interpersonal, "helping" occupations (e.g., teacher, counselor, clergy, trainer, nurse);
Enterprising: leadership, persuasion-related occupations (e.g., lawyer, personnel manager, salesperson);
Conventional: office-related occupations (e.g., bookkeeper, banker, secretary)

Some research by Campbell, Hyne, and Nilsen (1992) suggests that this set should be expanded to include a seventh dimension, defined by "adventurous" occupations that may involve confrontations with others (e.g., military personnel, law enforcement officer, professional athlete).

A review by Larson, Rottinghaus, and Borgen (2002; see also Barrick, Mount, & Gupta, 2003) summarized the results of over 20 previous studies that had examined the correlations between individuals' scores on scales measuring the Big Five and on scales measuring the six dimensions of occupational interests. The findings showed several moderately strong relations between personality and occupational interests:

Extraversion was correlated about .40 and .30 with Enterprising and Social interests, respectively;
Openness to Experience was correlated nearly .50 and .30 with Artistic and Investigative interests, respectively;
Conscientiousness was correlated about .25 with Conventional interests; and,
Agreeableness was correlated about .20 with Social interests.

The Big Five Emotional Stability factor did not correlate substantially with any of the interest dimensions, and the Realistic interest dimension did not correlate substantially with any of the personality dimensions.

Note that in each of the preceding cases, the relations between personality dimensions and vocational interest dimensions generally seem to be consistent with the content of those constructs. These results suggest that to some extent, an individual's vocational interests can be seen as a reflection of his or her personality. However, an individual's personality can give only a rough indication as to his or her likely pattern of vocational interests. As noted above, it will be interesting to see the results of future research that would actually compare the personalities of people who are employed in different types of occupations. Future studies might also examine the links of the HEXACO personality factors with the vocational interest dimensions, including the Adventuring dimension suggested by Campbell *et al.* (1992).

Other methods that have been examined as potential ways to reduce faking include the use of time limits on applicants' responses (Holden, Wood, & Tomashewski, 2001) and the use of items that require respondents to indicate which of several equally desirable (or undesirable) statements describes them most accurately (Jackson, Wroblewski, & Ashton, 2000). But perhaps the most likely way of overcoming the problem of faking will involve the use of *non-self-report* methods of assessing personality. All of the results described above were derived from self-reports, but it is possible that observer reports from persons who would have little reason to "fake" on behalf of the applicant—for example, previous employers or co-workers—would show higher levels of validity in predicting job performance. In fact, some evidence suggests that personality ratings from co-workers or supervisors can be at least as valid in predicting job performance as are personality self-ratings on the same characteristics (Mount, Barrick, & Strauss, 1994). Future research on personality and job performance is likely to involve a greater focus on observer reports, and not just self-reports, of personality.

Law-Abidingness versus Criminality

Criminal and other unethical activities cause enormous harm to their victims and to society at large, and one potential use of personality variables is to predict which persons are most likely to commit such actions. Of course, differences among people in the commission of criminal or unethical acts are likely to be due in considerable part to situational variables. For example, a person who would commit a crime under some circumstances—for example, when influenced by a particular social group, or when exposed to a particular temptation—might not commit a similar crime under other circumstances. But people do differ in the extent to which they abide by the laws and behave ethically, and personality is a plausible basis for these differences.

Many investigations of the links between personality and criminal activities are based on self-reports of both kinds of variables. When assessed under anonymous conditions—that is, when respondents perceive no risk of any punishment for admitting to unethical or illegal actions—such studies will likely provide an accurate indication of the relations between personality and crime. However, other investigations have used non-self-report methods of assessment, and in this section we will discuss results based on both types of studies.

The Role of Self-Control

One hypothesis about the personality basis of criminal activity comes from the work of two sociologists, Michael Gottfredson and Travis Hirschi. Considering crime as "acts of force or fraud undertaken in pursuit of self-interest" (Gottfredson & Hirschi, 1990, p. 15), those researchers tried to identify the crucial difference between criminals and noncriminals. According to those researchers, the critical variable is a lack of self-control: Criminals tend to act impulsively, failing to delay gratification and instead seeking immediate pleasure even at the risk of later punishment or other negative consequences. Interestingly, Gottfredson and Hirschi suggested that criminals are no more *motivated* to commit crimes than are noncriminals. That is, these researchers argued that noncriminals have the same selfish impulses that criminals have, but are better able to inhibit those impulses and delay gratification, choosing to cooperate and to work rather than to commit acts of force or fraud.

The description of self-control as given by Gottfredson and Hirschi (1990) is actually a bit more complicated than the preceding description, and there are some difficulties in measuring this variable (Marcus, 2004). But some recent research does give some interesting tests of the self-control hypothesis. For example, one study examined self-reports of personality and of criminal behavior among adolescents and university students in Spain (Romero, Gómez-Fraguela, Luengo, & Sobral, 2003). The researchers assessed several personality traits that are thought to be relevant to poor self-control, including impulsive risk taking, "preference for simple tasks," self-centeredness, preference for physical activities, and volatile temper. In addition, Romero *et al.* also obtained self-reports for several delinquent or criminal activities, representing categories of vandalism, theft, aggression, general rule breaking, academic dishonesty, and illegal drug use.

The results of the Romero *et al.* (2003) study showed that overall delinquent behavior was most strongly related to the characteristic of impulsive risk taking, with correlations averaging in the .40s across the two samples. (Other traits showed more modest relations and tended to be associated with specific kinds of delinquent acts. For example, self-centeredness and volatile temper both correlated in the .20s with aggressive acts.) Thus, the results of this study suggest that the willingness to take risks and the tendency *not* to inhibit one's impulses together have an important influence on criminal activity. Given that impulsive risk seeking is probably the trait that is most relevant, conceptually, to the construct of low self-control, these results do seem to be consistent with the hypothesis proposed by Gottfredson and Hirschi (1990).

Primary and Secondary Psychopathy

In contrast to the hypothesis of Gottfredson and Hirschi (1990), some other ideas about the links between personality and criminal behavior do include a role for differences in the *motivation* to commit crime, in addition to a role for lack of impulse control. For example, researchers have long observed that an important difference among criminals—even among the serious offenders called *psychopaths*—is that some have very poor self-control, whereas others are more coolly calculating and rational. Karpman (1948) used the term "primary psychopath" to refer to the latter kind of criminal, and called the former kind of criminal the "secondary psychopath." Consistent with this view, subsequent researchers who have studied the personality characteristics of criminals have found that those characteristics form two broad factors (e.g., Harpur, Hare, & Hakstian, 1989; Levenson, Kiehl, & Fitzpatrick, 1995) that show only modest positive correlations with each other. One group of characteristics, representing primary psychopathy, includes manipulation, deceit, grandiosity, callousness, and selfishness, whereas the other group of characteristics, representing secondary psychopathy, involves impulsivity, irresponsibility, lack of planning, and poor self-control.

In some studies, researchers have examined the relations of primary psychopathy and secondary psychopathy with criminal or delinquent behavior in samples of people, such as college students, who are generally not convicted criminals. These studies, based on anonymous self-reports, indicate that both sets of characteristics—primary and secondary psychopathy—are both positively correlated with delinquent activities, such as thefts, vandalism, driving while intoxicated, and others (Levenson *et al.*, 1995; McHoskey, Worzel, & Szyarto, 1998). These links are moderately strong, with correlations reaching the .40s, and suggest that both primary and secondary psychopathy need to be considered in order to predict criminal or delinquent behavior. That is, a person's likelihood of committing crimes depends both on how much he or she fails to control impulses, and also on his or her level of manipulativeness and selfishness.

The distinction between primary and secondary psychopathy has some interesting implications. One of these involves the behavior of persons who have high levels of one aspect of psychopathy, but low levels of the other. (Because the two kinds of psychopathy have modest positive correlations with each other, such persons will be somewhat unusual, but not extremely rare.) Consider a person who has high levels of primary psychopathic traits (such as deceitfulness, grandiosity, and selfishness) but low levels of secondary psychopathic traits (such as impulsivity and irresponsibility). Such a person will likely cause many difficulties for other people, by being exploitative and manipulative of others. However, such a person might be careful enough and self-controlled enough to avoid committing acts that would lead to criminal convictions (or at least to avoid committing such acts when he or she would be caught). Conversely, consider a person who has low levels of primary psychopathic traits but high levels of secondary psychopathic traits. Such a person would be unlikely to harm others deliberately while pursuing some selfish goals, yet he or she might nevertheless get into trouble with the authorities, for example, by impulsively committing a crime in response to some sudden provocation or some sudden temptation.

One question regarding primary and secondary psychopathy involves their relations with the major dimensions of personality, as organized within the Big Five or the HEXACO frameworks. For primary psychopathy, the relations with those broad personality factors have been studied along with two other, closely related traits: Machiavellianism (a cynical tendency to pursue one's interests by manipulating others) and narcissism (an inflated view of one's own importance, with a sense of entitlement and willingness to exploit others).[8] These three overlapping constructs of primary psychopathy, Machiavellianism, and narcissism are sometimes called the "Dark Triad" (Paulhus & Williams, 2002). These "Dark Triad" traits have been found to show moderately strong negative correlations (in the −.40s)

---

[8] Machiavellianism is most commonly measured using scales developed by Christie and Geis (1970). This construct is named after Niccolo Machiavelli, an Italian political philosopher of the late fifteenth and early sixteenth centuries, who advised rulers to use deceptive and ruthless tactics as a way to maintain and expand their personal power. Narcissism, as noted in the description of narcissistic personality disorder (Chapter 8), is named after a character in an ancient Greek myth who spent time admiring his own reflection in a pool of water.

BOX 9-2
Self-Esteem, Narcissism, and Aggression

How does self-esteem relate to aggressive and criminal behaviors? Are violent acts more likely to be committed by people who view themselves very negatively, or by people who view themselves very positively? To understand the relations between self-esteem and aggressive actions, it is important to realize that having low self-esteem is not exactly the opposite of having excessively high self-esteem. For example, a person who is narcissistic (see Chapter 8) tends to be conceited and arrogant, but such a person might also tend to have some feelings of inferiority or worthlessness. Similarly, even if a person rarely (if ever) feels inferior or worthless, he or she might not be at all conceited or arrogant. Therefore, it is important to consider low self-esteem and narcissism as two different traits—not as opposite ends of the same trait—when considering the relations of self-esteem with aggressive behavior.

When researchers have studied aggression in relation to both of the preceding traits, they have found that aggression is associated both with low self-esteem and also with narcissism (Donnellan, Trzesniewski, Robins, Moffitt, & Caspi, 2005; Paulhus, Robins, Trzesniewski, & Tracy, 2004). When both traits are considered together, their ability to predict aggressive tendencies is better than that of either trait alone. That is, the people who are most likely to commit aggressive acts are those who are susceptible to feelings of worthlessness and inferiority, but who are also inclined to have a conceited, arrogant sense of superiority over others. Conversely, the people that are least likely to commit aggressive acts are those who have adequate self-esteem (i.e., who do not feel inferior or worthless) without being narcissistic (i.e., without being self-important).

with the Big Five Agreeableness factor, but even stronger negative correlations (in the $-.60$s) with the HEXACO Honesty–Humility factor (Lee & Ashton, 2005). The strong relations with the latter dimension suggest that primary psychopathy (and the other two Dark Triad characteristics) can be understood largely as a low level of Honesty–Humility.

The relations of secondary psychopathy with the major personality dimensions are rather different from those of primary psychopathy. With regard to the Big Five factors, secondary psychopathy shows fairly strong negative correlations (about $-.50$) with Conscientiousness and Emotional Stability, and slightly weaker negative correlations with Agreeableness (Ross, Lutz, & Bailley, 2004). Relations with the HEXACO dimensions have not yet been examined, but would likely be broadly similar to those for the Big Five dimensions.

Life Satisfaction

In this chapter, we have considered the relations of personality with important outcome variables related to marriage and other relationships, to several health-related outcomes, to performance in school and at work, and to law-abiding versus criminal behavior. But another important variable that might be predicted by personality is simply that of life satisfaction—that is, a person's subjective evaluation of his or her own life. What aspects of one's personality can predict one's satisfaction with life?

Of course, one's life satisfaction at any given time is likely to depend on many variables that may be unrelated to one's personality. For example, the recent death of a loved one, the recent diagnosis of a serious illness, or the recent loss of a job would likely tend to lower one's current level of life satisfaction a great deal. Conversely, one's current level of life satisfaction is likely to be higher than usual if one has recently fallen in love or if one has recently achieved some much-desired success. However, there is evidence of some substantial stability to individual differences in life satisfaction: Even though one's level may rise or fall substantially in response to important events, some people have a general tendency to be more satisfied with life than others do, even across long periods of time (e.g., Diener, 2000).

For example, one study of American college students obtained correlations above .50 between life satisfaction levels measured 4 years apart. (Thus, a student who had an above-average level of life satisfaction at the beginning of college had about a 75% chance of having an above-average level at the end of college, and only about a 25% chance of having a below-average level.) Moreover, in one recent investigation of a sample of Dutch identical twins, fraternal twins, and nontwin siblings, life satisfaction was found to have a substantial genetic influence: Heritability was found to be almost .40 (Stubbe, Posthuma, Boomsma, & De Geus, 2005). Thus, even though one's level of life satisfaction will increase or decrease in response to important life events, there is still a tendency for some people to be consistently more satisfied with life than others are. This leaves open the possibility that personality characteristics might be related strongly to life satisfaction.

One study of American college students (Furr & Funder, 1998) examined the relations of a variety of personality traits with life satisfaction. Furr and Funder found that life satisfaction was strongly positively correlated with self-esteem (about .60) and to a lesser extent with cheerfulness (about .40) and with assertiveness and sociability (both above .30). In addition, life satisfaction showed strong negative correlations with depressiveness (about −.50) and to a lesser extent with anxiety (about −.30) and anger (about −.30). When these traits are considered in terms of the Big Five framework, the results show that life satisfaction is most strongly associated with high levels of Extraversion and of Emotional Stability. (In addition, life satisfaction also showed modest positive correlations, in the .20s, with Big Five Agreeableness and Conscientiousness.) These results were generally consistent even when personality was assessed by reports from the participants' parents and friends: That is, individuals' self-reports of life satisfaction were associated not only with their self-reported personalities, but also with their personalities as reported by their parents and friends.

The findings of the study by Furr and Funder (1998) suggest that an individual's satisfaction with life is to some considerable extent a function of his or her personality. In particular, persons who have a general disposition to feel positive emotions (e.g., cheerfulness, confidence) tend to have high life satisfaction; conversely, persons who have a general disposition to feel negative emotions (e.g., low self-esteem, depression, anxiety, anger) tend to have low life satisfaction. Note that these two dispositions are related independently to life satisfaction: If a person has a tendency to feel *both* positive and negative emotions rather strongly (or to feel both positive and negative emotions rather weakly), then he or she will likely have a roughly average level of life satisfaction (see Larsen &

BOX 9-3
Job Satisfaction

Earlier in this chapter, we examined the links between personality and satisfaction in one important domain of life, that of marriage. Researchers have also examined the relations between personality and satisfaction with other prominent domains of one's life, including job satisfaction. A review of many investigations (e.g., Judge, Heller, & Mount, 2002) indicated that job satisfaction was correlated with four of the Big Five factors—Extraversion, Emotional Stability, Agreeableness, and Conscientiousness. In combination, these four factors together correlate about .40 with job satisfaction. This result indicates that job satisfaction does depend to an important extent on personality, even though it likely also depends a great deal on characteristics of the job and also on the "fit" between a person and his or her job. There is already some evidence that people tend to be more satisfied with projects that are consistent with their personality characteristics, as, for example, when sociable people pursue social activities and goals (McGregor, McAdams, & Little, 2006).

Diener, 1987; Tellegen, Watson, & Clark, 1999). (Interestingly, women on average have a slight tendency to feel both positive emotions and negative emotions more strongly than do men; these tendencies apparently "cancel each other out," leaving virtually no difference between men and women in the average levels of life satisfaction.)

In a sense, it is not really surprising that life satisfaction tends to be high among people who feel positive emotions strongly and also among people who tend *not* to feel negative emotions strongly. Not only will these tendencies influence the way one evaluates one's life as a whole, but they may also influence the *experiences* one has in life: For example, a person who feels more positive than negative emotions may behave in such a way as to elicit more favorable reactions from others, and thus to develop better relationships and career outcomes. One question of interest for future studies will be to examine whether other personality traits can predict future life satisfaction many years later. For example, as found by Furr and Funder (1998), college students who are high in Conscientiousness traits have a slight tendency to be currently more satisfied with life, but it is also possible that Conscientiousness could also predict future life satisfaction, if traits such as organization and self-discipline tend to produce more favorable life events that improve various outcomes in one's life.

Summary and Conclusions

The relations between personality and the important life outcomes considered in this chapter can be summarized briefly as follows (see Table 9-1).

First, there is little tendency for spouses to be similar in personality; on average, a given husband and wife are likely to be little more similar to each other than to any other person. (As we will see in later chapters, though, there does exist some strong similarity between spouses for some other psychological characteristics.) However, some aspects of personality, such as Agreeableness or Emotional Stability, are related to marital satisfaction—both one's own and that of one's spouse.

TABLE 9-1
Summary of Relations between Personality Characteristics and Important Life Outcomes

Life outcome variable	Associated personality characteristics
Marital Satisfaction (one's own)	high Agreeableness
	high Emotional Stability
Marital Satisfaction (one's partner's)	high Agreeableness
	high Emotional Stability
Popularity/Status with peers (in young adults)	high Extraversion (men and women)
	high Emotional Stability (men only)
Substance Use	low Conscientiousness
	low Emotional Stability
Longevity	high dependability, low cheerfulness
Heart Disease	high hostility, high dominance
Academic Performance	high Conscientiousness (especially achievement motivation)
Job Performance	high Conscientiousness
	high proactivity
	high integrity
Law-Abidingness	low impulsivity/secondary psychopathy
	low exploitativeness/primary psychopathy
Life Satisfaction	high Extraversion
	high Emotional Stability
	high self-esteem
	high cheerfulness
	low depressiveness

See text for sources and for sizes of correlations. Names of Big Five factors are capitalized; names of more specific traits are in lowercase.

With regard to peer relationships, some research has shown that children who are popular with their peers tend to be sociable and nonaggressive. Among college students, popularity has been found to be associated with Extraversion and also (for male college students only) with Emotional Stability and physical attractiveness.

In the domain of health-related behaviors and outcomes, personality has been found to predict substance use, longevity, and heart disease. Persons with lower levels of Conscientiousness and of Emotional Stability are more likely to smoke and to abuse alcohol or illicit drugs. Traits of social dependability have been found to be moderately good predictors of longevity; also, some evidence suggests that cheerfulness is somewhat related to chances of earlier death, but other results have shown the opposite pattern. Higher risk of heart disease has been found to be associated with personality traits of hostility and dominance, but not (as had previously been thought) with the other "Type A" characteristics, such as time urgency or job involvement.

Performance in school and on the job are also associated with personality characteristics. The best predictors of academic performance are traits associated with the Conscientiousness factor, particularly achievement motivation. These Conscientiousness-related traits are also important for predicting job performance across the various types of jobs, as are the characteristics measured by integrity tests, which are associated with both Conscientiousness and the HEXACO Honesty–Humility factor.

Research on personality and law-abidingness has focused on low self-control as an important predictor of criminal activity. Other research has suggested that criminal activity is associated not only with traits of poor impulse control, but also with traits of willingness to exploit and manipulate others for personal gain (i.e., with low Honesty-Humility).

Finally, persons' ratings of their overall life satisfaction are associated with traits involving Extraversion and Emotional Stability, such as self-esteem, cheerfulness, and lack of anxious or depressive tendencies. This result suggests that people differ in their underlying tendency to feel satisfied with their lives, as these traits represent a tendency to feel positive emotions and also a tendency not to feel negative emotions.

Taken together, the findings described in this chapter suggest that personality does play a significant role in predicting important life outcomes. Those outcomes are certainly not influenced solely (or even primarily) by personality, but many of the important "results" of people's lives are at least partly a function of their personality characteristics.

Chapter 10

Mental Ability

The Domain of Mental Ability 210

**The Structure of Mental Ability:
One Dimension or Many? 211**

Spearman and the *g* Factor 214

Thurstone and Group Factors 217

g Plus Group Factors 218

**Developmental Change and Stability in
Mental Abilities 220**

Developmental Changes in Mean Levels of
Mental Ability 220

Stability of Mental Ability across the Life
Span 221

Biological Bases of Mental Ability 222

Brain Size 222

Nerve Conduction Velocity 223

Reaction Time 224

Inspection Time 226

Brain Waves: Averaged Evoked
Potentials 227

Brain Glucose Metabolism 228

**Genetic and Environmental Influences on
Mental Ability 228**

Genetic Influences 228

Womb Environment Influences 230

Other Environmental Influences:
Nutrition 231

**Evolutionary Function of Mental
Ability 234**

Mental Ability and Life Outcomes 237

Academic Achievement and
Performance 237

Job Performance, Occupational Status, and
Income 240

Longevity and Health 242

Law-Abidingness versus Criminality 243

Marriage: Assortative Mating 245

**Not All g-Loaded Tasks Are the
Same 245**

Novel versus Familiar Tasks: Fluid and
Crystallized Intelligence 246

Generational Changes in Mental Abilities:
The Flynn Effect 246

Reasoning with Numbers and Shapes versus
Understanding Verbal Concepts: Different
Relations with Personality 248

**Alternative Ideas about Mental
Abilities 249**

Gardner's "Theory of Multiple
Intelligences" 249

Sternberg's "Triarchic Theory of
Intelligence" 251

Emotional Intelligence 253

Summary and Conclusions 255

The Domain of Mental Ability

The topic of this chapter is mental ability—an area of human individual differences that is usually considered to be separate from that of personality. When we discuss personality variation, we are describing differences among people in their *typical behavioral tendencies*—that is, the ways they generally act, think, and feel in various situations. For example, we might try to find out how much different persons tend to socialize, to become angry, to learn new things, or to feel afraid. But when we discuss variation in mental abilities, we are not describing differences among people in these "styles" of behavior; instead, we are describing differences among people in their *maximum performance* in producing correct answers to various problems or questions. For example, we might try to find out how well different persons are able to understand written paragraphs, to solve arithmetic problems, or to figure out directions on a map.

In this chapter, we will explore several important questions about human mental abilities. In many ways, these questions are similar to those that we have addressed throughout this book in the context of personality variation. We will begin with the issue of the structure of mental abilities: Is there a general tendency for some people to be "smarter" than others across the full array of intellectual tasks? Or, is there a tendency for some people to be "smart" at some intellectual tasks and for other people to be "smart" at other such tasks?

After discussing the structure of mental abilities, we will consider a series of questions about the nature of mental ability. How do levels of mental ability change throughout the life span, and how stable are individual differences in mental ability across long periods of time? What are the biological variables that underlie variation among people in mental ability? Is this variation mainly attributable to genetic or to environmental differences? To the extent that the environment is involved, which aspects have the strongest impact on mental abilities?

We will then move on to the question of whether mental abilities have any important influences on real-life outcomes: Do scores on mental ability tests predict academic performance? Do they predict job performance or health and longevity? Being a good citizen? Whom we marry?

Next, we will examine the sometimes complex ways in which mental abilities are related to several other variables. For example, some aspects of mental ability are substantially related to certain personality characteristics, whereas other aspects are not. Similarly, some aspects of mental ability show large differences between the generations and large changes throughout the life span, whereas other aspects do not.

Finally, we will also consider some alternative ideas about mental ability that have achieved some popularity among the general public, such as the "triarchic theory of intelligence," the "theory of multiple intelligences," and "emotional intelligence." In particular, we will examine the evidence regarding the validity of these ideas.

But before we address these many questions, we should take a moment to clarify what we mean by "mental abilities." This is important, because if we want to study and to measure mental abilities, we will need to decide exactly what is included (and what is not included) within this domain. Generally, researchers who study mental ability have agreed that this domain should be assessed by tasks whose difficulty is due to their demands on mental processes, such as reasoning, understanding, imagining, and remembering. For example, the difficulty in understanding a written paragraph, in solving an arithmetic problem, or in figuring out a route on a map is in each case due to the demands placed on thinking-related skills. The researchers in this field have also agreed that the domain of mental abilities should *not* be assessed by tasks whose difficulty is due in part to their demands on physical skills or on sensory abilities. For example, the difficulty in throwing a javelin, in tying a knot, in hearing a very high-pitched sound, or in seeing a very dim light is in each case largely due to the demands these tasks place on physical or sensory abilities.

Besides focusing on tasks that assess purely mental abilities, researchers in this field also restrict their investigations to tasks that demand skills that are roughly equally familiar to all persons. For example, a test of arithmetic problem solving might be used, because almost everyone is familiar with these problems (at least after middle childhood); however, a test of calculus problem solving would not be used, because most people are not familiar with these problems. Similarly, a mental abilities researcher might measure reading comprehension in a language that was fully familiar to all of the research participants (assuming, of course, that they had all learned to read), but not in a language that some participants had studied and others had not. Figure 10-1 shows several examples of tasks that are used in tests of various mental abilities.

Also, there is one other point to mention before we examine in depth the topic of mental abilities. You might have noticed that, in the preceding paragraphs, the word "intelligence" has not been used, even though the topic considered here is frequently described by that term. The reason for referring to this domain as "mental ability" rather than "intelligence" is that this avoids raising the (rather meaningless) question of what intelligence "really" is. Frequently, when scientists describe mental abilities research with the word intelligence, many people object that this domain is not necessarily the same thing as intelligence. They might argue that intelligence is not really about solving the problems given on intelligence tests, many of which are either school-like tasks or artificial puzzles. They might suggest instead that intelligence is about achieving success in the competitive struggles of "real life" or (alternatively) about living in harmony with other people and with the natural surroundings. Perhaps you will agree with this objection, or perhaps you will disagree; but to avoid a pointless debate about the meaning of a word, we should make it clear that what we are trying to investigate is mental ability as described above: That is, the capacity to solve problems that demand thinking-related skills. After reading the summary provided in this chapter about the nature of mental abilities, their causes, and their consequences for the real world, you might think about whether or not you would describe those abilities as "intelligence." But let us put this aside for now, and begin discussing what scientists have learned about individual differences in mental ability.

The Structure of Mental Ability: One Dimension or Many?

Consider the four tasks that are shown in Figure 10-1. These four tasks are all parts of a widely used intelligence test called the Multidimensional Aptitude Battery (MAB; Jackson,

Vocabulary: Choose the alternative from A to E that is nearest in meaning to the word given.

Simple

A. hard   B. easy   C. example   D. the same   E. useful

Arithmetic: Solve the following problem.

If it costs $8 for two students to go to the theatre, how much will it cost for three students?

A. $10   B. $16   C. $12   D. $4   E. $6

Spatial: Choose one figure to the right of the vertical line which is the same as the figure on the left. One figure can be turned to look like the figure on the left; the others would have to be flipped over.

Picture Arrangement: Look at these pictures. Put them in the right order so that they will tell a story.

A.   1 2 4 3

B.   2 3 1 4

C.   1 4 3 2

D.   4 1 3 2

E.   4 3 2 1

1.   2.

3.   4.

FIGURE 10-1. Example items from four mental ability subtests of the Multidimensional Aptitude Battery. Source: Jackson (1984a). Reproduced by permission of SIGMA Assessment Systems, Inc. P. O. Box, 610984, Port Huron, MI 48061-0984.

1984a). The first task is a test called Vocabulary, which asks respondents to identify which of several alternative words is closest in meaning to the given word. In the second task, called Arithmetic, respondents must figure out how to solve an arithmetic problem and then correctly perform the needed calculations. The third task is called Spatial; this particular spatial test asks respondents to consider a given two-dimensional shape and to indicate which of several alternative shapes would match the given shape if it were flipped over (as opposed to merely being rotated). In the fourth task, called Picture Arrangement, respondents must figure out which sequence of comic strip panels would make the most meaningful story.

Consider these four tasks, and ask yourself this question: Would people who perform well at one of these tasks usually also perform well at the others, or would there be essentially zero correlations between levels of performance on the tasks? For example, do you believe that people with better verbal ability (measured by the Vocabulary task) would also have better ability in social interpretation (measured by the Picture Arrangement task), or not? Also, do you believe that people with better quantitative reasoning ability (measured by the Arithmetic task) would also have better ability in spatial orientation (measured by the Spatial task), or not? If you believe that there exists a *general* mental ability—an overall tendency to be "smart"—then you would expect some substantial positive correlations. On the other hand, if you believe that that there are several completely independent mental abilities—several completely different kinds of being "smart"—then you would expect the correlations to be close to zero. Later in this chapter, we will summarize the actual correlations among these tasks, as based on the scores of thousands of high school students who have taken the tests. But now let us examine the history of research on this question of the structure of mental abilities.

It was only in the late nineteenth century that scientists began the systematic study of mental ability. Some early researchers, such as James McKeen Cattell (in the United States) and Francis Galton (in England), believed that individual differences in intellectual abilities could be understood as the result of individual differences in various physical or sensory abilities. Therefore, they tried to determine whether the latter abilities—for example, lung capacity, grip strength, hearing acuity, or reaction time—would discriminate between persons who were believed to differ in intelligence. However, these researchers did not measure mental abilities directly.

The first researcher to develop tasks assessing mental abilities was Alfred Binet. His work was part of an effort by the French government to improve the educational system by helping teachers to identify which children were mentally retarded, so that these children could be given their own educational curriculum. Binet developed a variety of tasks that he used in measuring the mental ability of children—he used the word "intelligence"—and many of these really did demand mental abilities, such as thinking with numbers, words, and shapes. Binet's tests were rather successful in their intended purpose, and went on to be used in revised form in many other countries even to the present day. However, Binet himself did not try to examine empirically the major scientific questions about the nature of mental abilities, such as the crucial issue of whether there is a single major dimension of mental ability, or whether there are instead several independent varieties of mental ability.

Spearman and the *g* Factor

This question of the structure of mental abilities was investigated by Charles Spearman, the researcher who remains the most important figure in the history of the science of mental ability. An engineer by training, Spearman served for 15 years in the British Army, and then in 1897 began studying psychology in Germany under the supervision of Wilhelm Wundt—the first psychologist to conduct experimental research. At the same time, Spearman was also influenced by the work of Francis Galton—the first psychologist to study individual differences. Spearman became interested in the nature of mental ability, and he began to study it systematically when he returned to England, using students in English schools as his research participants.

At first, Spearman did not measure mental ability directly; instead, he examined students' grades in school, which he believed to be a reasonably good indicator of their mental ability. In order to determine whether or not there was a single mental ability that was responsible for students' performance across their courses, Spearman calculated correlations among the grades in various courses.[1] His results—as published in his classic article (Spearman, 1904)—showed that grades in the various courses tended to be substantially positively correlated with each other. For example, most students who achieved high grades in arithmetic also achieved high grades in Latin, and most students who achieved low grades in geometry also achieved low grades in French. This result suggested to Spearman that students' grades in these various courses were largely a reflection of the students' differing levels of a single, general mental ability. In other words, the fact that grades in each course were related to grades in every other course indicated that grades in every one of those courses were assessing something in common—presumably, a general, all-around academic ability.

In subsequent research (e.g., Spearman, 1927; Spearman & Jones, 1950), Spearman investigated this question by testing students directly on a variety of tasks intended to assess different aspects of mental ability. (This was an important step, because it could have been the case that students' grades were due not only to a general dimension of mental ability, but also to a general dimension of academic motivation, or to some other source.) Again, he found that students' scores on these various tasks tended to have substantial positive correlations with each other. For example, students who performed well at understanding the meanings of proverbs usually also performed well in identifying which of several shapes was unlike the others; similarly, students who performed poorly in solving arithmetic problems also performed poorly in figuring out analogies between various pairs of words.

---

[1] In fact, this was the first time that *anyone* had calculated correlations: It was Spearman himself who invented the correlation coefficient, in order to express how strongly (or weakly) different abilities were related to each other. Spearman's form of the correlation coefficient was calculated using individuals' ranks on the variables, rather than their actual scores. Nowadays, researchers usually use a form of the correlation coefficient, developed by Karl Pearson, that is based on individuals' scores rather than ranks.

These results therefore confirmed the findings based on school grades, suggesting again that a general mental ability was at work: The correlations among the various tasks indicated that performance on each task was influenced by a general mental ability.

Spearman's finding of positive correlations among the diverse mental ability tasks was important, given that it indicated the existence of a single, major dimension of mental ability. (Like Binet, Spearman did not hesitate to refer to mental ability as "intelligence," and he described this dimension as "general intelligence.") But this was not the only noteworthy aspect of his findings. Another important finding was that some tasks tended to show rather high correlations with the various other tasks, whereas other tasks tended to show rather low correlations with the various other tasks. This result led Spearman to suggest that performance on the former tasks was very strongly influenced by general mental ability; how well someone did on those tasks was a fairly good indication of their overall level of mental ability. Conversely, performance on the latter tasks was not so strongly influenced by general mental ability; how well someone did on those tasks was not such a good indication of their overall level of mental ability. As a way of summarizing the extent to which each task was correlated with the other tasks, Spearman used factor analysis (actually, he invented factor analysis, as he invented the correlation coefficient). When Spearman factor analyzed the correlations among the various subtests, he obtained one factor of general mental ability. The tasks that tended to show strong correlations with other tasks showed high loadings on that factor, and the tasks that tended to show weak correlations with other tasks showed lower loadings on that factor. Spearman referred to this factor as *g*, using the letter "g" to represent "general intelligence," and this abbreviation is still used today. The loadings of the various tasks on this *g* factor were described as the "*g*-loadings" of the subtests, and this terminology also remains in use to this day.

At this point, you might be wondering about the kinds of tasks that showed higher and lower *g*-loadings—that is, you might wonder *which* tasks were the best indicators of general mental ability (or, to use Spearman's term, general intelligence). For example, do *g*-loadings depend on the content of the task, such as whether it uses numbers, words, or shapes? Or, do *g*-loadings depend on the kind of mental process demanded by the task, such as whether it requires reasoning or memory or perception? By comparing the *g*-loadings of the various tasks, Spearman was able to answer these questions.

First, Spearman found that the content of the task did not matter. Among the most highly *g*-loaded tasks, some tasks were based on verbal content, others were based on numerical content, and still others were based on spatial or figural content. Among the tasks with low *g*-loadings, again there were some verbal tasks, some numerical tasks, and some spatial or figural tasks. Spearman considered this to be an important result, and he referred to it as "the principle of the indifference of the indicator." What he meant by this was that the content of the task (i.e., the indicator) was unimportant (i.e., indifferent) in determining whether the task would show a high *g*-loading or a low *g*-loading.

Second, Spearman found that the mental processes involved in the task did matter. Among the tasks with high *g*-loadings, Spearman found that most of these tasks involved reasoning in some form or other. For example, he found high *g*-loadings for tasks in which respondents had to figure out an analogy between two pairs of words, or the next number in a series of numbers, or the shape that was different from the other shapes in a group. In contrast, Spearman found that the tasks with low *g*-loadings involved simpler mental processes that were more automatic or involved following rules. For example, he found relatively low *g*-loadings for tasks involving *spelling* of words (rather than *comprehension* of word meanings), *calculation* of numbers (rather than *solving problems* involving numbers), or *simple comparison* of shapes (rather than *figuring out* how shapes were alike or unalike).

As was the case for Spearman's finding of "the principle of the indifference of the indicator," Spearman thought that the finding of high *g*-loadings for reasoning-based tasks was very important. In fact, he suggested that these reasoning tasks had some important similarities that generalized across the different kinds of content used by those tasks. According to Spearman, the highly *g*-loaded tasks mostly involved a process that he described as "the eduction of relations and correlates." (Note that the word is "eduction" without an "a"; it is not "education.")

As an example of this process of educing relations and correlates, consider the verbal analogy problem shown in Figure 10-2: "cat is to dog as kitten is to ? ". In solving this problem, you need to "educe" the *relation* between a cat and a kitten—that is, a kitten is a young cat—and then to "educe" the *correlate* of this relation for a dog—that is, a young dog is a puppy. Similarly, consider a number series problem such as the one shown in Figure 10-2, in which you need to figure out which number continues the series 1, 3, 5, 7, ... To solve this, you need to educe the relations between the numbers (in this case, each number is two larger than the number to its left), and then educe the correlate of this relation for the next number of the series (here, a number two greater than 7 is 9).

The same steps are involved in tasks such as matrix reasoning problems (also shown in Figure 10-2), in which you must notice the pattern of shapes within each cell of the matrix, figure out how the pattern of shapes changes from one cell to the next, and then apply this rule to figure out the pattern of shapes for the missing cell. Spearman's students, among them a man named John Raven, developed a test of this type (e.g., Raven, 1941), which they intended to be a very highly *g*-loaded task. This test is known as Raven's Matrices, and in its several versions it remains a widely used measure of general mental ability. The items of the Raven's Matrices test are somewhat different from that shown in Figure 10-2, but the basic principle is very similar. (All of the examples in Figure 10-2 are very easy ones, but as you can imagine, other items of these kinds can be very difficult.)

As we have discussed so far, Spearman discovered some important facts about human mental abilities. One important finding was his discovery of the positive correlations among all the diverse tasks assessing different aspects of mental ability, a fact that indicated the existence of a general factor of mental ability, or *g*. Another important result was that some of these tasks tended to show strong correlations with most other tasks (and thus had high loadings on the *g* factor), whereas other tasks tended to show weaker correlations (and thus had lower *g*-loadings). Finally, Spearman also found that highly *g*-loaded tasks could have any kind of content (i.e., numbers, words, shapes), but

Verbal Analogies	Number Series	Matrices	
cat is to dog as kitten is to ?	1 3 5 7 ?	XOX	OXO
		I O I	?

FIGURE 10-2. Examples of mental ability tasks requiring the eduction of relations and correlates. In each task, the respondent must find the answer by educing (inferring) the relations between the given parts of the item, and then educing (inferring) the missing part. See text for further explanation.

that those tasks frequently demanded reasoning of some kind, often involving the process of "educing relations and correlates."

Now, back to the question that we asked earlier in this chapter: The first four tasks shown in Figure 10-1 are all positively correlated with each other; that is, persons who do very well on one task are likely to perform well on another task also. All of the six correlations among these four tasks are roughly similar in size, ranging from .24 to .42 as found in a large sample of over 3000 high school students (Jackson, 1984a). If these four abilities are then factor analyzed, all four tasks show moderately high loadings on a *g* factor. This result is thus a nice illustration of Spearman's finding that a dimension of general mental ability is involved even in tasks that appear to be very different from each other.[2]

Thurstone and Group Factors

After Spearman's work was published, other researchers also began to investigate the structure of mental abilities. Some of the largest and most influential investigations were those of an American psychologist, Louis Thurstone. Like Spearman, Thurstone had originally been trained as an engineer before studying psychology; for a short time in 1912, Thurstone worked as an assistant to the famous inventor, Thomas Edison.

Much of Thurstone's research was motivated by his view that a *g* factor did not adequately explain the relations among various kinds of mental abilities. Instead, Thurstone suspected, tasks having similar content, or tasks requiring similar mental processes, would be very highly correlated with each other—that is, the correlations would be higher than one would expect based on their *g*-loadings. For example, two tasks that both require numerical ability (e.g., an addition task and a division task) would correlate very highly with each other, much more highly than with nonnumerical tasks. Similarly, two tasks that both require verbal ability (e.g., listing words that rhyme with a given word, and listing words that begin with a given letter) would also correlate very highly with each other, and again much more highly than with nonverbal tasks.

Thurstone believed that it would be possible to identify several important factors of mental ability, by factor analyzing a very large and diverse battery of mental ability tasks.

---

[2] The correlations are even higher when these abilities are measured by tasks that do not involve multiple-choice responses, but instead use a "one-on-one" interview-style testing format.

He and his assistants developed—with great creativity—dozens of tasks intended to assess a wide variety of abilities. After administering those tasks to large numbers of students, Thurstone (e.g., 1938) conducted factor analyses on the students' scores on those tasks. But unlike Spearman, Thurstone interpreted the results in terms of several factors, not just one "*g*" factor of general mental ability. On the basis of several investigations during the 1930s, Thurstone concluded that there were at least seven important factors of mental ability:

Verbal Fluency (ability to produce many words related to a given category);
Verbal Comprehension (ability to understand many words, alone or in the context of a written passage);
Numerical Facility (ability to work quickly with numbers);
Spatial Visualization (ability to imagine shapes from different perspectives);
Memory (ability to remember strings of information or paired associations);
Perceptual Speed (ability to notice quickly the similarities and differences between objects or symbols); and
Reasoning (ability to infer patterns, similar to "eduction of relations and correlates").

As noted by Thurstone, tasks measuring any one of these factors correlated particularly strongly with each other, and more strongly than with tasks measuring other mental abilities. These results suggested that "*g*" alone was not sufficient to explain the pattern of relations among different mental ability tasks.[3]

g Plus Group Factors

In spite of Thurstone's finding, however, an important fact still remained: All of the various tasks were positively correlated with each other, and therefore there were substantial correlations among the seven broad factors of mental ability that Thurstone had identified. (Note that this is different from the situation involving the personality dimensions described in Chapter 3; those personality factors are roughly uncorrelated with each other.) In other words, people who were above average in one of Thurstone's mental ability factors also tended to be above average in the others; therefore, there was still evidence of a general mental ability of the kind described by Thurstone.

Soon after Thurstone's results had been reported, several researchers worked to resolve the apparent contradiction between Spearman's finding of one general mental ability factor and Thurstone's finding of several mental ability factors. One approach was to examine several factors, as Thurstone had done, but then to conduct a second factor analysis, based

---

[3] In one of his manuscripts, Thurstone (1938) described the reaction of his research participants to the tests that he administered to them. In this case, the participants were undergraduate students at the University of Chicago, who had completed about 60 different tests in several sessions spanning a period of several days. At the end of the session, the students stood and applauded him and his assistants, apparently out of appreciation for the interesting tasks that they had been given. The participants took part in the investigation in return for information about their profile of mental abilities, and for suggestions regarding the kind of work that would be best suited to their profiles.

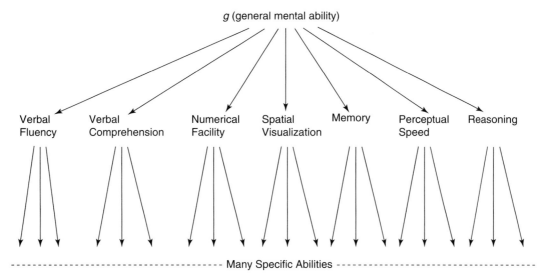

FIGURE 10-3. Hierarchical model of mental abilities, showing Thurstone's group factors at middle level.

on correlations among the several factors that were obtained from the first analysis (Burt, 1939; Eysenck, 1939; Vernon, 1950). In this way, the researchers could classify the many diverse mental ability tasks into a few broad factors of the kind found by Thurstone, but then they could in turn classify those factors into a *g* factor akin to that obtained by Spearman (see Figure 10-3). Using this approach, it was found that some of Thurstone's factors, particularly reasoning, had very high *g*-loadings. These results were therefore consistent with Spearman's findings about the tasks that had particularly high *g*-loadings.[4]

So, by the late 1930s, researchers had largely reached agreement about the structure of mental abilities. First, it was established that there did exist a *g* factor of general mental ability, which meant that people who performed well at one mental ability task were likely to perform well at other mental ability tasks. But in addition, it was established that there

---

[4] Another approach to resolving the differences between Thurstone's and Spearman's results used a somewhat different technique, but ended up with the same basic result. This alternative method (see, e.g., Holzinger & Swineford, 1939; Gustafsson, 2002) used a somewhat complex form of factor analysis to divide up each task into several parts. This technique would figure out, for any given task, (a) how much the task depended on the *g* factor of general mental ability, (b) how much it depended on the various mental ability factors identified by Thurstone, and (c) how much it depended on other, special characteristics that were unique to the test. When these results are averaged across all tasks, it is typically found that about 35% of overall performance on the test battery is due to the *g* factor of Spearman, about 20% is due to the several factors identified by Thurstone (but only about 3% or so for *each of those factors individually*), and about 45% is due to the many features unique to the tests individually (but only about 1 or 2% for *each test on its own*).

also existed several other, smaller factors of mental ability, each consisting of tasks that were similar in some important ways; this meant that people who performed well in one kind of task were especially likely to perform well in similar mental ability tasks. In most ways, however, the first conclusion is the more important one. This is partly because the *g* factor discovered by Spearman provides a simpler summary of individual differences in mental abilities than do the several factors discovered by Thurstone. Beyond this fact, however, the *g* factor has proved to be especially useful for predicting a wide array of important outcome variables, including academic performance, job performance, health, law-abidingness, and others. In a later section of this chapter, we will examine these correlates of the *g* factor in some detail. But first, let us consider some important questions about the nature and origins of *g*. How do levels of *g* change throughout the life span? How stable are individual differences in *g*? What are the biological bases of individual differences in *g*? Also, are those differences due mainly to hereditary variation or to environmental variation?

Before we begin addressing these questions, we should briefly discuss the relation of the well-known "IQ" tests to the *g* factor of personality. Most IQ tests consist of several subtests that assess different aspects of mental ability and are combined to produce an overall IQ score. (Some IQ tests instead consist of various items that are not organized into subtests, but that instead contribute directly to the overall score.) Individuals' IQ test scores are usually very strongly correlated with their levels of *g*, and for the purposes of this chapter we can treat "IQ" and *g* as being almost interchangeable. As noted in Chapter 1, most IQ tests are designed so that the average score is 100, and so that the standard deviation of scores is 15. An individual's IQ score is generally calculated in comparison with people of roughly his or her own age. (The label "IQ" stands for "intelligence quotient," a term that describes the method that was formerly used to calculate children's IQ scores: In the early days, those scores were computed by taking the child's "mental age"—as based on comparison of his or her test score to that of the average child of various other ages—and dividing this by the child's real, "chronological age," and multiplying the result by 100.)

Developmental Change and Stability in Mental Abilities

Now let us consider the development of mental abilities—particularly the *g* factor—across the life span. First, we will examine the ways in which the typical person changes in his or her level of *g*, and then we will examine the extent to which individual differences in *g*—that is, differences among people of the same age cohort—are stable across long periods of time.

Developmental Changes in Mean Levels of Mental Ability

When considering the changes in a typical person's level of *g* across the life span, we need to consider individuals' absolute levels of *g*, rather than levels of *g* in comparison with other people of the same age. The clearest findings from research on this question will probably seem rather obvious: On average, people's levels of *g* increase rapidly through childhood and continue to increase into late adolescence, and then decrease during old age. But the changes that occur *in between* the early and late stages of life—that is, between late adolescence and late middle age—are not so clear.

Some researchers have suggested that, on average, individuals' levels of mental abilities tend to remain about the same (or even increase slightly) throughout early and middle adulthood, before beginning to decline in late middle age and then declining more rapidly during old age (e.g., Rönnlund & Nilsson, 2006; Schaie, 1994). Other researchers have suggested that the pattern of changes in mental ability during adulthood is more complicated, and depends on which abilities are considered. Instead, they have argued (Horn & Cattell, 1966; Kaufman, 2001), people tend to maintain (or even increase slightly) their levels of abilities that are measured by familiar, school-like tasks (consider the Vocabulary and Arithmetic tasks of Figure 10-1). In contrast, those researchers have argued, people tend to decline substantially in their levels of abilities that are measured by less familiar, puzzle-like tasks (consider the Spatial and Picture Arrangement tasks of Figure 10-1). (These two categories of tasks are called "crystallized" and "fluid" abilities, respectively, and we will discuss them in more detail in a later section of this chapter.)

Which of these views is correct? So far, the answer is not clear, as few studies have assessed the abilities of a large group of people across a long period of time. Moreover, even when such studies have been conducted, it is possible that people's scores are influenced by their prior practice of taking the test on previous occasions. The investigation of this topic is still under way (e.g., Salthouse, 2005).

Stability of Mental Ability across the Life Span

Regardless of any changes in the people's average levels of mental abilities across the life span, there is also the question of whether or not *individual differences* in mental abilities are stable. As we discussed in Chapter 4 with regard to personality traits, the people of a given age cohort can undergo developmental changes in their levels of characteristics, yet still show the same relative standing in comparison with each other. With regard to mental abilities, the research evidence is clear: There does appear to be a high level of consistency across the life course in relative levels of mental ability, at least after late childhood.

Perhaps the most striking evidence of this comes from a study by Deary, Whiteman, Starr, Whalley, and Fox (2004), who administered an intelligence test to a sample of over 500 elderly Scottish adults. All of these participants—who were 79 or 80 years old at the time of testing—had taken the very same intelligence test nearly 7 decades earlier, when they were 11-year-old elementary school students. Deary *et al.* found that the participants' scores at 79 or 80 years of age were about one standard deviation unit higher than their scores at 11 years of age; interestingly, this indicates that the growth in mental ability during and after puberty was much greater than any decline in mental ability due to aging. But in spite of the increase in mental ability between 11 years of age and adulthood, the *differences among the participants* in mental ability remained remarkably stable across this interval of almost 7 decades: The correlation between test scores at 11 years old and test scores at almost 80 years old was about .65. This means that over 80% of the participants who were above average in mental ability at 11 years old were also above average when tested at nearly 80 years old. That is, the smartest 80-year-olds had usually been among the smartest 11-year-olds, and vice versa.

Biological Bases of Mental Ability

Given that people differ in their overall levels of mental ability—that is, in their levels of the *g* factor—the obvious question arises as to the biological basis of those individual differences. What is it about people's brains that make some of them smarter than others? Can we identify some biological variable that is associated with higher or lower levels of mental ability? As recently as the 1990s, there was relatively little research aimed at answering these questions (Vernon, 1991), but lately there have been many more investigations on this topic. In this section, we will consider some of the biological characteristics that have been examined as potential bases of individual differences in mental ability, particularly in the *g* factor.

Brain Size

If you try to think of some biological variable that might explain how smart people are, the one that comes to mind most readily is probably the size of the brain. In fact, the possibility that bigger brains are smarter brains seems almost *too* obvious, and many people seem to think that this idea has long since been refuted by psychologists. But what is the evidence regarding the links between brain size and *g*?[5]

To answer this question, we first need to know how these variables are measured. We have already discussed the measurement of *g*, but this leaves the question of how brain size can be measured. Until the late twentieth century, it was difficult for researchers to obtain a precise estimate of the brain sizes of one's research participants. As a result, researchers who wanted to find the relation between brain size and *g* had to rely on measurements of head size—which is substantially (but not perfectly!) correlated with brain size—rather than of brain size itself. They did this in the simple way that you might imagine, by using tape measures or callipers to measure the perimeter, height, width, and length of people's heads. Using these methods, researchers typically found that measurements of overall head size showed modest positive correlations, averaging about .20, with overall scores on mental ability tests, or on the *g* factor (Vernon, Wickett, Bazana, & Stelmack, 2000). Thus, this evidence suggested that the size of the brain probably did play some role in explaining individual differences in mental ability.

---

[5] Some people mistakenly believe that the idea of a relation between brain size and mental ability was long ago found to be false, and that it is no longer taken seriously by scientists. Although many people shared this belief during the late twentieth century—a time when several popular books claimed that brain size was unrelated to mental ability—they were too quick to discard the idea of a link between these variables, as the findings discussed below will make clear.

Since the 1980s, however, researchers have been able to measure the brain size of living persons in a much more direct way, by using a technique called magnetic resonance imaging—the MRI scan. An MRI scanner uses magnets and radio waves to produce accurate images of the brain, which allows researchers to measure brain volume. This method has been used frequently in studies of the relation between brain size and mental ability, and by 2005, at least 37 such studies had been conducted on a total of 1530 research participants (see McDaniel, 2005). The results of these investigations have been fairly consistent, and the overall pattern of findings is clear: Brain size is positively correlated with intelligence, with an average correlation of about .33 (McDaniel, 2005). As you will recall from our earlier chapters about the correlation coefficient, this would mean that more than 65% of people with above-average brain size will be above average in intelligence, whereas fewer than 35% of people with above-average brain size will be below average in intelligence.

In some sense, the research showing links between brain size and mental ability might actually underestimate the potential strength of those links. This is because the *overall* size of the brain might actually be less important than the sizes of certain regions of the brain. Keep in mind that much of your brain is not so directly involved in thinking, but is instead devoted to the day-to-day operations of your body. Therefore, even if two people have the same brain size overall, they might have different proportions of their total brain matter devoted to cognitive as opposed to noncognitive activity. However, it is not yet known whether or not there are indeed some regions of the brain whose sizes are especially strongly correlated with intelligence.[6]

Nerve Conduction Velocity

Another possible biological basis for individual differences in mental ability is the speed with which electrical impulses are transmitted between the cells of the brain and nervous systems. Even in the nineteenth century, researchers such as Galton believed that mental ability was based on the speed with which the brain could process information, and by the late twentieth century researchers were actually able to assess (albeit with some technical difficulties) the speed of the brain and nervous system. One such method of measuring the speed of nervous system transmissions involves the presentation of a visual stimulus (say, a quick flash of light) to the research participant, on whose head are placed various electrodes that record his or her brain waves; those recordings show a burst of brain wave activity as soon as the light is noticed by the brain. The researchers can record the precise

---

[6] At this point, you might be wondering whether or not these results actually indicate that larger brain size *causes* higher mental ability. Based on the correlational data described before, we cannot be certain that such a causal action exists; instead, it could be that being smarter tends to make one's brain larger, or that some other, third variable is influencing both brain size and mental ability *at the same time*. More research will be needed in the future to determine whether an increase in brain size can actually cause an increase in mental ability, but it does seem to be a very likely hypothesis.

amount of time between the appearance of the flash of light and the onset of brain wave activity. A shorter duration indicates a higher *nerve conduction velocity*—that is, a faster brain. Another method instead involves measuring the speed of the nervous system *outside* the brain, by applying some stimulus to the skin of the wrist, and then measuring the time taken for the resulting nervous system impulses to travel through the arm.

Several studies have examined the relations between nerve conduction velocity, as assessed in ways similar to those described above, and scores on mental ability tests. The results thus far have been inconsistent (see review by Jensen, 1998): Some investigations find substantial correlations, even in the .40s, between the *g* factor derived from the mental ability tests and the measurements of nerve conduction velocity, whereas other investigations find near-zero correlations. Overall, it does appear that there is some link between nerve conduction velocity and *g*, but the research to date has not shown a consistently strong link. It is possible that nerve conduction velocity is somewhat less important than had been expected by some researchers; on the other hand, it is also possible that improved measurement techniques for measuring nerve conduction velocity will reveal stronger relations than have been observed in studies so far.

Reaction Time

Like the variable of nerve conduction velocity described before, the variable of *reaction time* is also a potential indicator of the speed with which the brain and nervous system can operate, and has also been proposed as a possible basis for individual differences in mental ability. But whereas measurements of nerve conduction velocity involve assessment of an *automatic* response by the brain and nervous system to some stimulus, measurements of reaction time involve assessment of a *deliberate* response to such a stimulus—for example, the time taken to release a button in response to a flash of light. Note, however, that the response required in a reaction time task does not demand the complex thinking processes demanded by actual tests of mental ability.

Typically, a reaction time task of the kind used by mental ability researchers would work as follows. The research participant sits in front of a table on which there are several computerized features, including a lightbulb (currently turned off) and a "home" button (where the participant's hand is resting). The job of the research participant is to watch the lightbulb for a flash of light, and then to react as quickly as possible, by moving his or her hand from the home button to another button located in front of the light. The researcher can then measure, using an electronic sensor under the home button, the duration of time that elapsed between the onset of the flash of light and the removal of the participant's hand from the home button. This time interval is the reaction time of the participant.[7] (See Figure 10-4 for examples of reaction time tasks.)

---

[7] Note that this measurement is *not* based on the speed with which the participant's hand reaches the second button, *after* being raised from the home button. This other measurement, known as *movement time*, might be interesting in its own right, however; perhaps this variable would be implicated in athletic ability, for example.

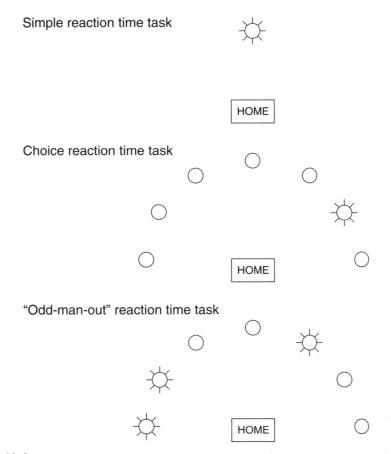

FIGURE 10-4.   Reaction time tasks. In each of the tasks, the respondent begins with his or her hand on the "home" button. When one or more of the lights flashes, he or she must move his or her hand as quickly as possible toward one of those flashing lights, according to the specific instructions of the task. In the simple reaction time task, there is only one light. In the choice reaction time task, any one of several lights might flash, and the respondent must move toward the light that does flash. In the "odd-man-out" reaction time task, three lights will flash (two adjacent and one other) and the respondent must move toward the other light. Reaction time is measured as the time taken to move one's hand *from the home button*, not as the time taken to move one's hand *to the light*.

Some reaction time tasks are more complicated than the basic task described above, which is known as a "simple" reaction time task. A different variation, known as a "choice" reaction time task, uses not one but several lightbulbs, any one of which might suddenly be turned on (see Figure 10-4). This task is difficult, because the participant must pay attention to more than one light, and also because the participant must "choose"—based on which light does actually flash—the correct direction in which to move his or her hand. Yet another variation is known as the "odd-man-out" reaction time task, in which there are several lightbulbs in front of the participant, three of which will suddenly flash together (see Figure 10-4). In this task, two of those three flashing bulbs are next to each other, but the third (the "odd man out") is separated from them by one or more nonflashing bulbs; the job of the participant is to move his or her hand toward the button that is immediately in front of the "odd-man-out" bulb.

Note that, when reaction times are measured using tasks such as these, each participant would be measured on several attempts for each task. This allows a reliable average score to be calculated for each participant on each reaction time task, which in turn allows a meaningful examination of correlations between reaction time and other variables, such as mental ability test scores and the *g* factor derived from them. When researchers have compared the reaction times and the *g* factor scores of their research participants, they have typically found correlations in the −.30s between the two variables. These correlations are based mainly on the "simple" reaction time tasks described above; when "choice" or "odd-man-out" tasks are used instead, the negative correlations become a bit stronger. (Apparently, the more complicated reaction time tasks are slightly better indicators of mental ability than are the simpler varieties.) These correlations indicate that slower reaction times are associated with lower scores on tests of mental ability, and they support the idea that the speed of the brain and nervous system is part of the basis for the *g* factor of mental ability (see, e.g., Detterman, 1987).

Inspection Time

Yet another way of measuring the speed of the brain is to assess the length of time that a stimulus must be present before the brain can notice that stimulus. The tasks that measure this duration are known as *inspection time* tasks, and they typically work as follows. A participant watches a blank screen on which two vertical lines are suddenly flashed for a brief interval, and then covered up by a "mask" pattern that eliminates afterimages from remaining in the eyes. One of those two vertical lines is much longer than the other, and the participant's job is simply to decide which line is the longer one (see Figure 10-5). This is an easy task, except that, if the interval during which the two lines are flashed is extremely short, then the participant may no longer be able to tell which line was the longer one. Typically, as the presentation interval becomes very short, the participant begins to make some mistakes, and if the interval becomes shorter still, the participant reaches a point at which he or she is basically guessing. The interesting feature of the inspection time task is that people differ widely in how long a time they require to be able to judge accurately which line is longer. This result was expected by researchers who have suggested that inspection time should be a good indicator of the basic speed of the brain, which in turn is likely to be an important basis of *g*.

Investigations of the relations between inspection time and mental ability have generally found fairly strong links, with correlations sometimes typically in the −.30s (Grudnik & Kranzler, 2001). This means that people who have longer inspection times (i.e., people who need a longer exposure time to be able to judge the line lengths) tend to have lower scores on mental ability tests and on the *g* factor of general mental ability. This result is particularly interesting, insofar as the inspection time task is very basic, requiring only the very simple decision as to which of two lines is longer. This supports the idea that mental

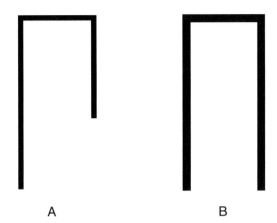

A   B

FIGURE 10-5. Inspection time task. Vertical lines are flashed for a brief period of time (A), then immediately covered by a mask (B). The participant's task is to indicate which line in (A), left or right, was longer. As the interval becomes very short, it becomes difficult to judge which line was longer (sometimes the longer line is on the left; sometimes on the right).

speed, as measured by these inspection time tasks, is strongly implicated in the *g* factor (e.g., Nettelbeck, 1987).

Brain Waves: Averaged Evoked Potentials

In addition to the variables associated with the speed with which the brain can process information, other features of the brain's functioning have also been examined in relation to mental ability (see review by Jensen, 1998). In particular, researchers have studied the electrical activity that occurs in the brain due to the activation of neurons (i.e., nerve cells; see Chapter 5). Because millions of nerve cells fire simultaneously, changes in the electrical potential of the brain are large enough to be measured by electrodes placed on the person's scalp. This technique, known as electroencephalography (EEG), records these changing electrical potentials as "brain waves" that fluctuate between positive and negative values. These waves can be described, for example, in terms of their size or amplitude (measured in microvolts) and also of their frequency (measured in cycles per second, or hertz). Researchers who examine EEG data in relation to mental ability can examine brain waves that occur spontaneously or naturally, but can also examine brain waves that occur in response to a specific stimulus, such as a clicking sound or a flashing light.

When measuring brain waves in response to a stimulus, researchers average the results across hundreds of waves, in order to obtain a reliable indication of the response of a given person's brain to that stimulus. These data are called "averaged evoked potentials," and it is these results that show the strongest relations with mental ability test scores (Jensen, 1998). Several studies have shown that higher levels of mental ability are associated with many features of averaged evoked potentials, including shorter latency (i.e., faster brain wave response to a stimulus), higher frequency, lower amplitude (i.e., less extreme response to a stimulus), and greater overall complexity of the waves. When various features of the averaged evoked potentials are combined into a single index, the correlations with *g* sometimes reach the .30s (Vernon *et al.*, 2000).

Brain Glucose Metabolism

Finally, another aspect of brain functioning that is related to mental ability is the rate at which the brain uses glucose, a simple form of carbohydrate that provides the main source of energy for the brain. Researchers can measure the amount of glucose consumed by the brain by injecting a small (and harmless) amount of radioactive glucose into the bloodstream, and then using a brain-scanning technique called positron emission tomography (PET). The PET scan detects gamma rays that are emitted by the radioactive form of glucose, and thereby produces an image that shows the amount of glucose being consumed, or metabolized, in different parts of the brain.

Several studies have been conducted in which researchers have measured the brain's rate of glucose use during the performance of some difficult mental tasks (see Jensen, 1998). In these studies, the researchers have examined the relations between brain glucose metabolism and scores on those tests of mental ability. The main finding of these investigations has been that individuals with higher levels of *g* tend to have brains that consume less glucose while performing mental ability tasks (e.g., Haier, 1993), with correlations at least as strong as those yielded by the other variables described in this section. In other words, the higher-*g* individuals appear to have brains that are more efficient, requiring less glucose to do the mental work of solving some cognitively difficult problem.

Genetic and Environmental Influences on Mental Ability

In Chapter 6, we discussed the methods by which researchers can estimate how much of the variation among individuals in any given trait is attributable to genetic (or heritable) variation, and how much is attributable to environmental variation. As noted in that chapter, research on the genetic and environmental origins of personality variation has suggested that, across various personality traits, about half of the variation is due to heritable differences. Of the remaining variation, it is the unique or nonshared environment (i.e., aspects of the environment that differ between individuals in the same family) that is the predominant influence on personality, rather than the common or shared environment (i.e., aspects of the environment that differ between families). But what is the situation for mental abilities? Are the results similar to those observed for personality characteristics?

Genetic Influences

The heritability of mental ability has been a widely studied topic for several decades. As has been the case for investigations of the heritability of personality, these studies have made use of various research designs, based on participant samples consisting of identical versus fraternal twins, twins or siblings raised apart, and adoptive siblings raised together. (Note that when these investigations are conducted, differences due to age are controlled by calculating individuals' levels of mental ability relative to the levels of other people of the same age.) The results of these studies have been fairly consistent, and can be summarized rather briefly.[8,9] However, as we will discuss next, there is typically a substantial difference between results based on data from adults and results based on data from children.

When studies using mental ability test scores from children are considered, the heritability of mental ability is typically about .45, and the effect of the common or shared environment is almost as strong, at about .35. In contrast, when studies using mental ability test scores from adults (or older adolescents) are considered, the heritability of mental ability is much higher, typically about .75, whereas the effect of the common or shared environment is much lower, sometimes approaching zero. (For a summary of this literature, see McGue, Bouchard, Iacono, & Lykken, 1993; see also Plomin & Spinath, 2004.) These findings indicate that differences among children in their levels of mental ability are attributable almost as much to their common environment—that is, to features of their family or household circumstances—as to their genetic inheritances. However, the findings also indicate that as children grow up, the differences among them in mental ability become less strongly related to the features of their common environments, and more strongly related to their genetic inheritances. In other words, the effect on one's mental ability of the family or household in which one is reared tends to become less important as one grows up, so that by adulthood one's level of mental ability is heavily dependent on one's genetic characteristics. It is as if one's level of mental ability can be raised (or lowered) during childhood by a particularly good (or poor) home environment, but then gradually returns to the level that one's genes tend to produce.

In considering the preceding findings about the heritability of mental ability, there are some important points to keep in mind. One issue is that of additive and nonadditive genetic variance, which we discussed in Chapter 6 in the context of personality characteristics. As you will recall from that chapter, the effects of genes on characteristics can be *additive* (whereby the combined effects of genes are simply the sums of the separate effects of each gene) or *nonadditive* (whereby the combined effects of genes are different from what would be expected based on the separate effects of each gene). When genetic influences are entirely additive, the similarity of identical twins (raised apart) is about twice that of fraternal twins (raised apart), because identical twins have twice as many

---

[8] These studies exclude persons who have a severe intellectual disability caused by brain damage or by abnormalities of the genes or chromosomes (e.g., persons with Down's syndrome).

[9] As will be discussed later in this chapter, there is some assortative mating—that is, a tendency for spouses to be similar to each other—for some aspects of mental ability. When calculating estimates of the heritability of intelligence, researchers take this assortative mating into account. As noted in Chapter 6, one assumption made in conducting heritability studies is that there is no assortative mating, but researchers can make adjustments in their calculations when assortative mating does occur.

genes in common as do fraternal twins. However, when genetic effects are partly nonadditive, the similarity of identical twins (raised apart) can be much more than twice that of fraternal twins (raised apart); this is because identical twins have all combinations of genes in common, whereas fraternal twins have few combinations of genes in common. (Even if you share 50% of your genes with someone, you will share much less than 50% of your combinations of genes with that person, because *any* difference between the two of you will mean a different combination. But if you have 100% of your genes in common with someone, then you must also have 100% of your combinations of genes in common with that person.)

As explained in Chapter 6, this distinction between additive and nonadditive genetic effects is important. When additive genetic effects are strong for a characteristic, then relatives will tend to have similar levels of that characteristic; that is, it will "run in the family." But when additive genetic effects are weak, then relatives will not be especially similar, and the characteristics will not run in the family very much. Thus, it is possible that a characteristic could show high heritability and yet not really "run in families," if the genetic influence on the trait was nonadditive.

What is the relative contribution of additive and nonadditive genetic influence to differences among people in mental ability? Results from many research studies conducted to date suggest that both influences are implicated about equally when calculated as described above (e.g., Devlin, Daniels, & Roeder, 1997): If overall heritability is estimated as being close to .70, then additive and nonadditive genetic influences both contribute about .35. These results are reflected in the fact that identical twins tend to be more than twice as similar in mental ability as are relatives who have only half their genes in common. For example, identical twins raised apart show mental ability correlations in the .70s, whereas the correlations for nontwin siblings raised apart (or for biological parents and their adopted-away children) are in the .20s. Thus, mental ability does run in families to some extent, but much of the genetic influence on personality is of the kind that does not run in families.

Womb Environment Influences

The logic of heritability studies is fairly straightforward, but there is an important way in which those investigations may overestimate the heritability of characteristics, including mental ability. The reason why heritability studies may overestimate heritability is the role of the womb environment, which we also discussed in Chapter 6 in the context of personality characteristics. Recall that heritability studies often use research designs that compare twins or siblings who have been raised apart; in this way, any similarity between twins or siblings cannot be attributed to the environment in which they were raised. However, this similarity might not be due entirely to the genetic relatedness of the twins or siblings; instead, it might be due in part to various features of the womb environment, such as the nutrients, toxins, and hormones to which the developing fetus is exposed. Because there are differences between mothers, and even between pregnancies of the same mother, in these aspects of the womb environment, it is possible that some part of the "genetic" influence on traits (including mental ability) is not genetic at all, but rather due to the womb environment.[10]

Some research has tried to separate womb environment influences from genetic influences. For example, if one compares *fraternal twin* pairs with *nontwin sibling* pairs, any extra similarity of fraternal twins over that of nontwin siblings might be due in large part to variation between pregnancies in the womb environment, because only the twins developed in the same womb *during the same pregnancy*. (Keep in mind that age differences in mental ability are statistically controlled in these studies, and will not affect the results.) Similarly, if one compares *nontwin sibling* pairs with *parent–child* pairs, any extra similarity of siblings over that of parent–child combinations might be due in large part to variation between mothers in the womb environment, because only the siblings developed *within the same mother's womb*. One investigation of womb environment effects (Devlin *et al.*, 1997) used the preceding approaches, and found that the influence of the womb environment on mental ability was about .20 when twins were considered, and .05 when nontwin siblings were considered. As a result, the authors suggested, the heritability of mental ability was about .25 lower than generally considered, probably less than .50 rather than .70. The reduction in the estimate for heritability is mainly in the nonadditive genetic influence, so that the additive and nonadditive genetic contributions are close to .35 and .15 rather than .35 and .35 as mentioned above.[11]

Other Environmental Influences: Nutrition

Although the genetic influences on personality are substantial, there are also many environmental variables that are known to influence mental ability. For example, levels of *g*

---

[10] Note that this problem does not apply to studies in which heritability is estimated by doubling the difference between (a) the correlation between identical twins and (b) the correlation between fraternal twins. This is because the twins of a given pair—whether identical or fraternal—have experienced the same mother's womb during the same pregnancy. Therefore, when we find the difference between these correlations, the effects of the womb environment are "cancelled out," and do not inflate the estimate of heritability. Interestingly, the estimates of heritability that are obtained by doubling the difference between identical twin correlations and fraternal twin correlations do tend to be lower than the estimates that are obtained by finding the correlation between identical twins raised apart. This suggests that the latter estimates of heritability may be somewhat inflated due to the effect of the womb environment.

[11] If you have previously read about the heritability of mental ability, you might have learned about the story of Cyril Burt, an English psychologist who conducted some heritability studies. Burt's results suggested a high degree of heritability of mental ability, but after his death, some researchers and journalists were suspicious that much of Burt's data may have been faked. Subsequently, there ensued a long-running debate that has perhaps not yet been resolved (e.g., Mackintosh, 1995). This is an interesting story, but it has little if any implication for the current state of knowledge about the heritability of mental ability: Many large-scale heritability studies have been conducted since Burt's death, and their results have generally been consistent with each other (and, to a large extent, with Burt's results).

BOX 10-1

Chorion Type as an Example of Womb Environment Influences on Mental Ability

The *chorion* is the outermost of the two membranes that surround the developing fetus. When two identical twins (i.e., monozygotic twins) are developing in their mother's womb, they might both be inside the same chorion, or each might be inside his or her own chorion. About two-thirds of identical twins have the same chorion (and thus are called *monochorionic monozygotic* twins), and about one-third have their own chorion (and thus are called *dichorionic* monozygotic twins). Because dichorionic twins receive nutrients from the mother through different blood vessels, they might be expected to receive different levels of those nutrients, and thus to show larger differences in mental ability than would monochorionic twins, who would be expected to receive nearly the same nutrient levels. A study by Jacobs *et al.* (2001) examined this hypothesis, by comparing the mental ability test scores for identical twin pairs who were monochorionic and for identical twin pairs who were dichorionic. The results indicated that both kinds of identical twins were very similar in their levels of mental ability, but that the dichorionic twins did show somewhat less similarity than did the monochorionic twins. This suggests that differences in chorion type—and the associated differences in prenatal nutrition—likely do have some effect on the development of the fetus. Chorion type thus represents an example of how the womb environment can influence mental ability.

are lower among children who have experienced fetal alcohol poisoning, lead poisoning, severe malnutrition, or brain damage (e.g., Neisser *et al.*, 1996). These problems are relatively rare within the broad middle classes of economically developed countries, within which most investigations of mental ability have been conducted. However, given that there is still an extremely wide variation in mental ability within those samples, this leaves us with the question of which aspects of the environment contribute to the variation in mental ability among healthy people in prosperous societies. But as discussed before, some aspects of the common environment do influence *g* during childhood, yet have little effect during adulthood. Therefore, in considering the influence of environmental variables on mental ability, we will focus on several nutrition-related variables, each of which has been suggested to have lasting influences on *g*—influences thought to persist even in late adolescence or in adulthood.

One aspect of the early environment that has been shown to be associated with levels of *g* even in adulthood is breast-feeding. This effect is illustrated by the results of a study by Mortensen, Michaelsen, Sanders, and Reinisch (2002), who investigated the intelligence test scores of nearly 1000 young Danish men and women. The researchers compared the intelligence test scores of adults who, as infants, had been breast-fed for different periods of time (as recalled by the mothers of those persons). Mortensen *et al.* found that longer duration of breast-feeding was associated with higher levels of *g*. Even when the researchers made statistical adjustments for differences in socioeconomic status and other variables, the difference was still substantial: Persons who had been breast-fed as infants for more than 6 months scored about 6 IQ points (about 0.4 standard deviations) higher, on average, than did persons who had been breast-fed for less than 1 month. These results suggest that breast-feeding may provide better nutrition to the developing infant, and thereby contribute to intellectual development. (Alternatively, it is possible that the mother–infant contact associated with breast-feeding, or some other variables, are responsible for this effect.)

The findings of Mortensen *et al.* (2002) suggest that breast-feeding may lead to higher levels of general mental ability in adulthood. However, there is also an alternative interpretation: Perhaps mothers with higher levels of *g* are more likely to breast-feed, and also likely to have children who inherit those high levels of *g*. In this way, the relation between breast-feeding and *g* might not be a causal link, but instead a reflection of the fact that smarter mothers tend both to breast-feed and also to have smart children. This hypothesis was recently tested by Der, Batty, and Deary (2006), who examined the mental ability test scores of over 5000 young adults and of the (more than 3000) mothers of those young adults.

The results obtained by Der *et al.* (2006) indicated that young adults who had been breast-fed as infants scored about 4 IQ points (more than one-quarter of a standard deviation) higher than did young adults who had not been breast-fed as children. However, it was also found that the mothers with higher IQ scores were more likely to have breast-fed their children than were the mothers with lower IQ scores. When the researchers controlled for the IQ scores of the mothers, they found that the difference was less than 1 IQ point, which is a very small amount. In other words, smarter mothers were more likely to breast-feed and were also more likely to have smarter children, but breast-feeding itself did not contribute much to mental ability test scores. For example, in families in which a mother breast-fed one child and did not breast-feed another child, there was typically no difference in mental ability test scores between those children. Thus, the findings of Der *et al.* suggest that breast-feeding might not contribute to higher levels of mental ability, at least when the infant was born at full term and at normal body weight. (It is still possible that breast-feeding would contribute to *g* when premature or low-birth-weight infants are considered.)

In addition to a possible role for nutrition during infancy, there is also the possibility that nutrition during gestation—that is, before birth—could be responsible for some of the variation among people in mental ability. Perhaps the levels of nutrients obtained by the developing fetus are associated with higher levels of intelligence in adulthood; this might be the case even when we consider societies in which very few pregnant mothers suffer from serious malnutrition. This possibility is supported by several lines of evidence involving the relations between birth weight (a plausible indicator of prenatal nutrition) and later intelligence test scores. One finding is that children who had a low birth weight (below about 2500 grams or 5.5 pounds) average about half of a standard deviation lower than do children of normal birth weight (Aylward, Pfeiffer, Wright, & Verhulst, 1988). But relatively few babies have low birth weights, and many of those babies are born prematurely, which raises the possibility that premature birth, rather than low birth weight itself, is partly responsible for the lower intelligence test scores. However, it has been consistently observed that twins—who as fetuses must share the nutrients available in the mothers' womb—tend on average to have lower intelligence test scores than do their nontwin siblings, with a difference of about five IQ points, or one-third of a standard deviation unit (Ronalds, De Stavola, & Leon, 2005).

The results described thus far in this section have examined the possibility that the levels of some nutrients during early childhood (or even in the womb) could influence later levels of mental ability. Some recent research has also tested the hypothesis that nutrient levels in adulthood may be associated with changes in levels of mental ability. One such investigation used data from the Scottish mental ability survey discussed earlier in this chapter. Starr, Pattie, Whiteman, Whalley, and Deary (2005) examined nearly 500 elderly adults who took intelligence tests at the age of 79 or 80 and for whom records were also available of their intelligence test scores at age 11. The researchers took small samples of blood from each participant to measure the levels of certain nutrients—specifically, folate (found in some legumes, fruits, and vegetables, and also in liver) and vitamin B_{12} (found in animal- but not plant-based foods). They then compared the participants' blood nutrient levels with the participants' change in intelligence test scores, relative to the scores of other participants; in other words, the researchers checked whether or not the nutrient levels were associated with a gain or loss in mental ability, relative to persons of one's own age. The results showed that folate levels had weak positive correlations with test scores both in childhood and in old age, but were not related to the change in those scores; in contrast, vitamin B_{12} was uncorrelated with test scores in childhood, but was weakly positively related to test scores in old age. The latter result suggests that lower levels of vitamin B_{12} are associated with a higher risk of a relative decline in mental ability between childhood and old age. Of the 18 participants with the lowest levels of vitamin B_{12}, seven (nearly 40%) declined more than one standard deviation unit in mental ability, whereas less than 20% of the other participants showed a decline of this size. These results do not establish that low B_{12} levels cause a cognitive decline, but they certainly do raise the possibility.

Evolutionary Function of Mental Ability

Let us now turn to the question of why the wide differences among people in mental ability have persisted across the generations. If we assume that persons with higher levels of mental ability (or any other kind of ability) would be those most likely to survive and reproduce, then it might be surprising that variation in mental ability has not disappeared. Instead, we might have expected that the level of ability should be uniformly high, because in any generation the persons whose genes tended to produce higher levels of ability would also have more surviving offspring. As a result, those genes would become more and more common in the succeeding generations, until finally only the "high-ability" genes would remain. But this has not happened; people who are perfectly normal can differ a great deal in their levels of *g* and other ability factors, and within any given group of people those differences are largely genetic in origin.

One likely reason why natural selection has not eliminated the genetic variation in mental ability is that there are important biological costs associated with higher levels of ability. That is, even though a high level of mental ability will likely provide many advantages in meeting the challenges of survival and reproduction and parenting, it also comes with some disadvantages. For example, the larger brain associated with higher levels of ability consumes more energy while at rest, requires a longer time to grow to maturity, and increases the risk of complications during childbirth. These disadvantages may tend to reduce the chances of survival and reproduction, thereby "canceling out" the advantages that would be provided by a larger, more able brain. (In addition, there may be some genes that increase mental ability while simultaneously causing some disease, the disadvantages of which would also tend to balance out or even outweigh the advantages of higher mental ability levels.)

If there are both advantages and disadvantages associated with higher levels of g or other aspects of mental ability, then the persistence of variation in the genetic basis of mental ability is not so surprising. But depending on various features of the environment, higher levels of ability may have more advantages than disadvantages overall, or vice versa. This can happen in two main ways, as described in Chapter 7. First, the ideal level of a given characteristic will differ from one place and one period to another (i.e., the "fluctuating optimum"). Also, the ideal level of that characteristic may also differ depending on the levels that other individuals have (i.e., "frequency-dependent selection").

Some researchers have already suggested some ways in which the fluctuating optimum or frequency-dependence might have operated on mental ability levels in human populations. With regard to the fluctuating optimum, Lynn (1987) suggested that during prehistoric times, colder climates would have tended to favor higher levels of mental ability, especially spatial ability. He suggested that in an "ice age" environment, individuals having a high level of spatial ability would have had an important advantage in such crucial tasks as designing and sewing warm clothing, making weapons for hunting large animals, and finding one's way across wide areas of wilderness while pursuing those animals. (Note that hunting would have been a particularly important source of food in a cold climate, because of the relative lack of plant food.) Lynn's suggestion is consistent with the finding that the Eskimo or Inuit people of the Arctic regions, who until recently lived mainly by hunting in that very cold environment, do tend to have high levels of spatial ability on average, as do persons of northeast Asian descent (e.g., Vernon, 1982). According to Lynn's idea, differences in climate from one region to another or from one time period to another would have led to differences in the average levels of spatial ability.

With regard to frequency-dependent selection, it has been suggested that the development of towns and cities, with the specialization of people into different types of occupations, might have been selected for higher levels of mental ability. In particular, high levels of verbal and numerical abilities would have given an important advantage in achieving success (and thus in surviving and reproducing), but only for those individuals who belonged to social classes whose occupations required the use of written words and numbers. For example, Cochran, Hardy, and Harpending (2006) noted that, on average, persons of Ashkenazi Jewish descent tend to have high levels of verbal and numerical ability. Those researchers attributed this to the fact that Jews in medieval and early modern Europe were restricted by law to several occupations that required verbal and numerical skills, and that this would have favored individuals who had higher levels of such skills.

Some researchers have suggested that patterns of sex differences in mental abilities can also be understood in terms of selection pressures that acted differently on men and women during prehistoric times. Specifically, men tend to average somewhat higher than do women in some aspects of spatial ability (especially those that require visualizing objects in three dimensions), whereas women tend to average somewhat higher than do men in some aspects of memory and of perceptual speed (i.e., noticing subtle differences between similar-looking objects); see Halpern (1997). (These differences are moderately large in size, sometimes favoring the higher-scoring sex by about one standard deviation unit.) One possible explanation for these differences is that they have resulted from selection for abilities required by the tasks that men and women tended to do during prehistoric times. According to this view, spatial visualization was needed for the mostly male task of hunting (which required spatial ability for weapon making and for tracking game), whereas perceptual speed and memory were needed for the mostly female task of gathering (which required perception and memory for distinguishing between similar-looking plants).[12]

When considering differences in average intelligence test scores between groups of people—for example, different social classes, ethnic or racial groups, sexes, or generations—it is important to keep in mind that the reasons for those between-group differences might not be the same as the reasons for differences within groups. For example, differences in mental ability between your generation and your great-grandparents' generation are probably not due in any large part to genetic differences, even though the differences in mental ability among persons *within* either generation are likely to be heavily influenced by genetic differences. Instead, the differences between the generations are likely to be due to some environmental variables (changes in the educational system, in the use of technology, in nutrition, etc.) that differ greatly between generations but that do not differ much among persons within a given generation. Likewise, genetic influences are responsible for much of the variation among people within a country in their levels of mental ability, but those influences might not be responsible for differences between countries in their peoples' average levels of mental ability. Instead, it is possible that differences that exist *between countries* (not within countries) in education, technology, nutrition, or other variables might be responsible for the differences in average mental ability levels. However, these are only hypotheses; it also remains possible that differences between groups in mental ability could have a genetic basis.

---

[12] There is some debate as to whether there exists any sex difference in *g*. Some researchers argue that there is no difference (e.g., Jensen, 1998); others argue that boys and girls do not differ, but that men have slightly higher levels on average than do women (e.g., Lynn, 1994). One interesting result has been that the *variation* in *g* is wider for men and boys than for women and girls: A study based on the data set involving 80,000 11-year-old Scottish schoolchildren (Deary, Thorpe, Wilson, Starr, & Whalley, 2003) showed no difference between boys and girls in their mean intelligence test scores, but found that there were more girls than boys at the middle levels of ability, and more boys than girls at both the high and low extremes. Among children with intelligence test scores in the *top* 1%, nearly 60% were boys and slightly more than 40% were girls, but among children with intelligence test scores in the *bottom* 1%, again almost 60% were boys and a little more than 40% were girls.

Mental Ability and Life Outcomes

Now that we have established the existence and the nature of a dimension of *general mental ability*—the *g* factor—we should next examine the role of this dimension in predicting outcomes of practical importance. You have probably already heard many arguments about this issue: For example, you have probably heard many times that IQ tests are not very important for predicting "success in the real world" or even for predicting academic achievement. This claim about the lack of predictive validity of IQ tests also applies to the *g* factor, which represents something very close to what is measured by IQ tests. So, let us now look at the evidence regarding the relations between *g* and a variety of important outcomes, such as academic achievement, job performance, occupational status, health and longevity, law-abiding behavior, and marriage.

Academic Achievement and Performance

First, let us consider academic achievement. Most people would probably expect that scores on mental ability tests would be at least somewhat predictive of success in school. Still, it is important to examine whether or not those tests (and the *g* factor derived from them) really are associated with grade point average and with the attainment of diplomas and degrees. The answer, as found consistently in hundreds of research studies over the past century, is that *g* does have a fairly strong relation with academic achievement. But the strength of that relation varies somewhat, depending on how academic achievement is measured and on the level of education being considered.

When large groups of students are tested for general mental ability, their resulting *g* scores tend to be correlated rather substantially with their grades in school. For example, among elementary school students, this correlation is often about .50 or .60 (e.g., Kaufman, 1979). This is a rather strong link: A correlation of .50 means that about 75% of the students with above-average *g* scores will also have above-average grades in school, whereas only about 25% will have below-average grades. What this tells us is that a high level of general mental ability is an important advantage in completing schoolwork successfully. Of course, *g* is not the only reason why students differ in their school grades: A correlation of .50 leaves a great deal of room for other variables, such as the motivation and effort of the student, to have major influences on school performance. Nevertheless, it is clear that, on average, students with higher levels of *g* tend to do better in school.

The relation between *g* and school performance, as just described, is based on grades assigned by teachers to their students. As you will recall from your own days in elementary and secondary school, those grades are generally based on students' performance on tests, on assignments of various kinds, on classroom presentations and participation, and even on the teacher's perceptions of "attitude and effort." But keep in mind that some of these aspects of student grades—apart from tests and some assignments—might not really be based on how deeply the student understands and applies the course material. Instead, some components of student grades—such as participating enthusiastically, making entertaining presentations to the class, handing in nicely decorated assignments, or just simply being well-behaved—might not have much to do with actual *academic achievement*. To the extent that this is the case, we might expect that the correlation between *g* and school grades could underestimate the strength of the link between *g* and real academic achievement. So, is this really the case?

The best way to check this possibility is to find the correlation between tests of *g*, on the one hand, and tests of academic achievement, on the other. In this way, we can see the extent to which students' levels of general mental ability really are associated with their mastery of course material. The results of many previous studies indicate that *g* is even more strongly related to academic achievement, as measured by actual tests, than to school grades. When tests of general mental ability and tests of academic achievement have been administered to large groups of students, the correlations tend to be in the .60s or even the .70s (e.g., Deary, Strand, Smith, & Fernandes, 2007).

The results as just summarized indicate that *g* is a very important predictor of academic achievement, particularly in the sense of acquiring a real understanding of course material, as assessed by standardized tests. But this might make you wonder whether the correlation between these tests might simply be due to some obvious similarities between them. In other words, could it be that the tests of general mental ability are simply measuring the same abilities as those measured by the tests of academic achievement, with the same kinds of test questions?

The answer to this question has two parts. First, there are some important differences between the tests that measure general mental ability and the tests that measure academic achievement. Tests of general mental ability involve questions that are not based directly on what is learned in school, or on a particular course of study; instead, the questions require problem solving or information of a general nature. In contrast, tests of academic achievement involve questions that are associated with the curriculum as taught in school, with a focus on specific skills that are practiced at certain grade levels. So, in this sense, the relations between *g* and academic achievement cannot be attributed to the similarity of the tests that measure these two variables.

On the other hand, however, there is still some similarity of content between tests of general mental ability and tests of academic achievement. In considerable part, the tests of *g* do involve working with numbers and words, as do the tests of academic achievement. This leads to the question of whether the mental ability tests can still predict academic achievement even when the mental ability tests are based on tasks that do not involve working with numbers and words. That is, could nonverbal tests of mental ability also predict performance on academic achievement tests (consider, e.g., the spatial or picture arrangement tasks of Figure 10-1, or the matrix reasoning task of Figure 10-2)? Again, the answer from previous research has been clear: Even the nonverbal tests of *g* do correlate moderately strongly with academic achievement tests. However, the correlations of nonverbal tests with achievement are typically around .40 (e.g., Sattler, 1988), which are lower than the correlations produced by tests that do involve words or numbers. This suggests that some part of the relation between tests of *g* and tests of academic achievement is due to the specific elements that the two kinds of tests have in common. For the most part, though, the relation is due to a real association between *general* mental ability and mastery of the school curriculum.

As mentioned before, the strength of the link between *g* and academic achievement also depends on the level of education that is being considered. In other words, the correlation between general mental ability and academic performance depends on whether we consider students at the elementary school level, at the secondary school level, or at the college and university level. But the differences may surprise you: The correlations between general mental ability and academic performance are actually stronger at the *lower* levels of education than in the higher levels. That is, *g* is better able to predict grades in elementary school than in secondary school, and better able to predict grades in secondary school than in college or university. In elementary school, *g* tends to correlate in the .60s with academic achievement, whereas in secondary school, the correlation tends to be in the .50s, and in college or university, in the .40s (Jensen, 1998). This result is perhaps a bit confusing, because it seems obvious that higher levels of education demand a higher level of general mental ability than do lower levels of education.

The reason for this result has to do with how much variation in mental ability there is at each level of education. To understand this, first consider an elementary school: The students at this level of education represent virtually the entire range of *g*, from the lowest levels to the highest. Therefore, because the students differ so widely in their levels of *g*, those differences can have a major influence on the students' grades. But now consider secondary school, at least at the levels when some students have dropped out of school. Because the students who drop out will tend, on average, to be considerably below average in general mental ability, a secondary school has less variation in *g* than an elementary school does. Therefore, there is less opportunity for *g* to influence secondary school grades. Similarly, if we consider a college or university setting, in which most students tend to be above average in general mental ability, there is even less variation in *g* than there is in secondary school; consequently, *g* is less important in predicting college or university grades than in predicting secondary school grades. (And again, the same pattern continues as we move on to the highest education levels, such as graduate schools or professional schools, for example, medicine, law, or business schools.)

Before leaving the topic of *g* and academic performance, there is one other finding to mention. In the preceding sections, we discussed how *g* was related to school grades and to achievement test scores. But a related question involves the relation between *g* and educational attainment, in the sense of "how far" one progresses in school: To what extent does *g* predict whether one will drop out of high school, as opposed to obtaining a high school diploma, or continuing on to obtain a college or university degree, or even a professional or graduate degree? Again, the correlations observed in many investigations have generally been rather strong, typically about .55 (Neisser *et al.*, 1996). Moreover, this correlation is observed even when *g* is measured during elementary school, when no one has yet dropped out. This means that the correlation is not simply due to an influence of staying in school on one's level of *g*. Thus, *g* has an important link with educational attainment: Although general mental ability is certainly not the only variable that determines how far one will pursue one's education, it is clearly an important predictor.

Most people would probably not be surprised to learn that high scores on tests of mental ability are associated with high levels of academic achievement. But many people would likely expect that academic achievement would be the *only* important variable that would be predicted by those tests. However, a wide range of evidence indicates that mental ability tests (and particularly the *g* factor that is the main common element of those tests) measure something that is far broader than simply the ability to perform well in school. Instead, scores on mental ability tests show moderately strong correlations with a diverse array of important variables. One such variable is job performance, which will be our next topic of discussion.

Job Performance, Occupational Status, and Income

What is it that makes some workers better at their job than other workers? For many jobs, of course, specific training and expertise is critically important, and a worker who does not have that training and expertise will simply be unable to perform satisfactorily. But beyond this rather obvious point, what characteristics of workers are associated with better work? As we have seen in previous chapters, personality plays an important role in job performance: Workers who are disciplined, organized, and diligent tend to do their jobs effectively and thoroughly, and workers who are honest and trustworthy tend to be "good citizens" on the job (a crucial consideration for many employers).

In addition to personality, however, there is also a role for raw *ability* to perform tasks well. Depending on the job, of course, the kind of ability that is needed may vary: Some jobs demand a strong back, some jobs demand nimble fingers, and so on. But almost all jobs involve at least some element of solving problems, making decisions, and learning the "tricks" of doing the job well. And this is exactly where the potential influence of mental ability comes into play: If the *g* factor really does represent a general mental ability (rather than just a narrow talent for taking tests), then workers who have high levels of *g* will likely be better able to solve problems, make decisions, and "learn the ropes" of their jobs. Those abilities, in turn, should mean a higher level of job performance.

This leads us to our next question: To what extent does *g* actually correlate with job performance? Recall from earlier chapters that, when researchers or employers want to assess job performance systematically, they have different ways of doing so. Sometimes they use some objective index of productivity, such as an actual measurement of the amount or accuracy of the completed work. But for many jobs, it is not so easy to measure this directly, and instead the main measure of job performance is a rating by the worker's supervisor (or, better still, by more than one supervisor). In any case, regardless of the precise way in which job performance is assessed, there is a consistent finding: *g* is correlated positively with job performance. That is, smarter workers tend on average to be better workers. This finding is one of the best established results in the social sciences, being based on reviews of hundreds of studies involving tens of thousands of workers across virtually all jobs and across a wide variety of settings (Hunter & Hunter, 1984; Schmidt & Hunter, 2004).

As you might expect, the importance of *g* as a predictor of job performance depends a great deal on the nature of the job. For some kinds of work, the cognitive elements are not so complex, and the element of problem solving, decision making, or rule learning is not so important. But for other kinds of work, the ability to make difficult decisions, solve complicated problems, and learn subtle "rules of thumb" is in constant demand. Typically, the correlation between *g* and job performance is rather modest, generally around .20, for those jobs that have relatively simple cognitive demands. Thus, for jobs that mainly involve a simple task (which is not to say an easy task!) that is repeated with little variation, higher levels of *g* translate into slightly better (but only slightly better) job performance. But this correlation increases as jobs become more complicated, and for those jobs that are the most cognitively demanding, the correlations often reach the .50s. Thus, for more complex jobs that require a great deal of thinking, a higher level of *g* translates into considerably better job performance; in fact, for the most complex jobs, a reasonably high level of *g* is almost a necessity for really good performance.

Related to the topic of *g* and job performance is the question of how *g* relates to various indicators of occupational achievement, such as the "status" of one's occupation and the income one earns. These variables, of course, depend in part on many variables other than one's level of mental ability (or, for that matter, how diligently one works). Even if we consider people who are equally smart and equally hardworking, we will find that some people deliberately seek out jobs that have high status and pay, whereas other people do not. And, many features of a given situation—economic conditions, "office politics," family connections, family responsibilities, and so on—will also influence the occupational status and income that individuals ultimately obtain. But in spite of these other important influences, there is still some room for *g* to influence occupational achievement (e.g., Jencks, 1979; Neisser *et al.*, 1996): The correlations are typically about .50 for occupational status (as rated on scales used by social scientists) and about .40 for income.

When discussing the relation between *g* and occupational achievement, there is one possible problem, however. If we find a correlation between the *g* factor and occupational achievement (i.e., status and income), it might mean that being smart helps one to get ahead in the world of work. But it might reflect something rather different: Perhaps people who are born into the higher classes of society tend to get better jobs and incomes simply by virtue of their social class, and at the same time tend to do better on mental ability tasks because of educational and environmental advantages when growing up. So, how can we figure out which of these possibilities gives the better explanation of the link between *g* and occupational achievement?

One way to do this is to use a statistic called a *partial correlation*, which allows the researcher to see how much two variables are correlated when the influence of a third variable is statistically removed. In this case, this means finding the correlation of *g* with status or with income, but then adjusting that correlation to control for the fact that both of those variables are related to the socioeconomic status at which a person started. (This is equivalent to finding the correlation between *g* and occupational status among people who have all started out with the same level of socioeconomic status in childhood.) When this procedure is applied, it is typically found that the correlations of *g* with these aspects of occupational achievement become weaker, but remain in the .30s (based on Jencks, 1979; Neisser *et al.*, 1996) or even in the .40s (Deary *et al.*, 2005). This indicates that, for the most part, the link between mental ability and occupational achievement reflects a real tendency for smarter people to gain higher-status jobs and higher incomes. But keep in mind, of course, that this is only a tendency: Recall that a correlation of .40 means that a person who is above average in g would have a 70% chance of being above average in occupational achievement, but would still have a 30% chance of being below average.

Longevity and Health

Are higher levels of mental ability associated with better health and a longer life span? One might expect that persons with higher levels of g would tend to make better health-related decisions and would also benefit from other variables associated with higher g, such as improved socioeconomic status. Medical researchers have long noted an association between socioeconomic status and health, but recently it has been suggested that this association reflects, in part, the influence of g on both of these variables (e.g., Gottfredson, 2004).

One of the largest investigations to examine the links between g and longevity was based on the longitudinal study (described earlier in this chapter) of Scottish people who had taken an intelligence test when they were 11 years old. Whalley and Deary (2001) examined the childhood mental ability scores of nearly 2800 people in relation to records of which of those people had died and at what age. The analyses showed that there was a substantial link between g and longevity within both sexes. Of women whose intelligence test scores as 11-year-olds had been in the top quarter of the sample, about 70% survived to the age of 75 years; for women whose scores had been in the bottom quarter of the sample, the proportion was only 45%. Among men, about 50% of those who had scored in the top quarter survived to the age of 75, versus only about 35% of those who had scored in the bottom quarter. (The somewhat smaller difference between higher-g and lower-g men, compared to that between higher-g and lower-g women, was due to the higher death rates of higher-g men during World War II; apparently, the higher-g men were more likely than lower-g men to have been killed during that war, probably because men who had lower levels of g were not selected for military service.)

In examining the relations between childhood g and longevity, Whalley and Deary (2001) also considered the possibility that this relation might have been due to the effects of the social class in which the participants were raised. Therefore, the researchers examined records of the participants' social class during childhood, as measured by the father's occupational status and by the overcrowdedness of the neighborhood in which the children grew up. But Whalley and Deary found that these variables could not explain the relation between mental ability and longevity. That is, even among children who grew up in a similar neighborhood and had fathers of similar occupational status, the children with higher levels of g tended to live longer than did the children with lower levels of g.

One question that arises from the results of Whalley and Deary (2001) is that of *why* it is that g tends to be associated with longevity. Several plausible explanations can be considered (Gottfredson & Deary, 2004). One possibility is that lower g in childhood could be due to some health-related problems that arise in childhood (or even before birth) and then ultimately lead to premature death. A similar possibility is that lower *g* in childhood could itself indicate that the body and brain are not functioning well overall (even apart from any specific illnesses), and hence predicts a lower likelihood of surviving to old age. Another possible explanation is that lower *g* is associated with a tendency to adopt unhealthy rather than healthy behaviors, with the consequence of increased risk of injury or death. Yet another possible explanation is that lower *g* is associated with a tendency to enter into unhealthy environments, such as hazardous or stressful occupations.

It is not yet known how well each of these explanations can account for the link between *g* and longevity. Some evidence does suggest, however, that the third explanation is at least partly responsible. In the Scottish study, participants with higher levels of *g* were more likely to have quit smoking than were participants with lower levels of *g*, and (probably as a result) were less likely to have died of lung cancer. This would only explain a small part of the relation between *g* and longevity, but other differences in behavior between high-*g* and low-*g* participants might also exist. For example, a study of Australian army veterans found that men who were low in *g* were several times more likely than were men high in *g* to have died in motor vehicle accidents (O'Toole & Stankov, 1992). (Of course, there is also a large element of randomness in motor vehicle accidents; *g* can only predict a somewhat increased risk of accident involvement.) Also, Gottfredson (2004) has documented results of several previous studies in which researchers have assessed patients' "health literacy" (i.e., knowledge and understanding of health-related information). Those studies show that patients with low levels of health literacy tend to misunderstand doctors' instructions, to take medication incorrectly, to have higher rates of hospital admissions, and to have lower levels of self-rated health. (These relations persist even when socioeconomic status is controlled.) Thus, it appears that at least part of the link between *g* and health, and between *g* and longevity, is attributable to the relation of *g* with behaviors that influence health.

Law-Abidingness versus Criminality

Crime rates differ widely across different times and different places, for a variety of reasons that are studied by social scientists. But at the level of *individuals*—that is, if we ask which persons in a given group or a given society are more likely to commit crimes— one clear finding is that there are some significant links between crime and low *g*. On average, persons convicted of criminal offences score almost two-thirds of a standard deviation unit below average on tests of mental ability (Hirschi & Hindelang, 1977; Wilson & Herrnstein, 1985). But this result raises an interesting question: Is it the case that persons who *commit crimes* have lower levels of *g*, or is it instead merely the case that persons who *are caught for having committed crimes* have lower levels of *g*?

The evidence suggests that the former is true. One study of about 650 New Zealand teenagers (Moffitt & Silva, 1988) obtained intelligence test scores, anonymous self-reports of delinquent behavior, and police records of arrests and other interventions for delinquency. In this way, the researchers identified three subsets of youths within this sample: One subset of 40 youths who had been in contact with the police because of delinquent behaviors; another subset of nearly 70 youths who had admitted committing equally serious delinquent acts but who had avoided contact with the police; and a final (much larger) subset of youths who had no police contact and no serious self-reported delinquency. Both of the delinquent groups averaged about one-half of a standard deviation lower in intelligence test scores than did the nondelinquent group; there was very little difference between the group that had had police contact and the group that had committed delinquent acts without coming to the attention of the police. Thus, the results of Moffitt and Silva suggest that the lower levels of *g* among criminals are a reflection of a difference between persons who commit and persons who do not commit crimes, rather than a difference between persons who are caught and persons who are not caught for committing crimes.

Another issue in interpreting the relation between *g* and law-abiding behavior is that of socioeconomic status. Given that lower socioeconomic status tends to be associated, to some extent, with higher rates of crime and with lower levels of *g*, you might wonder whether the negative relation between *g* and crime is attributable simply to low socioeconomic status. In other words, perhaps there is no relation between low *g* and crime if we consider only persons who have grown up in households of equal socioeconomic status.

However, the evidence suggests that this is not the case; instead, persons with higher levels of *g* tend to commit fewer crimes even when socioeconomic status is held constant. One investigation that showed this result was reported by Moffitt, Gabrielli, Mednick, and Schulsinger (1981), who studied a sample of over 4500 young men in Denmark. Of those men, nearly 8% had been convicted of one criminal offence, and another 5% had been convicted of two or more criminal offences. Using records of these men's socioeconomic status and intelligence test scores as collected years earlier, Moffitt *et al.* found that the number of criminal offences was correlated, weakly, with lower socioeconomic status ($r = -.11$), but somewhat more strongly with lower *g* ($r = -.19$). When Moffitt *et al.* controlled for socioeconomic status by calculating a partial correlation (see description earlier in this chapter), number of offences was still related to lower *g* ($r = -.17$). This means that even when we consider people who come from households having the same level of socioeconomic status, there is still a tendency for those who have lower levels of mental ability to be more likely to commit crimes.

Although the preceding results indicate an association between criminal activity and lower levels of *g*, it is important to keep in mind that this does not mean that persons with high levels of *g* do not commit crime at all. Although high-*g* individuals are less likely to commit crimes, there is some indication that those who do so tend to "select" crimes that have a higher probability of payoff and a lower probability of arrest. Moreover, there are some "white-collar" crimes—such as large-scale corporate fraud or government corruption—that presumably are committed mainly by high-*g* persons, because only persons with rather high levels of mental ability are able to achieve the positions in which one has the opportunity to commit those crimes.

The finding that persons with higher levels of *g* tend to be more law-abiding—and not simply better at avoiding being caught when breaking the law—raises the question of why this is the case. One possibility is that the cost/benefit ratio of criminal activity is higher for persons who have high levels of *g*, because those persons have better chances for educational and occupational success. In contrast, persons with lower levels of *g* may become frustrated by their somewhat poorer prospects for achieving success (Hirschi & Hindelang, 1977). But more generally, it may also be the case that high-*g* persons are more likely to recognize that committing a crime carries rather high risks of serious penalties and to judge the potential gains from crime as being insufficient to justify those potential losses.

Marriage: Assortative Mating

Another socially important variable that is associated with mental ability is that of marriage, or more specifically that of who marries whom. A consistent finding in several studies of the characteristics of spouses is that there is a tendency for spouses to be similar in some—but not all—aspects of mental ability; in other words, some aspects of mental ability do show substantial "assortative mating."

For example, recall from Chapter 9 the study by Watson *et al.* (2004) of the personality and other characteristics of married couples. Among the variables examined by Watson *et al.* were two mental ability tasks—a vocabulary test and a matrix reasoning test. Interestingly, even though vocabulary and matrix reasoning tend to be correlated with each other (both are strongly *g*-loaded tests), they revealed quite different results when correlations between spouses were considered. On the one hand, wives' and husbands' levels of vocabulary showed a fairly strong positive correlation, about .45. But on the other hand, wives' and husbands' levels of matrix reasoning were correlated only about .10. This result is consistent with previous findings, in which spouses have tended to show quite similar levels of verbal comprehension ability, but no particular similarity in mathematical reasoning ability (e.g., Botwin *et al.*, 1997).

Why should it be the case that spouses tend to be similar in verbal abilities, but not so similar in (equally *g*-loaded) nonverbal reasoning abilities? One likely explanation—as you might guess—is that two people will tend to have more rewarding conversations if they have similar levels of verbal ability, but that similar levels of nonverbal or mathematical reasoning ability are unlikely to contribute in an important way to any aspect of relationship quality.

Not All g-Loaded Tasks Are the Same

The topic of the previous section of this chapter was the link between mental abilities—especially the *g* factor—and various important life outcomes. This emphasis on *g* is appropriate: All mental abilities have at least moderate loadings on the *g* factor, and it is this dimension of general mental ability that usually shows the strongest relations with important criterion variables. As discussed earlier in this chapter, one of Spearman's important discoveries was that many very different tasks—for example, verbal knowledge, spatial visualization, or numerical reasoning—could all be good measures of *g*, and that a combination of such tasks would provide an excellent measure of *g*.

But in spite of the importance of *g*, it is not necessarily the case that all mental abilities, or even all mental abilities that have high *g*-loadings, will show the same pattern of relations with other variables, such as personality characteristics, or gender, or age. Instead, one task may correlate rather strongly with one of those variables, whereas another task—even a task with the same loading on the *g* factor—may be roughly uncorrelated with the same variable. In fact, we have already discussed an interesting example of this situation: Recall that husbands and wives tend to be rather similar to each other in their levels of vocabulary (a highly *g*-loaded task), but have no such tendency to be similar in their levels of nonverbal or mathematical reasoning (another highly *g*-loaded task). In the following section, we will describe some ways in which different kinds of mental ability—even highly *g*-loaded abilities—show quite different relations with other important variables.

Novel versus Familiar Tasks: Fluid and Crystallized Intelligence

One widely recognized difference among mental abilities involves the extent to which they involve "novel" versus "familiar" tasks. One way to think of this distinction is that the novel tasks tend to resemble puzzles or riddles, whereas the familiar tasks tend to resemble tests of the kind given in schools (even if the content of such tasks differs from that of school tests). For example, novel tasks would include tests such as Raven's Matrices and also tests such as "Similarities" (in which the respondent must identify the most important similarity between two elements, such as a banana and an orange). In contrast, familiar tasks would be tests of mathematical thinking (e.g., solving problems that require the use of some concepts in arithmetic or geometry) and of vocabulary or general knowledge.

This distinction between novel and familiar tasks was first discussed by Raymond Cattell, the same man who had conducted some early lexically based studies of personality structure (see Chapter 3). Cattell (e.g., 1971; Horn & Cattell, 1966) described the novel tasks as indicators of *fluid* ability and the familiar tasks as indicators of *crystallized* ability. These descriptions were based on Cattell's view that the novel tasks required a "fluid" or flexible response to a new situation, whereas the familiar tasks required the use of some "crystallized" or well-learned skills or knowledge.

The distinction between these two types of tasks is one that makes sense intuitively. However, when mental ability tests are factor analyzed in such a way as to produce two or more factors, those factors do not correspond perfectly to the division between novel and familiar tasks. In many cases, one factor includes tests that are verbal in content tend to make one factor, regardless of whether those tasks are somewhat novel (e.g., similarities) or highly familiar (e.g., vocabulary); one or more other factors contain tests that are numerical or spatial in content, again regardless of the novelty or familiarity of the tasks. So, the difference between fluid and crystallized ability, as originally described by Cattell, is not always supported empirically.

Generational Changes in Mental Abilities: The Flynn Effect

Nevertheless, there are some ways in which the difference between fluid and crystallized abilities is very meaningful. One striking case of this involves the ways in which people's performance on mental ability tasks has changed over the decades and generations. In many different countries, people today score much, much better on mental ability tasks than people did a few generations ago. In fact, on some tasks, there has been a steady increase in people's scores, such that people of a given age group (say, 18-year-olds, for example) in the year 2000 score about two standard deviation units higher than did people of the same age group in the year 1950. This means that if we could put the 18-year-olds from 1950 and from 2000 together, then about 85% of the 18-year-olds from 2000 would score above the average for the combined group, but only about 15% of the 18-year-olds from 1950 would do so. This is a very large increase!

But here is the strange thing about these improvements in test scores: The very large increases, as just described, have occurred only on the more novel tasks, such as Raven's Matrices or Similarities, which assess fluid intelligence (e.g., Flynn, 2006). In contrast, there have been very small increases (almost no increase at all) on the more familiar tasks, such as solving math problems or Vocabulary, which assess crystallized intelligence (Flynn, 2006). It is not clear why this pattern of increases has emerged, but a plausible reason has been proposed by James Flynn, the researcher who documented the improvements in test scores (Flynn, 1984, 1987). (This increase is now known as the "Flynn effect.") He has suggested that in modern times, people have been doing more and more of the kind of novel thinking that is used in puzzle- or riddle-solving tasks, and hence have been getting better at those tasks; in contrast, he has noted, people have not really had any greater exposure to the tasks involving skills or knowledge related to what is taught in school, because these tasks were already highly familiar even decades ago.

What is so strange about this? When you consider people of the same age who are tested at the same time, the difference between novel (fluid) and familiar (crystallized) tasks is sometimes almost impossible to notice. In other words, if you and your former high school classmates had all taken some mental ability tests on a given day, some people would have tended to do better than others across the various tests, regardless of whether those tests were puzzle- or riddle-like tasks as opposed to school-like tasks. But, if the class from 50 years earlier had taken the same tests, that class would likely have performed *far below your class* on the puzzle- or riddle-like tasks, yet *about the same as your class* on the school-like tasks. So, the distinction between novel and familiar tasks—between fluid and crystallized intelligence—can potentially be very important when we consider differences between groups of people who have grown up in rather different environments or at very different times. This occurs even though the distinction between those tasks is perhaps rather unimportant when we consider differences within a group of people who have grown up in roughly the same environment at the roughly same time.[13]

---

[13] One fascinating question that is raised by the pattern of increases in test scores is this: Are people "smarter" today than they were in previous generations? On one hand, it appears that they are *not* smarter, because the increases are not general to all of the mental ability tasks. For example, important abilities such as mathematical problem solving and verbal comprehension have not shown much improvement during the past several decades. But on the other hand, it appears that in one sense people *are* smarter, because they do have a much better ability to solve unusual problems that have a puzzle-like or riddle-like aspect to them. Flynn (2006) has speculated that this latter ability is very important in a modern economy and society, although it is difficult to evaluate the extent to which this is true.

Reasoning with Numbers and Shapes versus Understanding Verbal Concepts: Different Relations with Personality

As mentioned in the preceding section, factor analyses of mental ability tests often show a distinction between tasks that involve an understanding of verbal concepts and tasks that involve reasoning with numbers or with shapes and spaces. These factors tend to be correlated with each other—as always, there is a *g* factor of general intelligence—but still, some people are relatively strong in one factor or relatively weak in another. Notice that the numerical and spatial tasks both involve a kind of "mathematical" thinking, such as that used in arithmetic (numerical) or geometry (spatial). In contrast, the verbal ability tasks—such as vocabulary or similarities—instead require an understanding of some concept that is usually not very "mathematical," but instead involves events, places, people, living things, or substances.

This distinction between the "math reasoning" abilities (both numerical and spatial) and the "understanding of verbal concepts" abilities is revealed in a very interesting way—specifically, in the relations of those abilities with personality characteristics. For the most part, personality is not much related to mental abilities: Most of the major dimensions of personality as described earlier in this book are more or less uncorrelated with mental abilities (e.g., Ashton, Lee, Vernon, & Jang, 2000; Noftle & Robins, 2006). In other words, people who are "smarter," as assessed by mental ability tests, do not differ much in personality from people who are less smart.

But there is one important exception to this finding: For some kinds of mental ability, higher scores tend to be obtained by people who have higher levels of the personality traits associated with Openness to Experience, especially intellectual curiosity. Specifically, intellectually curious people tend to have higher levels of verbal ability than do people who are not so intellectually curious. In some studies, the relation has been rather strong, with correlations of more than .40 between inquisitiveness and tests of vocabulary or general knowledge. In contrast, however, intellectually curious people are about the same as less inquisitive people when it comes to spatial or numerical abilities, which show weaker correlations, only about .10, with tests that involve reasoning with shapes and numbers (Ashton *et al.*, 2000). The pattern is observed for the SAT subtests that are taken by high school students in the United States: Openness to Experience correlates almost .30 with the SAT Verbal subtest, but only about .05 with the SAT Mathematical subtest (Noftle & Robins, in press; see also Ackerman, Bowen, Beier & Kanfer, 2001).

So, why does this difference exist? Why is intellectual curiosity related rather strongly to verbal ability, but not so much to numerical or spatial ability? One likely explanation is that people who are intellectually curious—that is, people who enjoy learning and reading about various topics, such as literature, the arts, history, or science—simply tend to learn and understand many facts and many words. Conversely, people who are less inquisitive generally have less exposure to various facts and words, and thus tend not to develop such a deep and broad understanding of those concepts. But this effect of intellectual curiosity does not apply to the kind of numerical or spatial thinking required in solving mathematical problems: Apparently, intellectual curiosity may help one to learn words or facts, but it does not develop one's ability to solve problems that are of a numerical or spatial kind.

Alternative Ideas about Mental Abilities

This chapter has described the current state of knowledge in the field of mental abilities research, as revealed by many thousands of empirical studies conducted since the early twentieth century. But although the summary presented here represents the views shared by the large majority of researchers in this field, there are some contrasting ideas about the nature of mental abilities, and some of these ideas have become very popular in the media, in schools, and in the general public. In this section, we will take a look at some of these popular alternative views about the nature of mental abilities.

Gardner's "Theory of Multiple Intelligences"

Since the 1980s, a very popular perspective on mental abilities has been the "theory of multiple intelligences," as promoted in a series of books by Howard Gardner. Gardner (1983, 1999) has suggested that the *g* factor of mental ability is not particularly important for real-world outcomes, and that this factor emerges mainly because virtually all mental ability tests use a verbal format, which gives an advantage to people who are good at verbal skills.

Gardner has suggested that in fact there are eight very distinct kinds of intelligence: linguistic, logical–mathematical, spatial, musical, bodily–kinesthetic, interpersonal, intrapersonal, and naturalistic. The meaning of the first four of these "intelligences" is close to what is suggested by their names, as these refer to abilities in thinking with words, numbers, shapes, and musical sounds, respectively. Bodily–kinesthetic intelligence involves motor coordination, both at the level of the whole body (as in sports or in dancing) and also at the level of the hands or fingers (as in using small tools or instruments). Interpersonal intelligence refers to the ability to understand social situations and the behavior of other people, whereas intrapersonal intelligence refers to the ability to understand one's own behavior, thoughts, and feelings. Finally, naturalistic intelligence involves the ability to classify elements in the natural world (e.g., different species of animals or plants) according to the important similarities and differences among them.

The popularity of Gardner's model may be due in part to the very appealing idea that everyone has his or her own pattern of strengths or weaknesses. This emphasis on this diversity of abilities is in many ways more satisfying than is the idea that people differ in terms of a single major factor of general intelligence, or *g*. Notice, however, that several of the abilities considered by Gardner are not *purely mental* abilities, which have generally been the focus of other researchers. That is, most researchers in the field of mental abilities have excluded from their investigations those abilities that involve motor skills (as in bodily–kinesthetic intelligence), sensory acuteness (as in musical intelligence), or personality tendencies (as in interpersonal and especially intrapersonal intelligences).

This is not to say that these abilities are unimportant or uninteresting—obviously, these abilities play a major role in many human activities, and would be a worthwhile topic of study—yet their nonmental aspects tend to make them less relevant to the study of purely mental abilities.

What is the empirical evidence for Gardner's theory? There is not really any empirical evidence of the kind based on factor analysis, partly because Gardner has not developed tests to measure these various abilities. But researchers have long known that measures of many of Gardner's intelligences are indeed substantially correlated with each other, and have strong loadings on the *g* factor of general intelligence. Recall that in Figure 10-1 we showed several tests of mental ability; these tests happen to represent (in terms of Gardner's theory) the linguistic, logical–mathematical, spatial, and interpersonal forms of intelligence. As mentioned earlier in this chapter, those tests show moderate positive correlations with each other, and all of them show fairly high loadings on *g*. In addition, tests of naturalistic intelligence—for example, tests in which the respondent must decide which of several diagrams best represents the relations among various categories of objects—also correlate strongly with other mental ability tasks, and thus also load on the *g* factor (Visser, Ashton, & Vernon, 2006).

Now let us consider the other abilities described by Gardner. With regard to intrapersonal intelligence, it is very difficult to measure this form of ability, so its relations with other mental abilities are not really known. One recent attempt to assess the self-knowledge involved in intrapersonal intelligence was moderately successful, and suggested that this ability was only modestly related to the *g* factor (Visser *et al.*, 2006); hence, this ability might be considered as a separate talent of its own. As for musical intelligence, some studies have suggested that it correlates modestly with other mental abilities, and hence is moderately loaded on the *g* factor. Other data suggest that composers and performers of classical music often have very high levels of mental ability; some research suggests that the basic abilities to judge pitch and rhythm are apparently somewhat associated with *g*, but are partly a separate talent in their own right (Lynn, Wilson, & Gault, 1989). Finally, measures of bodily–kinesthetic intelligence tend to be correlated modestly with mental abilities, and hence have relatively low loadings on *g*. (Interestingly, the "athletic" physical skills involving the whole body are almost uncorrelated with the "dextrous" physical skills involving the hands and fingers, which suggests that there are actually at least two basic kinds of bodily–kinesthetic talent; Visser *et al.*, 2006.)

To sum up, the evidence from empirical studies of mental abilities largely contradicts Gardner's theory of multiple intelligences. First, the "intelligences" that involve purely mental abilities—linguistic, logical–mathematical, spatial, naturalistic, and perhaps interpersonal—are all substantially correlated with each other: People who are strong at one of these abilities tend to be strong at the others also. This indicates the existence of a strong factor of general mental ability that cuts across some very different kinds of mental ability tasks. (Moreover, this *g* factor cannot be explained by the "verbal" content of the tests used in assessing those abilities, because many of the spatial and logical–mathematical ability tasks are nonverbal in format.) Finally, with regard to the "intelligences" that are not purely mental, but instead have some sensory or physical aspect as well, these abilities are only modestly associated with *g*, but the nonmental aspects of these abilities suggest that they are better understood as separate talents—for example, musical, athletic, or manual—rather than as aspects of mental ability or intelligence.

Sternberg's "Triarchic Theory of Intelligence"

Another popular theory of intelligence is the "triarchic theory" proposed by Robert Sternberg. Sternberg (1985) has suggested that there are three fundamental aspects of mental ability, which he describes as *analytic intelligence, creative intelligence*, and *practical intelligence*. In Sternberg's framework, analytic intelligence corresponds closely to the kind of ability that is highly valued in school settings—that is, an ability to think logically and critically. In contrast, creative intelligence represents the ability to formulate new ideas and to gain original insights into problems. Finally, practical intelligence represents the ability to solve problems in the context of everyday life, and thus involves a kind of "street smarts" or a common-sense understanding of how the world works.

In order to evaluate the triarchic theory, it is necessary to find some way first to measure the three intelligences, and then to find the extent to which they are distinct from each other and the extent to which they can predict important criterion variables. If Sternberg's theory is valid, then it should be possible to obtain reliable measurements of all three of his proposed aspects of intelligence. In addition, those three variables should be largely independent of each other; that is, they should be only weakly intercorrelated. Moreover, each aspect of intelligence should predict its own distinct set of outcomes—for example, analytical intelligence should predict academic performance, creative intelligence should predict actual creative accomplishments (e.g., in artistic endeavors or in making innovations of some kind), and practical intelligence should predict "real-world" successes (e.g., in job performance or in dealing with everyday financial or social situations).

How has the triarchic theory fared thus far? Sternberg and his colleagues have attempted to measure practical intelligence in a variety of settings, typically by assessing the extent to which persons in a given occupation have managed to learn the best ways to succeed within their careers and organizations (e.g., Sternberg *et al.*, 2000). For example, Sternberg has developed tests to measure the extent to which people in various lines of work—including business managers, bank managers, army officers, university professors, and insurance salespersons—have figured out the "unwritten rules" or "tacit knowledge" of how to get ahead. Generally, these tests ask respondents to rank-order the usefulness of many possible actions that could be taken, in various job-related situations, to improve the chances of career advancement. The respondents' rankings of those actions can then be compared with the typical rankings as provided by people who have achieved a high level of success within the occupation in question—that is, by experts. Respondents whose rankings are most similar to those of the typical successful person are thus showing a high level of tacit knowledge, or of practical intelligence.

In some studies, Sternberg and his colleagues have reported some success for the tests of practical intelligence that they have developed for the occupations just listed (Sternberg *et al.*, 2000). That is, according to Sternberg and colleagues, those persons who perform well on these tests—in the sense of giving answers similar to those rated as good answers by experts in the specified job—tend to have higher levels of variables related to job performance. (However, the positive results reported by Sternberg and colleagues may be due in part to selective reporting—that is, of drawing attention only to the results that support the validity of tacit knowledge tests; see Gottfredson, 2003.) The finding of a link between "practical intelligence" tasks and job performance is actually similar to a well-established finding in industrial psychology. Researchers in that field have found that "situational judgment tests"—tasks that measure something very similar to "tacit knowledge" of Sternberg's practical intelligence—are moderately related to job performance (see McDaniel & Whetzel, 2005). But situational judgment tests are also related to *g* and to experience for the specific type of work in which those tests are designed. In other words, one's level of "situational judgment" or "practical intelligence" in a particular area is due partly to one's level of *g* and partly to one's level of experience in that area.

In addition to developing tests of practical intelligence that are specific to a particular job, Sternberg has also constructed measures of practical intelligence that involve questions of a more general nature (Sternberg, 1993). Those questions ask the respondent to choose the best solutions to various "real-life" problems involving, for example, awkward social situations, "best-buy" purchasing decisions, and finding one's way using a map. Sternberg developed his test of practical intelligence as part of an instrument that also included tests of analytical and creative intelligence. The availability of this test has thus allowed some investigation of the relations among the three kinds of intelligence, and a test of the extent to which the three are independent of each other.

One more recent study (Koke & Vernon, 2003) measured analytical, creative, and practical intelligence in a sample of 150 college students, using the intelligence test developed by Sternberg. In addition, Koke and Vernon also administered another well-known intelligence test (specifically, the Wonderlic Personnel test), and obtained records of the students' examination grades in a first-year psychology course. The results of this study showed that—contrary to Sternberg's theory—the three aspects of intelligence were substantially correlated with each other, with correlations ranging from about .35 to .50. This result indicates that people with high levels of analytical intelligence tend also to have high levels of creative intelligence and of practical intelligence, and vice versa. In addition, all three aspects of intelligence—not just analytical intelligence—correlated substantially (in the .30s and .40s) with intelligence as measured by the Wonderlic test. (When added together, the overall score for the three kinds of intelligence correlated about .55 with the Wonderlic test.) As for performance in the psychology course, all three aspects of intelligence—again, not just analytical—correlated in the .20s and .30s with course examination grades; when added together, the overall score on the three "triarchic" tests correlated about .40 with those grades, a value that was actually slightly higher than that yielded by the Wonderlic test. Thus, these results suggest that the three aspects of intelligence are not independent, but instead are all related to a general mental ability (or *g*) and are all related to criteria (such as academic performance) that depend, in part, on that general mental ability.

To summarize, there is not much evidence so far to support Sternberg's suggestion of three separate aspects of intelligence. The study by Koke and Vernon (2003) described above found that the analytical, creative, and practical aspects of intelligence were all substantially correlated with each other, and hence strongly related to an overall, general intelligence. Moreover, although there may be some validity for "practical intelligence" tests designed as predictors of performance in specific jobs, these tests are likely to measure a kind of "situational judgment" that depends on specific job experience in addition to general intelligence.

Emotional Intelligence

Since the 1990s, there has been a great deal of interest in the idea of "emotional intelligence." Promoted in best-selling books, this concept has received much attention in newspapers, radio, and TV, apparently because of the suggestion that emotional intelligence can be more important than the traditional concept of intelligence, which is generally measured using IQ tests of mental ability.

There have been two rather different approaches to the study and measurement of emotional intelligence. The original approach was developed by psychologists John Mayer and Peter Salovey, who studied emotional intelligence as an ability to perceive and understand one's emotions and those of others (e.g., Mayer & Salovey, 1993). A later approach was popularized by journalist Daniel Goleman, whose best-selling book on the topic (Goleman, 1995) described emotional intelligence in terms of an ability to regulate one's emotions. Let us consider these two ways of conceptualizing emotional intelligence, beginning with the more recent and widely popularized approach.

The concept of emotional intelligence as described by Goleman (e.g., 1995) involves an ability to regulate one's emotions, and includes such characteristics as self-control, self-confidence, trustworthiness, empathy, optimism, achievement orientation, conflict management, teamwork, and awareness of one's emotions. Some instruments have been developed to measure the various aspects of emotional intelligence as described here, and these generally rely on self-reports or on observer reports (e.g., Bar-On, 1997).

In reading the preceding description of emotional intelligence and its measurement, you might wonder how this concept differs from that of personality. Many psychologists have raised this same question, because most of the various characteristics related to emotional intelligence are generally viewed as socially desirable personality traits. When self-report measures of these emotional intelligence characteristics have been examined along with personality inventories, the results have shown strong correlations between emotional intelligence and familiar personality traits. For example, consider two investigations (Brackett & Mayer, 2003; Newsome, Day, & Catano, 2000) of the relations between emotional intelligence (measured using the inventory by Bar-On, 1997) and personality traits as assessed by traditional personality inventories. In both studies, emotional intelligence was negatively related to Neuroticism (or anxiety), and positively related to Extraversion and Conscientiousness (or self-control); the correlations were rather strong, with the highest well above .50.

Interestingly, both of the preceding studies were based on samples of college students, and both studies obtained information on the grade point average and the mental ability (i.e., IQ test scores) of the students. In both investigations, grade point average was correlated with IQ and with Conscientiousness (or self-control), but not with emotional intelligence; also, emotional intelligence was unrelated to test scores (Brackett & Mayer, 2003; Newsome *et al.*, 2000).

Thus, it appears that when emotional intelligence is measured using self-reports (or observer reports), it largely represents a blend of several desirable personality traits. Those traits—such as low anxiety, high extraversion, and high self-control—are important predictors of many important outcome variables, including one's subjective sense of life satisfaction (see Chapter 9). Therefore, emotional intelligence is also likely to be associated with well-being and psychological health, and some researchers have found emotional intelligence measures to be just as good as traditional personality scales in predicting those outcomes, if not somewhat better (Day, Therrien, & Carroll, 2005). But the validity of self-report emotional intelligence scales appears to be due to the fact that they assess several important personality traits, with a particular emphasis on traits that are associated with psychological health. What this means is that it is not really necessary to invent a new concept—"emotional intelligence"—to describe variables that are already familiar to personality psychologists.

The status of emotional intelligence is rather different when we consider it not as a collection of desirable personality traits, but rather as the ability to think accurately about emotions. As you will recall, this was the way in which emotional intelligence was originally defined by Salovey and Mayer (1990; Mayer & Salovey, 1993), the researchers who began much of the recent work on this topic. As described by Salovey and Mayer, emotional intelligence includes the abilities to monitor one's own emotions and those of others, to discriminate among various emotions, and to use information about emotions as a guide to one's own thinking and action. Accordingly, these researchers have developed a performance test whose items assess these abilities (Mayer, Salovey, & Caruso, 2002). For example, some items ask the respondent to indicate which emotions are expressed in pictures of people's faces (or even of landscapes or designs). Some other items ask the respondent to choose effective ways to manage their own emotions and the emotions of others within hypothetical situations. (Interestingly, women score higher on average than do men on this test, with a difference between one-half and one full standard deviation.)

In several studies, performance-based tests of emotional intelligence have been examined in relation to overall intelligence and to personality characteristics (e.g., Brackett & Mayer, 2003; Brackett, Mayer, & Warner, 2004). The results of these studies have indicated that emotional intelligence shows modest positive correlations with the personality dimensions of Big Five Agreeableness and Openness to Experience and also with verbal-based tests of mental ability. However, these correlations are rather modest, reaching only the .20s for the personality characteristics, and the .30s for verbal ability. These results suggest that emotional intelligence—when measured as an ability—can indeed be distinguished rather clearly from personality and from general mental ability, even though it is somewhat related to those other individual differences.

The preceding investigations were based on college student participants, and these studies also examined relations of emotional intelligence with some important outcome variables, such as drug and alcohol use, smoking, grade point average, and deviant behaviors (e.g., fighting, vandalism). Overall, the relations with emotional intelligence were rather weak, although low emotional intelligence was modestly associated with higher levels of deviance, even when personality and mental ability were held constant (Brackett & Mayer, 2003; Brackett *et al.*, 2004). These results suggest at least some potential for emotional intelligence—as measured by the actual ability to think about emotions—to predict some useful criterion variables. Future research might examine the validity of emotional intelligence for predicting outcomes that are more directly connected to emotional skills, such as success in interacting with other people in a variety of individual and group settings.

Summary and Conclusions

As described in this chapter, there are positive correlations among diverse tasks measuring many different kinds of mental ability; that is, on average, people who are relatively good at one mental ability task tend to be relatively good at any other mental ability task also. This indicates that the domain of mental abilities can be summarized in terms of a large factor of general mental ability, known as *g*. However, tasks measuring similar aspects of mental ability tend to correlate quite strongly with each other, and this indicates that, in addition to *g*, there are several smaller "group factors" of mental ability. Each of these corresponds to a different aspect of mental ability, such as spatial, numerical, or verbal abilities. Thus, whereas the *g* factor describes the individual's overall level of mental ability, the group factors provide some additional information about areas of relative strength or weakness.

Typically, people's levels of *g* tend to increase substantially throughout childhood and into adolescence, and then decline during old age. The pattern of changes in *g* between early adulthood and late middle age is less clear: Some researchers believe that some mental abilities begin to decline substantially after early adulthood, whereas other researchers believe that most mental abilities do not decline until late middle age. In any case, individual differences in *g* are very stable, even between childhood and old age: That is, children who are "smart" relative to their age peers will usually be "smart" relative to their age peers in old age.

Much research has been conducted in search of the biological bases of mental ability, particularly of the *g* factor. One consistent finding is that individuals with larger brains tend to have higher levels of *g*, with correlations typically in the .30s. The relations between *g* and nerve conduction velocity have been inconsistent, but *g* is typically correlated about .40 with faster reaction times, and shows similar relations with speed of inspection time (i.e., with the ability to discriminate between stimuli that are presented for only a vanishingly brief interval). In addition, *g* is also related to several features of averaged evoked potentials (i.e., brain waves in response to a stimulus). Finally, the brains of persons who have high levels of *g* tend to metabolize less glucose (i.e., consume less energy) when solving difficult mental tasks than do the brains of lower-*g* persons.

Research on the genetic and environmental origins of mental ability has been based on methods essentially the same as those described for personality, in Chapter 6. The results of many investigations suggest that the heritability of mental ability (or of the *g* factor) is typically in the .40s when assessed in children, but in the .70s when assessed in adults. The genetic contribution to variation in mental ability is partly additive and partly nonadditive in nature. The effects of the common environment on *g* show a pattern opposite to that of genetic effects: The common environment shows a moderately strong influence during childhood, with values in the .30s, but this declines almost to zero by adulthood. However, some recent studies suggest that variation in the womb environment—both between mothers and also between pregnancies of the same mother—is an important contributor to mental ability. The lack of attention to these womb effects may have led researchers to overestimate somewhat the heritability of mental ability, which might be only about .50. With regard to environmental influences on *g*, one possible influence is breast-feeding, but recent research suggests that the link between breast-feeding and mental ability is due to the tendency for mothers who are more intelligent to be both more likely to breast-feed and also more likely to have smarter children. During adulthood, lower levels of vitamin B_{12} intake appear to be associated with decreases in the level of *g*.

Scores on tests of mental ability—and on the *g* factor that is the main element of those tests—are related to a variety of "life outcome" variables of practical significance. Academic achievement and performance are substantially correlated with *g*: School grades typically correlate about .50 with *g* in elementary school, and somewhat lower at the secondary and postsecondary levels, because of the narrower range of mental ability among students at higher levels of education. Standardized tests of school achievement correlate even more strongly with *g*.

In the workplace, job performance is also related to *g*, with correlations typically in the .50s for performance in complex jobs and in the .20s for performance in simpler jobs. Individuals' levels of occupational status are also correlated with *g*, even when the individuals' parents' levels are controlled. Longevity is also modestly related to *g*, as individuals who score higher on mental ability tests tend to have longer-than-average life expectancies; this relation is likely due in part to health-related behaviors, as higher-*g* persons tend to have healthier patterns of behavior. Higher levels of *g* are also associated with lower levels of criminal or delinquent behavior, as measured both by arrest records and also by anonymous self-reports. There is also a moderately strong tendency for spouses of the same couple to be similar in their levels of verbal aspects of mental ability (i.e., there is "assortative mating" for verbal ability), but no such tendency exists for mathematical aspects of mental ability.

Tasks that are good indicators of *g* often relate in similar ways to other variables, but there are exceptions. For example, during the past century people's scores have increased greatly on tasks that resemble puzzles or riddles, but hardly at all on tasks that resemble school tests. Also, the personality trait of intellectual curiosity is correlated substantially with tasks assessing verbal knowledge, but hardly at all with tasks assessing mathematical problem solving.

Several popular theories of mental ability have been offered as alternatives or as supplements to traditional concepts of mental ability. Gardner's theory of multiple intelligences describes several areas of mental ability. Sternberg's triarchic theory includes analytical intelligence (similar to academic ability), creative intelligence, and practical intelligence (i.e., "street smarts" or common sense). Recent ideas about emotional intelligence emphasize either (a) a variety of socially desirable personality characteristics, or (b) the *ability* to understand the emotions and behavior of oneself and others. Thus far, Gardner's and Sternberg's theories have not shown important improvements on the traditional theories of mental ability, which are based on a *g* factor and on several group factors. Other investigations suggest that tests of emotional intelligence—tests based on the *ability* to think accurately in the context of emotions—may provide some predictive validity beyond that given by traditional measures of personality and mental abilities.

Chapter 11

Religion and Politics

Religion   260

Is Religiosity a Personality
  Characteristic?   260

Religiosity and the Major Dimensions of
  Personality   261

Developmental Change and Stability in
  Religiosity   264

Religiosity and Paranormal Beliefs   265

Religiosity and Life Outcomes   266

Politics   267

Right-Wing Authoritarianism   267

Social Dominance Orientation   269

Relations between Right-Wing
  Authoritarianism and Social
  Dominance Orientation   270

Two Dimensions of Political Attitudes   272

Political Attitudes and the Major Dimensions
  of Personality   273

Political Attitudes, Social Values, and
  Religion   274

Developmental Change and Stability in
  Political Attitudes   276

**Origins of Religious Beliefs and Political
  Attitudes: Biological Bases, Genetic
  and Environmental Influences, and
  Evolutionary Function   278**

Biological Bases   278

Genetic and Environmental Influences   278

Evolutionary Function   281

Summary and Conclusions   281

In this chapter we will consider religion and politics—two topics that you are not supposed to discuss in polite company. These topics are the source of much passion and conflict in people's lives, but they are also of great interest to psychologists. For the personality psychologist, several major questions come to mind. What are the main ways in which people differ in their religious beliefs and political attitudes? How are those beliefs and attitudes related to personality characteristics? Why do people differ so sharply in their religious and political orientations?

≡ *Religion*

Religion is of profound importance in the lives of millions of people, yet millions of others profess no religious beliefs at all. Although religiosity often differs greatly between generations and between nations,[1] there are also very large individual differences *within* societies in the extent of religious belief and practice. This raises the obvious question of whether *individual differences* in religiosity—that is, among persons who have grown up in the same society and at the same time—are associated with personality differences. Are some personality characteristics consistently and strongly related to religiosity? For example, are religious people more gentle, or more harsh? More open-minded, or more closed-minded?

Is Religiosity a Personality Characteristic?

Before answering the above questions, it is worth reflecting for a moment on a different question: Is religiosity itself a personality trait? There are certainly many ways in which religiosity is a kind of trait: It is manifested in a wide variety of correlated behaviors that are expressed in various situations (praying before going to bed, reading scriptures, watching religious television, observing dietary restrictions, attending weekly services, seeking advice from religious authorities, etc.). And, on an intuitive level, a person's religiosity (or lack thereof) seems to be a very important part of his or her personality, in the broad sense of the term, given that religiosity involves such a wide range of behaviors, thoughts, and feelings.

On the other hand, there are some important differences between religiosity and the personality traits that we have considered in previous chapters. One difference is that individual differences in religiosity depend on people's *beliefs*, whereas typical personality traits do not. That is, a person can only be really religious if he or she accepts some specific beliefs about the supernatural or spiritual world (e.g., the existence of God or of a soul); in contrast, a person's level of any of the various personality dimensions does not depend on his or her acceptance of any specific beliefs.[2]

Another important difference between religiosity and personality traits is the fact that religiosity—unlike any given personality trait—involves an entire *way of living* that is

---

[1] In this chapter, we will focus mostly on religiosity as expressed in Western societies, in which the religion of the majority is Christianity. This emphasis reflects the fact that most research on the topic of religiosity has been based on samples of Christians in Western countries. An important task for future research will be to find out whether or not the correlations of religiosity with other variables will be similar in non-Western or non-Christian countries.

[2] Related to the preceding point are some interesting features of the way that people's levels of religiosity are distributed (e.g., Ashton, Lee, & Goldberg, 2004; Paunonen, 2002). On self- or observer report personality trait scales, the items tend to be correlated modestly with each other, and the distribution of people's scores is roughly "normal," with most people close to the middle and with fewer and fewer people toward the extremes at either end (see Figure 1-1). But this tends not to be the case for self-report or observer report scales measuring religiosity. Instead, the items tend to be correlated very strongly with each other, and the scale scores show a nonnormal distribution in which there are many people who show extremely low or extremely high levels of religiosity.

BOX 11-1

Cross-Generational and Cross-National Differences in Religiosity

As you might expect, there is evidence of some very large differences in religiosity between generations and between countries or cultures. With regard to generational differences, some societies have shown rapid changes in their levels of religious belief and practice, as was strikingly apparent in many Western countries during the late twentieth century. A classic example is the Canadian province of Quebec: In the late 1950s, about 99% of French-speaking Quebec residents belonged to a Roman Catholic congregation; by 1990, the proportion had dropped to 18% (Bibby, 1993). With regard to national or cultural differences, the contrasts are equally striking. For example, a survey conducted in 2002 found that, in many African and Asian countries, more than 80% of the people considered religion to be an important part of their lives (Pew Global Attitudes Project, 2002). However, the proportion was less than 20% in some other Asian countries and in some European countries.

These differences between countries and generations are massive, and probably much greater than any such differences involving personality characteristics. Even though there may well be important variations across countries and generations in the major dimensions of personality, it seems unlikely that differences in, say, Emotionality or Agreeableness would be quite so large. As shown in the case of Quebec, a change in people's ideas about religious belief and practice can spread rapidly throughout a society, but a similarly rapid change in the general dispositions that make up personality has not yet been observed (see Box 7-3).

meant to bring the individual into harmony with some higher power (such as God). A person's religious beliefs may influence a diverse array of behaviors, and not only behaviors that are exclusively religious, such as praying or attending services. For example, highly religious people of any given religion may differ from nonreligious people in terms of what they eat, whom they marry, what they do with their money, what drugs they use, how they raise their children, whom they obey, when they fight, whom they help, and so on. Notice that although these kinds of behaviors can all be regulated by the rules of a given religion, they do not have much else, if anything, in common. In contrast to this situation for religious behaviors, the behaviors that are relevant to any given personality *do* tend to have some conceptual similarity. (For example, Conscientiousness is observed in behaviors such as organizing one's surroundings, checking for mistakes, working long hours, and planning one's schedule; similarly, Extraversion is observed in behaviors such as introducing oneself to others, speaking up in group meetings, expressing one's enthusiasm, and attending parties.) This reflects the fact that personality traits involve behaviors that go together "naturally," not as part of a system that provides a whole way of life.

Religiosity and the Major Dimensions of Personality

In considering how religiosity relates to the major dimensions of personality, we should first be clear about what we will mean by religiosity. As you have probably noticed, people who apparently follow various religious practices may have very different motivations for doing so: Some people's religious behavior is a reflection of their deepest beliefs, whereas for other people, expressions of religiosity are intended mainly for the purpose of "keeping up appearances" within their community. In other words, some people are genuinely religious in the sense that they would follow their religious practices even if no one were watching, whereas other people observe religious rituals simply to gain and maintain social approval. In the following sections, we will focus mainly on aspects of religiosity of the former kind; some researchers refer to this as *intrinsic* religiosity, because the person's religious activity is based on a view that religion is important in its own right, or intrinsically. Only when specifically noted will we consider the latter kind of religiosity; this other variety is often called *extrinsic* religiosity, because religion is treated as a way of obtaining other, or extrinsic goals, rather than as something important for its own sake. Now—keeping in mind that we will consider religiosity in the "intrinsic" sense just described—let us consider how religiosity relates to the major dimensions of personality.

Several studies have examined the links between religiosity and the Big Five dimensions of personality, and a more recent review of those studies (Saroglou, 2002) has summarized their results. Probably the most striking finding is that the relations tend to be weak: Religiosity is not strongly associated with any of the Big Five factors. There is, however, some tendency for people who are more religious to have higher levels of Agreeableness and of Conscientiousness, with correlations of about .20. (As noted by Saroglou, this means that a relatively religious person is 60% likely to be above average in Agreeableness or Conscientiousness, whereas the likelihood for a relatively nonreligious person is only 40%.) Thus, these results suggest that more religious people are somewhat "better behaved" than are nonreligious people, but again, the tendency is not especially strong. These results raise the interesting question of why religious people tend to be a bit higher in Agreeableness and in Conscientiousness. Are better-behaved people more likely to be attracted to religion? Or, does religion tend to make people better behaved? Or both? The relative importance of these influences has not yet been determined.[3,4]

In addition to the results described above, there are also some interesting relations between religiosity and the personality factor of Openness to Experience. Overall, religiosity is roughly uncorrelated with Openness to Experience, but this fact conceals some intriguing contrasts between two very different ways in which religiosity is expressed. First, consider what might be called *religious fundamentalism*, which involves a strict obedience and unquestioning devotion toward the rules and teachings of one's religion. Next, consider what might be called *spirituality*, which involves a sense of unity or togetherness with God and the universe and an intense *feeling* of religious fervor or inspiration.

Can you predict how these two aspects of religiosity are related to Openness to Experience? As reported in Saroglou's (2002) review, religious fundamentalism is correlated

---

[3] Incidentally, women tend to be slightly more religious than men are, with a difference of about one-quarter of a standard deviation unit (data from Paunonen, 2002).

[4] In case you were wondering about extrinsic religiosity, Saroglou's (2002) review indicated that its relations with the Big Five personality dimensions were very weak. However, it seems likely that other personality traits, such as those involving the need for social status, would be more strongly associated with extrinsic religiosity.

negatively with Openness to Experience, whereas spirituality is correlated *positively* with Openness to Experience. These results would seem to make sense if one considers the traits that make up the Openness to Experience factor in relation to these two expressions of religiosity. Persons high in Openness to Experience are inquisitive and unconventional, and these tendencies would likely lead them to question traditional religious teachings. But in addition, persons high in Openness are imaginative and feel a sense of awe toward nature, and these tendencies would likely lead them to seek a kind of spiritual unity with God or with the universe. (Note that the correlations as observed by Saroglou were rather weak—about .20 in absolute value—but that the relations can be considerably stronger depending on the scales that are used to measure fundamentalism or spirituality.)

Overall, these results suggest that the major dimensions of personality are not strongly related to religiosity. But this is perhaps not surprising if we realize that our level of religious belief and commitment is partly determined by the religiosity of the household in which we grow up. (We will discuss this influence of the shared or common environment in more detail later in the chapter.) If the religiosity of one's upbringing has a strong effect on one's level of religiosity, then there might not be so much variation left over for one's personality to explain. But what about those people whose level of religiosity differs sharply from that of the household in which they were raised? Is there anything special about the personalities of people who entirely abandon the religion with which they grew up, or of people who become deeply religious despite having had a thoroughly non-religious upbringing?

So far, only a few investigations have addressed this question. One interesting project by McCullough, Tsang, and Brion (2003) studied a sample of persons who had been identified as "gifted" children and who had later provided a variety of information about themselves during adulthood. The results showed that the children who had been raised in religious households tended to be more religious in adulthood (the correlation was in the .40s). But the strength of this relation differed according to personality, which had been assessed by teachers' ratings of the children on a series of variables. Those children who were rated as having been confident, optimistic, and emotionally stable showed a somewhat weaker tendency to have the same level of religiosity in adulthood as that with which they were raised (for this subset of persons, the correlation was in the .30s). But those children who were rated as having been insecure, pessimistic, and moody showed a somewhat stronger tendency to have the same level of religiosity in adulthood as that with which they were raised (for this subset of persons, the correlation was in the .50s). So, these results suggest that, even though there is a tendency to maintain the level of religiosity with which one was raised, this tendency is *especially* strong among people who are moody, and somewhat *less* strong (but still significant) among people who are stable. McCullough *et al.* suggested that this finding might be explained by a tendency for emotionally unstable persons to be strongly motivated to avoid the tension and conflict that would arise as a result of departing from the religious traditions (or the very non-religious traditions) of their families.

Another study of the personalities of people who are much more or much less religious than their parents is that of Altemeyer and Hunsberger (1997). These researchers did not collect any standardized measures of personality, but they conducted detailed interviews with several dozen persons who were either (a) very nonreligious despite having been raised in a very religious household, or (b) very religious despite having been raised in a very nonreligious household. Altemeyer and Hunsberger referred to the people who had abandoned their religion as "Amazing Apostates," and referred to the people who had spontaneously become very religious as "Amazing Believers." (Note that both of these kinds of individuals are quite rare, each representing less than 2% of the young adult population from which Altemeyer and Hunsberger identified them.)

The interviews revealed that the Amazing Apostates had generally experienced increasing doubts about their religion. These doubts were due to what they perceived as moral hypocrisy in religious people and as logical inconsistency and factual inaccuracy in religious teachings. Most of the Amazing Apostates were very good students in school, and upon having thought a great deal about their religion, they had eventually concluded that they no longer sincerely believed in that religion. With regard to the Amazing Believers, the conversion to religion had generally followed a period of intense personal crisis due, for example, to the death of a loved one or to problems with drug or alcohol use. The conversion of the Amazing Believers had been sudden and was characterized by emotion and passion rather than reason and reflection—thus opposite to the typical case of the Amazing Apostates—and suggests that the Amazing Believers had felt a strong need for a sense of community and structure in their lives.

Developmental Change and Stability in Religiosity

The studies described before are related to the questions of developmental change and stability in religiosity. As shown by McCullough *et al.* (2003) and Altemeyer and Hunsberger (1997), there is a tendency for people to maintain a level of religiosity that is fairly similar to that with which they were raised. In other words, people who are raised in more religious households tend to maintain a higher level of religiosity than do people who are raised in less religious households. But a couple of important questions remain. First, how do people's levels of religiosity typically change across the life span? That is, do people in general tend to become more religious or less religious during certain phases of their lives? Second, how much stability is there to individual differences in religiosity? Put another way, to what extent do the differences in religiosity levels among a group of people remain similar across the life span?

Some answers to these questions are provided from the same data set as that used in the McCullough *et al.* (2003) study that was described above. In a follow-up investigation, McCullough, Enders, Brion, and Jain (2005) examined the self-rated levels of religiosity of participants in an early study of gifted children. As part of this study, the participants were contacted at various times throughout their adulthood (specifically, about every 10 years between 1940, when the participants were 24 to 40 years old, and 1991). This allowed McCullough *et al.* (2005) to examine overall trends in the average level of religiosity across the life span, and it also allowed them to examine whether or not the participants' relative levels of religiosity were stable across the life span.

With regard to developmental change, the results showed a modest tendency for religiosity levels to increase between young adulthood and middle age, and then a slightly weaker tendency to decrease between middle age and old age. Overall, the average participant was very slightly more religious in old age than in young adulthood. But even these changes were not the same for all participants. Instead, McCullough *et al.* (2005) found that the participants showed three different patterns of change in religiosity: About 40% of participants showed the pattern described above; however, another 40% showed initially high levels of religiosity that gradually increased across the years; also, another 20% showed initially low levels of religiosity that remained low, or even decreased slightly, across the years.

Thus, the patterns of developmental change in religiosity do not show any dramatic changes for the average person, but there is some weak tendency for religiosity to be higher in middle age than in young adulthood or in old age. Future research will be needed to find out why these developmental changes occur, or even to find out whether these findings are true of people in general. (Remember that this was a sample of gifted children; in adulthood, these children were somewhat less religious on average than were people in the general population.)

The results of McCullough *et al.* (2005) also provide some information about stability in levels of religiosity—that is, the extent to which the differences among people in religiosity remain constant across the years. In general, there was a fairly high level of stability: Even across the half-century span between 1940 and 1991, the correlation between levels of religiosity at these two times was above .50. This suggests that, if someone were above average in religiosity as a young adult (i.e., relative to other young adults), then there would be a 75% chance that that person would remain above average in religiosity as an elderly adult (i.e., relative to other elderly adults), and only a 25% change that he or she would then be below average. Given the very long span of time involved, this does seem to be a rather high level of stability. (Over shorter time periods, the stability was higher, with correlations approaching .90 for religiosity self-ratings at times 10 years apart.)

Religiosity and Paranormal Beliefs

The topic of religiosity also raises the issue of other forms of beliefs in the supernatural. For example, some people feel very confident about the existence of ghosts, "psychic" powers, witchcraft, communication with the dead, extrasensory perception (ESP), and other occult forces. Other people, in contrast, are extremely skeptical about these *paranormal* phenomena. How do these paranormal beliefs relate to religious beliefs? Are religious people more or less likely to believe in the existence of paranormal phenomena such as those just described?

In trying to predict the relation between religious and paranormal beliefs, there are some reasons to expect a positive correlation. Both kinds of beliefs involve an acceptance of things that defy the known laws of nature, and that have not been verified by scientists. Therefore, you might expect that some people would be skeptical about any and all supernatural forces, whether those from religion or those from the paranormal or occult, whereas other people might be inclined to believe in all kinds of supernatural forces.

On the other hand, there are also reasons to expect a negative correlation between religious beliefs and paranormal beliefs. Even though religious belief generally involves an acceptance of some supernatural phenomena, such as a God or spirits, most religious organizations tend to discourage their members from believing in paranormal phenomena. As a result, you might predict very low levels of paranormal belief among the most religious people.

So, which prediction is correct? What is the relation between religious and paranormal beliefs? Most studies conducted so far (MacDonald, 2000; Rice, 2003) suggest these beliefs are more or less unrelated to each other, with correlations not far from zero. Thus, neither of the preceding predictions appears to be correct. However, it may be the case that the two tendencies cancel each other out: People who hold religious beliefs may have an *inclination* to hold paranormal beliefs, but the teachings of their religion may weaken those other kinds of supernatural beliefs.

Religiosity and Life Outcomes

Some potential advantages or disadvantages of religious belief might be understood by examining how religiosity is related to some important life outcomes in contemporary, modern societies. In particular, let us consider four variables: Health outcomes, life satisfaction, law-abidingness, and number of children.

First, many investigations have examined the links between religiosity and health, and the results of these studies have been summarized in a review by McCullough, Hoyt, Larson, Koenig, and Thoresen (2000). By averaging the results obtained across 42 studies, involving over 125,000 participants, McCullough *et al.* were able to estimate the extent to which religious involvement was associated with health outcomes, and particularly with the odds of survival during the period of the investigation. The results showed that persons who were more religious were about 25% less likely to die during the period of study than were persons who were less religious. This finding indicates a fairly important link between religiosity and longevity; however, it leaves open the question of *why* that link exists. For example, it might be the case that religious people tend to have healthier lifestyles, either because of adherence to the teachings of their religion or because of some tendency for people who live healthy lifestyles to be more oriented toward religion. It is also possible that social support from one's religious community has important benefits, whether psychological, financial, or otherwise, that help people to maintain health and to recover from illness. Another possibility is that religious people have a more optimistic or a more courageous outlook that helps them to withstand stress and to recover from illness; in particular, the practice of prayer or meditation may itself provide these benefits. One of the challenges for future research will be to explore the reasons for the link between religiosity and health outcomes.

Regarding the relations between religiosity and life satisfaction, some investigations report modest positive correlations of around .20 or .30 (Salsman, Brown, Brechting, & Carlson, 2005). In the study by Salsman *et al.*, this link between religiosity and life satisfaction was partly attributable to a tendency for more religious persons to be somewhat more optimistic and to have somewhat more social support than less religious persons.

Many studies have examined the links between religiosity and law-abidingness, and the results have been fairly consistent, usually showing a weak tendency for more-religious persons to commit fewer criminal or delinquent acts (Baier & Wright, 2001). The relation between religiosity and law-abidingness is small (about .10), and appears to operate through the development of conventional attitudes and the avoidance of delinquent peers (Simons, Simons, & Conger, 2004).

Finally, various lines of evidence suggest that higher levels of religiosity are associated with having larger numbers of children. At the level of the society as a whole, this link can be observed in many Roman Catholic countries that became much less religious during the second half of the twentieth century: When Italy, Spain, and Quebec experienced a decline in religious belief and activity, a sharp decline in the birthrate occurred also. (This likely reflects in part, but only in part, an abandonment of traditional Roman Catholic prohibition of birth control.) Within societies, there is also a tendency for the more religious persons to have the largest numbers of children (e.g., Balakrishnan & Chen, 1990).

Politics

Intuitively, it seems likely that personality should have some influence on one's political attitudes. Most of us would probably think that if we know an individual's personality in some depth, then we could have at least some rough idea as to his or her outlook on political issues. But before we can investigate the links between personality and politics, it would be helpful to examine the structure of political attitudes themselves—that is, to identify the main ways in which people differ in their orientations toward various kinds of political issues.

Right-Wing Authoritarianism

Much of our current knowledge on this topic of individual differences in political attitudes has been derived from the research of Bob Altemeyer. Altemeyer's work (e.g., 1981, 1988, 1996) has focused on a variable known as *Right-Wing Authoritarianism*, which he defines in terms of three related tendencies called *conventionalism, authoritarian submission*, and *authoritarian aggression*. As studied by Altemeyer, conventionalism refers to a strong adherence to the norms endorsed by society and the authorities. Authoritarian submission refers to obedience toward the authorities perceived as legitimate in one's society. Authoritarian aggression refers to hostility toward people or groups that are considered "deviant" or deserving of punishment.

Altemeyer's construct of Right-Wing Authoritarianism was partly based on some earlier efforts by several other psychologists who, in the years following World War II, had tried to develop scales to measure "fascist" tendencies (Adorno, Frenkel-Brunswik, Levinson, & Sanford, 1950). Those researchers—who had fled Nazi Germany shortly before World War II—believed that some personality characteristics or attitudes were associated with a tendency to support anti-Semitic policies and the fascist, authoritarian governments that implemented those policies. Adorno *et al.* developed a set of self-report items called the "F scale" (short for "Fascist scale") to measure these tendencies, but unfortunately there were several major problems with the F-scale.

One problem was that many of the items in this scale had nothing to do with authoritarianism at all, and instead assessed a mixture of variables such as cynicism, superstition, sexual repression, glorification of toughness, dislike of artistic sensitivity, and a tendency to "project" one's impulses onto others.[5] Adorno *et al.* had believed that authoritarian individuals would tend to show all of these tendencies; this belief was partly based on their own observations, and partly based on ideas derived from Sigmund Freud's writings about psychoanalysis. However, Adorno *et al.* were wrong: The diverse variables listed before were not much related to each other or to the core elements of authoritarianism that Altemeyer later identified.

Another problem with the F-scale was that it did not contain any reverse-keyed items (recall our earlier discussion in Chapter 2 about the use of reverse-keyed items). As a result, it was not clear whether persons who had high scores on the F-scale were really "fascists" having strongly authoritarian views, or whether they simply tended to "acquiesce" or agree when asked to respond to statements expressing various attitudes.

One interesting result of this problem of acquiescence was that F-scale scores tended to show strong negative correlations with educational level: Because the item statements seemed to be rather extreme generalizations, few educated people indicated strong agreement with those statements, whereas some less educated people (who may have had some difficulty in comprehending the items) did indicate agreement.[6]

Altemeyer (1981) developed an improved measure of authoritarianism—the Right-Wing Authoritarianism scale—by including some reverse-keyed items and by focusing on items that measured conventionalism, authoritarian submission, and authoritarian aggression, leaving aside the other kinds of items in the earlier F-scale. (See some example Right-Wing Authoritarianism items in Table 11-1.) This scale had better reliability than did the old F-scale, and it was also less strongly associated with educational level. In a series of studies, Altemeyer (1981, 1988, 1996) investigated the validity of the new Right-Wing Authoritarianism scale. Some of those studies examined the relations of Right-Wing Authoritarianism with willingness to punish others. For example, higher scores on the scale were associated with willingness to give harsh prison sentences to hypothetical criminals and to give stronger electric shocks to a participant who made mistakes in a learning experiment. In other studies, Altemeyer found that higher scores were also

---

[5] The idea of projection is that one might unconsciously have some socially undesirable impulse—for example, to behave aggressively, or to engage in some forbidden kind of sexual activity—and that in order to reduce the anxiety caused by having this forbidden urge, one might come to imagine that those impulses are held by other people, not by oneself.

[6] The problem of acquiescence tends to be more severe for political attitudes than for personality characteristics in general: Many people do not have any opinion at all on many issues, but few people have no idea about their own behavior.

TABLE 11-1

Example Items from the Right-Wing Authoritarianism and Social Dominance Orientation Scales

Right-Wing Authoritarianism

Obedience and respect for authority are the most important virtues children should learn.

Once our government leaders and the authorities condemn the dangerous elements in our society, it will be the duty of every patriotic citizen to help stomp out the rot that is destroying our country from within.

Young people sometimes get rebellious ideas, but as they grow up they ought to get over them and settle down.

Social Dominance Orientation

To get ahead in life, it is sometimes necessary to step on other groups.

If certain groups stayed in their place, we would have fewer problems.

It's probably a good thing that certain groups are at the top and other groups are at the bottom.

Sources: Altemeyer (1998); Sidanius and Pratto (1999).

associated with approval of restrictions on civil liberties, such as police raids and wiretaps conducted without warrants from a judge. In addition, another finding in Altemeyer's research was that higher scores on Right-Wing Authoritarianism were substantially correlated with "ethnocentrism"—a tendency to favor one's own ethnic group over other groups—and also with negative attitudes toward homosexuals.

From the point of view of our question about political attitudes, some of the interesting findings about the Right-Wing Authoritarianism scale involved its relations with political party preferences, with voting, and with attitudes on specific issues. Altemeyer (e.g., 1996) found (not surprisingly) that Right-Wing Authoritarianism was strongly correlated with preference for more "right-wing" political parties: In the United States, higher Right-Wing Authoritarianism scores were associated with preference for the Republicans over the Democrats, and in Canada higher scores were associated with preference for the Conservatives over the Liberals and (especially) the New Democratic Party. These differences were also observed among elected politicians in federal and in state or provincial legislatures.

Social Dominance Orientation

Based on the results of Altemeyer's work, many other researchers began to use the Right-Wing Authoritarianism scale as a basic measure of political attitudes. But in the 1990s, a second variable began to be studied in depth also, beginning with the work of Felicia Pratto and James Sidanius. They introduced a new construct, called *Social Dominance Orientation* (Pratto, Sidanius, Stallworth, & Malle, 1994), that captured some aspects of political attitudes that were not assessed by Right-Wing Authoritarianism. Overall, the two variables were similarly strong predictors of many important criteria, and together they were very effective in explaining a wide array of political attitudes.

The idea of Social Dominance Orientation is that people differ in their preference for hierarchy, as opposed to equality, in relations among social groups. That is, some people like the idea that some groups of people (e.g., ethnic or racial groups, religious groups, social classes, or sexes) should have higher status than others, whereas other people like the idea that all groups should be treated equally. In fact, most people in modern Western countries tend to favor equality over hierarchy, but there are large individual differences in the degree of this preference, and there are certainly some people who show a clear preference for hierarchy.

In developing the Social Dominance Orientation construct, Pratto and Sidanius began with the assumption that virtually all human societies have social hierarchies of some kind, and that those hierarchies assign different groups to higher or lower positions. In addition, Pratto and Sidanius perceived that people differ in their endorsement of attitudes (or ideologies) that justify those hierarchies. For example, some people might believe that the members of a lower social class or a disadvantaged ethnic group tend to be lazy or impulsive or unintelligent, and that their lower position is therefore natural or appropriate; in contrast, other people might reject these beliefs. The researchers reasoned that such attitudes could be important in explaining a wide array of more specific social and political attitudes. The Social Dominance Orientation scale was constructed to assess this general preference for social hierarchy versus social equality. (See some example Social Dominance Orientation items in Table 11-1.)

In their original study, Pratto *et al.* (1994) found that the Social Dominance Orientation scale was correlated substantially (typically about .40) with attitudes on a variety of specific issues. Higher Social Dominance Orientation scores were associated with lower levels of support for government social programs, for assistance for racial minorities, for environmental protection, and for limited defense spending. In subsequent investigations, other researchers (e.g., Altemeyer, 1998) found that both Social Dominance Orientation and Right-Wing Authoritarianism were associated with less favorable attitudes toward persons of other ethnic or racial groups and toward homosexual persons.

Relations between Right-Wing Authoritarianism and Social Dominance Orientation

These latter results raise the question of whether Social Dominance Orientation and Right-Wing Authoritarianism might be strongly correlated with each other, and hence whether they might be measuring a common underlying variable. Most investigations have shown some positive correlation between the two variables (Altemeyer, 1998; Whitley, 1999), but the size of these correlations (often about .20) is far too small to suggest that the two variables represent essentially the same thing.[7]

The fact that Right-Wing Authoritarianism and Social Dominance Orientation tend to be only modestly correlated with each other has interesting implications for the prediction

---

[7] In fact, the overlap between the variables might be due in large part to the authoritarian aggression aspect of Right-Wing Authoritarianism, rather than to the conventionalism or authoritarian submission aspects. Among the items of the Right-Wing Authoritarianism scale, it is the items that involve aggressive attitudes that tend to be positively correlated with the Social Dominance Orientation scale (Altemeyer, 1998).

of other variables, such as attitudes toward minority ethnic groups. When these two predictors are considered, each of them often shows fairly high correlations with the criterion variable, and in combination, the "multiple correlation" yielded by the two predictors is very high. This is because each scale is accounting for some aspect of the criterion variable that the other scale does not. For example, consider attitudes toward a particular ethnic minority group: Some people may have unfavorable attitudes toward that group because of a perception that this group's members tend to violate society's norms of proper behavior; in contrast, other people may have unfavorable attitudes because of a tendency to perceive all other ethnic groups as inferior to one's own. Because Right-Wing Authoritarianism (especially its conventionalism and submission aspects) assesses adherence to social norms, whereas Social Dominance Orientation assesses a general preference for inequality, the two variables together can account for a great deal of the variation among people in attitudes toward an ethnic minority group (e.g., Altemeyer, 1998; Duckitt, 2000).

The relations of Right-Wing Authoritarianism and Social Dominance Orientation with prejudice might be explained in part by the ways in which those two scales are related to one's perception of the world. Some studies have found an interesting difference between the two scales (e.g., Altemeyer, 1998; Duckitt, 2000; Duckitt, Wagner, Du Plessis, & Birnum, 2002). First, persons high in Right-Wing Authoritarianism tend to see the world as a *dangerous* place in which one's most important values and traditions are being threatened, whereas persons low in Right-Wing Authoritarianism tend to see the world as a safe place in which one's values are secure. In contrast, persons high in Social Dominance Orientation tend to see the world as a *competitive* place (a "jungle") in which people struggle for resources and power, whereas persons low in Social Dominance Orientation tend to see the world as a cooperative place in which people help and share with each other. Thus, the people with the most negative attitudes toward other groups would tend to be high in both Right-Wing Authoritarianism and Social Dominance Orientation: Those people would tend to see other groups as dangerous and as threatening, and also to see those groups as rivals in a competitive struggle. These two perceptions of the world are independent of each other—you can see the world as dangerous but not competitive, or vice versa—but if someone has both of these perceptions, then he or she is unlikely to have favorable views of other groups.

BOX 11-2
Right-Wing Authoritarianism and Social Dominance Orientation within Minority Groups

At this point, it is worth mentioning one interesting complication that emerges when interpreting an individual's levels of Right-Wing Authoritarianism and of Social Dominance Orientation. Scores on those two scales are probably more meaningful for persons who belong to the "majority" or "mainstream" groups of a society, and less meaningful for persons who belong to some "minority" or "underclass" groups. For example, imagine a person who tends to have a strong dislike for members of other ethnic groups. If this person belongs to the dominant ethnic group of a given society, then he or she will probably favor inequalities among groups, because it is his or her group that is "on top"; as a result, he or she will have a high level of Social Dominance Orientation.

(continues)

But if this person instead belongs to a subordinate ethnic group, then he or she will probably be strongly opposed to inequalities among groups, because his or her group is "on the bottom"; as a result, he or she will have a low level of Social Dominance Orientation.

As another example, consider someone who tends to conform to social norms and to be obedient toward authorities. If this person belongs to the majority group of a given society—a group whose norms are shared by the authorities of that society— then he or she will almost certainly have a high level of Right-Wing Authoritarianism. But suppose instead that this person belongs to a group that completely rejects the majority view; for example, suppose that

he or she was raised in a family and community that considered itself hostile to the norms of the majority and the authorities of that society. This person might then have a low level of Right-Wing Authoritarianism, because his or her conventionalism and submission would be oriented toward his or her family and community, and would be reflected in a rejection of the majority group's norms and authorities.

Of course, these examples do not undermine the validity of Right-Wing Authoritarianism or of Social Dominance Orientation for the large majority of the population. But, it is worth remembering that the meaning of an individual's scores on those variables may depend on his or her group membership, and not only on his or her own characteristics.

Two Dimensions of Political Attitudes

In trying to understand the structure of political attitudes, the finding that Right-Wing Authoritarianism and Social Dominance Orientation are relatively independent of each other is an important fact. The existence of two important but nearly uncorrelated variables might be somewhat surprising, because the traditional view of political attitudes suggests that there exists a single dimension of "left" versus "right."

But the existence of two major dimensions of political attitudes has also been found in studies that were not based on the Right-Wing Authoritarianism and Social Dominance Orientation scales. This result has also occurred, even more clearly, when factor analyses have been performed on people's responses to items asking their opinions on a variety of political issues. Two large factors were obtained in early studies by Ferguson (1939) and by Eysenck (1954), but also in more recent investigations. For example, another series of studies examined differences among people in their support or opposition toward various political policies (Ashton *et al.*, 2005). Factor analyses of these variables showed two factors of political attitudes that were called *Moral Regulation versus Individual Freedom* and *Compassion versus Competition*.

The issues that defined each of these two factors are shown in Table 11-2. First, the factor called Moral Regulation versus Individual Freedom involved the restriction versus legalization of various behaviors, and was defined by issues related to drug use, gambling, prostitution, homosexuality, abortion, and doctor-assisted suicide. As you might expect, this dimension tends to be correlated positively with Right-Wing Authoritarianism and with religious traditionalism, but uncorrelated with Social Dominance Orientation. Next, the factor called Compassion versus Competition involved the gentle versus harsh treatment of various "out-groups," and was defined by issues related to economic assistance for poor or unemployed people, sentencing of criminals, and relations with other ethnic groups and other countries. As suggested by this content, this factor tends to be correlated

TABLE 11-2

Some Political Issues That Load on the Factors of Moral Regulation versus Individual Freedom and of Compassion versus Competition

---

Moral Regulation (+) versus Individual Freedom (−)

Legalized abortion (−)
Doctor-assisted suicide for terminally ill patients (−)
Legalized marijuana (−)
"Red-light" districts for prostitutes (−)
Adoption rights for homosexual couples (−)
Prayer in public schools (+)
Ban on casino gambling (+)
Increased taxes on alcohol (+)
Increased restrictions on smoking (+)

Compassion (+) versus Competition (−)

Capital punishment for murder (−)
Reduced immigration levels (−)
Mandatory "workfare" for welfare recipients (−)
Harsher punishment for young criminal offenders (−)
Privatized health care system (−)
Publicly funded child day care system (+)
Increased aid to developing countries (+)
Land claims settlements for Native peoples (+)
Minority-language services from government (+)

Source: Ashton *et al.* (2005).

negatively with Social Dominance Orientation and with the authoritarian aggression aspect of Right-Wing Authoritarianism, but not with the authoritarian submission and conventionalism aspects of the latter variable.

Political Attitudes and the Major Dimensions of Personality

Next comes the question of how the differences among people in their political attitudes are related to the differences in their personalities. In other words, can we view political attitudes as an expression of personality characteristics? A few studies have examined the relations of scales such as Right Wing Authoritarianism and Social Dominance Orientation with the major dimensions of personality (e.g., M. C. Ashton, unpublished data; Heaven & Bucci, 2001), and these results are summarized below.

First, authoritarian or traditional attitudes are associated with substantially lower levels of Openness to Experience (correlations in the −.40s), but also with slightly higher levels of Conscientiousness (correlations close to .20). Thus, if we know a person's level of these personality dimensions, then we can have some idea of his or her level of authoritarianism. If we also know that person's level of religiosity (in the sense of "core" intrinsic religiosity as described before), then our estimate should be even more accurate, because religiosity is related to Right-Wing Authoritarianism without being related much to personality.

Next, attitudes favoring social equality (versus social dominance) correlate modestly with Big Five Agreeableness and with HEXACO Honesty–Humility, Agreeableness, and Emotionality; if these three personality dimensions are considered together, their combination correlates about .40 with the egalitarian or compassionate attitudes. Thus, we can see that personality is associated with this second dimension of political attitudes in a way that is intuitively plausible: Nicer people tend to be somewhat more humanitarian in their political views. In addition, Openness to Experience also has some modest relation with the more compassionate attitudes (correlation about .20).[8]

Political Attitudes, Social Values, and Religion

The finding of two major dimensions of political attitudes has an interesting parallel in a related area of research. Some investigators have examined individual differences in people's *social values*—that is, in the goals that people view as important guiding principles in their lives (e.g., Schwartz & Bilsky, 1987). Much of the research in this area has been conducted by the Israeli psychologist Shalom Schwartz, who in the 1980s began to expand on some earlier work by Milton Rokeach (e.g., Rokeach, 1973). Schwartz began by generating thorough lists of values that people might consider to be important, for example, "wisdom," "self-indulgence," "freedom," "environmental protection," "social power," and so on. He asked research participants in various countries to rate the personal importance of more than 50 such values. The results of these responses suggested that the various values could be grouped into about 10 categories. In turn, further analyses (based on techniques similar to factor analysis) suggested that those 10 types of values could be described in terms of two broad dimensions (see Figure 11-1).

One of the two broad dimensions of values in Schwartz's framework is called *Conservation versus Openness to Change*. In terms of the value types, Conservation values include *Conformity* (e.g., obedience, respect for parents/elders), *Security* (e.g., family safety, national security), and *Tradition* (e.g., devotion, respect for tradition). At the opposite pole, Openness to Change values include *Self-Direction* (e.g., freedom,

---

[8] Two cautions are worth mentioning here. First, it should not be assumed that a person who professes "compassionate" political attitudes is *necessarily* a kind person. In some cases, advocacy of such views can be less than fully sincere, and can serve instead as a tool for gaining personal power or prestige. (Recall the similar difference between "extrinsic" and "intrinsic" religiosity, as described earlier in this chapter.) Also, it should not be assumed that a person with moderately "uncompassionate" political attitudes is an unkind person. Some very nice people might genuinely come to conclude—whether rightly or wrongly—that extremely low levels of economic competition, of criminal punishment, and of ethnic self-interest tend to lead ultimately to problems that end up causing even greater suffering.

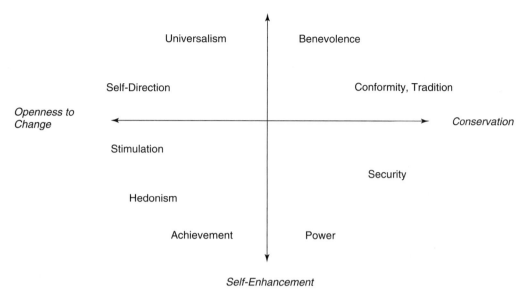

FIGURE 11-1. The two-dimensional arrangement of the 10 values identified by Schwartz.
Source: Schwartz (1992).

independence) and *Stimulation* (e.g., excitement, variety). According to Schwartz's research, people who view Conservation values as particularly important guiding principles in their lives tend to view Openness to Change values as less important, and vice versa.

The other broad dimension of values observed by Schwartz was one that he called *Self-Transcendence versus Self-Enhancement*. From the perspective of the value types described by Schwartz, Self-Transcendence values include *Benevolence* (e.g., helpfulness, loyalty) and *Universalism* (e.g., peace, equality). At the opposite pole of this dimension, Self-Enhancement values include *Power* (e.g., wealth, authority) and *Achievement* (e.g., success, ambition). (Note that one of Schwartz's value types, *Hedonism* (e.g., self-indulgence, enjoyment), is associated both with the Self-Enhancement pole of the first dimension and with the Openness to Change pole of the second dimension (see Figure 11-1).) Again, Schwartz's findings suggest that people who view Self-Transcendence values as particularly important guiding principles in their lives tend to view Self-Enhancement values as less important, and vice versa.

Based on the descriptions of the two dimensions of values described by Schwartz, you can probably predict how those dimensions will relate to the political attitudes variables described earlier in this section (see Ashton *et al.*, 2005; Choma, Ashton, & Hafer, 2007). First, Conservation (versus Openness to Change) values are correlated positively both with the political issues factor of Moral Regulation (versus Individual Freedom) and also

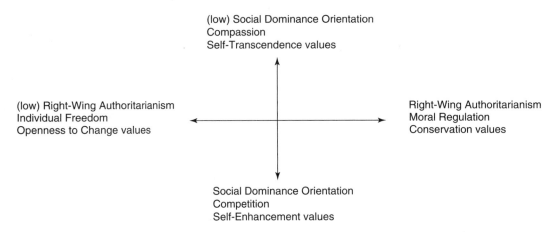

FIGURE 11-2. Two-dimensional arrangement of political attitude scales (Right-Wing Authoritarianism and Social Dominance Orientation), political issues factors (Moral Regulation versus Individual Freedom and Compassion versus Competition), and Schwartz's values dimensions (Conservation versus Openness to Change and Self-Transcendence versus Self-Enhancement). Source: Ashton *et al.* (2005), Choma *et al.* (2007).

with the Right-Wing Authoritarianism scale.[9] Also, Self-Transcendence (versus Self-Enhancement) values are correlated positively with the political issues factor of Compassion (versus Competition) and negatively with the Social Dominance Orientation scale.

So, as summarized in this chapter, political attitudes can be described in terms of two large dimensions. Figure 11-2 shows how the different variables are aligned: One dimension is shared by Right-Wing Authoritarian attitudes, by Moral Regulation (versus Individual Freedom) political issues, and by Conservation (versus Openness to Change) values. This dimension is also associated with religious traditionalism and with low levels of the Openness to Experience personality dimension. The other dimension is defined by (low) Social Dominance Orientation attitudes, by Compassion (versus Competition) political issues, and by Self-Transcendence (versus Self-Enhancement values). This dimension is also associated with personality dimensions involving sympathy or softheartedness, such as Big Five Agreeableness or the HEXACO Honesty–Humility, Agreeableness, and Emotionality factors.

Developmental Change and Stability in Political Attitudes

Relatively few studies have examined the patterns of developmental change and stability in political attitudes. However, some important data on this topic have been reported by

---

[9] Conservation values are also correlated with religiosity (Saroglou, Delpierre, & Dernelle, 2004), with religious people being higher in Conservation or lower in Openness to Change.

Altemeyer (1988, 1996) for the Right-Wing Authoritarianism scale. In one study, Altemeyer administered this scale to a sample of nearly 80 college students at the beginning of their first year of college and again at the end of their fourth year. Altemeyer found that authoritarianism levels tended to decrease on average, by an amount about equal to half of a standard deviation unit. This result could suggest that attending college tends to reduce one's level of authoritarianism. On the other hand, it is also possible that young adults in general tend to experience a decline in authoritarian attitudes during this period of life, regardless of college attendance. In order to find out whether or not college attendance itself is the important variable, it would be necessary to examine both students and nonstudents. Interestingly, though, Altemeyer found that the largest decreases in authoritarianism were observed for students in "liberal arts" programs. This finding suggests that the decline is due to being exposed to new ideas about people and society, as these ideas would likely be discussed by liberal arts students and professors.

Altemeyer (1988, 1996) also examined the changing levels of authoritarianism across the entire span of young adulthood, from the college years to the 30s. In two samples totaling nearly 180 persons, Altemeyer obtained Right-Wing Authoritarianism scale scores from first-year college students, and then obtained scores on the same scale from those same persons either 12 years or 18 years later, by which time they were in their 30s. The results showed that these persons' authoritarianism scores decreased somewhat across this period, but that the decrease was a bit less than that observed between the first and last years of college (as found in the study described in the previous paragraph). This suggests that authoritarianism levels remain stable, or perhaps even increase very slightly, during one's 20s or early 30s. One especially interesting finding of Altemeyer's study was that persons who had become parents tended to have authoritarianism scores that were about as high as they had been at the start of college, whereas persons who had not become parents showed authoritarianism scores that were somewhat lower than they had been at the start of college. This raises the possibility that the experience of being a parent tends to increase one's level of authoritarianism. Presumably, parents would be more likely to prefer a society that is oriented toward security and obedience than would people who do not have children.

In conducting the studies just described, Altemeyer (1988, 1996) was also able to examine the stability of Right-Wing Authoritarianism scores across long periods of time. In his study of students' authoritarianism scores at the beginning and end of their college careers, Altemeyer found that the correlation between scores across this 4-year period was .75. In his study of people's authoritarianism scores at the beginning of college and in their 30s (i.e., 12 or 18 years later), the correlation between scores was nearly .60. These results suggest that the differences among people in their authoritarianism scores are rather stable, even across a fairly long period of time during early adulthood. Put another way, most people who are more authoritarian than their peers before the age of 20 will also be more authoritarian than their peers after the age of 30. However, the levels of stability are not extremely high, and this indicates that some shifts do occur in people's relative levels of political attitudes during the period of young adulthood.

Origins of Religious Beliefs and Political Attitudes: Biological Bases, Genetic and Environmental Influences, and Evolutionary Function

In Chapters 5, 6, and 7, we examined some basic questions about why personality variation exists, as we explored the biological bases, the genetic and environmental origins, and the evolutionary adaptive functions of personality characteristics. But these same issues can also be considered with regard to individual differences in religious beliefs and political attitudes. Why is it that people differ in these important variables?

Biological Bases

Thus far, there has not been very much research examining the biological bases of individual differences in religious and political variables. However, an interesting recent study examined religious or spiritual beliefs, along with personality characteristics, in relation to one of the brain neurotransmitters, serotonin (Borg, Andreé, Söderström, & Farde, 2003). The researchers found that the persons whose brains showed a high density of serotonin receptors—places where serotonin can be removed from the regions where it is active—tended to be the same persons who believe in things that cannot be objectively demonstrated, such as supernatural beings or events. Borg *et al.* therefore suggested that, because serotonin tends to inhibit the experience of some kinds of sensory stimulation, people with low serotonin activity may experience sensory stimuli that are interpreted in spiritual or religious terms. However, this result was based on an extremely small sample of participants (only 15), so it will need to be tested in future research using much larger samples.

Genetic and Environmental Influences

In comparison, much more research has examined the genetic and environmental origins of variation in religiosity and in political attitudes. The results of these studies have been interesting, insofar as the findings differ in important ways from those observed for personality characteristics (see Chapter 6). The most striking of these differences involves the influence of the common or shared environment: This influence has tended to be very weak for personality traits, but has apparently been much stronger for religious and political variables.

Recall that for most personality traits, the shared environment has had a very small impact: Adopted persons do not resemble the parents or siblings of their adoptive family in terms of the personality dimensions that we have discussed. However, for religiosity, there is a fairly strong similarity between adopted persons and the parents and siblings of their adopted family. In a study of 650 adopted and nonadopted adolescents (Abrahamson, Baker, & Caspi, 2002), correlations above .40 were observed between the religiosity levels of relatives, with the values being almost as high for adoptive relatives as for biological relatives. A similar pattern of results, but with slightly weaker correlations, was also observed for conservatism of political attitudes.[10] This indicates that—at least during adolescence—the shared environment does influence religiosity and political attitudes substantially, even though it has little impact on the personality characteristics that we considered in the previous chapters.

There is some additional evidence, however, to indicate that the influence of the common or shared environment on religiosity and political attitudes, as observed in adolescents, tends to diminish as people reach adulthood. Koenig, McGue, Krueger, and Bouchard (2005) found that *fraternal* twins of the same pair tended to be very similar in religiosity when they were growing up together in the same household, but only moderately similar when they were in their 30s, after they had grown up and moved away. The correlation between fraternal twins' religiosity levels during adolescence was about .60, but this correlation had dropped to only slightly over .40 by the time the twins were in their 30s. In contrast, *identical* twins of the same pair did not show as much of a decrease in similarity of religiosity, with a decline from a correlation of nearly .70 when growing up to slightly over .60 when in their 30s. Note that for all of the twins (both identical and fraternal), the common environment in which they were raised was presumably having a much weaker effect in adulthood than during childhood or adolescence. However, Koenig *et al.* suggested that the genetic tendencies of the identical twins (which are indeed identical) were helping to maintain similar levels of religiosity, whereas this effect was not so strong for the fraternal twins (who are less genetically similar). On the basis of their results, Koenig *et al.* estimated that the heritability of religiosity is higher during adulthood (at least .40) than when growing up (under .15), and that, conversely, the effect of the common environment is lower during adulthood (under .20) than when growing up (at least .50).

A similar decline in the influence of the common environment (and a similar rise in the influence of heredity) was observed in another study that examined political attitudes (Eaves *et al.*, 1997). This study involved nearly 7000 twin pairs—roughly half identical and half fraternal—that included adolescents as well as young, middle-aged, and elderly adults. Eaves *et al.* assessed the levels of conservatism of each participant, using the same conservatism scale that Abrahamson *et al.* (2002) later used in the study described earlier in this section. Interestingly, the similarity in conservatism levels showed a very different pattern of change across age groups, depending on whether identical twins or fraternal twins were considered. Fraternal twins of the same pair tended to be rather similar in conservatism during their teenage years (correlations averaging in the .50s), but somewhat less so after the age of 20 (correlations averaging about .40). Identical twins of the same pair also tended to be rather similar in conservatism during their teenage years (correlations again averaging in the .50s); however, identical twins actually became somewhat *more* similar in conservatism after the age of 20 (correlations averaging above .60). These results suggest that common environment influences have strong effects on political attitudes prior to the age of 20, making fraternal twins of the same pair nearly as similar as identical twins of the same pair. After the age of 20, however, those common environment

---

[10] The conservatism scale used in this study was related to both aspects of conservatism as discussed in this chapter; that is, it contained items relevant both to authoritarian submission or moral regulation and also to social dominance orientation or competition.

influences weaken while genetic influences strengthen, with the result that fraternal twins become less similar in political attitudes whereas identical twins do not.

In investigating the effects of heredity and environment on religiosity and political attitudes, researchers also examine the extent to which spouses are similar in these variables. As explained in Chapter 6, if spouses tend to be alike in a trait that is influenced by genetic differences, then their children will have more than 50% of their genes in common with each other (and with each of their parents). As a result of the extra genetic similarity between siblings whose parents are similar to each other on a trait, researchers' estimates of the heritability of the trait may be inaccurate. (That is, the researchers might overestimate or underestimate the heritability, depending on the type of design used in their investigation; see Chapter 6.) In such a case, the researchers would need to make statistical adjustments to their heritability estimates, to account for the effects of assortative mating. However, in the case of personality characteristics, this is not really a problem, because there is very little assortative mating: As we discussed in Chapter 9, there is no important tendency for spouses to be similar (or dissimilar) in personality traits.

For religiosity and political attitudes, the situation is much different: People do tend to marry people whose level of religiosity and political views are similar to their own. There-fore, researchers must take this fact into account when examining the heritability of these variables by studying biological relatives. One example of the finding that spouses tend to be similar for religiosity and political attitudes comes from the study of spouses' character-istics by Watson *et al.* (2004). Recall that Watson *et al.* found near-zero correlations between spouses of the same couple for personality characteristics (see Chapter 9), and found moderately high correlations (about .45) between spouses for verbal intelligence (but not for nonverbal intelligence; see Chapter 10). However, Watson *et al.* also found very strong correlations between spouses for religiosity and for political conservatism. Religios-ity, as assessed by items regarding religious beliefs, practices, and the importance of reli-gion, showed correlations of about .75 between husbands and wives. Political conservatism, as assessed by items regarding attitudes toward issues related to authority, moral regulation, and traditional values, showed correlations approaching .65. This result is also similar to previous findings (e.g., Lykken & Tellegen, 1993), and it indicates that husbands and wives are very similar in their religious beliefs and political attitudes. Apparently, these variables play an important role in determining who will marry whom, as spouses are usually not very different from each other in these characteristics. This finding makes some sense: A person is more likely to enter into a close relationship with someone whose beliefs and attitudes about the world, society, life, and the supernatural are similar to one's own.[11]

---

[11] However, this does not necessarily mean that greater similarity beliefs and attitudes will lead to higher levels of marital satisfaction. In the study by Watson *et al.* (2004), there was a near-zero correlation between marital satisfaction and the degree of similarity between spouses in religiosity or political attitudes. That is, the spouses whose beliefs and attitudes were most similar were no more and no less satisfied with their marriages than were spouses whose beliefs and attitudes were least similar. Keep in mind, however, that because spouses tend to be similar to each other in religious beliefs and political attitudes, there are very few marriages in which the spouses are really opposite in those variables. It is possible that there would be lower levels of marital satisfaction for such marriages, but this is not actually known.

Evolutionary Function

Next, let us turn to the question of why individual differences in religiosity and in political attitudes have been maintained across the generations. In other words, why has the process of evolution by natural selection not eliminated variation in these characteristics, by favoring some single optimal level? For the time being, we can only speculate on this issue, but future research will allow some tests of hypotheses such as those outlined below. Here we will focus on adaptive trade-offs associated with the two broad dimensions that span the domains of religious beliefs, social values, and political attitudes.

Let us first consider the dimension that involves high versus low levels of religious traditionalism, conservation values, and authoritarian attitudes. One potential advantage for persons having higher levels of these characteristics is that, within any given group, those persons would likely receive more rewards and fewer punishments than would persons who are more nonconforming or rebellious.[12] In contrast, however, there would also be some disadvantages associated with being an obedient person: By strictly following the leaders of their group, they might make sacrifices that would be avoided by less obedient persons. (For example, in time of war, the persons who are more obedient toward authority might be more likely to be killed or otherwise affected by the conflict.) Presumably, when the customs and the leaders of a group are successful in promoting the society's interests, the persons who are most socially conservative will gain the most; when the group is unsuccessful, however, those same persons will lose the most.

Now let us consider the dimension that involves high versus low levels of self-enhancement values and of socially dominant attitudes. The likely benefit for individuals having high levels of these characteristics is that those persons would sometimes succeed in exploiting persons in other groups; for example, by conquering a neighboring group, or by enslaving some segment of their own society. However, these power-oriented individuals would also risk some heavy costs due to retaliation by those other groups, which would likely resist violently any attempts at being conquered or being enslaved. Thus, there is a trade-off associated with self-enhancement values and socially dominant attitudes, as persons having lower levels of these characteristics would tend to avoid both the benefits and the costs associated with higher levels. Depending on the relative strength of one's group—a variable that might sometimes be badly misjudged—individuals who encourage their group to dominate other groups might experience great gains or great losses.

Summary and Conclusions

In this chapter, we have examined religious beliefs and political attitudes, studying these variables in relation to personality characteristics and other individual differences. Although

---

[12] One evolutionary biologist (Wilson, 2002) has proposed that the primary function of organized religion is to encourage (and to enforce) cooperation within a group, which also has the consequence of making that group more effective in competition with other groups.

religiosity might perhaps be considered a personality characteristic in its own right, the central importance of *belief* sets religiosity aside from the major dimensions of personality. Religious belief generally shows weak correlations with those personality dimensions, but there are interesting links between Openness to Experience and religiosity: Persons high in Openness tend to have a greater sense of spirituality, and persons low in Openness tend to have a greater adherence to traditional religious teachings.

Some research suggests that, on average, people are slightly more religious during middle adulthood than during adolescence or during old age. Also, even though some people show sharp changes in their level of religiosity, the overall stability of individual differences in religiosity is rather high, even across a span of several decades. It is possible that people who have religious beliefs are *inclined* to believe in various other supernatural or paranormal phenomena, but established religions tend to discourage their followers from accepting those beliefs. Religiosity shows positive but weak associations with several life outcomes involving health, law-abidingness, and life satisfaction, and is also associated with having more children.

With regard to political attitudes, two of the most widely studied variables are Right-Wing Authoritarianism and Social Dominance Orientation. Right-Wing Authoritarianism involves a combination of conventional attitudes, submission to authorities, and aggression against targets designated by the authorities. Social Dominance Orientation involves a favorability to inequalities among groups, such that some groups would be dominant and others subordinate. Right-Wing Authoritarianism and Social Dominance Orientation are only modestly related to each other (and even this relation may be due to the authoritarian aggression aspect of Right-Wing Authoritarianism). Those two variables are related to the two factors that usually emerge in studies of attitudes toward political issues: A factor of Moral Regulation versus Individual Freedom is associated with Right-Wing Authoritarianism, and a factor of Compassion versus Competition is associated with (low) Social Dominance Orientation. Also, individual differences in social values—the abstract goals that serve as guiding principles in people's lives—can be summarized by two dimensions, "Conservation versus Openness to Change" and "Self-Transcendence versus Self-Enhancement." The former dimension is associated with Right-Wing Authoritarianism and with Moral Regulation versus Individual Freedom (as well as with religious traditionalism), and the latter dimension is associated with (low) Social Dominance Orientation and with Compassion versus Competition.

Although the developmental trends in political attitudes have not been studied in depth, the existing evidence suggests that one's level of Right-Wing Authoritarianism scores tends to decline during the college-age years, but tends to increase on becoming a parent. Individual differences in Right-Wing Authoritarianism show fairly high levels of stability between the college-age years and the 30s.

Thus far, there has not been much systematic research on the biological bases of religious beliefs and political attitudes, but some recent research has examined the role of neurotransmitters as influences on religiosity. Studies of the heritability of religious beliefs suggest that the genetic influence on religiosity increases between adolescence and middle age, whereas the influence of the common environment decreases during that interval. Religious beliefs and political attitudes show a high level of "assortative mating," with correlations between spouses in the .60s and .70s; that is, most people marry someone whose beliefs and attitudes are similar to their own.

Some speculations have been offered on the evolution of individual differences in the two major dimensions that underlie religious beliefs, social values, and political attitudes. Presumably, persons who follow traditional authority will receive more rewards and fewer punishments than will more nonconforming or rebellious persons; however, such obedience may be disadvantageous when the group and its leaders have unsuccessful policies. In addition, persons who strive to make their group dominant over other groups may well gain when such attempts are successful, but this is a risky strategy that could lead to heavy costs when other groups resist and retaliate.

Chapter 12

Sexuality

Major Dimensions of Sexuality 285

Sexuality and Personality 287

   Sexual Arousal and Personality 287

   Sexual Commitment and Personality 288

   Sexual Orientation and Personality 289

Origins of Variation in Sexuality: Genetic and Environmental Influences, Biological Bases, and Evolution 292

Sexual Commitment (or Restricted versus Unrestricted Sociosexuality) 294

   Genetic and Environmental Influences 294

Biological Bases 294

Evolutionary Function 295

Sexual Orientation 297

   Genetic and Environmental Influences and Biological Bases 297

   Evolutionary Function 301

Sexual Arousal 302

   Genetic and Environmental Influences 302

   Biological Bases 303

   Evolutionary Function 303

Summary and Conclusions 304

Sex, in case you did not notice, is an important part of the human condition. And just as people differ in their personality characteristics—that is, in their general patterns of behavior, thought, and feeling—so too do they differ in various aspects of their sexuality—that is, in their sexual behaviors, attitudes, and preferences. In this chapter, we will begin by identifying some important aspects of sexuality, and examining their relations with personality. We will then examine several important issues concerning the nature of these sexuality dimensions, including their biological bases, their genetic and environmental origins, and their evolutionary history.

Major Dimensions of Sexuality

To study individual differences in sexuality, it is useful to start by finding the basic ways in which people differ in their sexual behaviors, preferences, and attitudes—that is, by finding a way to summarize the many ways in which people differ in their sexuality. One approach to this problem is to adopt a lexically based strategy, one that is similar to that used in identifying the major dimensions of personality (see Chapter 3).

Using this lexical method, David Schmitt (Schmitt & Buss, 2000) identified a set of 67 familiar adjectives that describe various aspects of a person's sexuality. Schmitt and Buss then obtained self- and observer ratings on these adjectives from several hundred participants, including roughly similar numbers of men and women. When factor analyzed, the ratings on these adjectives produced a set of seven factors; however, several of those factors were correlated with each other, and could in turn be summarized in terms of only two very broad factors (Schmitt & Buss, 2000; D. P. Schmitt, personal communication, 2006). Because this two-factor solution provides a simple yet reasonably complete summary of human sexuality variation, we will focus on those two dimensions in the rest of this chapter. However, we will also consider one other important aspect of sexuality that, as Schmitt and Buss noted, was not well summarized by the two broad factors.

One of the two large dimensions obtained by Schmitt and Buss (2000) was labeled as *Sexual Arousal*. This factor was defined by adjectives such as *seductive, sensual, sexual, arousing, sexy,* and *erotic* versus (at the opposite pole) *celibate, abstinent,* and *prudish,* and thus represents individual differences in the tendency to feel sexually aroused, sexually attractive, and generally interested in sex.

The other of the two large dimensions found by Schmitt and Buss (2000) was called *Sexual Commitment*. This factor was defined by adjectives such as *devoted, loving, faithful,* and *monogamous* versus (at the opposite pole) *polygamous, promiscuous, loose,* and *unfaithful,* and thus represents individual differences in the inclination to be strongly committed or attached to one sex partner, as opposed to the inclination to prefer multiple partners or to be weakly devoted to any one partner.

Interestingly, some adjectives showed moderate loadings on both factors, and thus represented combinations or blends of these dimensions (see Figure 12-1). For example, adjectives such as *passionate, romantic,* and *affectionate* loaded about equally on the positive poles of both Sexual Arousal and Sexual Commitment; thus, these terms describe someone who has a high level of both factors. Some other adjectives, such as *obscene, vulgar,* and *indecent* loaded about equally on the positive pole of Sexual Arousal and on the negative pole of Sexual Commitment; thus, these terms describe someone who is high in sexual arousal but low in sexual commitment.

The two large factors just described showed quite different patterns of sex differences. For Sexual Arousal, there was virtually no difference between the average ratings for men and for women; however, for Sexual Commitment, there was a moderately large difference between the sexes, with women having higher ratings on average than did men. For example, terms such as *faithful* versus *unfaithful* showed sex differences of about two-thirds of a standard deviation overall.[1] This suggests that more than 60% of women, but less than 40% of men, have above average levels of Sexual Commitment. Note that, even though this represents a fairly substantial difference between the sexes, there is also

---

[1] When data from both men and women are analyzed together, the second factor is also defined by adjectives such as *feminine* versus *masculine*. This reflects the fact that women tended to be somewhat higher in Sexual Commitment than did men, and also that women generally rated themselves as feminine, whereas men generally rated themselves as masculine. If data are analyzed separately for each sex, then there is much less variation in ratings on *feminine* and *masculine*, and these terms do not load strongly on either of the two factors.

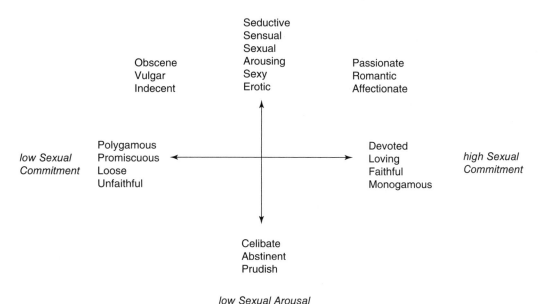

FIGURE 12-1. Graph showing loadings of sexuality adjectives on two factors of Sexual Arousal and Sexual Commitment.
Source: Schmitt and Buss (2000); D. P. Schmitt (personal communication, 2006).

a great deal of variation within each sex, with a considerable fraction of men who are high in Sexual Commitment, and a considerable fraction of women who are low.

As mentioned earlier in this section, there were some sexuality-related terms that did not show substantial loadings on either of these two large factors. These relatively few terms included *heterosexual* versus *homosexual* and *bisexual*, and thus describe a person's *sexual orientation*. Because this is obviously an important way in which people differ from each other, we will consider Sexual Orientation as an additional dimension of sexuality when we discuss relations with personality and other variables, later.

Now that we have identified some basic dimensions of sexuality, we can examine the question of how personality is related to sexuality. We will consider Sexual Arousal, Sexual Commitment, and Sexual Orientation, relying in part on results obtained by Schmitt and Buss (2000) and in part on results from other research studies.

Sexuality and Personality

Sexual Arousal and Personality

Along with the sexuality adjectives that Schmitt and Buss (2000) administered to their research participants were some scales measuring the Big Five personality factors. Of these characteristics, the one that showed the clearest links with Sexual Arousal was Extraversion, which correlated about .45 with this dimension of sexuality (Schmitt & Buss, 2000; D. P. Schmitt, personal communication, 2006). That is, people who were more extraverted tended to report a stronger sex drive and a stronger sense of being sexually attractive—to put it simply, the more extraverted people tended to feel sexier. Note that this correlation is moderately large: It means that more than 70% of people who have higher than average levels of Extraversion also have higher than average levels of feeling "sexy." In contrast, somewhat less than 30% of people who are below average in Extraversion are above average in the Sexual Arousal dimension. Thus, there is a fairly clear tendency for people who are outgoing and lively to feel a strong sex drive and a strong sense of being sexually attractive, although there are certainly some people with more shy or passive personalities who also feel very sexy.

Sexual Commitment and Personality

Next, with regard to Sexual Commitment, the findings of Schmitt and Buss (2000; D. P. Schmitt, personal communication, 2006) showed that the Big Five Agreeableness and Conscientiousness factors were correlated with this dimension of sexuality. In particular, higher levels of Agreeableness and higher levels of Conscientiousness were both associated with a stronger inclination to be faithful and devoted to a single partner, rather than to be promiscuous.[2] Both correlations were about .50, thus indicating a rather strong link between these personality characteristics and Sexual Commitment.

Some additional research that is relevant to Sexual Commitment has been based on a variable called *sociosexual orientation* (Simpson & Gangestad, 1991). (An important note: Do not confuse this with sexual orientation!) Simpson and Gangestad described sociosexual orientation as a dimension that has two opposing poles, "restricted" and "unrestricted." A person who has a *sociosexually restricted* orientation can be comfortable in a sexual relationship only if he or she feels a strong emotional bond with his or her partner. In contrast, a person who has a *sociosexually unrestricted* orientation can be perfectly willing to engage in sexual relations even in the absence of any emotional commitment to his or her partner. In short, people with an "unrestricted" orientation are very much willing to have sex without love, whereas people with a "restricted" orientation only want sex within a relationship that is based on love.

As can be seen from this description, the variable of sociosexual orientation closely resembles the Sexual Commitment factor, with a restricted orientation representing high

---

[2] The *opposite* pole of the Sexual Commitment dimension includes both unfaithfulness and promiscuity, even though these are not exactly the same thing. Although unfaithful people are likely to be promiscuous and vice versa, there could be exceptions: Imagine someone who has an ongoing extramarital affair with only one person, or imagine someone who has had many one-night stands but who has never actually cheated on a long-term partner. The personality variables associated with these two tendencies are slightly different; for example, promiscuity has a weak association with Extraversion, whereas unfaithfulness does not (Schmitt, 2004).

commitment, and an unrestricted orientation representing low commitment. Some research suggests that sociosexual orientation does show roughly the same relations with personality as does Sexual Commitment: Bourdage, Lee, Perry, and Ashton (in press) found that a restricted orientation was associated with higher levels of HEXACO Honesty–Humility and, to a lesser extent, higher levels of the HEXACO Emotionality, Conscientiousness, and Agreeableness factors. Similarly, Reise and Wright (1996) found that more socio-sexually unrestricted persons had somewhat higher levels of traits such as narcissism and psychopathy (which are related to low Honesty–Humility).

Sexual Orientation and Personality

As noted before, Sexual Orientation represents another aspect of sexuality, additional to the two broad dimensions of Sexual Arousal and Sexual Commitment. But one interesting difference between Sexual Orientation and the other two aspects of sexuality involves the distributions of people's levels of these variables. To see this, first consider Sexual Arousal: Some people have a very strong sex drive, whereas others have a very weak sex drive, and most people are somewhere in between. Or, consider Sexual Commitment: Most people are very devoted and monogamous, but many others are very unfaithful and pro-miscuous, and still others are somewhere in between. Thus, for both of those variables—as for personality characteristics and most other individual differences considered in this book—there is a continuous distribution of people along the entire length of a dimension that extends from one extreme to another.

Sexual Orientation is different from the preceding two dimensions, because the very large majority of people (both women and men) describe themselves as being entirely heterosexual in their preferences (see Bailey, Dunne, & Martin, 2000). Among both men and women, about 92% of people report having sexual fantasies and attractions that are entirely heterosexual (see Table 12-1). In contrast, only about 4% of men and 1% of women report having sexual fantasies or attractions that are mainly or completely homo-sexual; and in between, about 4% of men and 7% of women report having fantasies and attractions that are partly homosexual but equally or mainly heterosexual. Thus, for Sexual Orientation, most people are at one pole of the "dimension," with a few people at the other pole, and a few others in between.

But regardless of the distribution of the Sexual Orientation dimension, the question of how personality relates to sexual orientation is an interesting one. What differences are there, if any, between the average gay man and the average heterosexual man, or between the average lesbian and the average heterosexual woman? There exist many stereotypes about the personalities of gay men and of lesbians, but to what extent are these stereotypes true, if at all? What about the personalities of persons (of either sex) who describe themselves as bisexual?

Perhaps surprisingly, there is not very much research that has compared the personalities of heterosexual and nonheterosexual people. (One difficulty in conducting this research is that, because only a relatively small percentage of people is nonheterosexual, a typical research study that contains less than, say, 1000 participants will not really have a large enough sample of gay men or lesbians to allow meaningful comparisons.) But in the study by

TABLE 12-1

Proportions of Men and Women Reporting Sexual Fantasies and Attractions That Are Heterosexual and/or Homosexual

Sexual Fantasies and Attractions	Gender	
	Men (%)	Women (%)
Entirely heterosexual	92	92
Partly homosexual but equally or mainly heterosexual	4	7
Mainly or entirely homosexual	4	1

Source: Bailey, Dunne, and Martin (2000).

Schmitt and Buss (2000), nonheterosexual persons (of either sex) had somewhat higher levels of Openness to Experience, on average, than did heterosexual persons. However, the difference was not large, being equivalent to a correlation of less than .25. Another study by Lippa and Arad (1997) found results that were in the same direction, but even weaker in strength, especially among women. Thus, there is some limited evidence that Openness to Experience tends to be higher in nonheterosexual persons, but more research is needed on this question.

Interestingly, the possibility that Sexual Orientation may be associated with Openness to Experience is consistent with the fact that gay men, and to a lesser extent lesbians, are rather heavily represented in artistic occupations. (As described in Box 9-1, the dimension of "Artistic" vocational interests is fairly strongly correlated with Openness to Experience, which includes such personality traits as creativity and unconventionality.) One more recent survey of over 2000 respondents (Lewis & Seaman, 2004) found that 5.2% of gay men were professional artists, versus only 1.1% of heterosexual men, and that 2.2% of lesbians were professional artists, versus 1.4% of heterosexual women. (Lewis and Seaman included a variety of creative occupations within their "professional artists" category: Designers, musicians, composers, actors, directors, sculptors, painters, craft artists, print-makers, photographers, dancers, and other artists or performers.) These data suggest that gay men (and to considerably lesser extent, lesbians) are more strongly inclined toward artistic activities than are their heterosexual counterparts. Thus, an interesting hypothesis for future research is that homosexual persons (particularly gay men) will be higher, on average, than heterosexual persons in Openness to Experience.[3]

---

[3] Be careful not to misinterpret the preceding results: For example, even though gay men are more than four times as likely as heterosexual men to be employed in artistic occupations, this does *not* mean that most men in those occupations are gay. Because there are at least 10 times as many heterosexual men as there are gay men, most men who work as professional artists will be heterosexual. By the same token, even if (on average) homosexual persons are somewhat higher in Openness to Experience than are heterosexual persons, most people with high levels of Openness to Experience would still be heterosexual, simply because of the much greater numbers of heterosexual persons.

Besides Openness to Experience, there may be other personality characteristics that are associated with sexual orientation. One possibility is that gay men and lesbians will tend to have personality profiles that are somewhat "feminine" and "masculine," respectively. If so, then one might expect that the personality characteristics on which men and women tend to differ will also show differences between heterosexual and homosexual persons. For example, recall that the personality dimension of Emotionality—defined by traits such as vulnerability, fearfulness, and sentimentality—shows moderately large sex differences, with women being about a full standard deviation unit higher than men (see Box 7-1). Are there also differences in Emotionality according to sexual orientation, with gay men being higher on average than heterosexual men, and with lesbians being lower on average than heterosexual women?

This question has been addressed, indirectly, in studies that have assessed personality characteristics related to Emotionality. For example, women tend to average higher than do men on high-Emotionality traits involving the expression of affection and sensitivity, whereas the opposite result is observed for low-Emotionality traits involving independence and competitiveness. But when Lippa (2002; Lippa & Arad, 1997) compared gay men with heterosexual men and lesbians heterosexual women on these personality characteristics, the differences were rather small. On average, both gay men and lesbians were "in between" the average levels for heterosexual men and for heterosexual women. However, the differences between homosexual and heterosexual persons on these characteristics were often less than half of a standard deviation unit in size. Thus, although there may be some tendency for gay men to be higher in Emotionality traits than are heterosexual men, and for lesbians to be lower in Emotionality traits than are heterosexual women, an individual's levels of these traits do not give a good indication as to his or her sexual orientation.

Although the major dimensions of personality do not show particularly large differences between people of different sexual orientations, there are very large differences on interests in various activities, including occupational or vocational interests (see Box 9-1). Interestingly, the vocational interests that show the largest differences between men and women also tend to be the same ones that show the largest differences between heterosexual and homosexual persons of either sex (Lippa, 2002). For example, relative to heterosexual men, both heterosexual women and gay men tend to have considerably *higher* levels of interest in many traditionally "feminine" occupations, such as fashion design, and considerably *lower* levels of interest in many traditionally "masculine" occupations, such as mechanical work. Conversely, relative to heterosexual women, both heterosexual men and lesbians show the opposite pattern of interests. Thus, it appears that vocational interests are much more strongly associated with sexual orientation than are personality characteristics.[4]

---

[4] However, if we consider heterosexual persons *within* each sex, there is little if any relation among the various domains of interests that show differences between the sexes (Ashton & Lee, 2006). For example, men tend on average to be more interested in mechanical things and in sports than women are; however, men who are especially interested in mechanical things are no more likely *than other men* to be especially interested in sports. Similarly, women tend on average to be more interested in fashion and in child care than men are; however, women who are especially interested in fashion are no more likely *than other women* to be especially interested in child care.

BOX 12-1
Cross-Generational and Cross-National Differences in Sexuality

Sexuality can show wide variation across generations and across countries, much like the religious and political variables of the previous chapter. Some behaviors that are considered perfectly acceptable in one culture may be considered criminal in another; some attitudes that were almost universally shared in one generation may become very rare in the next. A few researchers have tried to study these differences systematically, to find out how (and how much) sexuality differs across times and places.

With regard to differences across generations or age cohorts, Wells and Twenge (2005) conducted a review of previous studies that had assessed the sexuality of young people in North America between the 1940s and late 1990s. They found that young people—especially young women—reported increasing favorability toward sexual activity throughout this period. For example, in the 1940s, only 12% of young women and 40% of young men indicated attitudes approving of premarital sex, but by the late 1990s, 73% of young women and 79% of young men indicated approval.

Regarding cross-national differences, Schmitt (2005) examined this topic in a study of 14,000 participants in 48 countries. Schmitt obtained self-reports on a scale designed to measure sociosexual orientation (i.e., "restricted" versus "unrestricted," as described before). The average levels of sociosexuality differed substantially across countries, and there were some fairly clear differences between regions of the world. Among the most "restricted" nations were those of east Asia, south Asia, and Africa; among the most "unrestricted" nations, in contrast, were several European countries. In between were nations in North America, Latin America, and the Middle East, as well as a few other European, Asian, and African countries. The differences between the most and least unrestricted countries were fairly large, amounting to more than one standard deviation unit. Interestingly, countries with higher fertility rates and higher childhood malnutrition tended to be more restricted overall. Schmitt interpreted this result as indicating that people tend to be more monogamous (and less promiscuous) when the demands of raising families are greater and more stressful.

A couple of cautions should be noted regarding the preceding cross-national comparisons. First, the participants in these various countries were college students, who in some countries represent a rather small and atypical fraction of the population. Also, the data are based on self-reports; consequently, differences between cultures in people's willingness to describe their sexual habits (even in an anonymous setting) might have influenced the results. Thus, the use of college student samples or of self-reports might to some extent distort the true picture of cross-cultural differences in sexual behavior.

One interesting aspect of the cross-national comparisons of sexuality involves the degree of sex differences observed in various countries. Within every one of the 48 countries studied by Schmitt (2005), men tended to be more "unrestricted" in attitudes than did women, with the difference averaging about three-quarters of a standard deviation unit. (This means that, in a typical country, men make up almost two-thirds of people who are more *unrestricted* than the "average" person, whereas women make up almost two-thirds of people who are more *restricted* than average.) Nations did differ, however, in the sizes of these sex differences, with somewhat smaller sex differences within countries that had greater equality of political status for men and women.

Origins of Variation in Sexuality: Genetic and Environmental Influences, Biological Bases, and Evolution

For sexuality, as for personality characteristics, there is the important issue of "nature versus nurture": Are individual differences in sexuality due mainly to genetic differences,

---

BOX 12-2
Religiosity and Sexuality

Most religions tend to disapprove of extramarital and premarital sex, and hence we might expect that religious persons would tend to be higher in Sexual Commitment or, in other words, more restricted in sociosexual orientation. Some investigations of the relations between religiosity and sexuality do indeed show a positive correlation between religiosity and Sexual Commitment. However, there is an interesting difference in results depending on whether *intrinsic* religiosity or *extrinsic* religiosity (see Chapter 11) is examined (Leak, 1993; Rowatt & Schmitt, 2003; Wulf, Prentice, Hansum, Ferrar, & Spilka, 1984). People who report being "intrinsically" religious—in other words, people who value religious contemplation, prayer, and scriptures for their own sake—tend to be more sexually committed, that is, less promiscuous or less unfaithful. In contrast, people who report being "extrinsically" religious—in other words, people who value participation in religion as a way of gaining social status, social contacts, or even rewards from God—actually tend to be less sexually committed, that is, more promiscuous and more unfaithful. Thus, people who are genuinely religious do tend to be somewhat higher in Sexual Commitment, whereas people who are religious only for the purpose of "keeping up appearances" tend to be lower in Sexual Commitment.

---

or to environmental differences? Some researchers have tried to answer these questions, by using methods very similar to those used in investigating the heritability of personality characteristics. In addition, researchers have examined the question of *how* those genetic or environmental influences might affect sexuality: What are the biological variables that contribute to differences among people in sexual behavior, and how do they operate? And finally, the existence of these individual differences leads to the question of why the variation in sexuality would persist across evolutionary time: In other words, what have been the "trade-offs" associated with higher and lower levels of each dimension of sexuality, as judged in terms of reproductive success?[5,6]

---

[5] Perhaps surprisingly, there has been little research on the topics of developmental change and stability in sexuality-related variables. One exception, however, is a study by Schmitt et al. (2002), who obtained self-reports of Sexual Arousal-related variables from large samples of men and women of widely varying ages. Schmitt et al. found that women's sexual arousal reached a peak in the early 30s, whereas men's sexual arousal reached a peak in the late 20s (not in the late teens, as many might expect). Another exception, as noted later in this chapter, is the finding that some characteristics observable during childhood can predict sexual orientation in adulthood. It will be interesting to see the results of future studies that use a longitudinal design, assessing the major dimensions of sexuality at several intervals across a span of many years in the same sample of persons.

[6] Keep in mind that in the following sections we will be discussing individual differences *within* a given society: If we consider instead differences *between* societies, such as those considered in Box 12-1, we might find rather different results. For example, cultural attitudes that influence sexuality can vary widely, and can change relatively quickly. These attitudes, and the environmental forces that produce them, are likely to be far more important than any genetic changes in explaining the trends in a society's sexuality. The same is true of changes in a society's levels of religiosity or of political attitudes, as discussed in Chapter 11.

Sexual Commitment (or Restricted versus Unrestricted Sociosexuality)

Genetic and Environmental Influences

Some of the largest investigations of the heritability of sexuality-related variables have been conducted in a sample of 4900 Australian twins. Using data from this sample, Bailey, Kirk, Zhu, Dunne, and Martin (2000) examined the genetic and environmental influences on sociosexuality. (As discussed before, "restricted" sociosexuality corresponds to high Sexual Commitment, and "unrestricted" sociosexuality corresponds to low Sexual Commitment.) Their results showed that the members of an identical twin pair were usually similar to each other in their level of unrestricted (versus restricted) sociosexuality: Correlations were above .50, both for male twin pairs and for female twin pairs. For the members of fraternal twin pairs, there was still some similarity, but the correlations were weaker, with values in the .30s for both male twin pairs and female twin pairs, and less than .20 for opposite-sex twin pairs.

Overall, the results of Bailey, Kirk, Zhu, Dunne, and Martin (2000) suggested that individual differences in sociosexuality were almost 50% heritable, and that the environmental influences were due not to the common environment, but almost entirely to the unique environment. In other words, sociosexuality variation is not caused by aspects of the environment that differ *between* one family and the next; instead, it is caused by genetic variation and by aspects of the environment that differ *within* each family. (As you will recall from Chapter 6, a similar pattern of results is observed for personality characteristics.) An important question for future research will be to find out exactly which features of the unique environment are those that influence sociosexuality.

Biological Bases

Now let us consider the possible biological bases of individual differences in Sexual Commitment. To some extent, we will understand the causes of variation in Sexual Commitment by understanding the causes of variation in the major dimensions of personality. As described earlier in this chapter, Sexual Commitment is related to several aspects of personality; therefore, if we can find the biological bases of those personality dimensions, then we will have at least a partial knowledge of the biological bases of Sexual Commitment. But as noted in Chapter 5, the causes of personality variation are not yet well understood, and therefore the causes of variation in Sexual Commitment also remain obscure.

Incidentally, one variable that might be considered as a possible contributor to lower levels of Sexual Commitment is the "male" hormone, testosterone. Some studies of young men have suggested at least modest links between higher levels of testosterone and higher numbers of sexual partners (e.g., Halpern, Udry, Campbell, Suchindran, & Mason, 1994; Bogaert & Fisher, 1995), and similar patterns might also exist among young women (Halpern, Udry, & Suchindran, 1997). However, these links with testosterone are somewhat weak, and might not be any stronger for sexuality in particular than for personality in general (see Chapter 5).

Evolutionary Function

Findings regarding the heritability and the biological bases of Sexual Commitment (or in sociosexuality) lead to the question of why the variation in sociosexuality has been maintained during the course of human evolution. This question has been considered in some detail by researchers, who have considered both the differences between the sexes and the differences among members of each sex.

Most researchers have agreed that some sex difference in sociosexuality would be expected, because of evolutionary forces that would have favored a more restricted orientation in women during prehistoric times. The reason for this is simple: Women can become pregnant. Consider the consequences for a prehistoric woman who has sex with a man who is *not* emotionally committed to her: If she becomes pregnant, then she will undergo a 9-month pregnancy, followed by childbirth and then a prolonged period of breast-feeding and intensive child care. During this period, she may find it very difficult to obtain enough food and to defend herself and her child, and she is unlikely to get any help from the man who impregnated her. As a result, the woman will have paid the heavy biological "cost" of reproduction, but her child may be unlikely to survive, and her own life may also be at considerable risk.

In contrast, suppose that our prehistoric woman has sex with a man who *is* emotionally committed to her: She will then likely obtain much help from him in the form of food and protection, and the chances that she and her child will survive may be rather high. Thus, the likelihood of having surviving offspring would have been greater for women who were sociosexually restricted, and therefore a restricted orientation would have predominated in later generations.

Now let us consider the consequences for a prehistoric man who has sex with a woman despite not being in a committed relationship with her. If she becomes pregnant, he will likely feel little inclination to help her or the child. If the child does not survive, then there is no biological "cost" to the man, who can still impregnate another woman; if the child instead does survive, then the man achieves some reproductive success at no cost. Therefore, men who were sociosexually unrestricted would not have been at the same disadvantage as unrestricted women would have been, and the unrestricted orientation would not have become so rare among men as among women.

The logic just described may be largely accurate, but it leaves unexplained an important fact about sociosexuality: Despite the difference between the sexes, there is still wide variation within each sex, with many men being restricted and many women being unrestricted. Why should this be the case? One strong possibility is that frequency-dependent selection (see Chapter 7) may be at work, preserving variation in sociosexuality both among women and among men.

First, let us consider women (see Gangestad & Simpson, 1990). As explained before, evolution would have tended to favor a more restricted sociosexuality among women than among men, because the biological cost of reproduction is so much greater for women than for men. But nevertheless, an unrestricted orientation might still have been advantageous for some women. Consider again a prehistoric woman who has sex with a man who is not emotionally committed to her. This unrestricted woman will not randomly choose any man to be her sex partner; instead, she will choose a man whom she (and probably most other women) would find to be attractive, physically and socially. Now, if the woman becomes pregnant, she is unlikely to receive any help from the man, and there is some large chance that the child will not survive. But there is also some chance that the child will survive, and if so, that child will inherit the father's genes, and will thereby inherit, to some extent, his attractiveness. If the child happens to be a boy, then he may well grow up to be a man whom women find to be very attractive. As a result, the mother will end up having many grandchildren, because her son may end up impregnating many different women. In this way, being sociosexually unrestricted could have been a successful "strategy" for some women. However, this "sexy son strategy" (as it is fittingly named) would not work if too many women were to use it: If many women were unrestricted, then the advantage gained by having a "sexy son" would no longer be so rare, and the unrestricted strategy would no longer possess any advantage. As a result, most women would still tend to be restricted in their sociosexuality.[7]

Now, let us consider men. As explained before, evolution would not have tended to favor restricted sexuality so strongly among men as among women, because the biological cost of reproduction is so much less for men than for women. However, a restricted orientation could still have had some important advantages for at least some men. Consider a prehistoric man who develops an emotional commitment to a woman with whom he then has sex: If this woman becomes pregnant, he will help to feed and protect her and her child, and thus the man's child is more likely to survive. Now, if this man had instead felt no such emotional attachment, he could have tried to have sex with various other women. But this is not guaranteed to be a successful "strategy": There may be much competition from other men for sexual access to women, and even if this man has some success in mating, he might not have any surviving children. Thus, for many men, a sociosexually restricted tendency would have been more successful. In this way frequency-dependent selection would maintain variation among men in sociosexual orientation: Some men would follow a restricted strategy, and others would follow an unrestricted strategy.

Finally, it is also possible that sociosexuality would be governed by the "fluctuating optimum" level of this trait, as influenced by features of the environment. For example, in environments in which it is very difficult for a woman to have surviving children without

---

[7] The word strategy is given in quotation marks because it is not meant to suggest a *conscious* strategy. That is, women (or men) would not have chosen their level of sociosexuality by deliberately calculating their likely reproductive success. On this point, it is worth keeping in mind that the "sexy son" hypothesis was developed originally to explain the sexual behavior of female *birds*, not of women (Weatherhead & Robertson, 1979).

the help of a man, a more restricted sociosexuality would be favored. In contrast, in environments in which it is somewhat easier for a woman to have surviving children without the help of a man, a more unrestricted sociosexuality would be favored.

Sexual Orientation

Genetic and Environmental Influences and Biological Bases

Difficulties in Estimating the Heritability of Sexual Orientation

Now let us consider the origins of sexual orientation: Are the differences between heterosexual and homosexual persons due mainly to genetic or to environmental differences between them? In other words, are some people "born straight" and others "born gay" and "born lesbian," or are people's sexual orientations determined by experiences during development? One difficulty in addressing this question is that, as discussed before, sexual orientation has a distribution much different from that of most other individual differences. As noted earlier in this chapter, slightly more than 90% of people describe themselves as completely heterosexual; as a result, even when researchers obtain a fairly large sample of research participants taken from the general population, they usually have only a small subsample of participants who have nonheterosexual orientations. With these small samples, it is difficult to have confidence in estimates of the heritability of sexual orientation.

Researchers have tried to obtain larger samples of participants for sexual orientation research by advertising their investigations toward homosexual persons who have twin siblings of the same sex. This approach has been successful in increasing the sample sizes, but it does create a potential problem: A homosexual twin is probably more likely to participate in such a research project if his or her twin is also homosexual. Because twins with different sexual orientations will therefore tend to be underrepresented, the researchers may get a misleadingly high estimate of the extent to which twins are similar in sexual orientation.

Some studies that used the preceding approach for obtaining participants had found that the similarity, or *concordance*, for sexual orientation in identical twins was rather high: If one twin was homosexual, then the other twin had about a 50% chance of being homosexual (Bailey & Pillard, 1991). However, results from the large Australian sample of twins—a sample taken randomly from the general population—found that the concordance of homosexuality was much lower: If one member of an identical twin pair was homosexual, then the other twin had about a 25% chance of being homosexual (Bailey, Dunne, & Martin, 2000). (For fraternal twins, the overall concordance of homosexuality was about 10%.) These results suggest that there may be a genetic basis for homosexuality, but because the size of the participant sample of this study was rather small, the results are very uncertain: There might be quite a strong genetic influence, or there might be virtually none at all. To allow accurate estimates of the heritability of sexual orientation, more data will be needed.

Causes of Sexual Orientation? "Exotic Becomes Erotic"

As described above, the results of the Australian twin study cannot allow clear conclusions regarding the heritability of sexual orientation. However, there was an interesting and more definite finding regarding the heritability of a characteristic that is closely linked to sexual orientation. Bailey, Dunne, and Martin (2000) asked the twins to recall some aspects of their behavior during childhood, in order to examine each individual's level of *childhood gender nonconformity*. Specifically, the researchers asked the participants to indicate their preference, as children, for activities that are typically preferred by boys and by girls. For example, boy-typical activities include playing with toy trucks or blocks or playing rough and tumble sports, whereas girl-typical activities include playing with dolls and with toy clothes. If a child tends to prefer the activities that are more typical of children of the opposite sex, then this is a case of child-hood gender nonconformity.

Previous investigations have found that childhood gender nonconformity is strongly correlated with sexual orientation in later life, as boys who prefer girl-typical activities are likely to become gay men, and girls who prefer boy-typical activities are somewhat likely to become lesbian women. (The link is not quite as strong among women as among men.) In the Australian twin study of Bailey, Dunne, and Martin (2000), the same pattern of results was found: Among men who reported a homosexual orientation, levels of child-hood gender nonconformity were about two standard deviation units higher than among men who reported a heterosexual orientation. (Men who were "bisexual," having a partly heterosexual and partly homosexual orientation, were about halfway in between in their levels of childhood gender nonconformity.) For women, the same pattern of differences was observed, but the effect sizes were somewhat smaller.

In studying heritability, childhood gender nonconformity is an easier variable to examine than is sexual orientation. This is because, even though most people behave largely in a gender-typical way during childhood, there exists a substantial fraction of people who have at least moderate levels of childhood gender nonconformity. In the study by Bailey, Dunne, and Martin (2000), the correlations between twins' levels of childhood gender nonconformity were fairly high for identical twins, but rather low for fraternal twins. Overall, those results suggest that the heritability of childhood gender nonconformity would be fairly high, probably close to 50%. Thus, it appears that childhood gender non-conformity—one of the best predictors of a person's eventual sexual orientation—is sub-stantially heritable, even though the evidence regarding the heritability of sexual orientation itself is less clear.

The finding that childhood gender nonconformity has a substantial genetic component is of some importance for an interesting theory of how sexual orientation develops. Childhood gender nonconformity plays a major role in what is called the "exotic becomes erotic" theory of sexual orientation, as developed by Daryl Bem (Bem, 1996). According to Bem, most children engage mainly in activities that are typical of their own sex, and thus tend to play and associate with children of the same sex as themselves. Bem suggests that, when children reach puberty, they then develop a sexual attraction toward the strange and unfamiliar "other" children: Boys become attracted to girls, and girls become attracted to boys. In this sense, members of the opposite sex appear to be mysterious and "exotic," and when puberty arrives, this becomes sexually attractive, or "erotic."

But what happens if a child is involved mainly in activities that are typical of the opposite sex? According to Bem (1996), people differ in the hormonal and other physiological characteristics that influence their level of male-typical or female-typical behavior during childhood. Depending on these hormonal and other causes, some boys will tend to prefer "girlish" activities, and some girls will tend to prefer "boyish" activities. As a result, the boys with girlish interests will tend to play with girls, and the girls with boyish interests will tend to play with boys. When puberty arrives, these gender-nonconforming persons will tend to see members of the same sex as the "exotic" ones, and will thus develop an "erotic" attraction toward them. That is, the boys who had girlish interests will now be attracted to other boys, and the girls who had boyish interests will now be attracted to other girls.

An alternative hypothesis is also possible: Perhaps childhood gender nonconformity is inherited genetically, and is influenced by the same genes that, after puberty, will cause a homosexual attraction. However, if sexual orientation itself is not quite as heritable as childhood gender nonconformity is, then it is more likely that the first hypothesis is correct—that is, it is more likely that some genes influence childhood gender nonconformity, which in turn influences sexual orientation (which may also be influenced by other, non-genetic variables). The results reported by Bailey, Dunne, and Martin (2000) are consistent with Bem's suggestion that childhood gender non-conformity is genetically influenced, and that it then leads to a homosexual orientation in adulthood.

Causes of Sexual Orientation? Number of Older Brothers

In addition to the possibility of genetic influences on sexual orientation, there is some evidence that some features of the environment are also involved, at least as far as men's sexual orientation is concerned. But the aspect of the environment that has shown the clearest relation with male sexual orientation is not one that you might expect. According to a series of recent studies by Anthony Bogaert (e.g., Blanchard & Bogaert, 1996; Bogaert, 2000, 2003a), the more older brothers a man has, the more likely he is to be gay. This does not mean that most men with several older brothers will be gay; on the contrary, most such men are heterosexual. But in several large studies, results have shown that the chances of a man having a homosexual orientation are about 38% higher for every older brother that he has. If, for example, the chances of being gay are 3% for a man with no older brothers, then the chances of being gay would be about 15% for a man with five older brothers.[8] According to other calculations (Cantor, Blanchard, Paterson, & Bogaert, 2002), about 1 in 7 gay men have acquired their sexual orientation through the influence of the number of older brothers.

---

[8] In case you are curious, this value is calculated as $.03 \times 1.38^5 = .03 \times 5.00 = .15$.

This effect is very interesting, and it raises an obvious question: *Why* is the number of older brothers associated with sexual orientation in men? One possible explanation would be that any kind of sexual play that might occur among brothers might have a lasting influence on a younger brother, causing him to develop a homosexual orientation. However, the evidence available so far does not support this hypothesis: The amount of same-sex sexual contact that a man experienced with his brothers as a young boy is not related to his sexual orientation in later life (Bogaert, 2003a).

Another possible explanation involves the personalities of younger brothers. Recall the hypothesis by Sulloway (1996) that later birth order is associated with higher levels of the personality dimension of Openness to Experience. This raises the possibility that younger brothers, as a result of being more open to experience, would be more likely to "experiment" with same-sex sexual behavior during their adolescent years, and would therefore have a greater chance of developing a homosexual orientation. However, the lack of any relation between early same-sex contact and later sexual orientation means that this hypothesis is unlikely to be correct.

Still another potential explanation is related to Bem's (1996) exotic becomes erotic theory. If some boys are born with a tendency to prefer "girlish" activities, then this childhood gender nonconformity could have stronger effects on the development of a boy if he has older brothers. That is, the more older brothers that a "feminine" boy has, the more he will be aware that he is different from other boys, and the more likely he will be to develop an attraction toward them. Although this hypothesis is plausible, the evidence so far does not support it: Even though childhood gender nonconformity is predictive of homosexual orientation in adulthood, this relation is no stronger *among* boys with many older brothers than it is *among* boys with no older brothers (Bogaert, 2003b).

The most likely explanation of the relation between number of older brothers and male sexual orientation is perhaps a surprising one, because it does not involve any aspects of the relationships among brothers. Even more surprising, it does not involve any features of the environment that operate during adolescence, or during childhood, or even during infancy. Instead, the explanation seems to lie in the environment of the mother's womb. According to this hypothesis (e.g., Blanchard & Bogaert, 1996; Bogaert, 2003a), some substances that are involved in the development of a male fetus may be recognized by the mother's body as "foreign" substances. If another male fetus is conceived during a later pregnancy, then the presence of this foreign substance will be remembered by the mother's body, which will then release antibodies that tend to counteract the effects of these substances. As a result of the antibodies, these substances involved in male fetal development might not operate at full strength, and the development of a "male-typical" brain—including the features that would later produce a heterosexual orientation—may not fully occur. This effect would become stronger with each additional pregnancy involving a son, and the likelihood that a male fetus would develop a homosexual orientation would increase each time.

One important aspect of the preceding hypothesis is that the mother's body would have no such reaction to a female fetus, because the substances involved in the development of a female fetus would not be recognized as "foreign." As a result, the number of older sisters would not be expected to relate to the development of a homosexual orientation among women. This is consistent with the evidence: A woman's likelihood of being lesbian is unrelated to the number of older sisters that she has (e.g., Bogaert, 2003a). Apparently, the effect of having older siblings of the same sex on one's sexual orientation is observed for men only.

As discussed before, the influence of number of older brothers on male sexual orientation is a consistent one, and can account for the sexual orientation of about one in seven gay men. However, this leaves unexplained the sexual orientation of most gay men, as well as that of all lesbians. Also, as noted earlier, the fact that even identical twins are often different from each other in sexual orientation indicates that genetic influences are unlikely to account for all of the variation in sexual orientation. This raises the question of what additional variables could explain sexual orientation, and one controversial explanation is that sexual orientation might be in some way transmitted, perhaps by a virus or a bacterium that does not cause any physical or mental illness. Some researchers (see Hooper, 1999) have suggested that this is the most likely explanation of male exclusive homosexuality (i.e., attraction to women only, as opposed to bisexuality, in which there is attraction to both sexes).

Evolutionary Function

According to Paul Ewald and Gregory Cochran (see Hooper, 1999), it is unlikely that genetic influences can explain male homosexuality, because any genes that tended to cause men to be attracted to other men rather than to women would rather quickly disappear from the population. The results of one study suggest that gay men have only about one-fifth the number of biological children that heterosexual men do (Bell & Weinberg, 1978). Perhaps this number would have been considerably higher during earlier eras, when social pressures might have caused more gay men to have married women and to have had children, but it still seems likely that gay men would have had substantially lower "reproductive success" than straight men would have had. Therefore, the genes causing homosexuality would have become less and less frequent with each generation, and would have soon disappeared altogether.

Alternatively, it has been proposed that even though gay men tend to have fewer children than do straight men, it might also be the case that the relatives of gay men might have more children than do the relatives of straight men. In other words, genes causing homosexuality (and hence, low reproductive success for gay men) might also cause gay men's relatives to have high reproductive success, therefore balancing out the effects of the gene on biological fitness. How might this work? One possibility is that perhaps gay men contribute heavily to the well-being of their siblings and to their siblings' children. However, these effects would have to be extremely strong to make up for the decreased number of children fathered by gay men. Also, the available evidence suggests that gay men do not contribute any more assistance to their siblings than straight do to their siblings, whether in terms of money, child care assistance, or emotional support (Bobrow & Bailey, 2001). Another possibility is that the same genes that sometimes cause male

---

BOX 12-3

The Evolution of Sex Differences in Vocational Interests?

As noted earlier in this chapter, there are some differences between heterosexual and homosexual persons of the same sex in their patterns of vocational interests, and these differences are similar in pattern (but smaller in size) to those observed between men and women. The areas of interest that show large differences between men and women are quite varied: Women tend to be higher than men in child care and fashion interests, whereas men tend to be higher than women in mechanical and military interests (e.g.,

Campbell *et al.*, 1992). These differences are very large—sometimes approaching two standard deviation units in size—and it is interesting to speculate on their possible evolutionary origins. For example, the sex differences in child development interests or in mechanical interests might reflect a prehistoric division of labor between men and women that existed throughout human prehistory, whereby women did more child care work and men did more work with tools. Also, the sex differences in fashion interests and in competitive interests might reflect different forms of competition within each sex, whereby women competed more through appearance and men competed more through combat.

---

homosexuality may also cause, in some unknown way, the relatives of gay men to have more children than do the relatives of straight men. One recent study (King *et al.*, 2005) did find that gay men tended to have more relatives than did straight men, but it is not clear that the difference was large enough to make up for the much smaller number of children fathered by gay men.

Sexual Arousal

Genetic and Environmental Influences

Finally, we have not yet examined the heritability of any variables that represent the dimension of Sexual Arousal. Apparently there are not yet any studies that have examined the heritability of sex drive or related characteristics. However, in one recent study, Dawood, Kirk, Bailey, Andrews, and Martin (2005) did investigate the heritability of orgasm frequency in women, using the Australian twin data that have been the basis of other heritability studies as described earlier in this chapter. The heritability of orgasm frequency, as occurring during sexual intercourse or during sexual contact other than intercourse, was between .30 and .40, and the heritability of orgasm during masturbation was about .50. (Presumably, the latter figure is higher because it does not depend on the contribution of a sex partner to the experience of orgasm.) These results indicate that differences among women in orgasm frequency have an important genetic basis, and suggest that the broad dimension of Sexual Arousal is also likely to be influenced substantially by genetic differences.

Biological Bases

Next, let us take a quick look at possible biological bases of individual differences in Sexual Arousal. As mentioned earlier in the section on Sexual Commitment, one way to understand the causes of variation in sexuality is to find the causes of the personality characteristics that are related to sexuality. In the case of Sexual Arousal, the moderately strong relations with Extraversion suggest that the biological bases of that personality dimension would also be involved in Sexual Arousal. But as we discussed in Chapter 5, there is a great deal to be learned about the biological bases of personality, and therefore we still have much to learn about the causes of individual differences in Sexual Arousal.

As was the case for Sexual Commitment, one potential cause of individual differences in Sexual Arousal is testosterone, the hormone that is associated with many aspects of sexual behavior. Some of the research findings described in that section—for example, studies linking testosterone to number of sex partners—might reflect high levels of Sexual Arousal as well as low levels of Sexual Commitment. But again, the links between testosterone levels and sexual behavior are not especially strong, at least within samples of healthy young adults.

One recent study examined the relations between Sexual Arousal and levels of the neurotransmitter called dopamine (see Chapter 5). This investigation (Ben Zion *et al.*, 2006) compared the self-reported levels of Sexual Arousal of persons who had different alleles (i.e., different versions) of a gene that influences dopamine levels. The researchers found that individuals who had the alleles associated with higher dopamine tended to be higher in Sexual Arousal than did individuals who had the alleles associated with lower dopamine levels. These results suggest that dopamine may have an influence not only on personality characteristics—such as the novelty-seeking-related traits suggested by Cloninger (see Chapter 5)—but also on this aspect of sexuality in particular. However, more research will be needed to verify these findings.

Evolutionary Function

These findings regarding the heritability and biological basis of Sexual Arousal also raise the challenging question of why genetic variation in this dimension would have been maintained throughout the human evolutionary past. Of course, persons having virtually no interest in sex might have been less likely to have had children, and so it is not difficult to imagine that genes causing a very low level of sexual arousability would tend to disappear from the population. But why are some people genetically inclined to be highly sexually arousable, and others so much less so? There is no clear evidence on this question so far, but the correlations between Sexual Arousal and Extraversion, as described before, suggest that the evolutionary forces that maintain Sexual Arousal might be analogous to those for Extraversion (see Chapter 7). That is, persons who have high levels of Sexual Arousal (or of Extraversion) are likely to be more attractive to potential mates, and may therefore have more opportunities to choose among potential mates. However, persons who have high levels of Sexual Arousal (or of Extraversion) are also likely to be at some risk for hostility from potential competitors, and are likely to have less time and energy for investment in work-related or other endeavors.

Summary and Conclusions

Let us summarize the major points of this chapter. First, research on the structure of individual differences in sexuality suggests at least three major aspects of sexuality, which can be called Sexual Arousal, Sexual Commitment, and Sexual Orientation. These aspects have distinctive patterns of correlations with dimensions of personality: Sexual Arousal is associated with Extraversion; Sexual Commitment is associated with several personality dimensions (in the HEXACO framework, Conscientiousness, Agreeableness, Emotionality, and Honesty–Humility); Sexual Orientation is (perhaps) associated with Openness to Experience. In addition, Sexual Commitment is associated with intrinsic religiosity, and Sexual Orientation is also related to vocational interests that show differences between men and women.

With regard to the origins of individual differences in sexuality, the biological bases of these dimensions are not yet well understood. Investigations of the heritability of these variables do suggest some genetic influences, but for Sexual Orientation it has been difficult to estimate the importance of these influences. It is possible that genetic influences on Sexual Orientation operate through childhood gender nonconformity, and it appears that Sexual Orientation in men is influenced by an environmental variable, specifically, the number of biological older brothers that a man has. Finally, speculations on the evolutionary origins of variation in sexuality dimensions are similar in nature to those for personality dimensions more generally, but again there is greater uncertainty with regard to Sexual Orientation.

Conclusions

What We Have Learned So Far   *305*   **Final Remarks**   *311*
What We Have Yet to Learn   *309*

Now we have come to the end of our exploration of personality traits and related individual differences. In surveying this field of study, we have examined a wide variety of questions. For some of these questions, the answers are already well understood, but for others, the answers are really not yet known. We can now summarize some of the important answers that have been gained from personality research, and some of the unanswered questions to be resolved in future study. These summaries are not meant to be exhaustive; many other answers and many other unanswered questions could also be listed. But the following review should bring attention to some of the highlights of the ongoing work in this intriguing discipline.

What We Have Learned So Far

We Can Describe People Meaningfully by Their Levels of Various Personality Traits

This point would seem obvious to most people, but there was a time when many psychologists believed that the whole idea of a personality trait was mistaken. As discussed in Chapter 2, some researchers suggested that the differences among people in their behavior showed very little consistency across situations. But it was soon demonstrated that there is a great deal of consistency, when we consider people's behavior "in the big picture," as aggregated or averaged across many situations. For example, the people who are the most impulsive in one situation might not be the most impulsive in another, but if you observe people's overall pattern of behavior across a wide variety of situations, you can easily tell which people are the most impulsive.

The fact that people can be described in terms of personality trait levels allows us to do two very important things. One is that we can summarize a given individual's personality in some detail by describing his or her personality in terms of various different traits, or characteristics. Another is that we can easily study the causes and the consequences of personality. For example, the relations between levels of a personality trait and some important life outcome variable could show us something about the practical significance of that aspect of personality. In the same way, the relations between levels of a personality trait and some biological variable (whether a neurotransmitter, hormone, or brain structure) could teach us something about the origins of that dimension of personality. (Of course, results such as these will not prove cause and effect, but they will give some likely hints.)

We Can Measure People's Personality Trait Levels Fairly Accurately Using Self- and Observer Report Personality Inventories

As noted in Chapter 2 and elsewhere in this book, there are some legitimate concerns about the limitations of self-report personality inventories. Nevertheless, the evidence shows that those instruments are reasonably valid indicators of the differences among individuals in their levels of various personality traits. Scores on self-report scales show meaningful correlations with direct observations of relevant behaviors and with scores on observer report scales (when the observers are persons who are well acquainted with the individuals who give the self-reports). Moreover, when observer reports of the same individual are given by two different observers, the correlations between those observer reports are moderately large, even when those persons do not know each other. The results of some studies suggest that observer reports may be slightly more accurate than self-reports in predicting behavior, particularly when observer reports are averaged across several persons who are well acquainted with the target person. Ideally, personality would be assessed most accurately using a combination of self-reports and several observer reports, but even self-reports alone appear to be good indicators of individuals' personalities.

Interestingly, self-report measures of personality retain much of their validity even when people provide those self-reports under conditions that tend to encourage unrealistically desirable responses, such as a job application. The problem of how to measure personality accurately in these "high-stakes" situations does pose a challenge for researchers, who continue to seek ways to improve personality assessment. But for the purposes of psychological research, and even for some purposes involving practical decision making, the use of self-reports and observer reports works rather well.

Personality Traits (and People's Personalities) Can Be Summarized in Terms of about Six Broad Dimensions

Although the domain of personality characteristics contains many hundreds of traits, a rough summary of personality can be given in terms of about six broad dimensions, or factors. (Until recently, the most widely accepted view has been that there are five major factors of personality, but much recent research has indicated that there are in fact six such factors.) One implication of this finding is that we can understand each personality trait, in considerable part, as an aspect of one of these broad dimensions of personality, or as a blend of two or more such dimensions. Another implication is that the personality of any given individual can be understood, in broad outline, as a combination of his or her levels of each of these dimensions. Because the number of combinations is extremely large, a great deal of information about an individual can be expressed using only half a dozen broad factors.

The identification of these major personality dimensions is very useful, because it allows personality to be assessed thoroughly and efficiently, and thereby makes it feasible to assess personality in research and in applied settings. But we should be careful not to oversimplify personality. Personality traits are not perfectly summarized in terms of the major factors, and as a result, some important outcome variables are predicted better by specific traits than by the more general dimensions to which those traits belong. Also, even though we can obtain a good overview of an individual's personality by assessing his or her levels of the broad factors, this obviously cannot entirely capture the essence of his or her personality.

Some Important Individual Differences—Including Some Aspects of Mental Ability, of Religiosity, and of Sexuality—Are Only Modestly Related to Personality Characteristics

The major dimensions of personality are related to individual differences in a variety of other areas of human individual differences, such as mental abilities, religious or political views, and sexuality. For example, higher levels of the Openness to Experience factor are associated to some extent with verbal ability, with spiritual religiosity (as opposed to religious fundamentalism), and (possibly) with sexual orientation. But relations such as these are not particularly strong, and so we cannot simply describe these characteristics as being expressions of the major personality factors. Instead, it appears that these other individual differences are important dimensions in their own right. Therefore, a complete portrait of an individual's psychological characteristics would need to include—in addition to the personality factors—his or her level of general mental ability (g), his or her level of religious belief, and his or her sexual orientation.

Personality and Other Psychological Individual Differences Are Moderately Heritable, and Are Not Much Influenced by the Common Environment

Perhaps the most surprising results observed in personality research have come from studies of the heritability of personality characteristics. One major finding of those investigations is that genetic differences account for about half (or perhaps more) of the personality variation among people. This genetic influence is partly of the "additive" kind, which means that genetic relatives will tend to have somewhat similar personalities; however, it is partly of the "nonadditive" kind, which means that a person will in some ways be quite different from genetic relatives (other than an identical twin).

A related finding of these studies involves the nature of environmental influences on personality: Persons raised in the same household tend to have only slightly more similar personalities than do persons raised in different households. This indicates that personality is influenced much more strongly by aspects of the environment that differ *within* families (i.e., among siblings *within the same family*) than by aspects of the environment that differ *between* families. Apparently, an individual's levels of the various personality traits are not much influenced by, for example, the socioeconomic status or the child-rearing style of his or her parents. This result has been something of a shock to many researchers who had assumed that personality would be heavily influenced by the household in which one was raised. Some recent research suggests that the effect of the common environment might not be quite so small after all, but it still appears to be weaker than most researchers would have guessed.

Somewhat different results have been observed for mental ability and for religiosity, which do show a substantial influence of the common (i.e., between family) environment, at least during earlier periods of development. However, the heritability of *g* increases, and the influence of the common environment decreases, as individuals progress from childhood to adulthood. A similar pattern of change occurs slightly later in the life span for religiosity, whereby genetic effects increase and common environment effects decrease between adolescence and later adulthood.

Personality and Other Psychological Individual Differences Are Moderately Predictive of Some Important Life Outcomes

Another conclusion that we can draw from research on personality and other individual differences is that *these variables do matter*, in the sense of being related to some important life outcomes. For example, persons who are generally achievement oriented do tend to get high marks in school and good performance ratings on the job. Similarly, persons who are generally dishonest and impulsive do tend to commit more delinquent and criminal acts. Also, persons who are impulsive and unstable are more likely to abuse drugs or alcohol, and persons who are hostile and dominant are more likely to suffer from heart disease. Finally, persons who are generally cheerful and calm tend to report higher levels of life satisfaction.

Several other important examples involve the *g* factor of general mental ability, which is a strong predictor not only of school performance but also of job performance; in addition, *g* is also related to health and longevity and to law-abidingness. Of course, individual differences such as personality factors and *g* cannot predict these outcomes with extremely high accuracy, because there are so many other variables that are involved. But it is clear that a person's levels of various personality traits have a considerable influence on the likelihood of many life outcomes.

Personality Does Not Predict Which People Will Marry Each Other, but Some Other Psychological Individual Differences Do

Despite the importance of personality as a predictor of life outcomes, it does not appear to be a good predictor of how married couples are formed. That is, for any given personality trait, the personalities of wives and husbands are roughly uncorrelated with each other; they tend to be neither similar nor opposite. However, marital satisfaction is related both to one's own personality and also to that of one's spouse: In general, people who are agreeable, even-tempered, and stable tend to be happier with their marriages and also to have spouses who feel the same way. Other psychological variables do show considerable "assortative mating"—that is, substantial similarity between the spouses of a given couple. In general, spouses tend to have fairly similar levels of verbal (but not mathematical) ability, and also to have very similar levels of religiosity and of political conservatism.

What We Have Yet to Learn

The Biological Bases of Personality Are Not Yet Well Understood (and Neither Is the Development or Evolution of Personality)

During the second half of the twentieth century, many researchers investigated the biological bases of personality, examining the links of brain structures, neurotransmitters, and hormones with levels of various personality traits. These studies have revealed some interesting findings, but have also indicated that the biological bases of personality are very complicated. Thus far, we do not yet have a good understanding of which biological variables influence which personality characteristics, or of how that influence works.

Identifying the biological bases of personality will be an important task for future personality researchers. In some related domains of human individual differences, there has already been some encouraging progress. With regard to mental ability, researchers have identified some biological variables (such as brain size, brain glucose consumption, etc.) that are substantially correlated with the g factor. We might hope to see similar progress during the next few decades in identifying the bases of the major personality dimensions. In some cases, the nature of the characteristics that define a dimension might provide some good clues as to how to find their biological origins. For example, Emotionality is strongly related to the tendency to cry, so we might learn about the Emotionality dimension by studying individual differences in the biological mechanisms that underlie crying. But it will likely be some time (if ever) before we can predict an individual's personality trait levels by measuring the levels of some biological variables—that is, of some substances or some kinds of activity—within his or her brain or body.

Related to this lack of any thorough understanding of the biological basis of personality, there is also a great deal to learn about the development of personality during childhood and about the evolutionary history of personality during the distant past. With regard to personality development, we noted in Chapter 4 the challenges involved in measuring personality during early childhood. This makes it difficult to identify the extent to which the major dimensions of personality—as observed in adulthood, adolescence, or even later childhood—emerge in the very early stages of life. For example, is it meaningful to describe, say, 3-year-olds in terms of dimensions such as Openness to Experience or Honesty–Humility? If so, in what ways are those dimensions expressed at that early age? To what extent is there stability of the individual differences in personality characteristics between early childhood and later life?

Some similar questions exist with regard to the evolutionary origins of personality. How "old" are the major dimensions of personality? One way to examine this question would be to determine whether or not we can identify these dimensions of individual differences within species that have differing degrees of relatedness to human beings. For example, can we identify dimensions such as Openness to Experience or Honesty–Humility among chimpanzees? Among dogs? There has recently been an increase in research on the personalities of animals, and future work may help us to identify how the various personality dimensions emerged during the distant past.

The Specific Features of the Unique Environment That Influence Personality Trait Levels Are Not Yet Known

As noted before, the research evidence suggests that environmental influences on personality are more of the "unique" (i.e., nonshared, or within family) variety than of the "common" (i.e., shared, or between family) variety. But this leaves open the question as to *which* aspects of the unique environment are the ones that have the strongest impact on personality.

Some researchers have suggested that an individual's birth order—that is, whether he or she is the youngest or oldest sibling in the household—might influence personality even in adulthood, but the existing evidence suggests that this has only a small effect on personality trait levels. Another hypothesis is that peer influences have a lasting influence on personality, but it is difficult to measure peer influences, and the little existing research suggests a relatively modest effect of the peer environment on personality. However, much more research will be needed to establish how strong these influences are, and to identify any other aspects of the unique environment that might influence personality. (In fact, it is even possible that the unique environment has a weaker influence than has been suggested by some research studies, given some recent findings which suggest that heritability may be even higher than previously believed, or that the common environment might make some noteworthy contribution after all.) In any case, we have a lot to learn about the ways in which the unique environment does (and does not) influence personality.

The Nature and Evolution of Geographical and Historical Differences in Personality Are Not Yet Known, nor Is the Role of Personality in Cultural Differences

In Chapter 7, we discussed some examples of differences in the average levels of some personality characteristics across different geographical areas or different historical periods. But we still have only a limited knowledge of this variation in personality between regions or between generations. (This is partly due to the difficulty in making meaningful comparisons between self- or observer reports obtained within different societies, because the people presumably use the other members *of their own society* as a basis for comparison.) One important aim for future research will be to find some ways to compare personality trait levels across different regions and generations. By learning about the geography and history of personality, we might figure out which circumstances will favor higher or lower levels of any dimension; or, we might see that some characteristics tend to have the same average level even across very different settings. In addition, we will likely gain a better understanding of how personality relates to culture: For example, is the culture of a given society influenced by the personality characteristics of its people? Or, is the "typical" personality of a society influenced by the culture? If we can learn more about how the average levels of personality characteristics tend to vary (or tend not to vary) across places and times, we will thereby learn about the nature of personality and also about the differences and similarities among various cultures.

Final Remarks

The science of personality is a very special field of study, because personality—unlike the vast majority of the sciences—is a subject that is so much a part of our own lives as human beings. We all have a personality, we all observe each other's personality, we all communicate about personality, and we all make decisions based on personality. Because personality seems so specially and uniquely human, this tends to make us think of it as something beyond scientific study. But the story of this book has been that it is possible to investigate personality in a systematic way—and thus to find clear answers to some fundamental questions that, until recently, were considered suitable only for philosophical speculation. Although the measurement of personality does pose some rather tricky challenges, researchers who are careful and creative in their methods can learn a great deal about the psychological differences among people. In short, personality can be studied as a science—a human science.

References

Abrahamson, A. C., Baker, L. A., & Caspi, A. (2002). Rebellious teens? Genetic and environmental influences on the social attitudes of adolescents. *Journal of Personality and Social Psychology*, *83*, 1392–1408.

Ackerman, P. L., Bowen, K. R., Beier, M. E., & Kanfer, R. (2001). Determinants of individual differences and gender differences in knowledge. *Journal of Educational Psychology*, *93*, 797–825.

Adorno, T. W., Frenkel-Brunswik, E., Levinson, D. J., & Sanford, R. N. (1950). *The authoritarian personality*. New York: Harper and Row.

Allport, G. W. (1937). *Personality: A psychological interpretation*. New York: Holt, Rinehart, & Winston.

Allport, G. W., & Odbert, H. S. (1936). Trait-names: A psycho-lexical study. *Psychological Monographs*, *47* (1, Whole No. 211).

Altemeyer, B. (1981). *Right-wing authoritarianism*. Winnipeg: University of Manitoba Press.

Altemeyer, B. (1988). *Enemies of freedom: Understanding right-wing authoritarianism*. San Francisco: Jossey-Bass.

Altemeyer, B. (1996). *The authoritarian specter*. Cambridge, MA: Harvard University Press.

Altemeyer, B. (1998). The other "authoritarian personality." In M. P. Zanna (Ed.), *Advances in experimental social psychology* (Vol. 30) (pp. 47–92). San Diego: Academic Press.

Altemeyer, B., & Hunsberger, B. (1997). *Amazing conversions: Why some turn to faith and others abandon religion*. New York: Prometheus.

American Psychiatric Association (1987). *Diagnostic and statistical manual of mental disorders: DSM-III-R*. Washington, DC: American Psychiatric Association.

American Psychiatric Association (1994). *Diagnostic and statistical manual of mental disorders: DSM-IV*. Washington, DC: American Psychiatric Association.

Anderson, C., John, O. P., Keltner, D., & Kring, A. M. (2001). Who attains social status? Effects of personality and physical attractiveness in social groups. *Journal of Personality and Social Psychology*, *81*, 116–132.

Ashton, M. C., Danso, H. A., Maio, G. R., Esses, V. M., Bond, M. H., & Keung, D. K-Y. (2005). Two dimensions of political attitudes and their individual difference correlates: A cross-cultural perspective. In R. M. Sorrentino, D. Cohen, J. Olson, & M. Zanna (Eds.), *Culture and social behavior: The Ontario Symposium* (pp. 1–29). Hillsdale, NJ: Erlbaum.

Ashton, M. C., Jackson, D. N., Helmes, E., Paunonen, S. V. (1998). Joint factor analysis of the Personality Research Form and the Jackson Personality Inventory: Comparisons with the Big Five. *Journal of Research in Personality*, *32*, 243–250.

Ashton, M. C., & Lee, K. (2001). A theoretical basis for the major dimensions of personality. *European Journal of Personality*, *15*, 327–353.

Ashton, M. C., & Lee, K. (2005a). A defence of the lexical approach to the study of personality structure. *European Journal of Personality*, *19*, 5–24.

Ashton, M. C., & Lee, K. (2005b). Honesty–Humility, the Big Five, and the Five-Factor Model. *Journal of Personality*, *73*, 1321–1353.

Ashton, M. C., & Lee, K. (2006). *Gender-related occupational interests do not define a masculinity—femininity factor.* Manuscript submitted for publication.

Ashton, M. C., & Lee, K. (2007). Empirical, theoretical, and practical advantages of the HEXACO model of personality structure. *Personality and Social Psychology Bulletin, 11,* 150–166.

Ashton, M. C., Lee, K., & Goldberg, L. R. (2004). A hierarchical analysis of 1,710 English personality-descriptive adjectives. *Journal of Personality and Social Psychology, 87,* 707–721.

Ashton, M. C., Lee, K., de Vries, R. E., Szarota, P., Marcus, B., Wasti, S. A., Church, A. T., & Katigbak, M. (2006). *Lexical studies of personality structure: A comparison of six-factor solutions.* Paper presented at the 13th European Conference on Personality, Athens, Greece.

Ashton, M. C., Lee, K., & Paunonen, S. V. (2002). What is the central feature of Extraversion? Social attention versus reward sensitivity. *Journal of Personality and Social Psychology, 83,* 245–252.

Ashton, M. C., Lee, K., Perugini, M., Szarota, P., de Vries, R. E., Di Blas, L., Boies, K., & De Raad, B. (2004). A six-factor structure of personality-descriptive adjectives: Solutions from psycholexical studies in seven languages. *Journal of Personality and Social Psychology, 86,* 356–366.

Ashton, M. C., Lee, K., Vernon, P. A., & Jang, K. L. (2000). Fluid intelligence, crystallized intelligence, and the Openness/Intellect factor. *Journal of Research in Personality, 34,* 198–207.

Ashton, S. G., & Goldberg, L. R. (1973). In response to Jackson's challenge: The comparative validity of personality scales constructed by the external (empirical) strategy and scales developed intuitively by experts, novices, and laymen. *Journal of Research in Personality, 7,* 1–20.

Aylward, G. P., Pfeiffer, S. I., Wright, A., & Verhulst, S. J. (1988). Outcome studies of low birth weight infants published in the last decade: A meta-analysis. *Journal of Pediatrics, 115,* 515–520.

Baier, C. J., & Wright, B. R. E. (2001). "If you love me, keep my commandments": A meta-analysis of the effect of religion on crime. *Journal of Research in Crime and Delinquency, 38,* 3–21.

Bailey, J. M., Dunne, M. P., & Martin, N. G. (2000). Genetic and environmental influences on sexual orientation and its correlates in an Australian twin sample. *Journal of Personality and Social Psychology, 78,* 524–536.

Bailey, J. M., Kirk, K. M., Zhu, G., Dunne, M. P., & Martin, N. G. (2000). Do individual differences in sociosexuality represent genetic or environmentally contingent strategies? Evidence from the Australian twin registry. *Journal of Personality and Social Psychology, 78,* 537–545.

Bailey, J. M., & Pillard, R. C. (1991). A genetic study of male sexual orientation. *Archives of General Psychiatry, 48,* 1089–1096.

Balakrishnan, T. R., & Chen, J. (1990). Religiosity, nuptiality and reproduction in Canada. *Canadian Review of Sociology and Anthropology, 27,* 316–340.

Bar-On, R. (1997). *The Bar-On Emotional Quotient Inventory: A test of emotional intelligence.* Toronto: Multi-Health Systems.

Barrick, M. R., & Mount, M. K. (1991). The Big Five personality dimensions and job performance: A meta-analysis. *Personnel Psychology, 44,* 1–26.

Barrick, M. R., Mount, M. K., & Gupta, R. (2003). Meta-analysis of the relationship between the five-factor model of personality and Holland's occupational types. *Personnel Psychology, 56,* 45–74.

Bartholomew, K., & Horowitz, L. M. (1991). Attachment styles among young adults: A test of a four-category model. *Journal of Personality and Social Psychology, 61,* 226–244.

Baumgarten, F. (1933). Die Charaktereigenschaften. [The character traits.] *Beiträge zur Charakter- und Persönlichkeitsforschung* (Whole No. 1). Bern: A. Francke.

Bell, A. P., & Weinberg, M. (1978). *Homosexualities: A study of diversity among men and women.* New York: Simon and Schuster.

Bem, D. J. (1996). Exotic becomes erotic: A developmental theory of sexual orientation. *Psychological Review, 103,* 320–335.

Ben Zion, I. Z., Tessler, R., Cohen, L., Lerer, E., Raz, Y., Bachner-Melman, R., Gritsenko, I., Nemanov, L., Zohar, A. H., Belmaker, R. H., Benjamin, J., & Ebstein, R. P. (2006). Polymorphisms in the dopamine D4 receptor gene (DRD4) contribute to individual differences in human sexual behavior: Desire, arousal and sexual function. *Molecular Psychiatry, 11,* 782–786.

Benjamin, J., Li, L., Patterson, C., Greenberg, B. D., Murphy, D. L., & Hamer, D. H. (1996). Population and familial association between the D4 dopamine receptor gene and measures of novelty seeking. *Nature Genetics, 12,* 81–84.

Berenbaum, S. A., & Hines, M. (1992). Early androgens are related to childhood sex–typed toy preferences. *Psychological Science, 3*, 203–206.

Bernhardt, P. C., Dabbs, J. M., Jr., Fielden, J., & Lutter, C. (1998). Testosterone changes during vicarious experiences of winning and losing among fans at sporting events. *Physiology and Behavior, 65*, 59–62.

Bibby, R. W. (1993). *Unknown gods: The ongoing story of religion in Canada.* Toronto: Stoddart.

Blanchard, R., & Bogaert, A. F. (1996). Homosexuality in men and number of older brothers. *American Journal of Psychiatry, 153*, 27–31.

Bobrow, D., & Bailey, J. M. (2001). Is male homosexuality maintained via kin selection? *Evolution and Human Behavior, 22*, 361–368.

Bogaert, A. F. (2000). Birth order and sexual orientation in a national probability sample. *Journal of Sex Research, 37*, 361–368.

Bogaert, A. F. (2003a). Number of older brothers and sexual orientation: New tests and the attraction/behavior distinction in two national probability samples. *Journal of Personality and Social Psychology, 84*, 644–652.

Bogaert, A. F. (2003b). Interaction of older brothers and sex-typing in the prediction of sexual orientation in men. *Archives of Sexual Behavior, 32*, 129–134.

Bogaert, A. F., & Fisher, W. A. (1995). Predictors of university men's numbers of sexual partners. *Journal of Sex Research, 32*, 119–130.

Bogg, T., & Roberts, B. W. (2004). Conscientiousness and health-related behaviors: A meta-analysis of the leading behavioral contributors to mortality. *Psychological Bulletin, 130*, 887–919.

Borg, J., Andrée, B., Söderstrom, H., & Farde, L. (2003). The serotonin system and spiritual experiences. *American Journal of Psychiatry, 160*, 1965–1969.

Borkenau, P., Riemann, R., Angleitner, A., & Spinath, F. M. (2001). Genetic and environmental influences on observed personality: Evidence from the German Observational Study of Adult Twins. *Journal of Personality and Social Psychology, 80*, 655–668.

Bottlender, M., & Soyka, M. (2005). Outpatient alcoholism treatment: Predictors of outcome after 3 years. *Drug and Alcohol Dependence, 80*, 83–89.

Botwin, M. D., Buss, D. M., & Shackelford, T. K. (1997). Personality and mate preferences: Five factors in mate selection and marital satisfaction. *Journal of Personality, 65*, 107–136.

Bouchard, T. J., Jr., & Loehlin, J. C. (2001). Genes, evolution, and personality. *Behavior Genetics, 31*, 243–273.

Bouchard, T. J., Jr., Lykken, D. T., McGue, M., Segal, N. L., & Tellegen, A. (1990). Sources of human psychological differences: The Minnesota study of twins reared apart. *Science, 250*, 223–228.

Bourdage, J. S., Lee, K., Perry, A., & Ashton, M. (in press). Big Five and HEXACO model correlates of sexuality. *Personality and Individual Differences.*

Brackett, M. A., & Mayer, J. D. (2003). Convergent, discriminant, and incremental validity of competing measures of emotional intelligence. *Personality and Social Psychology Bulletin, 29*, 1147–1158.

Brackett, M. A., Mayer, J. D., & Warner, R. M. (2004). Emotional intelligence and its relation to everyday behavior. *Personality and Individual Differences, 36*, 1387–1402.

Brennan, K., Clark, C. L., & Shaver, P. R. (1998). Self-report measurement of adult attachment: An integrative overview. In J. A. Simpson & W. S. Rholes (Eds.), *Attachment theory and close relationships* (pp. 46–76). New York: Guilford.

Burd, L., Klug, M. G., Coumbe, M. J., & Kerbeshian, J. (2003). Children and adults with attention-deficit hyperactivity disorder: 1. Prevalence and cost of care. *Journal of Child Neurology, 18*, 555–561.

Burisch, M. (1984). Approaches to personality inventory construction: A comparison of merits. *American Psychologist, 39*, 214–227.

Burt, C. (1939). The relations of educational abilities. *British Journal of Educational Psychology, 9*, 55–71.

Buss, D. M. (1996). Social adaptation and five major factors of personality. In J. S. Wiggins (Ed.), *The Five-Factor Model of Personality* (pp. 180–207). New York: Guilford.

Buss, D. M., & Greiling, H. (1999). Adaptive individual differences. *Journal of Personality, 67*, 209–243.

Cabot, P. S. de Q. (1938). The relationship between personality and physique. *Psychological Bulletin, 35*, 710.

Campbell, A. (1999). Staying alive: Evolution, culture, and women's intrasexual aggression. *Behavioral and Brain Sciences, 22*, 223–252.

Campbell, D. P., & Holland, J. L. (1972). A merger in vocational interest research: Applying Holland's theory to Strong's data. *Journal of Vocational Behavior, 2*, 353–376.

Campbell, D. P., Hyne, S. A., & Nilsen, D. L. (1992). *Manual for the Campbell Interest and Skill Survey.* Minneapolis, MN: National Computer Systems.

Camperio Ciani, A. S., Capiluppi, C., Veronese, A., & Sartori, G. (2007). The adaptive value of personality differences revealed by small island population dymanics. *European Journal of Personality, 21,* 3–22.

Cantor, J. M., Blanchard, R., Paterson, A. D., & Bogaert, A. F. (2002). How many gay men owe their sexual orientation to fraternal birth order? *Archives of Sexual Behavior, 31,* 63–71.

Carver, C. S., & White, T. L. (1994). Behavioral inhibition, behavioral activation, and affective responses to impending reward and punishment: The BIS/BAS scales. *Journal of Personality and Social Psychology, 67,* 319–333.

Cashdan, E. (1980). Egalitarianism among hunters and gatherers. *American Anthropologist, 82,* 116–120.

Caspi, A., Roberts, B. W., & Shiner, R. L. (2005). Personality development: Stability and change. *Annual Review of Psychology, 56,* 453–484.

Castellanos, F. X., Giedd, J. N., Marsh, W. L., Hamburger, S. D., Vaituzis, A. C., Dickstein, D. P., Sarfatti, S. E., Vauss, Y. C., Snell, J. W., Lange, N., Kaysen, D., Krain, A. L., Ritchie, G. F., Rajapakse, J. C., & Rapoport, J. L. (1996). Quantitative brain magnetic resonance imaging in attention-deficit hyperactivity disorder. Archives of General Psychiatry, 53, 607–616.

Cattell, R. B. (1947). Confirmation and clarification of primary personality factors. *Psychometrika, 12,* 197–220.

Cattell, R. B. (1971). *Abilities: Their structure, growth, and action.* Oxford, England: Houghton Mifflin.

Chen, C., Burton, M., Greenberger, E., & Dmitrieva, J. (1999). Population migration and the variation of dopamine D4 receptor (DRD4) allele frequencies around the globe. *Evolution and Human Behavior, 20,* 309–324.

Child, I. L. (1950). The relation of somatotype to self-ratings on Sheldon's temperamental traits. *Journal of Personality, 18,* 440–453.

Choma, B. L., Ashton, M. C., & Hafer, C. L. (2007). *Conceptualizing political orientation among political candidates: The tale of two dimensions.* Manuscript submitted for publication.

Christie, R., & Geis, F. L. (1970). *Studies in Machiavellianism.* New York: Academic Press.

Clark, L. A. (1993). *Manual for the Schedule of Adaptive and Non-Adaptive Personality.* Minneapolis: University of Minnesota Press.

Clark, L. A., & Livesley, W. J. (2002). Two approaches to identifying the dimensions of personality disorder: Convergence on the Five-Factor Model. In P. T. Costa, Jr., & T. A. Widiger (Eds.), *Personality disorders and the Five-Factor Model of personality* (2nd ed.) (pp. 161–176). Washington, DC: American Psychological Association.

Clark, L. A., Livesley, W. J., Schroeder, M. L., & Irish, S. L. (1996). Convergence of two systems for assessing specific traits of personality disorder. *Psychological Assessment, 8,* 294–303.

Cloninger, C. R. (1987). A systematic method for clinical description and classification of personality disorders: A proposal. *Archives of General Psychiatry, 44,* 573–588.

Cloninger, C. R., Przybeck, T. R., Svrakic, D. M., & Wetzel, R. D. (1994). *The Temperament and Character Inventory (TCI): A guide to its development and use.* St. Louis, MO: Center for Psychobiology of Personality, Washington University.

Cloninger, C. R., Svrakic, D. M., & Przybeck, T. R. (1993). A psychobiological model of temperament and character. *Archives of General Psychiatry, 50,* 975–990.

Cochran, G., Hardy, J., & Harpending, H. (2006). Natural history of Ashkenazi intelligence. *Journal of Biosocial Science, 38,* 659–693.

Cohen, D. (1996). Law, social policy, and violence: The impact of regional cultures. *Journal of Personality and Social Psychology, 70,* 961–978.

Cohen, D., Nisbett, R. E., Bowdle, R. F., & Schwarz, N. (1996). Insult, aggression, and the southern culture of honor: An "experimental ethnography." *Journal of Personality and Social Psychology, 70,* 945–960.

Comings, D. E., Gade-Andavolu, R., Gonzalez, N., Wu, S., Muhleman, D., Blake, H., Mann, M., Dietz, G., Saucier, G., & MacMurray, J. P. (2000). A multivariate analysis of 59 candidate genes in personality traits: The Temperament and Character Inventory. *Clinical Genetics, 58,* 375–385.

Conn, S. R., & Rieke, M. L. (1994). *The 16PF fifth edition technical manual.* Champaign, IL: Institute for Personality and Ability Testing.

Cooper, T., Detre, T., & Weiss, S. M. (1981). Coronary-prone behavior and coronary heart disease: A critical review. *Circulation, 63*, 1199–1215.

Costa, P. T., Jr., & McCrae, R. R. (1985). *The NEO Personality Inventory Manual*. Odessa, FL: Psychological Assessment Resources.

Costa, P. T., Jr., & McCrae, R. R. (1988a). From catalog to classification: Murray's needs and the Five-Factor Model. *Journal of Personality and Social Psychology, 55*, 258–265.

Costa, P. T., Jr., & McCrae, R. R. (1988b). Personality in adulthood: A six-year longitudinal study of self-reports and spouse ratings on the NEO Personality Inventory. *Journal of Personality and Social Psychology, 54*, 853–863.

Costa, P. T., Jr., & McCrae, R. R. (1992a). Four ways five factors are basic. *Personality and Individual Differences, 13*, 653–665.

Costa, P. T., Jr., & McCrae, R. R. (1992b). *NEO Personality Inventory–Revised (NEO-PI-R) and NEO Five-Factor Inventory (NEO-FFI) Professional Manual*. Odessa, FL: Psychological Assessment Resources.

Costa, P. T., Jr., & McCrae, R. R. (1992c). Trait psychology comes of age. In T. B. Sonderegger (Ed.), *Nebraska Symposium on Motivation 1991: Psychology and Aging. Current Theory and Research in Motivation* (Vol. 39) (pp. 169–204). Lincoln, NE: University of Nebraska Press.

Cramer, K. M., & Imaike, E. (2002). Personality, blood type, and the Five-Factor Model. *Personality and Individual Differences, 32*, 621–626.

Crant, J. M. (1995). The Proactive Personality Scale and job performance among real estate agents. *Journal of Applied Psychology, 80*, 532–537.

Cunningham, M. R., Wong, D. T., & Barbee, A. P. (1994). Self-presentation dynamics on overt integrity tests: Experimental studies of the Reid Report. *Journal of Applied Psychology, 79*, 643–658.

Cutshall, C., & Watson, D. (2004). The Phobic Stimuli Response Scales: A new self-report measure of fear. *Behaviour Research and Therapy, 42*, 1193–1201.

Dabbs, J. M., Jr., Alford, E. C., & Fielden, J. A. (1998). Trial lawyers and testosterone: Blue-collar talent in a white-collar world. *Journal of Applied Social Psychology, 28*, 84–94.

Dabbs, J. M., Jr., Carr, T. S., Frady, R. L., & Riad, J. K. (1995). Testosterone, crime, and misbehavior among 693 prison inmates. *Personality and Individual Differences, 18*, 627–633.

Dabbs, J. M., Jr., Hargrove, M. F., & Heusel, C. (1996). Testosterone differences among college fraternities: Well-behaved vs. rambunctious. *Personality and Individual Differences, 20*, 157–161.

Dabbs, J. M., Jr., & Mohammed, S. (1992). Male and female salivary testosterone concentrations before and after sexual activity. *Physiology and Behavior, 52*, 195–197.

Dahlstrom, W. G., Hopkins, D., Dahlstrom, L., Jackson, E., & Cumella, E. (1996). MMPI findings on astrological and other folklore concepts of personality. *Psychological Reports, 78*, 1059–1070.

Danner, D. D., Snowdon, D. A., & Friesen, W. V. (2001). Positive emotions in early life and longevity: Findings from the nun study. *Journal of Personality and Social Psychology, 80*, 804–813.

Darwin, C. (1859). *On the origin of species by means of natural selection, or the preservation of favoured races in the struggle for life*. London: John Murray.

Dawood, K., Kirk, K. M., Bailey, J. M., Andrews, P. W., & Martin, N. G. (2005). Genetic and environmental influences on frequency of orgasm in women. *Twin Research, 8*, 27–33.

Day, A. L., Therrien, D. L., & Carroll, S. A. (2005). Predicting psychological health: Assessing the predictive validity of emotional intelligence beyond personality, type A behaviour, and daily hassles. *European Journal of Personality, 19*, 519–536.

de Vries, R. E., Lee, K., & Ashton, M. C. (in press). The Dutch HEXACO Personality Inventory: Psychometric properties, self-other agreement, and relations with psychopathy among low and high acquaintanceship dyads. *Journal of Personality Assessment*.

Deary, I. J., Strand, S., Smith, P., & Fernandes, C. (2007). Intelligence and educational achievement. *Intelligence, 35*, 13–21

Deary, I. J., Taylor, M. D., Hart, C. L., Wilson, V., Smith, G. D., Blane, D., & Starr, J. M. (2005). Intergenerational social mobility and mid-life status attainment: Influences of childhood intelligence, childhood social factors, and education. *Intelligence, 33*, 455–472.

Deary, I. J., Thorpe, G., Wilson, V., Starr, J. M., & Whalley, L. J. (2003). Population sex differences in IQ at age 11: The Scottish Mental Survey 1932. *Intelligence, 31*, 533–542.

Deary, I. J., Whiteman, M. C., Starr, J. M., Whalley, L. J., & Fox, H. C. (2004). The impact of childhood intelligence on later life: Following up the Scottish Mental Surveys of 1932 and 1947. *Journal of Personality and Social Psychology, 86*, 130–147.

Der, G., Batty, G. D., & Deary, I. J. (2006). Effect of breast feeding on intelligence in children: Prospective study, sibling pairs analysis, and meta-analysis. *British Medical Journal*, doi:10.1136/bmj.38978.699583.55 (published 4 October 2006).

Detterman, D. K. (1987). What does reaction time tell us about intelligence? In P. A. Vernon (Ed.), *Speed of information-processing and intelligence* (pp. 177–200). Westport, CT: Ablex.

Devlin, B., Daniels, M., & Roeder, K. (1997). The heritability of IQ. *Nature, 388*, 468–471.

Diener, E. (2000). Subjective well-being: The science of happiness and a proposal for a national index. *American Psychologist, 55*, 34–43.

Digman, J. M., & Takemoto-Chock, N. K. (1981). Factors in the natural language of personality: Re-analysis, comparison, and interpretation of six major studies. *Multivariate Behavioral Research, 16*, 149–170.

Donnellan, M. B., Trzesniewski, K. H., Robins, R. W., Moffitt, T. E., & Caspi, A. (2005). Low self-esteem is related to aggression, antisocial behavior, and delinquency. *Psychological Science, 16*, 328–335.

Duckitt, J. (2000). Culture, personality, and prejudice. In S. Renshon & J. Duckitt (Eds.), *Political psychology: Cultural and cross-cultural foundations* (pp. 89–107). New York: New York University Press.

Duckitt, J., Wagner, C., du Plessis, I., & Birum, I. (2002). The psychological basis of ideology and prejudice: Testing a dual process model. *Journal of Personality and Social Psychology, 83*, 75–93.

Eaves, L., Martin, N., Heath, A., Schieken, R., Meyer, J., Silberg, J., Neale, M., & Corey, L. (1997). Age changes in the causes of individual differences in conservatism. *Behavioral Genetics, 27*, 121–124.

Edwards, A. G. P., & Armitage, P. (1992). An experiment to test the discriminating ability of graphologists. *Personality and Individual Differences, 13*, 69–74.

Elkins, I. J., King, S. M., McGue, M., & Iacono, W. G. (2006). Personality traits and the development of nicotine, alcohol, and illicit drug disorders: Prospective links from adolescence to young adulthood. *Journal of Abnormal Psychology, 115*, 26–39.

Epstein, S. (1979). The stability of behavior: I. On predicting most of the people much of the time. *Journal of Personality and Social Psychology, 37*, 1097–1126.

Exner, J. E. (1974). *The Rorschach: A comprehensive system. Volume 1*. New York: Wiley.

Eysenck, H. J. (1939). Primary mental abilities. *British Journal of Educational Psychology, 9*, 270–275.

Eysenck, H. J. (1947). *Dimensions of personality*. London: Routledge and Kegan Paul.

Eysenck, H. J. (1954). *The psychology of politics*. London: Routledge and Kegan Paul.

Eysenck, H. J. (1970). *The structure of human personality* (3rd ed.). London: Methuen.

Eysenck, H. J., & Eysenck, S. B. G. (1975). Manual of the Eysenck Personality Questionnaire. San Diego: EdITS.

Eysenck, H. J., & Wilson, G. D. (1991). *The Eysenck Personality Profiler*. London: Corporate Assessment Network.

Eysenck, S. B. G., & Eysenck, H. J. (1967). Salivary response to lemon juice as a measure of introversion. *Perceptual and Motor Skills, 24*, 1047–1053.

Eysenck, S. B. G., & Eysenck, H. J. (1968). The measurement of psychoticism: A study of factor stability and reliability. *British Journal of Social and Clinical Psychology, 7*, 286–294.

Ferguson, L. W. (1939). Primary social attitudes. *Journal of Psychology, 8*, 217–223.

Finn, S. E. (1986). Stability of personality self-ratings over 30 years: Evidence for an age/cohort interaction. *Journal of Personality and Social Psychology, 50*, 813–818.

Fleeson, W. (2004). Moving personality beyond the person-situation debate: The challenge and the opportunity of within-person variability. *Current Directions in Psychological Science, 13*, 83–87.

Flynn, J. R. (1984). The mean IQ of Americans: Massive gains 1932 to 1978. *Psychological Bulletin, 95*, 29–51.

Flynn, J. R. (1987). Massive IQ gains in 14 nations: What IQ tests really measure. *Psychological Bulletin, 101*, 171–191.

Flynn, J. R. (1991). *Asian Americans: Achievement beyond IQ*. Hillsdale, NJ: Erlbaum.

Flynn, J. R. (2006). [Efeito Flynn: Repensando a inteligência e seus efeitos.] [The Flynn Effect: Rethinking intelligence and what effects it.] In C. Flores-Mendoza & R. Colom (Eds.), *Introduçao à psicologia das diferenças individuais* (pp. 387–411) *[Introduction to the psychology of individual differences]*. Porto Alegre, Brazil: ArtMed.

Friedman, H. S., Tucker, J. S., Schwartz, J. E., Martin, L. R., Tomlinson-Keasey, C., Wingard, D. L., & Criqui, M. H. (1995). Childhood Conscientiousness and longevity: Health behaviors and cause of death. *Journal of Personality and Social Psychology*, *68*, 696–703.

Friedman, H. S., Tucker, J. S., Tomlinson-Keasey, C., Schwartz, J. E., Wingard, D. L., & Criqui, M. H. (1993). Does childhood personality predict longevity? *Journal of Personality and Social Psychology*, *65*, 176–185.

Friedman, M., & Rosenman, R. H. (1959). Association of a specific overt behavior pattern with increases in blood cholesterol, blood clotting time, incidence of arcus senilis, and clinical coronary artery disease. *Journal of the American Medical Association*, *169*, 1286–1296.

Funder, D. C., Kolar, D. W., & Blackman, M. C. (1995). On the basis of agreement among judges of personality: Interpersonal relations, similarity, and acquaintanceship. *Journal of Personality and Social Psychology*, *69*, 656–672.

Furnham, A., Chamorro-Premuzic, T., & Callahan, I. (2003). Does graphology predict personality and intelligence? *Individual Differences Research*, *1*, 78–94.

Furr, R. M., & Funder, D. C. (1998). A multimodal analysis of personal negativity. *Journal of Personality and Social Psychology*, *74*, 1580–1591.

Furukawa, T. (1930). A study of temperament and blood groups. *Journal of Social Psychology*, *1*, 494–509.

Galton, F. (1884). Measurement of character. *Fortnightly Review*, *36*, 179–183.

Gangestad, S. W., & Simpson, J. A. (1990). Toward an evolutionary history of female sociosexual variation. *Journal of Personality*, *58*, 69–96.

Gardner, H. (1983). *Frames of mind*. New York: BasicBooks.

Gardner, H. (1999). *Intelligence reframed*. New York: BasicBooks.

Geen, R. G. (1984). Preferred stimulation levels in introverts: Effects on arousal and performance. *Journal of Personality and Social Psychology*, *46*, 1303–1312.

Gilmore, D. D. (1990). *Manhood in the making*. New Haven, CT: Yale University Press.

Gleitman, H. (1986). *Psychology* (2nd ed.). New York: Norton.

Goffin, R. D., & Christiansen, N. D. (2003). Correcting personality tests for faking: A review of popular personality tests and an initial survey of researchers. *International Journal of Selection and Assessment*, *11*, 340–344.

Goldberg, L. R. (1990). An alternative "Description of personality": The Big-Five factor structure. *Journal of Personality and Social Psychology*, *59*, 1216–1229.

Goldberg, L. R. (1999). A broad-bandwidth, public-domain, personality inventory measuring the lower-level facets of several five-factor models. In I. Mervielde, I. Deary, F. De Fruyt, & F. Ostendorf (Eds.), *Personality psychology in Europe* (Vol. 7) (pp. 7–28). The Netherlands: Tilburg University Press.

Goleman, D. (1995). *Emotional intelligence*. New York: Bantam.

Gosling, S. D., Kwan, V. S. Y., & John, O. P. (2003). A dog's got personality: A cross-species comparative approach to personality judgments in dogs and humans. *Journal of Personality and Social Psychology*, *85*, 1161–1169.

Gottfredson, L. S. (2003). Dissecting practical intelligence theory: Its claims and evidence. *Intelligence*, *31*, 343–397.

Gottfredson, L. S. (2004). Intelligence: Is it the epidemiologists' elusive "fundamental cause" of social class inequalities in health? *Journal of Personality and Social Psychology*, *86*, 174–199.

Gottfredson, L. S., & Deary, I. J. (2004). Intelligence predicts health and longevity, but why? *Current Directions in Psychological Science*, *13*, 1–4.

Gottfredson, M. R., & Hirschi, T. (1990). *A general theory of crime*. Stanford, CA: Stanford University Press.

Gough, H. G. (1996). *California Psychological Inventory* (3rd ed.). Palo Alto: CA. Consulting Psychologists Press.

Gray, J. A. (1981). A critique of Eysenck's theory of personality. In H. J. Eysenck (Ed.), *A model for personality* (pp. 246–276). New York: Springer-Verlag.

Gray, J. A. (1987). Perspectives on anxiety and impulsivity: A commentary. *Journal of Research in Personality*, *21*, 493–509.

Grudnik, J. L., & Kranzler, J. H. (2001). Meta-analysis of the relationship between intelligence and inspection time. *Intelligence, 29,* 523–535.

Gustafsson, J.-E. (2002). Measurement from a hierarchical point of view. In H. I. Braun, D. N. Jackson, & D. E. Wiley (Eds.), *The role of constructs in psychological and educational measurement* (pp. 73–95). Mahwah, NJ: Erlbaum.

Haier, R. J. (1993). Cerebral glucose metabolism and intelligence. In P. A. Vernon (Ed.), *Biological approaches to the study of human intelligence* (pp. 317–331). Norwood, NJ: Ablex.

Halpern, C. T., Udry, J. R., Campbell, B., Suchindran, C., & Mason, G. A. (1994). Testosterone and religiosity as predictors of sexual attitudes and activity among adolescent males: A biosocial model. *Journal of Biosocial Science, 26,* 217–234.

Halpern, C. T., Udry, J. R., & Suchindran, C. (1997). Testosterone predicts initiation of coitus in adolescent females. *Psychosomatic Medicine, 59,* 161–171.

Halpern, D. F. (1997). Sex differences in intelligence: Implications for education. *American Psychologist, 52,* 1091–1102.

Halverson, C. F., Havill, V. L., Deal, J., Baker, S. R., Victor, J. B., Pavlopoulos, V., Besevegis, E., & Wen, L. (2003). Personality structure as derived from parental ratings of free descriptions of children: The inventory of child individual differences. *Journal of Personality, 71,* 995–1026.

Hamilton, W. D. (1964). The genetical evolution of social behavior. I, II. *Journal of Theoretical Biology, 7,* 1–52.

Hampson, S. E., Goldberg, L. R., Vogt, T. M., & Dubanoski, J. P. (2006). Forty years on: Teachers' assessments of children's personality traits predict self-reported health behaviors and outcomes at midlife. *Health Psychology, 25,* 57–64.

Harpur, T. J., Hare, R. D., & Hakstian, A. R. (1989). Two-factor conceptualization of psychopathy: Construct validity and assessment implications. *Psychological Assessment, 1,* 6–17.

Harris, J. R. (1995). Where is the child's environment? A group socialization theory of development. *Psychological Review, 102,* 458–489.

Harris, J. R. (1998). *The nurture assumption: Why children turn out the way they do.* New York: Free Press.

Hartshorne, H., & May, M. A. (1928). *Studies in the nature of character: Volume 1. Studies in deceit.* New York: Macmillan.

Heaven, P. C. L., & Bucci, S. (2001). Right-wing authoritarianism, social dominance and personality: An analysis using the IPIP measure. *European Journal of Personality, 15,* 49–56.

Hirschi, T., & Hindelang, M. J. (1977). Intelligence and delinquency: A revisionist review. *American Sociological Review, 42,* 571–587.

Hofstee, W. K. B., De Raad, B., & Goldberg, L. R. (1992). Integration of the Big Five and circumplex approaches to trait structure. *Journal of Personality and Social Psychology, 63,* 146–163.

Hogan, J., & Holland, B. (2003). Using theory to evaluate personality and job-performance relations: A socioanalytic perspective. *Journal of Applied Psychology, 88,* 100–112.

Hogan, R. (1996). A socioanalytic perspective on the Five-Factor Model. In J. S. Wiggins (Ed.), *The Five-Factor Model of Personality* (pp. 163–179). New York: Guilford.

Hogan, R., & Hogan, J. (1995). *Hogan Personality Inventory* (2nd ed.). Tulsa, OK: Hogan Assessment Systems.

Holden, R. R., Wood, L. L., & Tomashewski, L. (2001). Do response time limitations counteract the effect of faking on personality inventory validity? *Journal of Personality and Social Psychology, 81,* 160–169.

Holland, J. L. (1966). *The psychology of vocational choice.* Waltham, MA: Blaisdell.

Holzinger, K. J., & Swineford, F. (1939). A study in factor analysis: The stability of a bi-factor solution. *Supplementary educational monographs,* No. 48. Chicago: University of Chicago, Department of Education.

Hooper, J. (1999, February). A new germ theory. *Atlantic Monthly, 283,* 41–53.

Horn, J. L., & Cattell, R. B. (1966). Refinement and test of the theory of fluid and crystallized general intelligences. *Journal of Educational Psychology, 57,* 253–270.

Houston, B. K., Babyak, M. A., Chesney, M. A., Black, G., & Ragland, D. R. (1997). Social dominance and 22-year all-cause mortality in men. *Psychosomatic Medicine, 59,* 5–12.

Hunter, J. E., & Hunter, R. F. (1984). Validity and utility of alternative predictors of job performance. *Psychological Bulletin, 96,* 72–98.

Hurtz, G. M., & Donovan, J. J. (2000). Personality and job performance: The Big Five revisited. *Journal of Applied Psychology, 85*, 869–879.

Jackson, D. N. (1975). The relative validity of scales prepared by naïve item writers and those based on empirical methods of personality scale construction. *Educational and Psychological Measurement, 35*, 361–370.

Jackson, D. N. (1984a). *Multidimensional Aptitude Battery manual*. Port Huron, MI: Research Psychologists Press.

Jackson, D. N. (1984b). *Personality Research Form manual* (3rd ed.). Port Huron, MI: Research Psychologists Press.

Jackson, D. N. (1994). *Jackson Personality Inventory—Revised manual*. Port Huron, MI: Sigma Assessment Systems.

Jackson, D. N., & Paunonen, S. V. (1985). Construct validity and the predictability of behavior. *Journal of Personality and Social Psychology, 49*, 554–570.

Jackson, D. N., Wroblewski, V. R., & Ashton, M. C. (2000). The impact of faking on integrity tests: Does forced-choice offer a solution? *Human Performance, 13*, 371–388.

Jacobs, N., Van Gestel, S., Derom, S., Thiery, E., Vernon, P., Derom, R., & Vlietinck, R. (2001). Heritability estimates of intelligence in twins: Effect of chorion type. *Behavior Genetics, 31*, 209–217.

Jefferson, T., Jr., Herbst, J. H., & McCrae, R. R. (1998). Associations between birth order and personality traits: Evidence from self-reports and observer ratings. *Journal of Research in Personality, 32*, 498–509.

Jencks, C. (1979). *Who gets ahead? The determinants of economic success in America*. New York: Basic Books.

Jensen, A. R. (1998). *The g factor: The science of mental ability*. Westport, CT: Praeger.

John, O. P., Donahue, E. M., & Kentle, R. L. (1991). *The "Big Five" Inventory—Versions 4a and 54*. Berkeley: University of California, Berkeley, Institute of Personality and Social Research.

Judge, T. A., Heller, D., & Mount, M. K. (2002). Five-Factor Model of personality and job satisfaction: A meta-analysis. *Journal of Applied Psychology, 87*, 530–541.

Judge, T. A., Higgins, C. A., Thoresen, C. J., & Barrick, M. R. (1999). The Big Five personality traits, general mental ability, and career success across the life span. *Personnel Psychology, 52*, 621–652.

Kasl, S. V., Brooks, G. W., & Rodgers, W. L. (1970a). Serum uric acid and cholesterol in achievement behavior and motivation: I. The relationship to ability, grades, test performance, and motivation. *Journal of the American Medical Association, 213*, 1158–1164.

Karpman, B. (1948). The myth of the psychopathic personality. *American Journal of Psychaitry, 103*, 523–534.

Kasl, S. V., Brooks, G. W., & Rodgers, W. L. (1970b). Serum uric acid and cholesterol in achievement behavior and motivation: II. The relationship to college attendance, extracurricular and social activities, and vocational aspirations. *Journal of the American Medical Association, 213*, 1291–1300.

Kaufman, A. S. (1979). *Intelligent testing with the WISC-R*. New York: Wiley.

Kaufman, A. S. (2001). WAIS-III IQs, Horn's theory, and generational changes from young adulthood to old age. *Intelligence, 29*, 131–167.

King, J. E., & Figueredo, A. J. (1997). The five-factor model plus dominance in chimpanzee personality. *Journal of Research in Personality, 31*, 257–271.

King, M., Green, J., Osborn, D. P. J., Arkell, J., Hetherton, J., & Pereira, E. (2005). Family size in white gay and heterosexual men. *Archives of Sexual Behavior, 34*, 117–122.

Knudson, R. M., & Golding, S. L. (1974). Comparative validity of traditional versus S—R format inventories of interpersonal behavior. *Journal of Research in Personality, 8*, 111–127.

Koenig, L. B., McGue, M., Krueger, R. F., & Bouchard, T. J., Jr. (2005). Genetic and environmental influences on religiousness: Findings for retrospective and current religiousness ratings. *Journal of Personality, 73*, 471–488.

Koke, L. C., & Vernon, P. A. (2003). The Sternberg Triarchic Abilities Test (STAT) as a measure of academic achievement and general intelligence. *Personality and Individual Differences, 35*, 1803–1807.

Kolar, D. W., Funder, D. C., & Colvin, C. R. (1996). Comparing the accuracy of personality judgments by the self and knowledgeable others. *Journal of Personality, 64*, 311–337.

Kretschmer, E. (1925). *Physique and character*. Oxford: Kegan Paul.

Krueger, R. F. (2005). Continuity of Axes I and II: Toward a unified model of personality, personality disorders, and clinical disorders. *Journal of Personality Disorders, 19*, 233–261.

Lahey, B. B., Applegate, B., Waldman, I. D., Loft, J. D., Hankin, B. L., & Rick, J. (2004). The structure of child and adolescent psychopathology: Generating new hypotheses. *Journal of Abnormal Psychology, 113*, 358–385.

Lamb, M. E., Chuang, S. S., Wessels, H., Broberg, A. G., & Hwang, C. P. (2002). Emergence and construct validation of the Big Five factors in early childhood: A longitudinal analysis of their ontogeny in Sweden. *Child Development, 73*, 1517–1524.

Larsen, R. J., & Diener, E. (1987). Affect intensity as an individual difference characteristic: A review. *Journal of Research in Personality, 21*, 1–39.

Larson, L. M., Rottinghaus, P. J., & Borgen, F. H. (2002). Meta-analysis of Big Six interests and Big Five personality factors. *Journal of Vocational Behavior, 61*, 217–239.

Leak, G. K. (1993). Relationship between religious orientation and love styles, sexual attitudes, and sexual behaviors. *Journal of Psychology and Theology, 21*, 315–318.

Lee, K., & Ashton, M. C. (2004). Psychometric properties of the HEXACO Personality Inventory. *Multivariate Behavioral Research, 39*, 329–358.

Lee, K., & Ashton, M. C. (2005). Psychopathy, Machiavellianism, and Narcissism in the Five-Factor Model and the HEXACO model of personality structure. *Personality and Individual Differences, 38*, 1571–1582.

Lee, K., & Ashton, M. C. (2006a). Further assessment of the HEXACO Personality Inventory: Two new facet scales and an observer report form. *Psychological Assessment, 18*, 182–191.

Lee, K., & Ashton, M. C. (2006b). *Re-analysis of the structure of the Greek personality lexicon.* Unpublished manuscript.

Lee, K., Ashton, M. C., & de Vries, R. E. (2005a). Explaining workplace delinquency and integrity with the HEXACO and Five-Factor Models of personality structure. *Human Performance, 18*, 179–197.

Lee, K., Ashton, M. C., & de Vries, R. E. (2005b). *Six factors in the Croatian personality lexicon.* Unpublished manuscript.

Lee, K., Ogunfowora, B., & Ashton, M. C. (2005). Personality traits beyond the Big Five: Are they within the HEXACO space? *Journal of Personality, 73*, 1437–1463.

Lesch, K.-P., Bengel, D., Heils, A., Sabol, S. Z., Greenberg, B. D., Petri, S., Benjamin, J., Müller, C. R., Hamer, D. H., & Murphy, D. L. (1996). Association of anxiety-related traits with a polymorphism in the serotonin transporter gene regulatory region. *Science, 274*, 1527–1531.

Levenson, M. R., Kiehl, K. A., & Fitzpatrick, C. M. (1995). Assessing psychopathic attributes in a noninstitutionalized population. *Journal of Personality and Social Psychology, 68*, 151–158.

Lewis, G. B., & Seaman, B. A. (2004). Sexual orientation and demand for the arts. *Social Science Quarterly, 85*, 523–538.

Lippa, R. A. (2002). Gender-related traits of heterosexual and homosexual men and women. *Archives of Sexual Behavior, 31*, 83–98.

Lippa, R., & Arad, S. (1997). The structure of sexual orientation and its relation to masculinity, femininity, and gender diagnosticity: Different for men and women. *Sex Roles, 37*, 187–208.

Livesley, W. J., & Jackson, D. N. (in press). *Manual for the Dimensional Assessment of Personality Pathology—Basic questionnaire.* Port Huron, MI: Sigma Assessment Systems.

Loehlin, J. C. (1997). A test of J. R. Harris's theory of peer influences in personality. *Journal of Personality and Social Psychology, 72*, 1197–1201.

Loehlin, J. C. (2005). Resemblance in personality and attitudes between parents and their children: Genetic and environmental contributions. In S. Bowles, H. Gintis, & M. Osborne Groves (Eds.), *Unequal chances: Family background and economic success* (pp. 192–207). Princeton, NJ: Princeton University Press.

Loehlin, J. C., & Nichols, R. C. (1976). *Heredity, environment, and personality: A study of 850 sets of twins.* Austin, TX: University of Texas Press.

Loney, B. R., Butler, M. A., Lima, E. N., Counts, C. A., & Eckel, L. A. (2006). The relation between salivary cortisol, callous-unemotional traits, and conduct problems in an adolescent non-referred sample. *Journal of Child Psychology and Psychiatry, 47*, 30–36.

Lounsbury, J. W., Sundstrom, E., Loveland, J. M., & Gibson, L. W. (2003). Intelligence, "Big Five" personality traits, and work drive as predictors of course grade. *Personality and Individual Differences, 35*, 1231–1239.

Lykken, D. T., & Tellegen, A. (1993). Is human mating adventitious or the result of lawful choice? A twin study of mate selection. *Journal of Personality and Social Psychology, 65*, 56–68.

Lynn, R. (1987). The intelligence of the Mongoloids: A psychometric, evolutionary, and neurological theory. *Personality and Individual Differences, 11*, 755–756.

Lynn, R. (1994). Sex differences in intelligence and brain size: A paradox resolved. *Personality and Individual Differences, 17*, 257–271.

Lynn, R., Wilson, R. G., & Gault, A. (1989). Simple musical tests as measures of Spearman's *g*. *Personality and Individual Differences, 10*, 25–28.

MacDonald, D. A. (2000). Spirituality: Description, measurement, and relation to the Five-Factor Model of personality. *Journal of Personality, 68*, 153–197.

MacDonald, K. (1995). Evolution, the Five-Factor Model, and levels of personality. *Journal of Personality, 63*, 525–567.

MacDonald, K. (1998). Evolution, culture, and the Five-Factor Model. *Journal of Cross-Cultural Psychology, 29*, 119–149.

Mackintosh, N. (Ed.) (1995). *Cyril Burt: Fraud or framed?* New York: Oxford University Press.

Manicavasagar, V., Silove, D., Wagner, R., & Drobny, J. (2003). A self-report questionnaire for measuring separation anxiety in adulthood. *Comprehensive Psychiatry, 44*, 146–153.

Marcus, B. (2004). Self-control in the general theory of crime: Theoretical implications of a measurement problem. *Theoretical Criminology, 8*, 33–55.

Marcus, B., Lee, K., & Ashton, M. C. (2007). Personality dimensions explaining relationships between personality dimensions and counterproductive behavior: Big Five, or one in addition? *Personnel Psychology, 60*, 1–34.

Martin, L. R., Friedman, H. S., Tucker, J. S., Tomlinson-Keasey, C., Criqui, M. H., & Schwartz, J. E. (2002). A life-course perspective on childhood cheerfulness and its relation to mortality risk. *Personality and Social Psychology Bulletin, 28*, 1155–1165.

Mattia, J. I., & Zimmerman, M. (2001). Epidemiology. In W. J. Livesley (Ed.), *Handbook of personality disorders: Theory, research, and treatment*. New York: Guilford.

Mayer, J. D., & Salovey, P. (1993). The intelligence of emotional intelligence. *Intelligence, 17*, 433–442.

Mayer, J. D., Salovey, P., & Caruso, D. (2002). *Mayer–Salovey–Caruso Emotional Intelligence Test (MSCEIT), Version 2.0*. Toronto: Multi-Health Systems.

McCrae, R. R. (2002). NEO-PI-R data from 36 cultures: Further intercultural comparisons. In R. R. McCrae & J. Allik (Eds.), *The Five-Factor Model of personality across cultures*. New York: Kluwer.

McCrae, R. R., & Costa, P. T., Jr. (1989). Re-interpreting the Myers–Briggs Type Indicator from the perspective of the five-factor model of personality. *Journal of Personality, 57*, 17–40.

McCrae, R. R., & Costa, P. T., Jr. (1997). Personality trait structure as a human universal. *American Psychologist, 52*, 509–516.

McCrae, R. R., Costa, P. T., Jr., Terracciano, A., Parker, W. D., Mills, C. J., De Fruyt, F., & Mervielde, I. (2002). Personality trait development from age 12 to age 18: Longitudinal, cross-sectional, and cross-cultural analyses. *Journal of Personality and Social Psychology, 83*, 1456–1468.

McCrae, R. R., & Terracciano, A. (2006). National character and personality. *Current Directions in Psychological Science, 15*, 156–161.

McCrae, R. R., Terracciano, A., & 78 Members of the Personality Profiles of Cultures Project. (2005). Universal features of personality traits from the observer's perspective: Data from 50 countries. *Journal of Personality and Social Psychology, 88*, 547–561.

McCrae, R. R., Yik, M. S. M., Trapnell, P. D., Bond, M. H., & Paulhus, D. P. (1998). Interpreting personality profiles across cultures: Bilingual, acculturation, and peer rating studies of Chinese undergraduates. *Journal of Personality and Social Psychology, 74*, 1041–1055.

McCrae, R. R., Zonderman, A. B., Costa, P. T., Jr., Bond, M. H., & Paunonen, S. V. (1996). Evaluating replicability of factors in the Revised NEO Personality Inventory: Confirmatory factor analysis versus Procrustes rotation. *Journal of Personality and Social Psychology, 70*, 552–566.

McCullough, M. E., Enders, C. K., Brion, S., & Jain, A. R. (2005). The varieties of religious development in adulthood: A longitudinal investigation of religion and rational choice. *Journal of Personality and Social Psychology, 89,* 78–89.

McCullough, M. E., Hoyt, W. T., Larson, D. B., Koenig, H. G., & Thoresen, C. (2000). Religious involvement and mortality: A meta-analytic review. *Health Psychology, 19,* 211–222.

McCullough, M. E., Tsang, J.-E., & Brion, S. (2003). Personality traits in adolescence as predictors of religiousness in early adulthood: Findings from the Terman longitudinal study. *Personality and Social Psychology Bulletin, 29,* 980–991.

McDaniel, M. (2005). Big-brained people are smarter: A meta-analysis of the relationship between in vivo brain volume and intelligence. *Intelligence, 33,* 347–346.

McDaniel, M., & Whetzel, D. L. (2005). Situational judgment test research: Informing the debate on practical intelligence theory. *Intelligence, 33,* 515–525.

McGregor, I., McAdams, D. P., & Little, B. R. (2006). Personal projects, life stories, and happiness: On being true to traits. *Journal of Research in Personality, 40,* 551–572.

McGue, M., Bouchard, T. J., Jr., Iacono, W. G., & Lykken, D. T. (1993). Behavior genetics of cognitive ability: A life-span perspective. In R. Plomin & G. E. McClearn (Eds.), *Nature, nurture, and psychology* (pp. 59–76). Washington, DC: American Psychological Association.

McHoskey, J. W., Worzel, W., & Szyarto, C. (1998). Machiavellianism and psychopathy. *Journal of Personality and Social Psychology, 74,* 192–210.

Metsäpelto, R. L., & Pulkkinen, L. (2003). Personality traits and parenting: Neuroticism, extraversion, and openness to experience as discriminative factors. *European Journal of Personality, 17,* 59–78.

Michigan Department of Education (1989). *The Michigan Employability Survey.* Ann Arbor, MI: Author.

Miller, T. Q., Smith, T. W., Turner, C. W., Guijarro, M. L., & Hallet, A. J. (1996). Meta-analytic review of research on hostility and physical health. *Psychological Bulletin, 119,* 322–348.

Mischel, W. (1968). *Personality and assessment.* New York: Wiley.

Mischel, W., & Peake, P. K. (1982). Beyond déjà vu in the search for cross-situational consistency. *Psychological Review, 89,* 730–755.

Moffitt, T. E., Gabrielli, W. F., Mednick, S. A., & Schulsinger, F. (1981). Socioeconomic status, IQ, and delinquency. *Journal of Abnormal Psychology, 90,* 152–156.

Moffitt, T. E., & Silva, P. A. (1988). IQ and delinquency: A direct test of the differential detection hypothesis. *Journal of Abnormal Psychology, 97,* 330–333.

Mortensen, E. L., Michaelsen, K. F., Sanders, S. A., & Reinisch, J. M. (2002). The association between duration of breastfeeding and adult intelligence. *Journal of the American Medical Association, 287,* 2365–2371.

Mount, M. K., Barrick, M. R., & Strauss, J. P. (1994). Validity of observer ratings of the Big Five personality factors. *Journal of Applied Psychology, 79,* 272–280.

Murray, H. A. (1943). *Thematic Apperception Test manual.* Cambridge, MA: Harvard University Press.

Myers, I. B., & McCaulley, M. H. (1985). *Manual: A guide to the development and use of the Myers–Briggs Type Indicator.* Palo Alto, CA: Consulting Psychologists Press.

Nathan, B. R., & Alexander, R. A. (1988). A comparison of criteria for test validation: A meta-analytic investigation. *Personnel Psychology, 41,* 517–535.

Neisser, U., Boodoo, G., Bouchard, T. J., Jr., Boykin, A. W., Brody, N., Ceci, S. J., Halpern, D. F., Loehlin, J. C., Perloff, R., Sternberg, R. J., & Urbina, S. (1996). Intelligence: Knowns and unknowns. *American Psychologist, 51,* 77–101.

Nettelbeck, T. (1987). Inspection time and intelligence. In P. A. Vernon (Ed.), *Speed of information-processing and intelligence* (pp. 295–346). Westport, CT: Ablex.

Nettle, D. (2006). The evolution of personality variation in humans and other animals. *American Psychologist, 61,* 622–631.

Neuman, R. J., Sitdhiraksa, N., Reich, W., Ji, T. H.-C., Joyner, C. A., Sun, L.-W., & Todd, R. D. (2005). Estimation of DSM-IV and latent class-defined ADHD subtypes in a population-based sample of child and adolescent twins. *Twin Research and Human Genetics, 8,* 392–401.

Newcomb, A. F., Bukowski, W. M., & Pattee, L. (1993). Children's peer relations: A meta-analytic review of popular, rejected, neglected, controversial, and average sociometric status. *Psychological Bulletin, 113,* 99–128.

Newsome, S., Day, A. L., & Catano, V. M. (2000). Assessing the predictive validity of emotional intelligence. *Personality and Individual Differences, 29,* 1005–1016.

Nisbett, R. E. (1993). Violence and U.S. regional culture. *American Psychologist, 48,* 441–449.

Noftle, E. E., & Robins, R. W. (in press). Personality predictors of academic outcomes: Big Five correlates of GPA and SAT scores. *Journal of Personality and Social Psychology.*

Noftle, E. E., & Shaver, P. R. (2006). Attachment dimensions and the Big Five personality traits: Associations and comparative ability to predict relationship quality. *Journal of Research in Personality, 40,* 179–208.

Norman, W. (1967). *2800 personality trait descriptors: Normative operating characteristics for a university population.* Ann Arbor, MI: University of Michigan.

Ones, D. S., Viswesvaran, C., & Schmidt, F. L. (1993). Comprehensive meta-analysis of integrity test validities: Findings and implications for personnel selection and theories of job performance. *Journal of Applied Psychology, 78,* 679–703.

Osler, W. (1910). The Lumelin Lectures on angina pectoris. *Lancet, 1,* 839–844.

O'Toole, B. I., & Stankov, L. (1992). Ultimate validity of psychological tests. *Personality and Individual Differences, 13,* 699–716.

Paulhus, D. L., Robins, R. W., Trzesniewski, K. H., & Tracy, J. L. (2004). Two replicable suppressor situations in personality research. *Multivariate Behavioral Research, 39,* 303–328.

Paulhus, D. L., Trapnell, P. D., & Chen, D. (1999). Birth order effects on personality and achievement within families. *Psychological Science, 10,* 482–488.

Paulhus, D. L., & Williams, K. M. (2002). The Dark Triad of personality: Narcissism, Machiavellianism, and psychopathy. *Journal of Research in Personality, 36,* 556–563.

Paunonen, S. V. (2002). *Design and construction of the Supernumerary Personality Inventory* (Research Bulletin #763). London, ON: University of Western Ontario.

Paunonen, S. V., & Ashton, M. C. (2001a). Big Five factors and facets and the prediction of behavior. *Journal of Personality and Social Psychology, 81,* 524–539.

Paunonen, S. V., & Ashton, M. C. (2001b). Big Five predictors of academic achievement. *Journal of Research in Personality, 35,* 78–90.

Paunonen, S. V., Jackson, D. N., & Keinonen, M. (1990). The structured nonverbal assessment of personality. *Journal of Personality, 58,* 481–502.

Perugini, M., Gallucci, M., Presaghi, F., & Ercolani, A. P. (2003). The personal norm of reciprocity. *European Journal of Personality, 17,* 251–283.

Pew Global Attitudes Project (2002). *Among wealthy nations U.S. stands alone in its embrace of religion.* Washington, DC: Pew Research Center for the People and the Press.

Plomin, R. C., & Caspi, A. (1999). Behavioral genetics and personality. In L. A. Pervin & O. P. John (Eds.), *Handbook of personality: Theory and research* (2nd ed.) (pp. 251–276). New York: Guilford.

Plomin, R., & DeFries, J. C. (1985). *Origins of individual differences in infancy: The Colorado Adoption Project.* New York: Academic Press.

Plomin, R., DeFries, J. C., & Fulker, D. W. (1988). *Nature and nurture during infancy and early childhood.* New York: Cambridge University Press.

Plomin, R., & Spinath, F. M. (2004). Intelligence: Genetics, genes, and genomics. *Journal of Personality and Social Psychology, 86,* 112–129.

Pope, H. G., & Katz, D. L. (1994). Psychiatric and medical effects of anabolic-androgenic steroid use: A controlled study of 160 athletes. *Archives of General Psychiatry, 51,* 375–382.

Pope, H. G., Kouri, E. M., & Hudson, J. I. (2000). Effects of supraphysiologic doses of testosterone on mood and aggression in normal men: A randomized controlled trial. *Archives of General Psychiatry, 57,* 133–140.

Pratto, F., Sidanius, J., Stallworth, L. M., & Malle, B. F. (1994). Social dominance orientation: A personality variable predicting social and political attitudes. *Journal of Personality and Social Psychology, 67,* 741–763.

Raven, J. C. (1941). Standardisation of progressive matrices. *British Journal of Medical Psychology, 19,* 137–150.

Reinisch, J. M. (1981). Prenatal exposure to synthetic progestins increases potential for aggression in humans. *Science, 211,* 1171–1173.

Reise, S. P., & Wright, T. M. (1996). Personality traits, cluster B personality disorders, and sociosexuality. *Journal of Research in Personality, 30,* 128–136.

Rice, T. W. (2003). Believe it or not: Religious and paranormal beliefs in the United States. *Journal for the Scientific Study of Religion, 42,* 95–106.

Riemann, R., Angleitner, A., & Strelau, J. (1997). Genetic and environmental influences on personality: A study of twins reared together using the self- and peer-report NEO-FFI scales. *Journal of Personality, 65,* 449–475.

Roberts, B. W., Caspi, A., & Moffitt, T. (2001). The kids are alright: Growth and stability in personality development from adolescence to adulthood. *Journal of Personality, 81,* 670–683.

Roberts, B. W., & DelVecchio, W. F. (2000). The rank-order consistency of personality traits from childhood to old age: A quantitative review of longitudinal studies. *Psychological Bulletin, 126,* 3–25.

Roberts, B. W., Walton, K. E., & Viechtbauer, W. (2006). Patterns of mean-level change in personality traits across the life course: A meta-analysis of longitudinal studies. *Psychological Bulletin, 132,* 1–25.

Robins, R. W., Fraley, R. C., Roberts, B. W., & Trzesniewski, K. (2001). A longitudinal study of personality change in young adulthood. *Journal of Personality, 73,* 489–521.

Robins, R. W., & Trzesniewski, K. (2005). Self-esteem development across the lifespan. *Current Directions in Psychological Science, 14,* 158–162.

Rogers, M., & Glendon, A. I. (2003). Blood type and personality. *Personality and Individual Differences, 34,* 1099–1112.

Rokeach, M. (1973). *The nature of human values.* New York: Free Press.

Romero, E., Gómez-Fraguela, J. A., Luengo, M. A., & Sobral, J. (2003). The self-control construct in the general theory of crime: An investigation in terms of personality psychology. *Psychology, Crime, and Law, 9,* 61–86.

Ronalds, G. A., De Stavola, B. L., & Leon, D. A. (2005). The cognitive cost of being a twin: Evidence from comparisons within families in the Aberdeen children of the 1950s cohort study. *British Medical Journal, 331,* 1306.

Rönnlund, M., & Nilsson, M.-G. (2006). Adult life-span patterns in WAIS-R Block Design performance: Cross-sectional versus longitudinal age gradients and relations to demographic factors. *Intelligence, 34,* 63–78.

Rorschach, H. (1921). *Psychodiagnostics: A diagnostic test based on perception.* New York: Grune & Stratton.

Rosenblitt, J. C., Soler, H., Johnson, S. E., & Quadagno, D. M. (2001). Sensation seeking and hormones in men and women: Exploring the link. *Hormones and Behavior, 40,* 396–402.

Rosenthal, R., & Rubin, D. B. (1982). A simple, general purpose display of magnitude of experimental effect. *Journal of Educational Psychology, 74,* 166–169.

Ross, S. R., Lutz, C. J., & Bailley, S. E. (2004). Psychopathy and the Five-Factor Model in a noninstitutionalized sample: A domain and facet level analysis. *Journal of Psychopathology and Behavioral Assessment, 26,* 213–223.

Rosse, J. G., Stecher, M. D., Miller, J. L., & Levin, R. A. (1998). The impact of response distortion on preemployment personality testing and hiring decisions. *Journal of Applied Psychology, 83,* 634–644.

Rothbart, M. K., & Bates, J. E. (1998). Temperament. In W. Damon & N. Eisenberg (Eds.), *Handbook of child psychology: Social, emotional, and personality development* (5th ed.) (Vol. 3) (pp. 105–176). New York: Wiley.

Rowatt, W. C., & Schmitt, D. P. (2003). Associations between religious orientation and varieties of sexual experience. *Journal for the Scientific Study of Religion, 42,* 455–465.

Ruch, W. (1992). Pavlov's types of nervous system, Eysenck's typology and the Hippocrates–Galen temperaments: An empirical examination of the asserted correspondence between three temperament typologies. *Personality and Individual Differences, 13,* 1259–1271.

Rushton, J. P., Brainerd, C. J., & Pressley, M. (1983). Behavioral development and construct validity: The principle of aggregation. *Psychological Bulletin, 94*, 18–38.

Rusting, C. L., & Larsen, R. J. (1999). Clarifying Gray's theory of personality: A response to Pickering, Corr, and Gray. *Personality and Individaul Differences, 24*, 200–213.

Sackett, P. R., & Harris, M. M. (1984). Honesty testing for personnel selection: A review and critique. *Personnel Psychology, 37*, 221–245.

Salovey, P., & Mayer, J. D. (1990). Emotional intelligence. *Imagination, Cognition, and Personality, 9*, 185–211.

Salsman, J. M., Brown, T. L., Brechting, E. H., & Carlson, C. R. (2005). The link between religion and spirituality and emotional adjustment: The mediating role of optimism and social support. *Personality and Social Psychology Bulletin, 31*, 522–535.

Salthouse, T. A. (2005). Book Review: Developmental influences on adult intelligence: The Seattle Longitudinal Study. *Intelligence, 33*, 551–554.

Saroglou, V. (2002). Religion and the five factors of personality: A meta-analytic review. *Personality and Individual Differences, 32*, 15–25.

Saroglou, V., Delpierre, V., & Dernelle, R. (2004). Values and religiosity: A meta-analysis of studies using Schwartz's model. *Personality and Individual Differences, 37*, 721–734.

Sattler, J. M. (1988). *Assessment of children* (3rd ed.). San Diego: Sattler.

Saucier, G. (1992). Benchmarks: Integrating affective and interpersonal circles with the Big-Five personality factors. *Journal of Personality and Social Psychology, 62*, 1025–1035.

Saucier, G., & Goldberg, L. R. (1996). Evidence for the Big Five in analyses of familiar English personality adjectives. *European Journal of Personality, 10*, 61–77.

Scarr, S., & Carter-Saltzman, L. (1979). Twin method: Defense of a critical assumption. *Behavior Genetics, 9*, 527–542.

Schaie, K. W. (1994). The course of adult intellectual development. *American Psychologist, 49*, 304–313.

Schmidt, F. L., & Hunter, J. (2004). General mental ability in the world of work: Occupational attainment and job performance. *Journal of Personality and Social Psychology, 86*, 162–173.

Schmitt, D. P. (2004). The Big Five related to risky sexual behaviour across 10 world regions: Differential personality associations of sexual promiscuity and relationship infidelity. *European Journal of Personality, 18*, 301–319.

Schmitt, D. P. (2005). Sociosexuality from Argentina to Zimbabwe: A 48-nation study of sex, culture, and strategies of human mating. *Behavioral and Brain Sciences, 28*, 247–311.

Schmitt, D. P., & Buss, D. M. (2000). Sexual dimensions of person description: Beyond or subsumed by the Big Five? *Journal of Research in Personality, 34*, 141–177.

Schmitt, D. P., Shackelford, T. K., Duntley, J., Tooke, W., Buss, D. M., Fisher, M. L., Lavallée, M., & Vasey, P. (2002). Is there an early-30s peak in female sexual desire? Cross-sectional evidence from the United States and Canada. *Canadian Journal of Human Sexuality, 11*, 1–18.

Schwartz, S. H., & Bilsky, W. (1987). Toward a universal psychological structure of human values. *Journal of Personality and Social Psychology, 53*, 550–562.

Sheldon, W. H. (1940). *The varieties of human physique*. Oxford: Harper.

Sheldon, W. H. (1942). *The varieties of temperament*. Oxford: Harper.

Shiner, R. L., & Caspi, A. (2003). Personality differences in childhood and adolescence: Measurement, development, and consequences. *Journal of Child Psychology and Psychiatry, 44*, 2–32.

Sidanius, J., & Pratto, F. (1999). *Social dominance: An intergroup theory of social hierarchy and oppression*. New York: Cambridge University Press.

Simons, L. G., Simons, R. L., & Conger, R. D. (2004). Identifying the mechanisms whereby family religiosity influences the probability of adolescent antisocial behavior. *Journal of Comparative Family Studies, 35*, 547–563.

Simpson, J. A., & Gangestad, S. W. (1991). Individual differences in sociosexuality: Evidence for convergent and discriminant validity. *Journal of Personality and Social Psychology, 60*, 870–883.

Smith, T. W., & Ruiz, J. M. (2002). Coronary heart disease. In A. J. Christensen & M. H. Antoni (Eds.), *Chronic medical disorders: Behavioral medicine's perspective* (pp. 83–111). Malden, MA: Blackwell.

Smith, T. W., & Spiro III, A. (2002). Personality, health, and aging: Prolegomenon for the next generation. *Journal of Research in Personality, 36*, 363–394.

Spangler, W. D. (1992). Validity of questionnaire and TAT measures of need for achievement: Two meta-analyses. *Psychological Bulletin, 112*, 140–154.

Spearman, C. (1904). "General intelligence," objectively determined and measured. *American Journal of Psychology, 15*, 201–292.

Spearman, C. (1927). *The abilities of man.* Oxford, England: Macmillan.

Spearman, C., & Jones, L. W. (1950). *Human ability.* Oxford, England: Macmillan.

Starr, J. M., Pattie, A., Whiteman, M. C., Whalley, L. J., & Deary, I. J. (2005). Vitamin B_{12}, serum folate, and cognitive change from age 11 to age 79. *Journal of Neurology, Neurosurgery, and Psychiatry, 76*, 219–292.

Sternberg, R. J. (1985). *Beyond IQ: A triarchic theory of human intelligence.* New York: Cambridge University Press.

Sternberg, R. J. (1993). *The Sternberg Triarchic Abilities Test (Level H).* Unpublished test.

Sternberg, R. J., Forsythe, G. B., Hedlund, J., Horvath, J. A., Wagner, R. K., Williams, W. M., Snook, S. A., & Grigorenko, E. L. (2000). *Practical intelligence in everyday life.* New York: Cambridge University Press.

Strelau, J., Angleitner, A., Bantelmann, J., & Ruch, W. (1990). The Strelau Temperament Inventory— Revised (STI-R): Theoretical considerations and scale development. *European Journal of Personality, 4*, 209–235.

Stubbe, J. H., Posthuma, D., Boomsma, D. I., & De Geus, E. J. C. (2005). Heritability of life satisfaction in adults: A twin-family study. *Psychological Medicine, 35*, 1581–1588.

Sulloway, F. J. (1995). Birth order and evolutionary psychology: A meta-analytic overview. *Psychological Inquiry, 6*, 75–80.

Sulloway, F. J. (1996). *Born to rebel: Birth order, family dynamics, and creative lives.* New York: Pantheon.

Taylor, S. E., Klein, L. C., Lewis, B. P., Gruenewald, T. L., Gurung, R. A. R., & Updegraff, J. A. (2000). Biobehavioral responses to stress in females: Tend-and-befriend, not fight-or-flight. *Psychological Review, 107*, 411–429.

Tellegen, A. (in press). *MPQ (Multidimensional Personality Questionnaire): Manual for administration, scoring, and interpretation.* Minneapolis, MN: University of Minnesota Press.

Tellegen, A., Watson, D., & Clark, L. A. (1999). On the dimensional and hierarchical structure of affect. *Psychological Science, 10*, 297–303.

Terman, L. M. (1925). *Genetic studies of genius. Medical and physical traits of a thousand gifted children.* Oxford, England: Stanford University Press.

Terracciano, A., & Costa, P. T., Jr. (2004). Smoking and the Five-Factor Model of personality. *Addiction, 99*, 472–481.

Tett, R. P., Jackson, D. N., & Rothstein, M. G. (1991). Personality measures as predictors of job performance: A meta-analytic review. *Personnel Psychology, 44*, 703–742.

Tett, R. P., & Palmer, C. A. (1997). The validity of handwriting elements in relation to self-report personality trait measures. *Personality and Individual Differences, 22*, 11–18.

Thurstone, L. L. (1938). Primary mental abilities. *Psychometric Monographs*, No. 1. Chicago: University of Chicago Press.

Townsend, F. (2000). Birth order and rebelliousness: Reconstructing the research in Born to Rebel. *Politics and the Life Sciences, 19*, 135–156.

Trivers, R. L. (1971). The evolution of reciprocal altruism. *Quarterly Review of Biology, 46*, 35–57.

Tupes, E. C., & Christal, R. E. (1961). *Recurrent personality factors based on trait ratings.* (USAF Tech. Rep. No. 61–97). U.S. Air Force: Lackland Air Force Base, TX.

Tupes, E. C., & Christal, R. E. (1992). Recurrent personality factors based on trait ratings. *Journal of Personality, 60*, 225–251.

Twenge, J. M. (2000). The age of anxiety? Birth cohort change in anxiety and Neuroticism, 1952–1993. *Journal of Personality and Social Psychology, 79*, 1007–1021.

Twenge, J. M. (2001). Birth cohort changes in Extraversion: A cross-temporal meta-analysis, 1966–1993. *Personality and Individual Differences, 30*, 745–748.

Vernon, P. A. (1991). Studying intelligence the hard way. *Intelligence, 15*, 389–395.

Vernon, P. A., Wickett, J. C., Bazana, P. G., & Stelmack, R. M. (2000). *The neuropsychology and psychophysiology of human intelligence*. In R. J. Sternberg (Ed.), Handbook of intelligence (pp. 245–264). New York: Cambridge University Press.

Vernon, P. E. (1950). *The structure of human abilities*. London: Methuen.

Vernon, P. E. (1982). *The abilities and achievements of the Orientals in North America*. New York: Academic Press.

Visser, B. A., Ashton, M. C., & Vernon, P. A. (2006). Beyond *g*: Putting multiple intelligences theory to the test. *Intelligence, 34*, 487–502.

Walton, K. E., & Roberts, B. W. (2004). On the relationship between substance use and personality traits: Abstainers are not maladjusted. *Journal of Research in Personality, 38*, 515–535.

Wasti, S. A., Lee, K., Ashton, M. C., & Somer, O. (in press). The Turkish personality lexicon and the HEXACO model of personality structure. *Journal of Cross-Cultural Psychology*.

Watson, D., Klohnen, E. C., Casillas, A., Nus Simms, E., Haig, J., & Berry, D. S. (2004). Match makers and deal breakers: Analyses of assortative mating in newlywed couples. *Journal of Personality, 72*, 1029–1068.

Weatherhead, P. J., & Robertson, R. J. (1979). Offspring quality and polygyny threshold: The "sexy son" hypothesis. *American Naturalist, 113*, 201–208.

Weiss, A., King, J. E., & Perkins, L. (2006). Personality and subjective well-being in orangutans (*Pongo pygmaeus* and *Pongo abelii*). *Journal of Personality and Social Psychology, 90*, 501–511.

Wells, B. E., & Twenge, J. M. (2005). Changes in young people's sexual behavior and attitudes, 1943–1999: A cross-temporal meta-analysis. *Review of General Psychology, 9*, 249–261.

Whalley, L. J., & Deary, I. J. (2001). Longitudinal cohort study of childhood IQ and survival up to age 76. *British Medical Journal, 322*, 819.

Whiteman, M. C., Deary, I. J., & Fowkes, F. G. R. (2000). Personality and health: Cardiovascular disease. In S. E. Hampson (Ed.), *Advances in personality psychology* (Vol. 1) (pp. 157–198). New York: Psychology Press.

Whitley, B. E., Jr. (1999). Right-wing authoritarianism, social dominance orientation, and prejudice. *Journal of Personality and Social Psychology, 77*, 126–134.

Widiger, T. A. (2003). Personality disorder and Axis I psychopathology: The problematic boundary of Axis I and II. *Journal of Personality Disorders, 17*, 90–108.

Widiger, T. A., Costa, P. T., Jr., & McCrae, R. R. (2002). A proposal for Axis II: Diagnosing personality disorders using the Five-Factor Model. In P. T. Costa, Jr., & T. A. Widiger (Eds.), *Personality disorders and the Five-Factor Model of personality* (2nd ed.) (pp. 431–456). Washington, DC: American Psychological Association.

Wilson, D. S. (1994). Adaptive genetic variation and human evolutionary psychology. *Ethology and Sociobiology, 15*, 219–235.

Wilson, D. S. (2002). *Darwin's cathedral: Evolution, religion, and the nature of society*. Chicago: University of Chicago Press.

Wilson, J. Q., & Herrnstein, R. J. (1985). *Crime and human nature*. New York: Simon and Schuster.

Wood, J. M., Lilienfeld, S. O., Garb, H. N., & Nezworski, M. T. (2000). The Rorschach Test in clinical diagnosis: A critical review, with a backward look at Garfield (1947). *Journal of Clinical Psychology, 56*, 395–430.

Wu, K., Lindsted, K. D., & Lee, J. W. (2005). Blood type and the five factors of personality in Asia. *Personality and Individual Differences, 38*, 797–808.

Wulf, J., Prentice, D., Hansum, D., Ferrar, A., & Spilka, B. (1984). Religiosity and sexual attitudes and behaviors among evangelical Christian singles. *Review of Religious Research, 26*, 119–131.

Zak, P. J., Kurzban, R., & Matzner, W. T. (2005). Oxytocin is associated with human trustworthiness. *Hormones and Behavior, 48*, 522–527.

Zametkin, A. J., Nordahl, T. E., Gross, M., King, A. C., Semple, W. E., Rumsey, J., Hamburger, S., & Cohen, R. M. (1990). Cerebral glucose metabolism in adults with hyperactivity of childhood onset. *New England Journal of Medicine, 323*, 1361–1366.

Zelenski, J. M., & Larsen, R. J. (1999). Susceptibility to affect: A comparison of three personality taxonomies. *Journal of Personality, 67*, 761–791.

Zuckerman, M. (2005). *Psychobiology of personality* (2nd ed.). New York: Cambridge University Press.

Zuckerman, M., Kuhlman, D. M., & Camac, C. (1988). What lies beyond E and N? Factor analyses of scales believed to measure basic dimensions of personality. *Journal of Personality and Social Psychology, 54*, 96–107.

Zuckerman, M., Kuhlman, D. M., Joireman, J., Teta, P., & Kraft, M. (1993). A comparison of three structural models of personality: The Big Three, the Big Five, and the Alternative Five. *Journal of Personality and Social Psychology, 65*, 757–768.

Zuckerman, M., Kuhlman, D. M., Thornquist, M., & Kiers, H. (1991). Five (or three) robust questionnaire scale factors of personality without culture. *Personality and Individual Differences, 12*, 929–941.

Index

A

Academic performance
  Mental abilities and, 237–240, 251–252,
    254–256
  Personality and, 74, 193–194
Additive genetic variation, defined, 117–119
ADHD, *see* Attention-Deficit/Hyperactivity Disorder
Adoption
  Equal environments assumption, 131–132
  in research on heritability of personality, 115–123,
    128–131, 136–139
  in research on heritability of mental abilities,
    229–230
  in research on heritability of religiosity or political
    attitudes, 278
  Selective placement, 130–131
  Variation among adopting households, 129–131
Aggregation, principle of, 30–32
Aggression
  and evolutionary interpretation of personality
    dimensions, 148–150
  and liking or disliking by other children, 187
  Relations with Self-control traits, 201
  Relations with Narcissism and self-esteem, 203
Agreeableness
  in Big Five or Five-Factor Model, 62–66
  in cross-language lexical studies and HEXACO
    model, 67–72
  see also Big Five; HEXACO model
Agriculture, 155, 158, 159
Alcohol use, 188–189
Alleles, 99, 118, 134, 143, 159, 303
Alpha (coefficient alpha), 13
Altruism
  and evolutionary interpretation of personality
    dimensions, 148–151

Analysis of Variance
  in calculating similarity of relatives, 115
  in person-situation debate, 33–34
Animals, personality dimensions in, 94, 161
ANOVA, *see* Analysis of Variance
Antisocial personality disorder, 165, 166
  see also Psychopathy
Anxiety (in Gray's Reinforcement Sensitivity
    Theory), 101–103
Apes, personality dimensions in, 161
ARAS, *see* Ascending Reticular Activating System
Arousal
  in Eysenck's theory of biological basis of
    personality, 101–105
  see also Sexual Arousal
Ascending Reticular Activating System, 101–102
Ashkenazi Jews, 235
Assimilation effects, 125–126
Assortative mating (and spousal similarity), 127,
    182–183, 245, 280
Astrological sign, 110–111
Attachment styles, 185–186
Attention-Deficit/Hyperactivity Disorder (ADHD),
    171–172
  Biological bases, 106
Authoritarianism, *see* Right-Wing Authoritarianism
Averaged evoked potentials, 227–228
Avoidant personality disorder, 165, 167

B

Behavioral Activation System, 100, 103
Behavioral Inhibition System, 100, 103
BESD, *see* Binomial Effect Size Display
Big Five personality factors, 62–64
  Attachment styles, 186
  Basis of Five-Factor Model, 64–66

Birth order, 133
Change during adulthood, 80–81
Childhood, 86–89
Descriptions and discovery, 62–64
Evolutionary adaptive trade-offs, 153
Job performance, 196–197
Job satisfaction, 205
Life outcomes summary, 206
Life satisfaction, 204–205
Marital satisfaction, 184
Occupational choice, 199
Parenting styles, 186
Peer relationships (popularity and status), 187
Personality disorder symptoms, 177–178
Political attitudes, 276
Psychopathy, 202–203
Relations with Cloninger's dimensions, 97
Relations with cross-language lexical (and
    HEXACO) factors, 66–72
Relations with Zuckerman's dimensions, 105
Religiosity, 262
Sexuality dimensions, 287–288
Spousal similarity, 183
Stability during adulthood and adolescence, 85
Binomial Effect Size Display (BESD), 6–9
Biodata, 23–24
Assessment of cross-national differences, 161
Biological bases
Mental ability, 222–228
Personality, 93–112
Religiosity and political attitudes, 278
Sexuality dimensions, 292–295, 297–301, 303
Birth order
Personality differences, 132–134
Sexual orientation, 299–301
Birth weight
and mental ability, 233
Blood type, 110
Body type, 95
Borderline personality disorder, 165–166
Brain glucose metabolism, 228
Brain size, 222–223
Brain structures
in Eysenck's theory of biological basis of
    personality, 101–102
in Gray's Reinforcement Sensitivity Theory, 99–101
Brain waves (averaged evoked potentials), 227–228
Breast-feeding, and mental abilities, 232–233
Bushman (San), 155–156

C
California Psychological Inventory (CPI), 41–42
Change, *see* Developmental change; *see* Stability

Characteristics, personality *see* Personality traits
Childhood gender nonconformity, 298–300
Children, number of
Religiosity, 267
Chinese (and Chinese immigrants), 158–159, 161
Chorion type, 232
Cloninger's theory of biological basis of personality,
    97–99
Coefficient alpha, 13
Common (shared) environment, defined, 120–121
Compassion versus Competition (dimension of
    political attitudes), 272–276
Conduct disorder, 173
    see also Antisocial personality disorder;
        Psychopathy
Conscientiousness
Biological bases, 106
in Big Five or Five-Factor Model, 62–66
in cross-language lexical studies and HEXACO
    model, 67–72
see also Big Five; HEXACO model
Construct validity, 19–20
Content validity, 16–18
Contrast effects, 125–126, 131
Convergent validity, 18–19
Correlation coefficient, 5–9
Intraclass, 115
Rank-order, invention by Spearman, 214
Cortisol, 106, 108–109
Criminality, *see* Law-abidingness versus criminality
Criterion validity, 18–19
Cronbach's alpha, 13
Cross-generational differences
Mental abilities ("Flynn effect"), 246–247
Personality, 160–161
Religiosity, 261
Sexuality dimensions, 292
Cross-national differences
Personality, 160–161
Religiosity, 261
Sexuality dimensions, 292
Crystallized ability, 221, 246–247
Cultural differences, *see* Cross-national differences

D
Dependent personality disorder, 165, 167–168
Depressive personality disorder (proposed), 169–170
Developmental change
Mental abilities, 220–221
Personality, during adolescence and adulthood,
    80–82
Personality, during childhood, 88
Political attitudes, 276–277

Religiosity, 264–265
Sexuality, 293
Diagnostic and Statistical Manual of Mental
    Disorders—IV (DSM-IV), 164–179
Direct Observations, 22–23
    Assessment of cross-national differences, 161
Discriminant validity, 18–19
Dizygotic (DZ) twins, *see* Twins
Dogs
    Pavlov's temperament types of, 94
    Personality dimensions in, 161
Dominance, genetic, 118
Dopamine
    Cloninger's theory, 97–99
    Migration and nomadism, 159
    Molecular genetic studies, 134
    Sexual arousal, 303
DRD4 gene, 134
Drug use, 188–189
DSM-IV, 164–179

E
Ectomorphs, 95
EEG, *see* Electroencephalogram
Electroencephalogram (EEG), 227–228
Emotional intelligence, 253–255
Emotional Stability
    in Big Five or Five-Factor Model (as opposite
        pole of Neuroticism), 62–66
    in cross-language lexical studies and HEXACO
        model, 67–72
    in Eysenck's theory of biological basis of
        personality (as opposite pole of Neuroticism),
        101–103
    see also Big Five; Emotionality
Emotionality
    in cross-language lexical studies and HEXACO
        model, 67–72
    Sex differences, 151
    see also HEXACO model; Emotional Stability
Empirical strategy of test construction, 36–38, 41
Endomorphs, 95
Engagement,
    and evolutionary interpretation of personality
        factors, 148, 151–152
Environmental influences
    Common (shared) and unique (non-shared),
        120–121
    Mental abilities, 228–234
        Nutrition (including breastfeeding), 231–234
        Womb (uterine) effects (including chorion type),
        230–231
    Personality, 120–134

Birth order, 133–134
    Parental treatment, 132–133
    Peer groups, 132–133
    Womb (uterine) effects, 128–129
Religiosity or political attitudes, 278–280
Sexuality dimensions, 294, 298–301, 302
    Birth order, 299–301
    Childhood peer groups, 298–299
see also Environmental influences, specific
    examples
Epistasis, 118
Equal environments assumption, 131–132
Eskimo (Inuit), 235
Evolution
    Natural selection, 142–144
    Reproductive success (fitness), 142, 154
    Sexual selection, 143
Evolutionary function of variation,
    Mental abilities, 234–236
    Personality, 142–162
    Religiosity and political attitudes, 281
    Sexuality, 295–297, 301–302, 303–304
    Vocational interests, 302
"Exotic becomes erotic" theory of sexual orientation,
    298–299
Extraversion
    in Big Five or Five-Factor Model, 62–66
    in cross-language lexical studies and HEXACO
        model, 67–72
    in Eysenck's theory of biological basis of
        personality, 101–103
    see also Big Five; HEXACO model
Extrinsic religiosity, 261–262, 293
Eysenck Personality Profiler (EPP), 42
Eysenck Personality Questionnaire (EPQ), 42
Eysenck's theory of biological basis of personality,
    101–105

F
F-scale, 268
Factor analysis
    Description of, 54–59
    in construction of personality inventories, 39, 41
    in mental abilities research, 211–220
    in personality research, 59–73, 105
    in political attitudes and values research, 273–276
    in sexuality research, 285–287
Factor-analytic strategy of test construction, 39, 41
Factor loadings, *see* Factor analysis
Faking, in personality self-reports, 198–200
Farming, 155, 158, 159
Femininity, 291
    see also Sex Differences; Sexual Orientation

Fetus, *see* Womb environment

"Fight-or-Flight" system, 100–101, 103

Fitness, *see* reproductive success

Five-Factor Model, 64–66

   see also Big Five personality factors

5-HTTLPR gene, 134

Fluctuating optimum, 145–147, 153–159, 235, 296–297

Fluid ability, 221, 246–247

"Flynn effect", 246–247

fMRI, *see* Functional Magnetic Resonance Imaging

Fraternal twins, *see* Twins

Frequency dependence, 146–147, 153–159, 235, 295–296

Friendships, 186–187

Functional Magnetic Resonance Imaging (fMRI)

   in Attention-Deficit/Hyperactivity Disorder research, 106

   see also Magnetic Resonance Imaging (MRI)

G

g factor

   Discovery and description, 214–220

   see also Mental abilities

Gathering, 155–156, 236

Gender differences, *see* Sex differences

Generational differences, *see* Cross-generational differences

Genes, *see* Heritability; Molecular Genetic Studies

Genetic influence on traits, *see* Heritability

Genotype-environment correlations, 135–137

Genotype-environment interactions (active, passive, reactive/evocative), 137–139

Glucose consumption of brain

   Relations with Attention-Deficit/Hyperactivity Disorder, 106

   Relations with mental abilities, 228

"Go" system, 101–103

Grade-point average, *see* Academic performance

Graphology, *see* Handwriting style

Gray's Reinforcement Sensitivity Theory, 99–103

GRE, 5

Group factors

   Discovery and description, 217–220

   see also Mental abilities

H

Handwriting style, 110

Happiness, *see* Life satisfaction

Harm-Avoidance (in Cloninger's theory), 97–100

Health and longevity

   Personality and, 187–192

Mental abilities and, 242–243

Religiosity and, 266

Heart disease, 191–192

Herding, 155

Heritability (Genetic influence on traits)

   Additive and non-additive, defined, 117–119

   Broad versus narrow sense, defined, 119

   Methods of calculating, 116–120

   of mental abilities, 228–230

   of personality, 121–132

   of religiosity and political attitudes, 278–280

   of sexuality dimensions, 294, 297–301, 302

Heterosexuality, *see* Sexual Orientation

HEXACO personality factors, 66–72

   Change during adulthood, 80–81

   Childhood, 86–87

   Descriptions and discovery, 66–72

   Evolutionary adaptive trade-offs of factors, 148–159

   Integrity tests, 197

   Marital satisfaction, 184

   Occupational choice, 199

   Political attitudes, 274–276

   Psychopathy, 202–203

   Relations with Cloninger's dimensions, 97

   Relations with Big Five and Five-Factor Model factors, 66–72

   Sexuality dimensions, 289

   Spousal similarity, 185

   Stability during later adulthood, 86

HEXACO Personality Inventory(—Revised) (HEXACO-PI(-R)), 44

   List of traits measured by, 71

   in research on trait stability, 83

   see also HEXACO personality factors

Histrionic personality disorder, 165, 167

Hogan Personality Inventory (HPI), 42

Homosexuality, *see* Sexual Orientation

Honesty-Humility

   in cross-language lexical studies and HEXACO model, 67–72

   see also HEXACO model

Hormones, 106–110, 192, 294, 299, 303

Humors (in classical and medieval philosophy), 93–94

Hunting, 155–156, 159, 235–236

I

Identical twins, *see* Twins

Idiographic approach, xxi–xxiii

Impulsivity (in Gray's Reinforcement Sensitivity theory), 101–103

Income, 240–242

Inspection time, 226–227
Integrity tests, 197–198
Intellect/Imagination(/Unconventionality)
    in Big Five or Five-Factor Model, 62–66
    in cross-language lexical studies and HEXACO
        model, 67–72
    see also Openness to Experience; *see also* Big
        Five; HEXACO model
Inter-rater (inter-observer) reliability, 14–15
Internal-consistency reliability, 10–13
International Personality Item Pool (IPIP), 44–45
Intelligence
    see Mental abilities
Intrinsic religiosity, 261–262, 293
Introversion (i.e., low Extraversion), *see*
    Extraversion
Inuit, 235
IQ, 2–5, 220, 232–233, 237, 253–254
    see also Mental abilities
Irish-American immigrants, 158
Italians, mainlanders and islanders, 159
Items, *see* Reliability; Validity; Structured personality
    inventories

J
Jackson Personality Inventory (JPI), 43, 161
Jews, Ashkenazi, 235
Job choice, 199
    see also Vocational interests
Job performance
    Personality and, 194–200
    Mental abilities and, 240–242
Job satisfaction, 205

K
Kin altruism, 148–151

L
Languages, *see* Lexical approach to study of
    personality structure
Law-abidingness versus criminality
    Mental abilities and, 243–245
    Personality and, 200–203
    Religiosity and, 267
"Lemon juice test", 103
Levels of measurement, 2–3
Lexical approach to study of personality structure,
    60–73
    see also Sexuality, dimensions of
Lexical hypothesis, *see* Lexical approach to study of
    personality structure
Life outcomes
    Personality and, 181–207

Mental abilities and, 237–245
Religiosity and, 266–267
see also Academic performance; Children,
    number of; Health and longevity; Income;
    Job Performance; Law-abidingness
    versus criminality; Life Satisfaction;
    Marriage; Occupational Status; Peer
    Relationships
Life satisfaction,
    Personality and, 203–205
    Religiosity and, 266
Limbic system, 102
Longevity, *see* Health and longevity
Longitudinal research design
    in mental abilities research, 220–222, 232–234,
        239–243
    in personality research, 79–85, 88–90
    in religiosity or political attitudes research,
        263–265, 276–277

M
MAB, *see* Multidimensional Aptitude Battery
Machiavellianism, 202–203
Magnetic Resonance Imaging (MRI)
    in mental abilities research, 223
    see also Functional Magnetic Resonance Imaging
        (fMRI)
Marriage
    Assortative mating (spousal similarity)
        Assumptions in heritability studies, 127
        Personality, 182–183
        Mental abilities, 245
        Religiosity and political attitudes, 280
    Marital satisfaction, 183–184, 280
Masculinity, 291
    see also Sex Differences; Sexual Orientation
Mathematical ability, *see* Numerical ability;
    Reasoning; Spatial ability
Memory, 215, 218–219, 236
Mental abilities
    Academic performance, 237–240
    Assortative mating, 245
    Biological bases, 222–228
        Brain glucose metabolism, 228
        Brain size, 222–223
        Brain waves: Averaged evoked potentials,
            227–228
        Inspection time, 226–227
        Nerve conduction velocity, 223–224
        Reaction time, 224–226
    Birth weight, 233
    Cross-generational differences in, 246–247
    Crystallized abilities, 221, 246–247

Developmental change, 220–221
Domain of, as distinct from personality and
    non-mental abilities, 210–211
Emotional intelligence, 253–255
Environmental influences, 228–234
    Breast-feeding, 232–233
    Chorion type, 232
    Nutrition in adulthood, 234
    Womb environment, 230–231
Evolutionary function of variation, 234–236
Fluid abilities, 221, 246–247
g factor, 214–220
Group factors, 217–220
Health, 242–243
Heritability (genetic influence), 228–229
Income, 240–242
Job performance, 240–242
"Intelligence", 211
Law-abidingness versus criminality, 243–245
Longevity, 242–243
Occupational status, 240–242
Openness to Experience, 248–249
Personality, 248–249
Sex differences, 236
Stability across lifespan, 221–222
Structure of, 211–220
Mesomorphs, 95
Methods of measurement, 20–24
    see also Self-Reports; Observer Reports; Direct
        Observation; Biodata
Migration, 159
Molecular genetic studies, 134
Monozygotic (MZ) twins, *see* Twins
Moral Regulation versus Individual Freedom
        (dimension of political attitudes), 272–276
Mortality, *see* Health and longevity
MRI, *see* Magnetic Resonance Imaging
Multidimensional Aptitude Battery (MAB),
        211–213, 217
Multidimensional Personality Questionnaire (MPQ),
        43, 103
Multiple Intelligences, Theory of, 249–251
Mutations, genetic, 143–145
Myers-Briggs Type Indicator (MBTI), 42–43

N
Narcissism, 202–203
    see also Narcissistic personality disorder
Narcissistic personality disorder, 165, 167
Narrow traits, validity of, 74
National differences, *see* Cross-national
        differences
Natural selection, 142–144

Nature-versus-nurture debate, 114
    see also Heritability (Genetic influences);
        Environmental influences
Negatively-keyed items, 35–36
Negativistic personality disorder (proposed),
        169–170
NEO Five-Factor Inventory (NEO-FFI), 44
NEO Personality Inventory—Revised (NEO-PI-R),
        44
    List of traits measured by, 65
    in research on trait stability, 83
    see also Big Five personality factors; Five-Factor
        Model; Structured personality inventories,
        Commonly used
Nerve conduction velocity, *see* Mental abilities,
        biological bases
Neurons, 96
Neuroticism (i.e., low Emotional Stability)
    see Emotional Stability
Neurotransmitters, 96–99, 134, 159, 278, 303
Nomadism, 159
Nomothetic approach, xxi–xxiii
Non-additive genetic variation, defined, 117–119
Non-shared (unique) environment, defined, 120–121
Nonverbal Personality Questionnaire (NPQ), 43–44
Norepinephrine, 97–99
Normal distribution, 4, 260
Novelty-seeking
    in Cloninger's theory, 97–100
    Migration and nomadism, 159
Numerical ability, 215–219, 235, 245–249
Nutrition, and mental abilities, 231–234

O
Observer ratings, *see* Observer reports
Observer reports
    Agreement with self-reports and reports from
        other observer, 45–47
    Faking, 200
    Issues about use in heritability studies, 115,
        124–126
    Method of measurement, 21, 23–24
    Observer ratings, compared with, 21
    Validity in predicting behavior, 48–49
Obsessive-compulsive personality disorder, 165, 168
Occasions, variation in behavior across, 15–16, 30
Occupational choice, 199
    see also Vocational interests
Occupational status, 240–242
Openness to Change versus Conservation (dimension
        of values), 274–276
Openness to Experience
    in Big Five or Five-Factor Model, 62–66

in cross-language lexical studies and HEXACO model, 67–72

see also Intellect/Imagination(/Unconventionality) factor of lexical studies

see also Big Five; HEXACO model

Oppositional-defiant disorder, 171–173

Other reports, *see* Observer reports

Oxytocin, 106, 109–110

P

Parallel-forms reliability, 13

Paranoid personality disorder, 165, 166

Paranormal beliefs, 166, 265–266

Parental investment, 148–151, 295–297

Parental treatment, as influence on personality, 132–133

Parenting styles, personality correlates of, 186

Passive-aggressive personality disorder (proposed), 169–170

Peer groups, as influence on personality, 132–133

Peer relationships, personality correlates of, 186–187

Peer reports, *see* Observer reports

Perceptual ability, 218–219, 236

Person-by-situation interactions, *see* Person-situation debate

Person-situation debate, 30–34

Personality characteristics, *see* Personality traits

Personality disorders, 163–179

Alternative systems for diagnosis, 176–178

Descriptions and classification of disorders listed in DSM-IV, 165–169

Descriptions of disorders considered for DSM-IV, 169–171

Descriptions of other personality-related disorders, 171–174

Idea of, 163–164

Problems with concept, 174–175

see also entries for specific disorders

Personality Research Form (PRF), 43

Personality structure, 53–74

in childhood, 86–88

see also Big Five personality factors; Five-Factor Model; HEXACO personality factors

Personality traits (general concept)

Distinguished from other psychological characteristics, 29–30, 210, 260–261, 285

Evidence of existence, 30–34

Idea of, 27–29

Measurement of, by structured inventories, 34–45

Person-situation debate, 30–34

PET, *see* Positron Emission Tomography

Phobias, 171, 173

Physique, 95

Political attitudes, 267–281

Assortative mating, 280

Developmental change, 276–277

Environmental influences, 280

Evolution, 281

Heritability (genetic influence), 278–280

Relations with personality, 273–274

Relations with values and religiosity, 274–276

Stability, 276–277

Structure, 267–273

Popularity, 186–187

Positron Emission Tomography (PET), 228

Prenatal environment, *see* Womb environment

Primary psychopathy, 201–203

Proactive personality, 196–197

Projective tests, 49–50

Psychopathy, 201–203

see also Antisocial personality disorder

Psychoticism, 101–103, 105

Q

Quality of measurement, *see* Reliability and/or Validity

R

r, *see* Correlation coefficient

Rational strategy of test construction, 39–41

Raven's Matrices, 216, 246–247

Reaction time, 224–226

Reasoning, 211–219, 238, 245–248

Recessiveness, genetic, 118

Reciprocal altruism, 148–150

Reinforcement Sensitivity Theory, 99–103

Reliability, 9–16

Inter-rater (inter-observer) reliability, 14–15

Internal-consistency reliability, 10–13

Parallel forms reliability, 13

Split-half reliability, 13

Test-retest reliability, 15–16

Religiosity, 260–267, 274–276, 278–281

Assortative mating, 280

Biological bases, 278

Children, number of, 267

Developmental change, 264–265

Distinct from personality characteristic, 260–261

Environmental influences, 278–280

Evolution, 281

Extrinsic, 261–262, 293

Fundamentalism, 262–263

Health and longevity, 266

Heritability (genetic influence), 278–280

Intrinsic, 261–262, 293

Law-abidingness (versus criminality), 267

Life satisfaction, 266
Paranormal beliefs, 265–266
Personality, 261–264
Political attitudes, 274–276
Sexuality, 293
Spirituality, 262–263
Stability, 264–265
Religious fundamentalism, 262–263
see also Religiosity
Reproductive success, 142–159, 234–236, 293–296, 301, 304
Reverse-keyed items, 35–36
Reward dependence, in Cloninger's theory, 97–100
Right-Wing Authoritarianism, 267–277
Rorschach test, 49–50

S
Sadistic personality disorder (proposed), 169–170
San (Bushman), 155–156
SAT, 5, 248
Schizoid personality disorder, 165
Schizotypal personality disorder, 165–166
Secondary psychopathy, 201–203
Self-defeating personality disorder (proposed), 169–170
Self-esteem
Developmental change and stability, 89
Relations with Narcissism and aggressive behavior, 203
Self-ratings, *see* Self-reports
Self-reports
Agreement with observer reports, 45–47
Faking, 198–200
Issues about use in heritability studies, 115, 124–126
Method of measurement, 20–21, 23–24
Self-ratings, compared with, 21
Validity in predicting behavior, 48–49
Self-transcendence versus Self-enhancement (dimension of values), 274–276
Separation Anxiety disorder, 171–172
Serotonin
in Cloninger's theory, 97–99
molecular genetic studies, 134
Religiosity, 278
Sex differences
Life satisfaction, 205
Mental abilities, 236
Personality (Emotionality factor), 151
Religiosity, 262
Sexuality dimensions, 286–287, 289–291
Vocational (occupational) interests, 302
Sexual Arousal, 285–289, 302–304

Sexual Commitment, 285–289, 294–297
Sexual Orientation, 285–291, 297–302
Sexual selection, 143
Sexuality, 285–304
Biological bases, 292–295, 297–301, 303
Cross-generational and cross-national differences, 292
Developmental change, 293
Dimensions of,
Sexual Arousal, 285–289, 302–304
Sexual Commitment (and Sociosexuality), 285–289, 294–297
Sexual Orientation, 285–291, 297–302
Environmental influences, 292–294, 297–302
Evolutionary function, 295–297, 301–302, 303–304
Heritability (genetic influence), 294, 297–302
Personality, 287–291
Religiosity, 293
Sex differences, 286–287, 289–291
"Sexy son" hypothesis, 296
Shared (common) environment, defined, 120–121
Siblings, in research on heritability of characteristics
Mental abilities, 229–233
Personality, 116–136
Religiosity and political attitudes, 278–280
Sexuality dimensions, 297
see also Birth order
Simple phobias, *see* Specific phobias
16 Personality Factors Questionnaire (16PF), 42
Smoking, 188–189, 243
Social Dominance Orientation, 269–277
Social values, 274–276
Sociosexuality, *see* Sexuality, dimensions of, Sexual Commitment
South American Indians, 159
Spatial ability, 212–213, 215, 218–221, 235–236, 238, 245–250
Spearman-Brown formula, 13, 15
Spearman's *g*, *see* Mental abilities; *see also g* factor
Specific phobias, 171, 173
Spirituality, 262–263
Split-half reliability, 13
Stability (in sense of short-term Test-retest reliability), 15–16
Stability of characteristics
Mental abilities, 220–222
Personality
During adulthood and adolescence, 82–85
During childhood, 89–90
Religiosity, 264–265
Political attitudes, 276–277
Sexuality dimensions, 293

Standard deviation, 3–5
Standard scores, 3–5
Status (with peers), 186–187
"Stop" system, 101–103
Structured personality inventories, 34–49
  Commonly used
    California Psychological Inventory (CPI), 41–42
    Eysenck Personality Profiler (EPP), 42
    Eysenck Personality Questionnaire (EPQ), 42
    HEXACO Personality Inventory(-Revised) (HEXACO-PI(-R)), 44, 71, 83
    Hogan Personality Inventory (HPI), 42
    International Personality Item Pool (IPIP), 44–45
    Jackson Personality Inventory (JPI), 43, 161
    Multidimensional Personality Questionnaire (MPQ), 43, 103
    Myers-Briggs Type Indicator (MBTI), 42–43
    NEO Five-Factor Inventory (NEO-FFI), 44
    NEO Personality Inventory—Revised (NEO-PI-R), 44, 65, 83
    Nonverbal Personality Questionnaire (NPQ), 43–44
    Personality Research Form (PRF), 43
    16 Personality Factors Questionnaire (16PF), 42
    Temperament and Character Inventory (TCI), 43
  Response scale formats, 34
  Reverse-coded (negatively-keyed) items, 35–36
  Scale scores, calculation of, 34–36
  Strategies of construction, 36–41
    Empirical, 36–38, 41
    Factor-analytic, 39, 41
    Rational, 39–41
Substance use, 188–189

T
Tahiti islanders, 157
TAT, *see* Thematic Apperception Test
Temperament
  Biological bases, 93–112
  Children, 87–77
  Comparison with personality, 88
  Dogs, 94
Temperament and Character Inventory (TCI), 43
Terman longitudinal study of gifted children, 189–190
Test construction strategies
  Empirical, 36–38, 41
  Factor-analytic, 39, 41
  Rational, 39–41
Test-retest reliability, 15–16
Testosterone, 106–108, 294, 303
Thematic Apperception Test (TAT), 50
Traits, *see* Personality traits
Triarchic Theory of Intelligence, 251–253
Truk islanders, 157
Twins, in research on heritability of characteristics,
  Chorion type, 232
  Equal environments assumption, 131–132
  Fraternal (Dizygotic, DZ), defined, 117
  Identical (Monozygotic, MZ), defined, 117
  Personality, 116–137
  Mental abilities, 229–233
  Religiosity and political attitudes, 278–280
  Sexuality dimensions, 294, 297–298, 301–302
"Type A" personality, 192

U
Unique (non-shared) environment, defined, 120–121
Uric acid, 106
Uterine environment, 128–129, 230–231

V
Validity, 16–20
  Construct validity, 19–20
  Content validity, 16–18
  Criterion validity (convergent and discriminant), 18–19
  of self- and observer report inventories, 48–49
Values, social, 274–276
Verbal ability, 217–219, 235, 245–250, 254, 280
Vocational interests
  Personality, 199
  Sex differences, 302
  Sexual orientation, 291

W
Womb environment, 128–129, 230–231
Wonderlic Personnel Test, 252

Z
z-scores, 3–5
Zuckerman's model of biological basis of personality, 105